MANDATORY SUSTAINABILITY REQUIREMENTS IN EU PUBLIC PROCUREMENT LAW

This book provides the first comprehensive appraisal of the paradigm shift towards mandatory sustainability requirements in EU public procurement law.

Traditionally, EU public procurement law focused on 'how to buy', dictating procedural rules to overcome discrimination within the internal market. Mandatory green and social requirements mean that the EU will limit the discretionary power for public buyers by pushing them to acquire more sustainable goods and services to achieve sustainable development goals and fight climate change.

Based on legal analysis informed by economic perspectives, the book contributes to an understanding and critical discussion of the EU legislator's move towards regulating 'what to buy'. The book discusses the Public Procurement Directives and various other recast or new sectoral rules in light of the European Green Deal. The paradigm shift is analysed from different viewpoints, including subsidiarity, alternative regulation, economics and public purchasing.

The book includes novel sectoral studies on transport, food, clothing, and construction. Chapters on national mandatory requirements in Italy, the Netherlands, Spain, and more, offer case studies and highlight lessons learnt.

This is an essential book for professionals working with public procurement law in academia and practice, and to those engaged in achieving public policy objectives in light of climate change and social injustice.

Mandatory Sustainability Requirements in EU Public Procurement Law

Reflections on a Paradigm Shift

Edited by
Willem Janssen
and
Roberto Caranta

•HART•
OXFORD • LONDON • NEW YORK • NEW DELHI • SYDNEY

HART PUBLISHING

Bloomsbury Publishing Plc

Kemp House, Chawley Park, Cumnor Hill, Oxford, OX2 9PH, UK

1385 Broadway, New York, NY 10018, USA

29 Earlsfort Terrace, Dublin 2, Ireland

HART PUBLISHING, the Hart/Stag logo, BLOOMSBURY and the Diana logo are trademarks of Bloomsbury Publishing Plc

First published in Great Britain 2023

A catalogue record for this book is available from the British Library.

A catalogue record for this book is available from the Library of Congress.

Library of Congress Control Number: 2023938290

ISBN: HB: 978-1-50996-395-9
ePDF: 978-1-50996-397-3
ePub: 978-1-50996-396-6

Typeset by Compuscript Ltd, Shannon

ACKNOWLEDGEMENTS

The future of academia is team science. We fully subscribe to this vital belief that collaboration leverages joint expertise and leads to better outcomes for society as a whole, as opposed to individual and outdated approaches to the sciences.

For this book in particular, this has translated into a team with diversity of thought from different academic disciplines, including European and national law complemented with perspectives from public purchasing and economics, a gender-balance, a spread of different backgrounds across the European Union, and many established and upcoming talents from academic institutions and private practice. When aiming to provide an understanding and a discussion of the development towards mandatory sustainability requirements, we found ourselves humbled by the enthusiasm to work on this book.

With this approach and team in mind, it is clear that this book is the result of a *joint* effort. We are grateful to the support by the Centre for Regulation and Enforcement in Europe (RENFORCE), which accommodated our collective discussions at Utrecht University's Law School in June 2022. Similarly, many of the authors involved continue to thrive within the context of the ITN SAPIENS (H2020 – MSCA ITN: Grant 956696, sapiensnetwork.eu/). Over the course of the last one and a half years, the cross-cutting feedback on draft chapters and the discussions between all authors that followed after the Utrecht workshop has undoubtedly increased the academic quality of the book. We are grateful to have worked with such a fun, excellent and engaging group of authors. We hope this book will be a valuable addition to the existing excellent scholarship and research on Sustainable Public Procurement, and if it is, it is thanks to this team and its joint efforts.

We thank the two reviewers for improving our book proposal in the early stages of this project, Roberta Bassi and Verity Stuart for their enthusiasm to take on this book at Hart Publishing and for their guidance in getting it across the finish line. Finally, we are indebted to Ezgi Uysal (Turin University) for her editorial work in the final stages of this book. She kept the project on track and was diligent in her effort to streamline the contents and layout. We thank her for her assistance.

Willem Janssen and Roberto Caranta

CONTENTS

PART 2
SECTORAL SCRUTINY – MANDATORY SUSTAINABILITY REQUIREMENTS IN CURRENT AND FUTURE EU (SECTORAL) REGULATION

PART 3
MEMBER STATE EXPERIENCES – MANDATORY SUSTAINABILITY REQUIREMENTS ON THE MEMBER STATE LEVEL

PART 4
FUTURE PERSPECTIVES – THE FUTURE OF SUSTAINABLE PUBLIC PROCUREMENT

ABOUT THE AUTHORS

Marta Andhov is an Associate Professor in Public Procurement Law at the University of Copenhagen Faculty of Law and a researcher at the Centre for Private Governance (CEPRI) in Denmark. Marta's work focuses on EU public procurement law and public contracts with special focus on sustainability and public-private law intersection withing public contracts.

Chris Backes is professor of Environmental Law at Utrecht University in the Netherlands. He studied law, politics and Dutch at different German universities. Backes specialises in sustainability law and environmental law, and more especially in biodiversity law and the law of the circular economy.

Marlon Boeve is professor of Environmental and Planning Law at the Faculty of Architecture and the Built Environment, TU Delft and Assistant Professor at the Utrecht Centre for Water, Oceans and Sustainability Law and the Institute of Constitutional, Administrative Law and Legal Theory, Utrecht University in the Netherlands. Her research focuses on European and national environmental law and spatial planning Law and the Law for a Circular Economy.

Giulia Botta is a Ph.D. candidate at the University of Milan (Italy) in the program 'Law, Economics, Ethics for Sustainable Development' and she is an Associate Program Officer at the International Training Center of ILO, in the Sustainable Procurement Cluster. Her research interests are in public procurement and its interconnection with sustainable development and business and human rights.

Roberto Caranta is professor with the Law Department of the University of Turin (Italy) and coordinator of Sustainability and Procurement in International, European, and National Systems (SAPIENS) International Training Network. Roberto has a long track record of research on comparative law, public procurement and specifically on SPP.

Enrique Carreras is a Ph.D. candidate in Economics at the University of Turin (Italy) and a Marie Curie Ph.D. Fellow in the Sustainability and Procurement in International, European, and National Systems (SAPIENS) International Training Network. He is mainly focused on applied economics methods to study supply chain sustainability.

Maria José Plana Casado is Assistant Professor in the LAW group at Wageningen University (WUR, the Netherlands). Her research focuses on Food and Agricultural Law in the European Union and the US. Using a holistic approach, it also encompasses relevant underlying issues such as digital technologies (ie, e-commerce and big data), ethics in public procurement (ie, sustainability in school lunch programmes), and food waste and taxation.

Dorothy Gruyaert is an Assistant Professor at the KU Leuven and KULAK Law Faculty, Belgium. She is a member of both the Leuven Centre for Public Law and the Institute for Property Law. Her research domain is Law and Sustainability, with a particular focus on the built environment, and touches upon the boundaries between private law and public law, in particular between property and administrative law.

Paul Heijnsbroek is a lawyer at Straatman Koster advocaten in the Netherlands. He specialises in procurement law and state aid law, including procurement obligations regarding land sales by the government.

Willem Janssen is an Associate Professor in European and Dutch Public Procurement Law at Utrecht University's Law School, and a researcher at the Centre for Public Procurement (UUCePP) and the Centre for Regulation and Enforcement in Europe (RENFORCE) in the Netherlands. Willem's work focuses on EU and Dutch public procurement law from the perspectives of efficiency, effectiveness, climate change and social injustice.

Małgorzata Koszewska works as Associate Professor at the Institute of Marketing and Sustainable Development, of Faculty of Organization and Management at the Lodz University of Technology in Poland. Her research interests concentrate on sustainability aspects in the textile and clothing market.

Ximena Lazo Vitoria is a Lecturer in Law and Coordinator of the Green Public Procurement Research Group at The University of Alcalá in Spain. She also advises the Spanish Ministry of Environment in this field. She researches public-private partnerships and concessions, and her most recent publication (2022) focuses on public procurement and climate change.

François Lichère is Professor of public law at the University of Jean Moulin Lyon 3 (France), a public procurement expert and Director of the Chair of public contracts law. He has published numerous books and articles, in French and in English, mainly concerning public law contracts and economy and public law.

Jeanne Svensky Ligte is a PhD student in Management and Quality Studies at the Institute of Marketing and Sustainable Development, Lodz University of Technology (Poland). She is also a fellow at MSCA-ITN 'SAPIENS Network' Project. Her research focused on public buyer behaviour toward circular textile products and services.

Federica Muscaritoli is a Marie Curie PhD Fellow in the ITN *Sustainability and Procurement in International, European, and National Systems (SAPIENS)* Network and at the Faculty of Law, University of Copenhagen (Denmark). Her PhD project investigates 'Sustainable Procurement Tools to Fight Climate Change'.

Ruben Nicolas is a PhD candidate in Sustainable Public Procurement at the Utrecht University School of Economics in the Netherlands, and affiliated to the interdisciplinary Centre for Public Procurement. His research sheds light on Sustainable Public Procurement uptake and behaviour by contracting public authorities and the procurement practices that contribute to sustainable development.

Veerle Pissierssens is a public law lawyer in Belgium, who has worked her entire career in international law offices. Veerle has extensive experience in advising both public and private parties on public law related matter, with a specific focus on public procurement. Over the years she has advised parties in international, European and national public procurement files. In her day-to-day practice she assists parties in both transactional and litigious matters.

Hanna Schebesta is Associate Professor in the LAW group at Wageningen University (WUR, the Netherlands). Her specialty areas are WTO and EU law, in particular regulation, procedural law and liability, private standardisation and public procurement law.

Fredo Schotanus is a full professor of Public Procurement at the School of Economics of Utrecht University in the Netherlands, co-founder and board member of the Centre for Public Procurement, and principal consultant at Significant Synergy. Fredo's work focuses on sustainable and effective public procurement.

Abby Semple is the principal consultant at Public Procurement Analysis and a senior consultant and trainer at Greenville Procurement Partners in Ireland. Her main focus is on the environmental and social impact of public contracts and how these can be meaningfully addressed through the procurement process.

Oriane Sulpice is an Associate Professor in Public law at the University Lumière Lyon 2 (France). Oriane's work focuses on the implementation of environmental law and urban planning law by local authorities.

Ton van den Brink is full professor as well as Jean Monnet chair of EU legislative studies and member of the board of Utrecht Centre of Shared Regulation and enforcement in Europe (RENFORCE), Utrecht University.

Davide Vannoni is a full professor of Applied Economics at the Department of Economics and Statistics of the University of Torino (Italy), Fellow at the Collegio Carlo Alberto (Torino) and Research Fellow at IRCrES. Davide's work focuses on analysing firms' strategies, on studying their effect on firm performance, and on evaluating the economic impact of policy interventions, among which SPP.

ABBREVIATIONS/ACRONYMS

CAMs	Minimum Environmental Requirements (Criteri Ambientali Minimi)
Classic Directive	Directive 2014/24/EU
CJEU; Court	Court of Justice of the European Union
EEA	European Economic Area
EU	European Union
EU Commission; Commission	European Commission
GHG	Greenhouse Gas
GPP	Green Public Procurement
IPCC	Intergovernmental Panel on Climate Change
LCC	Life Cycle Costing
Mandatory sustainability requirement	Mandatory green and/or social requirement
MEAT	Most Economically Advantageous Tender
Member State; MS	Member State of the European Union
Public Procurement Directives	Directive 2014/24/EU, Directive 2014/23/EU and Directive 2014/25/EU
Remedies Directive	Directive 89/665
SDGs	Sustainable Development Goals
SMEs	Small and Medium-Sized Enterprises
SPI	Sustainable Products Initiative
SPP	Sustainable Public Procurement
SRPP	Socially Responsible Public Procurement
TEU	Treaty on the European Union
TFEU	Treaty on the Functioning of the European Union
UN	United Nations

TABLE OF CASES

COURT OF JUSTICE OF THE EU

AG OPINIONS

DOMESTIC CASES

France

United Kingdom

TABLE OF LEGISLATION

ILO

UNITED NATIONS

WTO

EU LAW

Treaties

Regulations

Directives

Recommendations

Protocols

Interinstitutional Agreement

Parliament Motions

Legislative Proposals and Soft Law

PART 1

Foundations of the Paradigm Shift: Towards Mandatory Sustainability Requirements in EU Public Procurement

1

Shifting Towards Mandatory Sustainability Requirements in EU Public Procurement Law: Context, Relevance and a Typology

WILLEM JANSSEN

I. Introduction

The need to tackle climate change and social injustice has consistently climbed political and policy agendas. Both have been acknowledged in a myriad of international and European instruments, such as the UN Sustainable Development Goals (SDGs) and, more recently, the European Green Deal.[1] The latter appears to make the EU more ambitious than ever in its environmental objectives, aiming to make Europe the first climate-neutral continent by 2050.[2] In a legal sense, the EU has, for instance, vested the protection of the environment in both the Treaty on the European Union (TEU) and Treaty on the Functioning of the European Union (TFEU).[3] The same is true for the social agenda of the EU.[4] Despite the clear-cut urgency for modern-day society to transition to a more sustainable way of inhabiting this planet whilst ensuring social equality, the achievement of the SDGs or the Green Deal still seems like a distant future, which was underlined again by the Intergovernmental Panel on Climate Change (IPCC) report of April 2022 that alarmingly stated 'it is now, or never'.[5] Social injustice issues, for instance, related to

[1] United Nations, *Transforming Our World: The 2030 Agenda for Sustainable Development*, 2015; European Green Deal COM(2019) 640).

[2] European Green Deal, 4.

[3] See, for instance, Art 11 and Arts 191–193 TFEU.

[4] Art 9 TFEU.

[5] Intergovernmental Panel on Climate Change, *IPPC Press Release*, 4 April 2022.

(climate-related) migration, are strongly interwoven with climate action, thereby stressing the need for an integrated approach in light of sustainable development.[6]

Similar to the reference in number 12.7 of the SDGs, public procurement is often advanced in the EU as an instrument to aid the fight against climate change and social injustice.[7] This book addresses the pressing and fundamental question of how contracting authorities in the EU are regulated at present or should be regulated in the future when it comes to sustainable public procurement. In other words, the objective of this volume is, thus, to understand and discuss the role of SPP and EU public procurement law in light of the development from *voluntary* legal requirements towards *mandatory* sustainability requirements. Transforming the law from voluntary to mandatory requirements requires a paradigm shift that demands deep academic scrutiny, particularly as the EU already appears to be moving in this direction through the proposals in the European Green Deal. Up until now, this transformation has received little and incoherent attention in the literature, despite possible systemic changes in EU law and the actors involved, such as contracting authorities, market participants and the courts.[8]

This chapter attempts to provide a foundation for this debate in the future by discussing the focus on SPP in public procurement (section II), the voluntary nature of SPP within EU public procurement law (section III), the relevance of the long-lasting debate on the alleged mandatory sustainability requirements in the Directive 2014/24 (section IV), the newly sparked interest that the European Green Deal has created for mandatory requirements in the SPP context (section V), and finally by providing a typology for different types of mandatory sustainability requirements to guide the debate in the future (section VI). The chapter concludes with some final thoughts (section VII).

II. Sustainable Public Procurement as a Force for Good

Over the years, sustainable public procurement has gained increased attention at the policy and legislative levels in the EU. It is seen as a means to 'kill two birds with one stone' or – better said in a more animal-friendly manner – to 'feed two birds with one scone'. Accordingly, public procurement procedures should ultimately not only fulfil the needs of public authorities in their role as contracting authorities,

[6] Accordingly, 'sustainable' in this volume broadly includes the environmental and the social angle in light of an economic integration context.

[7] M Monti, *A New Strategy for the Single Market*, Report to the President of the European Commission, (2010) 76.

[8] The discussion has so far focussed primarily on if mandatory requirements are effective, and if a current obligation can already be identified in the law, which is discussed further in sections II and III.

such as the purchase of ICT services or the construction of infrastructure, but also contribute to a just and inclusive society.[9] The use of public procurement in this way has also been long embraced by the European Commission, which explicitly places the EU Member States and their contracting authorities in a pivotal position for the achievement of its sustainable and social agenda.[10] SPP concerns a broad focus on all elements of sustainable development, rather than focusing on a single aspect, such as the environment in Green Public Procurement (GPP) or on social aspects through Socially Responsible Public Procurement (SRPP).[11] The Commission defines GPP as 'a process whereby public authorities seek to procure goods, services, and works with a reduced environmental impact throughout their life-cycle compared to goods, services, and works with the same primary function that would otherwise be procured'.[12] Whereas SRPP is defined as something that 'is about achieving positive social outcomes in public contracts' or that it 'aims to address the impact on society of the goods, services and works purchased by the public sector' as a driver towards, amongst other things, like 'promoting employment opportunities and social inclusion', 'providing opportunities for social economy enterprises', 'supporting compliance with social and labour rights'.[13] This role of SPP as a force to contribute to the 'good' in society has been referred to as the 'instrumental', 'horizontal' or 'strategic' role of public procurement in the literature.[14] It is no surprise that procurement is placed in this position because contracting authorities potentially have an enormous influence on how markets are shaped by using their purchasing power to influence corporate behaviour and competition by aiming to contract with the sustainable part of the private sector when purchasing public works, supplies and services.[15] This trendsetting potential on the market is supported by public procurement's share of the EU GDP, which consistently ranges between 14–19 per cent. In other words, Member States and their contracting authorities are placed in a vital position, where they can stimulate market demand towards more sustainable outcomes.

[9] ER Manunza, 'De kunst van het kiezen' [2017] *Ars Aequi* 66.

[10] Europe 2020: A Strategy for Smart, Sustainable and Inclusive Growth COM(2010) 2020.

[11] B Sjåfjell and A Wiesbrock (eds), *Sustainable Public Procurement Under EU Law* (Cambridge, Cambridge University Press, 2016); R Caranta and M Trybus (eds), *The Law of Green and Social Procurement in Europe* (Copenhagen, DJØF, 2010).

[12] See Public Procurement for a Better Environment COM(2008) 400, 4.

[13] European Commission, 'Making Socially Responsible Public Procurement Work: 71 Good Practices' (2020), 4–5.

[14] S Arrowsmith, 'The Purposes of the EU Procurement Directives: Ends, Means and the Implications for National Regulatory Space for Commercial and Horizontal Procurement Policies' (2012) 14 *Cambridge Yearbook of European Legal Studies* 34; M Trybus, 'Supporting Social Considerations through Public Procurement: A Legal Perspective' in M Trybus, G Piga and T Tatrai (eds), *Public Procurement Policy* (London, Routledge, 2016).

[15] A Wiesbrock, 'An Obligation for Sustainable Procurement? Gauging the Potential Impact of Article 11 TFEU on Public Contracting in the EU' (2013) 40 *Legal Issues of Economic Integration* 105.

III. The Voluntary Legal Nature of Sustainability in EU Public Procurement Law

The discussions on the status of sustainability in EU public procurement law, and the given leeway to favour a focus on sustainability in a public procurement procedure, can be placed in the debate on self-organisation and EU public procurement law. Self-organisation broadly refers to the discretionary power of a Member State and its public authorities to organise itself as it sees fit.[16] Essentially, this boils down to a traditional EU law question on how EU law influences and limits the discretion of contracting authorities on the Member State level.

The starting point of the influence of EU public procurement law is that it only comes into effect once the *decision* to procure has been made, whereas the decision itself to either 'make, buy or ally' remains unaffected by its legal limitations. In other words, self-organisation must be understood as entailing the discretion of contracting authorities to determine the exact status and emphasis on environmental and social objectives in the procurement cycle. The EU Commission is also adamant that contracting authorities are free to choose what they wish to procure. In its Handbook on Buying Green, the Commission emphasises that 'public authorities are in principle free to define the subject matter of the contract in a way that meets their needs'.[17] As such, *what* is bought is outside the sphere of EU public procurement law, which was also confirmed by the questions that the Commission raised in the 2011 Green Paper on if EU law should also regulate *what* instead of only *how* to buy.[18]

With the above context in mind, it is no surprise that the focus of the debate on the position of sustainability within EU public procurement law in the last two decades has been on the question if sustainability *can* be included – and under what conditions – instead of that it *must* be included. In this sense, the milestone case of *Concordia Bus* confirmed that the preservation of the environment can indeed be included in the criteria of a procurement procedure:

> It follows from the above considerations that, where the contracting authority decides to award a contract to the tenderer who submits the economically most advantageous tender, in accordance with Article 36(1)(a) of Directive 92/50, it may take criteria relating to the preservation of the environment into consideration, provided that they are linked to the subject-matter of the contract, do not confer an unrestricted freedom of choice on the authority, are expressly mentioned in the contract documents or the

[16] WA Janssen, *EU Public Procurement Law & Self-organisation: A Nexus of Tensions & Reconciliations* (The Hague, Eleven Publishers, 2018) 3.

[17] Buying Green 3rd edn.

[18] Green Paper on the Modernisation of EU Public Procurement Policy COM(2011) 15, 6; C McCrudden, *Buying Social Justice: Equality, Government Procurement and Legal Change* (Oxford, Oxford University Press, 2007).

tender notice, and comply with all the fundamental principles of Community law, in particular the principle of non-discrimination.[19]

Throughout the years, this standpoint was further confirmed in milestone Court of Justice of the European Union (CJEU) cases *Wienstrom* and *Max Havelaar*.[20] However, it was not just the CJEU that paved the way to accommodate environmental and social objectives in EU public procurement law.[21] The EU legislator has been at the forefront of solidifying the possibility to include sustainability considerations when it revamped the Public Procurement Directives in 2014. Scholarship agrees that the reforms have resulted in more legal discretion or certainty to procure based on these considerations, such as the introduction of the possibility to award contracts based on the lowest life cycle costs, the expansion of the possibility to award reserved contracts to sheltered workshops or social enterprises, or the enhanced legal clarity that has been given for the use of eco-labels.[22] If one were to consider the current landscape, it is clear that sustainability and social objectives can feature as a consideration in *all* the stages of the procurement cycle: these considerations can be specified in the subject matter of the contract in the pre-procurement stage and explored in market consultations; they can take the shape of technical specifications that must be met by the bidders to participate in the procurement process; at the selection stage, where the past environmental crime record of an economic operator may lead to exclusion; they can be taken into account in the award criteria with a focus on quality or lowest life-cycle costs; and by including them in the contractual conditions.[23] Temporary exclusion of a maximum 12 months featured as well in proposed legislation on greenwashing.[24] In any of these stages, environmental and social considerations remain a voluntary possibility for contracting authorities, who can choose to use these considerations as the compass of their procurement process. The limitations derived from EU public procurement law are applicable to these possibilities and built upon the principles of equality, transparency, and proportionality, either derived from the Public Procurement Directives or the free movement rules.

[19] Case C-513/99 *Concordia Bus Finland Oy Ab, formerly Stagecoach Finland Oy Ab v Helsingin kaupunki and HKL-Bussiliikenne*, ECLI:EU:C:2002:495, [1998] ECR I-07213 para 64.

[20] Case C-448/01 *EVN AG and Wienstrom GmbH v Republik Österreich*, ECLI:EU:C:2003:651, [2003] ECR I-14527.

[21] WA Janssen, 'On Discretion & Sustainability in EU Public Procurement Law: From Room for Diversity to Unity?' in T van den Brink and V Passalaqua (eds), *Diversity and Unity in the European Union* (Edward Elgar, forthcoming, 2023).

[22] See, for instance, S Arrowsmith, 'A Taxonomy of Horizontal Policies in Public Procurement' in S Arrowsmith and P Kunzlik (eds), *Social and Environmental Policies in EC Procurement Law: New Directives and New Directions* (Cambridge, Cambridge University Press, 2009) 108; R Caranta, 'The Changes to the Public Contract Directives and the Story They Tell about How EU Law Works' (2015) 52 *Common Market Law Review* 391.

[23] Arts 20, 57, 67, 68, 70 and 77 Classic Directive.

[24] Proposal for a Green Claims Directive COM(2023) 166; see also the Proposal for a Regulation on deforestation-free products COM/2021/706 final.

IV. The Current Debate about Mandatory Requirements in the Context of the Classic Directive

Despite the above conclusion that EU public procurement law concerns itself with 'how to buy' instead of 'what to buy', the question can still be posed – and it has been posed in literature – if such requirements do indeed exist in the Classic Directive. This section discusses the potential mandatory nature of Articles 18(2), 69 and 42(1) of Directive 2014/24 on the EU level.[25] Needless to say, the debate on Article 11 TFEU as the integration provision, is also relevant for this discussion but is discussed elsewhere and appears to not contain a mandatory requirement for contracting authorities.[26] It seems, though, that these provisions cannot be deemed to be effective in mandating sustainable public procurement, which is discussed further below.

A. Compliance with Environmental, Social and Labour Law – Article 18(2) Classic Directive

The most prominent part of the debate on the mandatory environmental or social nature of EU public procurement law concerns Article 18(2) Classic Directive. This provision states that

> Member States shall take appropriate measures to ensure that in the performance of public contracts operators comply with applicable obligations in the fields of environmental, social and labour law established by Union law, national law, collective agreements.[27]

The existing obligations, mentioned in Article 18(2) of the Classic Directive, are broadly described. It contains not only an exhaustive list of international law conventions, but also a non-exhaustive reference to European law and local laws to which the bidder is subjected.[28] For international law, reference is made to Annex X with a number of social and environmental law conventions, such as

[25] Accordingly, it will not delve into the Member State level in which those requirements exist in a variety of legal forms, such as the Netherlands, Italy and Spain.

[26] Wiesbrock (n 15); M Andrecka and KP Mitkidis, 'Sustainability Requirements in EU Public and Private Procurement – a Right or an Obligation' (2017) 1 *Nordic Journal of Commercial Law* 55; M Wasmeier, 'The Integration of Environmental Protection as a General Rule for Interpreting Community Law' (2001) 38 *Common Market Law Review* 159, 161. It seems, however, that Art 11 is solely directed at the EU institutions, thereby not providing a relevant point of reference when discussing mandatory requirements. WA Janssen, 'Verplicht Maatschappelijk Verantwoord Aanbesteden: een eerste Verkenning van een Paradigmaverandering' [2020] *Tijdschrift Aanbestedingsrecht & Staatssteunrecht* 1, 24; K Pouikli, 'Towards Mandatory Green Public Procurement (GPP) Requirements Under the EU Green Deal: Reconsidering the Role of Public Procurement as an Environmental Policy Tool' [2021] *ERA Forum* 699, 715.

[27] Andrecka and Mitkidis (n 26) 69–70.

[28] A Semple, 'Living Wages in Public Contracts: Impact of the RegioPost Judgment and the Proposed Revisions to the Posted Workers Directive' in A Sanchez Graells (ed), *Smart Public Procurement and Labour Standards* (Oxford, Hart Publishing, 2018) 83.

ILO Conventions of the International Labour Organisation on forced or compulsory labour, discrimination in respect of employment and occupation, and child labour, or conventions on transboundary movements of hazardous wastes and on substances that deplete the ozone layer. Article 18(2) of the Directive is typically considered as an instrument for more social and environmentally friendly public procurement because it introduces a general obligation to enforce existing rules related to, for instance, social dumping and violations of environmental law. As such, the duty provided for under Article 18(2) is seen as a ramification of overriding EU political and legal obligations to achieve sustainable development.[29]

Andhov articulates the obligations flowing from Article 18(2) Classic Directive as another limitation to a contracting authority's right to procure sustainably.[30] To that end, she confirms the obligatory character of the Directive. However, I argue that the extent of the legal obligation imposed under Article 18(2) is debatable, especially since the article only refers to 'appropriate measures' to be taken by the Member States, not contracting authorities. It is, thus, a requirement directed at national legislatures. In other words, contracting authorities are not subjected to this obligation. In addition, the article is, in fact, rather open-ended, since it requires a definition of the type of positive obligation that is expected (that is, what is an 'appropriate measure').[31] Furthermore, it only imposes an obligation by reference to very broad fields of international, European and national law. The true nature of this measure must, therefore, be assessed on the national level by a viewing of national legislation. Additionally, while it has been argued that Article 18(2) creates a general principle of EU law, the article only refers to very specific areas (such as labour law and environmental law), instead of enjoying the broad application that general principles typically enjoy, such as the principle of equality mentioned in Article 18(1). Therefore, as argued by Arrowsmith, the general principle hypothesis must be discarded.[32] Likewise, an extension or further specification of the obligations under this article is unlikely to be found in the national implementations of the Directive.[33] A brief look at the Dutch legislature's approach showcases a reference to the implementation of other legislative acts and urges economics operators to find the information that will allow them to abide by the broad set of legislative measures that are mentioned, thereby not adding much more arguments in favour of an obligation, let alone an effective obligation. The conclusion on the possibility to construe an obligation based on Article 18(2) of the Directive must, however, still side with Andhov's own analysis, which found

[29] M Andhov, 'Contracting Authorities and Strategic Goals of Public Procurement – A Relationship Defined by Discretion?' in S Bogojević, X Groussot and J Hettne (eds), *Discretion in EU Public Procurement Law* (Oxford, Hart Publishing, 2019) 134.

[30] ibid 127.

[31] Andrecka and Mitkidis (n 26) 80.

[32] S Arrowsmith, *The Law of Public and Utilities Procurement*, 3rd edn (London, Sweet & Maxwell, 2014) 631.

[33] A Wiesbrock, 'Socially Responsible Public Procurement – European Value or National Choice?' in B Sjåfjell and A Wiesbrock (eds), *Sustainable Public Procurement Under EU Law* (Cambridge, Cambridge University Press, 2015).

that 'the ambiguity of the provision is disappointing, and suggests that, failing a proactive approach on the part of the Member States, Article 18(2) may become just a policy statement rather than a valuable legal provision'.[34]

More recently, the debate on Article 18(2) gained new traction due to the CJEU's conclusions in the *Tim* case. I argue that this case does not appear to alter the above conclusion.[35] In this case, the Court was asked to assess Italian legislation that automatically excluded an economic operator from participation in a public procurement procedure if one of its subcontractors did not fulfil the standards relating to the right to work for people with disabilities. When assessing the legality of this Italian implementation of Article 18(2), the Court referred to this article as being of 'cardinal value' and as a 'principle', thereby seemingly attributing serious weight to this provision. Whereas the Dutch translation refers somewhat confusingly to 'in principle', one might argue that this case introduced a sustainability principle within the context of EU public procurement law.

However, the context of this case seems important and appears to significantly limit its impact. Vital is that these wordings were included to justify the existence of the Italian law under scrutiny. Accordingly, it meant that it was used purposefully by the Court as an argument to justify that Article 18(2) requires national legislatures to include 'appropriate measures' to give effect to the above-mentioned national, European and international obligations (in light of social law in this case). Thus, the Court seemingly did nothing more than conclude that the Italian law in question was considered 'an appropriate measure' instead of aiming to change the course of EU public procurement law all together via the introduction of a new and impactful sustainability principle. This conclusion is further supported by the continuation of the Court's reasoning referring to the link between exclusion grounds and Article 18(2):

> Combined with the specific objective of Article 57(4)(a) of Directive 2014/24, which is to ensure compliance with obligations under environmental, social and labour law, the objective relating to the reliability of the economic operator must enable the Member States to grant the contracting authority the option, or even the obligation, to regard as reliable only those economic operators who, when drawing up their tenders, have exercised the care and diligence required to ensure that, in the course of performance of the contract, the obligations concerned are complied with in all circumstances, whether by themselves or by the subcontractors to whom they intend to entrust part of that performance.[36]

Accordingly, the CJEU concludes that Article 57(4)(a) Directive 2014/24 does not preclude national legislation under which the contracting authority has the option, or even the obligation, to exclude the economic operator who submitted the tender from participation in the contract award procedure where the ground for

[34] Andhov (n 29).

[35] Case C-395/18 *Tim SpA – Direzione e coordinamento Vivendi SA v Consip SpA and Ministero dell'Economia e delle Finanze Case* ECLI:EU:C:2020:58, [2020].

[36] ibid paras 39–41.

exclusion referred to in that provision is found in respect of one of the subcontractors mentioned in that operator's tender, instead of adopting a broader conclusion to support the existence of a sustainability principle. Hence, Article 18(2) Classic Directive itself cannot be deemed to be an effective mandatory sustainability requirement directed at contracting authorities, unless it is voluntarily triggered further by Article 57(1)(f) Directive 2014/24.

B. Dismissal of Abnormally Low Tenders – Article 69(3) Classic Directive

As a corollary of Article 18(2), Article 69 of the Directive imposes an obligation to reject abnormally low tenders if they are non-compliant with Article 18(2).[37] This article seems to be the most concrete and only mandatory sustainability requirement within the scope of this Directive. Again, reference is made to Article 18(2), but in this case the legal consequences of this provision are clear. The bid must be rejected if the contracting authority has established that the tender is abnormally low, because it does not comply with the obligations referred to in Article 18(2). Thus, the policy objectives to be pursued are defined (these are hidden in the laws and regulations mentioned in Article 18(2)), and the discretion of the contracting authority to fulfil this obligation is regulated.

The required causality between an infringement of Article 18(2) of the Directive and the abnormally low tender, however, may lead to problems of proof in practice. Particularly when it comes to large global economic operators with long supply chains, it may be difficult for contracting authorities to demonstrate not only the existence of an abnormally low tender, but also a violation of environmental, social or labour laws abroad. Moreover, it will be even more challenging, if not impossible, to prove that one is caused by the other. For instance, the challenge will be to prove that the illegitimate dumping of toxic waste, or that the use of child labour, resulted in an abnormally low tender. In addition, the question is what to do with other factors that led to the existence of a low bid. Hence, the discussion of a partial causal link further complicates the effectiveness of this article in practice. Finally, 'normal' bids (ie, bids that are not abnormally low) that are the result of an infringement of Article 18(2) Classic Directive do not fall within the scope of this article. Questionable is, nonetheless, how courts would deal with this in practice, as they might also consider a mere rejection based on motivation by a tenderer already sufficient. Furthermore, malicious economic operators might even be inclined to place a higher bid to avoid being rejected entirely. As a consequence, this article has no effect on the vast majority of public procurement procedures, which might still not be sustainable. Accordingly, this provision

[37] Andhov (n 29) 127.

is indeed a mandatory requirement to procure sustainable and social outcomes, but it does appear ineffective.

C. Accessibility Requirements – Article 42(1) Classic Directive

A less discussed provision in the context of mandatory requirements is Article 42 Classic Directive. This provision states that:

> For all procurement which is intended for use by natural persons, whether general public or staff of the contracting authority, the technical specifications shall, except in duly justified cases, be drawn up so as to take into account accessibility criteria for persons with disabilities or design for all users.

Accordingly, technical specifications 'shall' be drawn up into as to take into account accessibility criteria for all procurements. Accordingly, this is a mandatory social requirement. Contracting authorities have, however, significant leeway as to what to do with this requirement, because it is unclear what 'take into account' means, particularly now that 'except in duly justified cases' also provides room for exemptions. This requirement was also included in the predecessor of this Directive but in a different wording.[38] The most significant difference between the two Directives is, however, the reference to

> Where mandatory accessibility requirements are adopted by a legal act of the Union, technical specifications shall, as far as accessibility criteria for persons with disabilities or design for all users are concerned, be defined by reference thereto.

Particularly relevant here is the European Accessibility Directive that also cross-references to Article 42(1). This Directive aims to contribute to an improvement of the internal market when it comes to accessibility requirements for products and services by eliminating barriers to the free movement of accessible products and services arising from divergent accessibility requirements in the Member States. It considers that:

> This Directive should establish mandatory accessibility requirements for products and services covered by it.

The reference to 'should' is somewhat unclear, because this Directive clearly poses accessibility requirements, when it comes to amongst other things, harmonisation of standards, alteration of products, and specific obligations for importers and manufacturers. For clarity's sake, the rules on accessibility for disabled persons are also referred to in light of exclusion grounds in the preamble of this Directive. The link is made here, however, via Article 18(2) and the violation of 'social obligations, including rules on accessibility for disabled persons or other forms of

[38] Art 23 Directive 2004/18/EC: 'Whenever possible these technical specifications should be defined so as to take into account accessibility criteria for people with disabilities or design for all users.'

grave professional misconduct'.[39] Finally, this requirement is interesting as well as it is one of the very few social requirements that currently exist. As detailed in this book, it appears that the social legislative agenda is gaining less importance compared to the environmental one due to the European Green Deal, as discussed in the next section.

V. The Relevance of the Paradigm Shift Ahead: The Need to Discuss the Development from Voluntary to Mandatory Sustainability Requirements

With the ineffectiveness (or at least unclarity) of the above-described requirements in the procurement context, it is clear that effectuating any legislative paradigm change in the EU towards mandatory sustainability requirements requires scrutiny on many levels to ensure coherency, consistency and certainty of the law.[40] Should the status quo indeed be changed on a substantial scale, then it mandates broad academic, political and societal discussion. The EU slate is not entirely voluntary, however. As Semple rightly notes, the Clean Vehicles Directive, initially adopted in 2009 and amended in 2019, was and is the prime example of sectoral mandatory requirements that limit the discretionary power of contracting authorities.[41] Whereas the earlier version obligated the use of technical specifications or award criteria relating to the lifecycle and environmental impact of a vehicle, the current version contains. The reformed version of this Directive changed this mandatory approach by including minimum procurement targets and got rid of the minimum procurement criteria approach (ie, technical specifications or award criteria, including the mandatory life-cycle costing method).[42]

Whereas the predominant part of the consulted stakeholders was not in favour of regulating 'what to buy' in response to the 2010 Green Paper, it appears that the times have changed since then.[43] For future days to come, the European Green Deal appears as the motor for the initial legislative paradigm shift by stating that 'public authorities, including the EU institutions, should lead by example and ensure that their procurement is green'. The Commission will propose further legislation and guidance on green public purchasing.[44] Accordingly, public procurement procedures continue to fulfil an essential role in greening the EU, but the Commission is willing to go a step further than merely a European emphasis on possibilities to

[39] Recital 101 Classic Directive (n 23).

[40] Janssen (n 26) 26.

[41] Directive amending Clean Vehicles Directive.

[42] ibid Art 5.

[43] European Commission, 'Green Paper on the Modernisation of EU Public Procurement Policy Towards a More Efficient European Procurement Market, Synthesis of Replies', (2011).

[44] European Green Deal (n 2) 8.

procure sustainable and social outcomes. The compelling reference to 'ensure' in this paragraph appears to have been made consciously by the Commission, which was confirmed by a reading of the European Green Deal Investment Plan. In this plan, the Commission announced it would 'propose minimum mandatory green criteria or targets for public procurements in sectoral initiatives, EU funding or product-specific legislation'. Accordingly, it is now clear that this is what was meant by the notion that the Commission 'will propose further legislation and guidance on green public purchasing'.[45] Whilst continuing to provide policy and practical support to contracting authorities, it becomes clear that the Commission considers three types of concrete obligations, namely targets, mandatory green criteria and product requirements in the context of public procurement with a clear focus on GPP rather than the broader SPP concept discussed before.

As noted by Andhov and Muscaritoli, this new European approach has since become apparent in many of the Commission's proposals with specific provisions related to green procurement, including a revamped Batteries Regulation, a revamped Construction Products Regulation, a revamped Ecodesign Regulation, and a revamped Energy Efficiency Directive.[46] It is clear that the transport, clothing and construction sectors will be affected by this development, and that requirements for the food sector and potentially others appear to be on their way.[47]

Interestingly, however, many of the preliminary questions that would proceed with a paradigm shift still remain under-researched. The authors of this volume provide a critical appraisal of the status quo, highlighting the potential and pitfalls of this development, and the future ahead for mandatory requirements. The economic underpinning of the effectiveness of mandatory requirements requires attention, considering alternatives such as taxation or subsidies require attention.[48] As Carreras and Vannoni state in this regard

> the decision to go towards more stringency in GPP and/or in SRPP should be mainly a political one and should consider not only costs, but also moral, legal, and societal obligations to protect the environment and to let citizens live in a more inclusive society.[49]

The call to be mindful of the economic effectiveness is also echoed by Nicolas and Schotanus, who explore in addition to mandatory requirements towards options

[45] ibid 6.

[46] M Andhov and F Muscaritoli, 'Climate Change and Public Procurement: Are We Shifting the Legal Discourse?', ch 2 in this volume.

[47] European Parliament, 'Motion for a European Parliament Resolution on a Farm to Fork Strategy for a Fair, Healthy and Environmentally-friendly Food System', 2020/2260(INI) (2021) para 102.

[48] For a critical perspective, see KM Halonen, 'Is Public Procurement Fit for Reaching Sustainability Goals? A Law and Economics Approach to Green Public Procurement' (2021) 28 *Maastricht Journal for European and Comparative Law* 535; S Lundberg, PO Marklund, and E Strömbäck 'Is Environmental Policy by Public Procurement Effective?' (2016) 44 *Public Finance Review* 478 and an overview of arguments in favour of the transition, see L Mélon, 'More Than a Nudge? Arguments and Tools for Mandating Green Public Procurement in the EU' (2020) 12 *Sustainability* 988.

[49] E Carreras and D Vannoni, 'Mandatory Requirements in Sustainable Public Procurement: The Economic Perspective', ch 4 in this volume.

that public purchasing sciences offer to further professionalise contracting authorities by noting 'In addition to mandatory requirements, better enabling sharing and copying best practices can improve SPP uptake in the short to middle term and also feed into professionalization.'[50]

Building on the question of whether a broad preliminary assessment has actually occurred prior to the proposals launched by the EU Commission, Van den Brink analyses what the role of the principle of subsidiarity has been in relation to what regulatory level is placed in the best position to introduce mandatory requirements (the EU or its Member States). His findings are somewhat daunting as he concludes that 'Subsidiarity generally thus fails to reach its potential as a balancing principle for EU and national competence.'[51] This will become more interesting now that the legislative approaches in these proposals differ substantially. Whereas some offer a delegated act to legislate sustainability levels to the Commission, others oblige the use of technical specifications and award criteria, which underlines the need for a typology as detailed in section VI.[52] For this reason, it will prove also important, once a balance between voluntary and mandatory requirements is made, to consider the benefits of regulating the producer instead of the procurer as discussed by Backes and Boeve.[53]

Furthermore, the subsequent important question will be if horizontal cross-cutting legislation will be more fruitful or if sectoral approaches must be taken. In this context, Semple explores transport-related legislation, including the Clean Vehicles Directive and the Proposal for a Batteries Regulation, and considers amongst other things, the importance of an effective legislative scope of requirements and the need to include practice and the perspective of contracting authorities in their design.[54] In addition to detailing the specifics of the construction sector in this context, Gruyaeart and Pissierssens consider as well the need to discuss enforcement of mandatory requirements by stating that 'as long as this is supported by clear contract management and enforcement during the execution phase'.[55] Schebesta and Plana Casado highlight the need to consider if the substance of mandatory requirements can even be sufficiently defined and thus regulated, particularly when it comes to food procurement.[56] Furthermore,

[50] F Schotanus and R Nicholas, 'Coercive, Memetic and Normative Influences on the Uptake of Sustainable Public Procurement: An Institutional Perspective', ch 5 in this volume.

[51] T van den Brink, 'Subsidiarity Lost Along the Way? EU Public Procurement Legislation on the Road to Sustainability', ch 3 in this volume.

[52] See respectively, Proposal for a Regulation on Ecodesign for Sustainable Products COM(2022) 142; Proposal for a Batteries Regulation (COM)2020 798.

[53] C Backes and M Boeve, 'Regulating the Producer instead of the Procurer – The EU Sustainable Products Initiative and Extended Producer Responsibility as Ways to Foster the Transition to a Circular Economy', ch 6 in this volume.

[54] A Semple, 'Charge of the Light Brigade? The Clean Vehicles Directive and the Batteries Regulation', ch 7 in this volume.

[55] D Gruyaert and V Pissierssens, 'Transforming the Construction Sector through Minimum Requirements', ch 10 in this volume.

[56] H Schebesta and MJ Plana Casado, 'Food: Mandatory EU Public Procurement Criteria for Food after the Farm to Fork Strategy', ch 8 in this volume.

Koszewska and Svensky Ligte detail the discussion on mandatory requirements in light of the textiles industry, and emphasise the importance of other sectoral pieces of legislation, but do also consider the absence of a focus on social requirements.[57]

Interestingly, much could in the future be learnt from the experiences of some of the Member States, who already have taken the step toward regulating 'what to buy' on the national level. Most prominent is the Italian example in which the voluntary EU GPP criteria have been transposed into mandatory requirements on the national level for 18 product categories, which is generally seen as a positive experience by Botta.[58] As Heijnsbroek considers the Dutch experiences (before the courts) with a 'comply or explain' regime requires contracting authorities to explain any choice for the lowest price or cost, and the mandatory requirement to achieve as much societal value as possible for public expenditures, which appears rather symbolic instead of effectively mandating sustainable procurement.[59] Lazo Vitoria discusses a plethora of mandatory requirements that have been introduced on the national and regional level in Spain, even though litigation is not present yet, it proves a fruitful discussion of procurement and climate-related obligations.[60]

Finally, the question comes up relating to remedies. What will change if mandatory sustainability requirements come to the forefront instead of voluntary possibilities? Lichère and Sulpice detail various routes of litigation, and question even the role of public interest litigation as a future option for NGOs and other interested parties claiming that these requirements have not (sufficiently) been met.[61]

VI. Guiding the Debate Ahead: A Typology of Mandatory Sustainability Requirements

At present, mandatory environmental and social requirements currently exist or are in the making at the European or Member State level. The following initial exercise proposes a first categorisation of mandatory sustainability requirements to streamline the discussion in the future as the paradigm shift further materialises.

[57] M Koszewska and JS Ligte, 'Textiles and Clothing: Mandatory Social Requirements as the Way Forward?', ch 9 in this volume.

[58] G Botta, 'Italy: Leading the Way towards Mandatory Sustainable Public Procurement through Minimum Environmental Criteria', ch 11 in this volume.

[59] P Heijnsbroek, 'The Netherlands: Obligations to Justify the Lowest Price and to Create as Much Societal Value as Possible', ch 12 in this volume.

[60] X Lazo-Vitoria, 'Spain: Transitioning towards Sustainable Public Procurement Mandatory Requirements', ch 13 in this volume.

[61] F Lichère and O Sulpice, 'Mandatory Requirements in Public Procurement Law: The Role of Remedies, Courts and Public Interest Litigation', ch 14 in this volume.

A. Mandatory Sustainability Requirements

A mandatory sustainability requirement – a legal environmental or social requirement that directs the decision-making process of a national, regional or local authority, often in their role as a contracting authority, either in the form of: 1) minimum mandatory public procurement requirements; 2) target; or 3) product specific legislation. A mandatory requirement, thus, limits the discretionary power of this authority to freely choose what goods, works and services to purchase on the market. These requirements can be found in primary law, the Public Procurement Directives and/or other secondary legislation in the EU. The opposite of mandatory requirements is those of a voluntary nature, such as the current EU GPP criteria introduced by the EU Commission.[62]

B. Minimum Mandatory Public Procurement Requirements

A minimum mandatory public procurement requirement is a legal requirement that directs the decision-making process of a national, regional or local authority, often in their role as a contracting authority, in a mandatory manner by specifying a contracting authority's demand in an environmental or social manner (substantive) or by mandating the competitive set-up of a public procurement procedure in environmental or social manner (procedurally). Furthermore, these requirements can be horizontal or sectoral. Combinations of the above distinctive features are also possible (ie, a sectoral substantive requirement).

C. Substantive or Procedural Mandatory Requirements

A substantive requirement directs the environmental or social level that is required in a public procurement procedure. For instance, this can be regulated by the law prescribing technical specifications or award criteria. An example of this is the mentioned Article 42 of the Classic Directive in terms of accessibility requirements or the Italian GPP minimum criteria, which prescribe mandatory technical specifications or the mandated use of a life-cycle calculation method (if chosen as an award criteria) in the old Clean Vehicles Directive of 2009.[63] Specific award criteria in terms of sustainability have, for instance, also been foreseen by the Proposal for a Net Zero Act and by the Proposal for a Regulation on Critical Raw Materials, which would mean that contracting authorities could in the future be required by national implementation plans to include recycled

[62] EU GPP Criteria at ec.europa.eu/environment/gpp/eu_gpp_criteria_en.htm.
[63] See Directive amending Clean Vehicles Directive (n 40); Art 34 of the Italian Public Contracts Code (Codice dei Contratti Pubblici).

content in their award criteria.[64] Contrarily, a procedural requirement only directs the competitive set-up of a public procurement procedure. An example of this is the Dutch example of the 'comply or explain' requirement, which obligates a contracting authority to motivate the choice for the lowest price as an award criterion, or the general duty to include one or more environmental criteria and/or technical specifications in the set-up of a procedure without depicting their substantive nature, such as is included in Spain.[65]

D. Horizontal or Sectoral Mandatory Requirements

A horizontal requirement is introduced for all types of public procurement by contracting authorities. An example is the Dutch requirement to procure 'as much societal value as possible for public expenditures' which applies to all procurements, irrespective of their nature.[66] Contrary to this, sectoral requirements are established particularly for a specific sector. An example of this is the approach taken in the Proposal for a Batteries Regulation and the 2019 Clean Vehicles Directive, which respectively regulate batteries and vehicles relevant to the transport sector.

E. Targets

A target requires national, regional or local public authorities, often in their role as contracting authorities, to gear their (procurement) activities towards achieving an environmental or social objective within a certain timeframe, which is often expressed in percentages or a general volume. Targets can be directly focused on public procurement, thereby making contracting authorities responsible for their achievement, or have a broader focus, meaning that public procurement can play an indirect role in achieving them alongside other activities. An example of a public procurement-specific target is the 2019 Clean Vehicles Directive, which was discussed before, with Member State-specific targets related to public procurement of vehicles (ie, 38,5 per cent of heavy vehicles must be bought in line with the Directive by 2025) or a regional target for Dutch municipalities in their role as contracting authorities to procure 80 per cent of their total annual spend in a sustainable manner.[67] Examples of broader targets with a potential indirect effect on public procurement are those included on the international level

[64] Proposal for a Net Zero Industry Act COM(2023) 161) Art 19. Proposal for a Regulation on critical raw materials COM(2023) 160).

[65] Aanbestedingswet 2012 Art 1.5; Law 9/2017 Arts 35.1.c and Spanish RD-L 3/2020 Art 53.1.c.

[66] P Heijnsbroek, 'The Netherlands: Obligations to Justify the Lowest Price and to Create as Much Societal Value as Possible', ch 12 in this volume.

[67] Paris Agreement under the United Nations Framework Convention on Climate Change (Paris, 12 December 2015).

(ie, Paris Agreement: limiting global warming below two degrees), European level (ie, European Green Deal, no net emissions of greenhouse gases by 2050), or on the national level (ie, the Dutch agreement to be climate neutral by 2050).[68]

F. Product Specific Legislation

This type of mandatory requirement regulates the product or the producer from an environmental or social perspective, not the behaviour of national, regional or local public authorities or their public procurement process. Accordingly, the procurement of goods, services and works is indirectly affected, because the supply on the market becomes entirely or partially more sustainable or social. This often concerns a more traditional integration method in the EU. An example of this type of regulation is the Proposal for a Regulation on Ecodesign for Sustainable Products. Still, product-specific legislation may foresee more or less sustainable products may be sold on the internal market while mandating contracting authorities to buy more sustainable ones (the proposal for a new Regulation *does* have a minimum public procurement requirement angle in Article 58).

VII. Conclusion

The commitment to sustainable development in the EU political agenda has permeated the fabric of EU public procurement law. This field has changed over the years into a legal framework that is increasingly tolerant and encouraging towards Member States that wish to pursue sustainability and social objectives through public procurement procedures. Contracting authorities may indeed, integrate these objectives in any stage of the procurement cycle. Current times, however, call for a discussion about moving from regulating 'how to buy' towards 'what to buy' in the EU.

As a preliminary step, this chapter has introduced the context in which SPP takes its place in public procurement law. The discussion in Articles 18(2), 69 and 42(1) of the Classic Directive has shown that these provisions are either not obligatory, or that they are not effective in the sense that they are unlikely to have any real effect in the public procurement context for now.

Despite this conclusion on the status quo, it does appear that this field of law is on the brink of change, fuelled by the European Green Deal, and is developing towards the introduction of many and diversified types of sectoral mandatory environmental and social requirements. Accordingly, the time is right to critically

[68] Dutch Klimaatwet, Stb. 2019, 254.

assess it, and to debate its effectiveness and need in light of pressing issues in society, which is particularly relevant given the immense potential of contracting authorities' purchasing power across the EU. The materialisation of this paradigm shift is still in progress, but the first contours are becoming clearer. A coherent discussion of the many facets related to mandatory sustainable and social requirements, partially highlighted in this chapter, is lacking up until now. Deviating away from the status quo in a legal sense requires fundamental scrutiny of the relationship between sustainability and EU public procurement law. Each chapter that follows in this book provides a piece of the missing puzzle to coherently discuss this topic. It aims to provide a first coherent understanding of mandatory sustainability requirements, to critically discuss it, and ultimately to ensure that EU public procurement law remains – or becomes more – effective in the fight against climate change and social injustice in the future.

2

Climate Change and Public Procurement: Are We Shifting the Legal Discourse?

MARTA ANDHOV AND FEDERICA MUSCARITOLI*

I. Introduction

Climate Change, understood as the modification of environmental conditions of the planet through the increase of the earth's temperature due to the greenhouse effect is recognised by overwhelming scientific consensus as an existential threat to our future.[1] The consensus is followed by the realisation that it is no longer good enough to sit back and wait for environmental legislation alone to address climate change. This is clearly seen in actions taken by the European Commission, which communicates the need to shift to new sustainable economies and market models with its Green Deal. In addition, various legal disciplines require adaptation and expansion of their interpretation to meet the current realities and recognise the scale of climate change issues – such as human rights law in the aftermath of the *Urgenda* case or constitutional law following the *Neubauer* case.[2]

Public procurement can be a particularly powerful strategic tool due to its size and value. The state's purchasing power can create new market behaviours and shift the existing ones towards low emission and, in the longer-term neutral emission consumption and production. Contracting authorities, who promote and use climate mitigation measures in public procurement, provide the private sector with real incentives for developing innovative green technologies and products, with effects ideally felt beyond their public contracts. This can not only

* This project has received funding from the European Union's Horizon 2020 research and innovation programme under the Marie Skłodowska-Curie grant agreement No 956696.

[1] The World Economic Forum's Global Risks Report 2022 ranked extreme weather and climate action failure among the top three global threats for the immediate future at www.weforum.org/agenda/2022/09/climate-change-severe-impacts-lives/.

[2] *State of the Netherlands v Urgenda Foundation*, Hoge Raad der Nederlanden [Supreme Court of the Netherlands], Dec. 12, 2019, Case No. [2015] HAZA C/09/00456689; BVerfG, Order of the First Senate of 24 March 2021-1 BvR 2656/18 -, paras 1-270.

contribute to the competitiveness of economic operators in the internal market, but also enhance – in the long run – the competitiveness of the EU economy.[3] Thus, public procurement can be a highly relevant lever in the hands of Member States and their contracting authorities to contribute to climate change mitigation. However, public procurement law will always play a supporting role, as in many cases, environmental regulation and enforcement will play a more appropriate leading role in fighting climate change.[4] This is seen in renewed interest in environmental legislation in the EU with the recently adopted Climate Law or at the national level with the adoption of climate acts in France, Spain, Portugal, Denmark and Italy.[5] In the latter, the Constitution has even recognised the duty to protect the environment.[6]

While EU public procurement law has several goals, it would be incorrect and too far-reaching to claim one of them is to fight climate change. Nevertheless, the EU procurement legislative framework must 'do its part' in contributing to the required *green transition*. That is mainly because of the responsibility of governments often vested in constitutions to ensure public health and longevity of societies that leads to a general responsibility to act, which also extends to public procurement. A further reason is also the scale of public procurement and the fact that taxpayers' money is spent through it. Finally, public procurement is an expression of Member States' choices. It would be inconsistent and contradictory to expect governments to regulate climate mitigation but ignore it when buying from the commercial market. Not to mention that governments and contracting authorities are not private companies but institutions that work for the public interest ensuring good governance. By implication, ensuring sustainable development is written into the function of governments and contracting authorities and thus should not be excluded from its public procurements. Public procurement should not stand in the way of genuine and proportionate climate mitigation initiatives, but also, Member States cannot be oblivious to the negative consequences of its procurements as one of the biggest buyers.

The above has been recognised to some extent. Over the last two decades, climate mitigation found its way also to the EU public procurement world. First, through the Court of Justice of the European Union (CJEU) case law, namely the landmark *Concordia Bus* case, which legitimised using criteria such as lower levels of nitrogen oxide emissions (climate mitigation consideration) as part of

[3] A New Circular Economy Action Plan COM(2020) 98.

[4] For the main challenges Member States encountered in the implementation of GPP, see Commission, 'Report on Implementation and Best Practices of National Procurement Policies in the Internal Market', COM(2021) 245 final, 8.

[5] EU Climate Law; Denmark: *Lov om klima nr 965 af 26/06/2020*, modified in 2021 by Act nr 2580; France: *Loi climat et resilience (Loi n.º 2021-1104)*, of 22 August 2021; Spain: *Ley 7/2021*, of 20 May, *de cambio climático y transición energética*; Portugal the *Lei de Bases do Clima (Lei n.º 98/2021)*, of 31 December 2021.

[6] In February 2022, Italy introduced amendments to its Constitution, adding the protection of the environment and biodiversity to its fundamental principles (Art 9) and stipulating that private economic initiative may not harm either the environment or health (Art 41).

the award criteria. Since then, climate mitigation considerations have found their way into the wording of Directive 2014/24 (Classic Directive), yet in a limited fashion.[7] Recital 2 of the latter indicates that one of its objectives is to enable 'procurers to make better use of public procurement in support of common societal goals such as climate change.[8] This argument is aligned with Arrowsmith, who notes that the 'prominence given to these objectives in the initial recitals may, in future cases, affect the interpretations of the directives adopted by the CJEU'.[9] Under the Classic Directive, climate change mitigation is only explicitly mentioned once when discussing the cost of environmental externalities under Article 68 on Life Cycle Costing (LCC). Though, reference to broader environmental considerations, which also cover climate change mitigation, is much more prevalent in the scope of the Directive.[10]

Traditionally, we look to the Public Procurement Directives as a source of rights and obligations in public procurement. However, following the Green Deal, we can observe a trend shift where various other areas of law introduce obligations influencing public procurement. This chapter focuses on this new development by considering one of such areas of law, namely climate change law. We explore how climate change is addressed in the law and its relationship with public procurement in the EU. The chapter is structured in the following manner. First, the conceptual framework for the chapter is given. We consider what climate change is and how we can characterise Low Emissions Public Procurement (LEPP). Next, the chapter examines EU legal sources regulating climate change law, particularly Article 11 Treaty on the Functioning of the European Union (TFEU) and the newly introduced EU Climate Law. Afterwards, we investigate the relevant sectoral legislation and consider whether established targets can constitute an obligation in public procurement. Finally, the chapter closes with conclusions.

II. What is Climate Change?

Climate change is a phenomenon that implies the modification of environmental conditions on our planet. It is generally associated with phenomena such as floods, heavy rains, heatwaves, and droughts, but also with melting ice, ocean

[7] Regarding renewable energy sources: Case C-448/01 *EVN AG and Wienstrom GmbH v Republik Österreich* ECLI:EU:C:2003:651, [2003] ECR I-14527; On eco-label considering climate environmental impacts and energy consumption, see Case C-368/10 *Commission v Kingdom of the Netherlands* ECLI:EU:C:2012:284, [2012] ECR I-284.

[8] See B Martinez Romera and R Caranta, 'EU Public Procurement Law: Purchasing beyond Price in the Age of Climate Change' (2017) 12 *European Procurement and Public Private Partnership Law Review* 281.

[9] S Arrowsmith, *The Law of Public and Utilities Procurement vol 2,* 3rd edn (London, Sweet & Maxwell, 2018) 720.

[10] Arts 18(2), 42, 56(1), 57(4)(a), 62, 67, 69(2)(d), 70 and 71 Classic Directive. For a discussion of these provisions, see W Janssen, 'Shifting towards Mandatory Sustainability Requirements in EU Public Procurement Law: Context, Relevance and a Typology', ch 1 in this volume.

acidification, and loss of biodiversity. Although the earth has always been subject to long-term temperature variations, the most consistent and unstoppable increase in temperature has been detected starting from the eighteenth century, the era of the first industrial revolution and the early stage of globalisation and mass production.[11] The latter generates a higher concentration of GHG in the atmosphere, so-called 'emissions', mainly carbon dioxide (CO_2), methane (CH_4), nitrous oxide (N_2O), and fluorinated gases, which increase the earth's temperature through the greenhouse effect. Emissions prevalently derive from energy consumption, agriculture, forestry and land use, transport and construction.[12] Recently, the Intergovernmental Panel on Climate Change (IPCC) reaffirmed that these atmospheric changes are mainly caused by human activity and that, if not curbed in 28 years, they are likely to increase the number of environmental catastrophes.[13] We can already see the devastating consequences of the atmospheric changes, for example, severe floods in Germany (2021) that caused 243 deaths and led to an economic loss of approximately 38 billion euros.[14]

The global response to climate change threats consists of two main lines of action: climate change mitigation and climate change adaptation. Climate mitigation is oriented at reducing emissions through alternative solutions (eg, electric vehicles instead of gasoline vehicles) or through offsetting (for a given amount of gas emitted, an equal amount of gas is absorbed, eg, by planting trees). Instead, climate adaptation aims to 'minimise damage' through infrastructural interventions (eg, dams, drainage systems, artificial ponds, green roofs).[15] In this chapter, we focus solely on climate change mitigation.

When discussing climate change mitigation, the national targets have been expressed through the terms 'carbon neutral', 'net-zero emissions', or 'zero carbon/emissions'. As indicated earlier, carbon refers to the main GHG, that is, CO_2, while 'emissions' is the umbrella term for all GHG. 'Neutral' and 'net zero' are synonyms, which indicate that for a total amount of GHGs emitted, the same amount is also removed from the atmosphere through offsets. Natural or artificial carbon sinks can absorb carbon, while sequestration of other gases must be

[11] S Manabe and AJ Broccoli, *Beyond Global Warming: How Numerical Models Revealed the Secrets of Climate Change* (Princeton, Princeton University Press 2020) 30.

[12] R Shukla, J Skea, R Slade, A Al Khourdajie, R van Diemen, D McCollum, M Pathak, S Some, P Vyas, R Fradera, M Belkacemi, A Hasija, G Lisboa, S Luz and J Malley, (eds), *IPCC, 2022: Summary for Policymakers. In: Climate Change 2022: Mitigation of Climate Change. Contribution of Working Group III to the Sixth Assessment Report of the Intergovernmental Panel on Climate Change* (Cambridge University Press, Cambridge, UK and New York, NY, US) 7.

[13] PR Shukla, et al, *IPCC, 2019: Climate Change and Land: an IPCC Special Report on Climate Change, Desertification, Land Degradation, Sustainable Land Management, Food Security, and Greenhouse Gas Fluxes in Terrestrial Ecosystems* (Cambridge, Cambridge University Press 2019) 36.

[14] K Kramer, and J Ware, 'Counting the Cost of 2021: A Year of Climate Breakdown' in M Delmotte et al, (eds) *IPCC, 2021: Summary for Policymakers. Climate Change 2021: The Physical Science Basis. Contribution of Working Group I to the Sixth Assessment Report of the Intergovernmental Panel on Climate Change* (Cambridge, Cambridge University Press, 2021).

[15] See E Woerdman, M Roggenkamp and M Holwerda (eds), *Essential EU Climate Law* (Cheltenham, Edward Elgar Publishing, 2021).

cut off at the source. The target of 'zero emissions' or 'zero carbon' is very ambitious, implying cutting all emissions at the source. As this is yet a distant goal in the context of public procurement, we focus on 'low emissions' in this chapter, meaning decreasing its scale.

III. What is Low Emission Public Procurement?

Over the decades, public procurement has been used as a policy instrument to pursue various goals, including environmental protection (GPP) or broader sustainability (SPP).[16] SPP prioritises purchasing products or services with the most positive environmental, social and economic impact possible over the entire life cycle. By doing so, SPP seeks to balance three components of sustainable development. This approach can be characterised as taking a long-term perspective on the consequences of the public buyer's purchasing decision. The SPP approach highlights that *green transition* cannot be considered in a vacuum and must be accompanied by a *just transition*. While we pursue mitigating climate change and phasing out coal, we need to remember the importance of the social dimension as the *green transition* may affect, for example, coal mining regions leading to unemployment. We must alleviate the negative socio-economic impact of the transition. Consequently, as the third leg of sustainable development, the social dimension focuses on the pledge 'no person and no place left behind'.[17]

Conceptually GPP is narrower than SPP. It is a sub-category covering two elements of sustainable development: economics and the environment. In the EU context, the Commission defined GPP as 'a process whereby public authorities seek to procure goods, services, and works with a reduced environmental impact throughout their life-cycle compared to goods, services, and works with the same primary function that would otherwise be procured'.[18]

The question is where to position LEPP in the range of the existing concepts of SPP and GPP, what it is, and why it is important to establish a separate concept. By focusing on LEPP, we aspire to create a common understanding and a reference point and delineate what we discuss in this chapter. SPP and GPP concepts cover the considerations of LEPP, but they go beyond climate mitigation alone. Regarding SPP, LEPP will inevitably lack a direct focus on the social dimension.

[16] See B Sjåfjell B and A Wiesbrock (eds), *Sustainable Public Procurement Under EU Law* (Cambridge, Cambridge University Press, 2016); R Caranta and M Trybus (eds), *The Law of Green and Social Procurement in Europe* (Copenhagen, DJØF, 2010); S Arrowsmith, 'The Purpose of the EU Procurement Directives: Ends, Means and the Implications for National Regulatory Space for Commercial and Horizontal Procurement Policies' (2012) 14 *Cambridge Yearbook of European Legal Studies* 1; P Kunzlik, 'Neoliberalism and the European Public Procurement Regime' (2013) 15 *Cambridge Yearbook of European Legal Studies* 283.

[17] European Green Deal COM(2019) 640.

[18] See Public Procurement for a Better Environment COM(2008) 400, 4.

It can be argued that climate mitigation considerations will be indirectly, but inherently connected with the social angle as: a) access to a healthy environment has been declared a human right by the UN Human Rights Council;[19] b) climate mitigation is ultimately about the self-preservation of humankind; and c) success in climate mitigation leads to improved living conditions. However, the social considerations will not necessarily find their way into the LEPP concept.

A. Why Should We Not Just Stick with the Concept of GPP?

Similar to SPP, the GPP is a broader concept than LEPP. The GPP covers LEPP, but also includes aspects such as protecting biodiversity, limiting the generation of waste, and limiting the use of pesticides and fertilisers related to protecting the environment but is not directly linked to emissions and mitigating climate change. Consequently, some aspects of the Commission's GPP definition are problematic from the perspective of climate mitigation, namely the reference to 'environmental impact' as it covers a broader group of impacts, not just climate change, and 'throughout their life-cycle' which is a broad concept and does not ensure a consistent reduction of the emissions.

Environmental impact is the effect on the environment resulting from a given activity. It is a multifaceted concept due to the wide range of various impacts and the ways of measuring them. Examples include climate change, human toxicity, ecotoxicity, ocean acidification, and water depletion.[20] The GPP definition is vague regarding how the reduction of related environmental impacts is to be calculated. More importantly, the definition does not specify how much that impact needs to be reduced, implying that any level of reduction, even minimal, falls under the definition.

The second aspect of the GPP definition that is problematic from a climate-mitigation perspective concerns using the wording 'throughout their life-cycle' when referring to the environmental impact of a supply, service, or work to be purchased. The Commission emphasises that the wording means the environmental impacts should be considered in all stages, from the cradle to the grave of the purchase.[21] What is not clear is whether the reduction of the environmental impact can be viewed from an overall perspective – this can be a reduction only at one stage of the life cycle, for example, transport – or it requires a reduction of the emissions to happen at every individual stage of the life cycle – for example, harvesting, manufacturing, packaging, distribution, and disposal.

[19] UN General Assembly in July 2022, following the Human Rights Council in October 2021.

[20] M Hauschild, 'Environmental Impact' in L Laperrière and G Reinhart (eds), *CIRP Encyclopaedia of Production Engineering* (Heidelberg, Springer, 2019).

[21] Art 2(20) Classic Directive and European Green Deal (n 17) 2.

Reducing emissions for each life cycle stage can only happen if an LCC methodology is applied in public procurement. LCC is a 'financial appraisal tool' that quantifies environmental externalities and monetises them accordingly.[22] LCC is not mentioned in the GPP's definition as a required pricing methodology. This is unfortunate from a climate mitigation perspective as, unsurprisingly, the tendency is for contracting authorities to opt for the lowest-priced option.[23] The latter does not provide an opportunity to assess various costs generated from the purchase, especially the negative environmental externalities, excluding the possibility of quantifying CO_2 or CO_{2eq} emissions – the fundamental elements from the climate mitigation perspective.[24] The reduction of emissions could be demanded as part of technical specifications. However, this could be challenging as it could lead to narrowing competition, particularly in immature markets. Not to mention that technical specification establishes the ceiling requirement while applying it in award criteria provides scalability and allows to reward those bidders that can provide the highest reduction possible.

An example can visualise the issue. A contracting authority wants to buy bananas for local canteens and wants the procurement to be green. Therefore, it decides that bananas should be organic. The technical specifications require that bananas bear an ecolabel or an equivalent means of proof, which certifies that no pesticides have been used to grow them – bananas carrying an ecolabel fall under the general characteristic of the GPP definition.[25] Nonetheless, the environmental benefit derived from organic farming is lost by the negative environmental externalities caused by transportation – considering that the contracting authority is based in Denmark, and bananas are usually imported from South America. Therefore, while buying organic bananas falls under the definition of GPP, it will not be a low-emission purchase.[26]

Reducing the emissions footprint of public contracts cannot be done through public procurement without considering environmental externalities. It is also not preferred to reduce the emissions on a singular occasion. If we are to take the goal of mitigating climate seriously, the reduction should be continuous and systematic.

[22] JJ Czarnezki and S Van Garsse, 'What is Life-cycle Costing?' in M Andhov, R Caranta and A Wiesbrock (eds), *Cost and EU Public Procurement Law: Lifecycle Costing for Sustainability* (Oxford, Routledge, 2019) 7.

[23] A Renda et al, *The Uptake of Green Public Procurement in the EU27* (2012). Submitted to the European Commission, DG Environment. Centre for European Policy Studies, College of Europe, 37.

[24] CO_{2eq} stands for carbon dioxide equivalent. It refers to the other gases responsible for global warming, ie, Methane (CH_4), Nitrous oxide (N_2O), Hydrofluorocarbons (HFCs), Perfluorocarbons (PFCs), Sulfur hexafluoride, Nitrogen trifluoride (NF_3). All these gases have a different impact on global warming, depending on the amount in the atmosphere and its measure through the GWP (global warming potential).

[25] Public Procurement for a Better Environment (n 18) 24 and 31. See also EU GPP criteria on food SWD(2019) 366.

[26] The example of bananas cannot be considered exhaustive. Other examples of LEPP that are not linked to transport-related environmental externalities are, eg, the choice not to buy a product or service that is not absolutely necessary (see Arrowsmith (n 9) 706) or to buy second-hand/recycled products.

In this chapter, we focus on LEPP, which we characterise as

> public procurement whereby public authorities seek to procure goods, services and works with the primary policy objective of contributing to climate mitigation. When awarding public contracts, LEPP requires applying an LCC methodology – or equivalent approach for emissions quantification. The LEPP seeks the best price-quality option, providing the lowest emissions and requires quantifying and reporting the emission and their reduction derived from the purchase.

The optimum is to seek continuous and systematic emission reduction at each stage of the life cycle of works, services or supply. However, we understand that public procurement is still far away from reaching that goal. Therefore, while not ideal, procurement can still be characterised as LEPP if the emission reduction is measured and achieved in one or more life cycle stages, such as the duration of a public contract.

The main limitation of the analysis in this chapter is that it does not analyse how the LEPP relates to other environmental or social objectives, perhaps to their detriment. For example, the decision to install a wind turbine plant will significantly impact biodiversity. Therefore, there is a need for further research on this intersection.

IV. How do We Address Climate Change in the Law?

Climate law can be considered a relatively new area of law. The first attempts to regulate climate change can be traced to the early 1990s leading to the adoption of the United Nations Framework Convention on Climate Change (UNFCCC), which aimed to stabilise 'greenhouse gas concentration in the atmosphere at a level that would prevent dangerous anthropogenic interference with the climate system'.[27] In 1997, the first binding quantified emission limitation agreement on climate change action was signed, the so-called Kyoto Protocol.[28] The latter established the objective of reducing global levels of GHG by at least five per cent between 2008–12. The protocol applied only to developed countries, including the EU and its Member States, for six specific GHG and entered into force only in 2005.[29] The Paris Agreement was adopted in 2015. It has a broader global reach and generally refers to all anthropogenic emissions. The goal of the Paris Agreement is to 'strengthen the global response to the threat of climate change'.[30] It sets specific long-term goals of keeping the increase in

[27] Art 2 of the United Nations Framework Convention on Climate Change (New York, 9 May 1992).

[28] Kyoto Protocol to the United Nations Framework Convention on Climate Change, 1997, FCCC/CP/L.7/; UNFCC, 'What Is the Kyoto Protocol?' at unfccc.int/kyoto_protocol.

[29] Art 2(2) Kyoto Protocol to the United Nations Framework Convention on Climate Change (Kyoto, 11 December 1997).

[30] Art 2 of Paris Agreement under the United Nations Framework Convention on Climate Change (Paris, 12 December 2015).

global average temperature 'well below two degrees than pre-industrial levels by 2030 with the purpose of implementing national legally binding measures'.[31] While international climate law establishes the normative climate framework that supports the joint decision-making between states, it does not consist of binding substantive rules.[32]

Climate change is only referred to once in EU primary law. Article 191(1) TFEU refers to the policy objectives of the Union, stating:

> promoting measures at the international level to deal with regional or worldwide environmental problems and, in particular, combating climate change.

Besides this, there are no specific climate change-related provisions. However, climate mitigation is one of the several dimensions of environmental protection and is covered by the umbrella provisions of environmental protection law, among them Article 11 TFEU.

A. The Environmental Integration Principle – Article 11

The TFEU establishes the so-called environmental integration principle in Article 11:

> Environmental protection requirements must be integrated into the definition and implementation of the Union's policies and activities, particularly with a view to promoting sustainable development.

Alongside Articles 191 and 193 TFEU, Article 11 explicitly states the EU's obligation to take an active role in combating the actions that harm the environment, which without question also includes climate change. Consequently, we refer to environmental protection in this section with a focus on climate mitigation whilst acknowledging here that environmental protection is indeed a broader concept.

Article 11 TFEU is considered simultaneously one of the EU's general objectives and a principle.[33] This provision provides a 'standard of interpretation' seen in the CJEU rulings, for example, the C-513/99 *Concordia* and C-379/98 *Preussen*

[31] ibid Art 2(a).

[32] CD Tvarnø, 'The New Era of Climate Law in Denmark and in the EU' (2022) 28 *EPL* 121.

[33] See A Wiesbrock and B Sjåfjell, 'The Importance of Article 11 TFEU for Regulating Business in the EU: Securing the Very Basis of Our Existence' in B Sjåfjell and A Wiesbrock (eds), *The Greening of European Business under EU Law: Taking Article 11 TFEU Seriously* (London, Routledge, 2014); M Klamert, 'Title II Provisions Having General Application' in M Kellerbauer, M Klamert and J Tomkin (eds), *The EU Treaties and the Charter of Fundamental Rights: A Commentary* (Oxford, Oxford University Press, 2019); M Klamert, 'Article 11 TFEU' in M Kellerbauer, M Klamert and J Tomkin (eds), *The EU Treaties and the Charter of Fundamental Rights: A Commentary* (Oxford, Oxford University Press, 2019).

Elektra cases.[34] In the latter case, concerning the rules of free movement and state aid, the Court highlighted that

> the use of renewable energy sources for producing electricity is useful for protecting the environment in so far as it contributes to the reduction in emissions of greenhouse gases which are amongst the main causes of climate change which the European Community and its Member States have pledged to combat.[35]

Advocate General Jacobs stated in this case that Article 11 is not merely a political statement but explicitly formulates legal obligations.[36] Due to the nature of Article 11, it can potentially restrict certain fundamental rights or principles, such as the free movement of goods.[37] This is demonstrated by *Commission v Denmark*, where the CJEU affirmed that 'the protection of the environment is a mandatory requirement which may limit the application of Article 30 [now Article 34 TFEU] of the Treaty'.[38] In other words, climate mitigation as a mandatory requirement following from Article 11 may limit free movement law in the EU. However, as indicated elsewhere, the challenge lies in the significant ambiguity regarding the scope and effects of the obligations arising from Article 11 TFEU. Unfortunately, there is very limited case law to provide further guidance.[39]

Regarding the scope of Article 11, two climate mitigation duties are established: the procedural duty of 'integration' and the nature of what is to be integrated being the 'environmental protection requirements'.

Article 11 TFEU refers to the integration within the Union's 'policies and activities'. Sjåfjell argues that 'activities' include legislative procedure, and consequently, during the law-making process, Article 11 should influence *the choice and the formulation of the rules* of the legislation.[40] This opinion is not shared by Jans and Vedder, who link the scope of Article 11 just to policies, stating that 'activities' are utilised just as a reinforcing expression for 'policies'.[41] The second duty regards integrating 'environmental protection requirements', which covers

[34] 'Standard of interpretation' is an expression used by M Klamert, 'Title II Provisions Having General Application' in M Kellerbauer, M Klamert and J Tomkin (eds), *The EU Treaties and the Charter of Fundamental Rights: A Commentary* (Oxford, Oxford University Press, 2019) 378.

[35] Case C-379/98 *PreussenElektra AG v Schhleswag AG* ECLI:EU:C:2001:160, [2001] ECR I-2099.

[36] Opinion of Advocate General Jacobs in the Case C-379/98 *PreussenElektra* ECLI:EU:C:2000:585, [2001] ECR I-2099231.

[37] Art 34 TFEU; T Lock, 'Article 37 CFR' in M Kellerbauer, M Klamert and J Tomkin (eds), *The EU Treaties and the Charter of Fundamental Rights: A Commentary* (Oxford, Oxford University Press, 2019) on Case T-634/13 *Arctic Paper Mochenwangen v Commission* ECLI:EU:T:2014:828, [2014] para 72.

[38] Case C-302/86 *Commission of the European Communities v Kingdom of Denmark* ECLI:EU:C:1988:421, [1988] ECR 460 para 9.

[39] M Andrecka and KP Mitkidis, 'Sustainability Requirements in EU Public and Private Procurement – A Right or an Obligation' (2017) 1 *Nordic Journal of Commercial Law* 55, 79.

[40] B Sjåfjell, 'The Legal Significance of Article 11 TFEU for EU Institutions and Member States' in B Sjåfjell and A Wiesbrock (eds), *Greening of European Business under EU Law: Taking Article 11 TFEU Seriously* (London, Routledge, 2014).

[41] JH Jans and H Vedder, *European Environmental Law – After Lisbon*, 4th edn (Amsterdam, Europa Law Publishing, 2012) 22–23.

climate mitigation. The definition of 'requirement' informs that it is compulsory, a necessary condition.[42] Thus, based on Sjåfjell's interpretation, Article 11 creates a material duty for climate mitigation requirements in law-making. According to Jans' and Vedder's interpretation, Article 11 seeks for that compulsory condition to be met by policies that are not obligatory by their legal nature. We believe that Sjåfjell's argument that, ultimately, the obligation extends to law-making is preferable as it ensures the internal coherence of the provision.

The procedural duty in Article 11 TFEU points to its transversal character, which stresses that climate change concerns a complex and interrelated natural world that is impacted by most human actions. Thus, every regulatory measure that affects the natural world shall comply with climate mitigation requirements (top-down approach). As Nowag argues, the *ratio legis* of Article 11 implies that the duty of environmental integration (climate mitigation) is even stronger in the legal areas where it is most at risk or most easily neglected, such as competition law or commercial law, which public procurement law is part of.[43]

Regarding the scope of Article 11 TFEU's obligatory character, the article is addressed to the Union. Nowag suggests that as one of the objectives of the Union, Article 11 creates a need for all EU institutions to act for its realisation, judicial and legislative bodies included.[44] Thus, it creates climate mitigation requirements to be applied by the EU institution in the law-making when drafting, for example, Public Procurement Directives or Financial Regulation. This obligation is potentially fulfilled by integrating climate mitigation requirements into the scope of the law requiring compliance with existing EU and national climate change laws under Article 18(2) Classic Directive and its equivalent Article 166(2) in the Financial Regulation. Regarding the Classic Directive, Article 11 TFEU is explicitly referred to in Recital 91 of the Directive.[45]

Besides the law making, the obligation from Article 11 also applies to the 'activities'. As the addressee is the Union, the EU institutions shall apply climate mitigation requirements into their activities, inter alia, when designing their procurements. The wording of Article 11 is vague, but a common interpretation is that it only applies to EU institutions. Consequently, it is presumably impossible to derive a minimum mandatory climate mitigation requirement directly from Article 11 as binding contracting authorities in their procurements.[46]

[42] Oxford Languages Google's English Dictionary. Also 'Any demands, constraints, needs, necessities needed to be met' (Black's Law Dictionary, 2nd edn.).

[43] J Nowag, 'The Sky is the Limit: On the Drafting of Article 11 TFEU's Integration Obligation and its Intended Reach' in B Sjåfjell and A Wiesbrock (eds), *The Greening of European Business Under EU Law: Taking Article 11 TFEU Seriously* (London, Routledge, 2015) 28–29.

[44] ibid.

[45] See M Andhov, 'Article 18(2) Public Procurement Principles' in R Caranta and A Sanchez-Graells (eds), *Commentary on Directive 2014/24/EU* (Cheltenham, Edward Elgar Publishing, 2021); Janssen (n 1).

[46] A Wiesbrock, 'An Obligation for Sustainable Procurement? Gauging the Potential Impact of Article 11 TFEU on Public Contracting in the EU' (2013) 40 *Legal Issues of Economic Integration* 105.

B. The New EU Climate Law

Under the 'Fit for 55' package, the Commission is leading the revamping of the entire climate and energy framework, which takes the front stage after the Green Deal commitment to achieve climate neutrality by 2050. A path is set towards realising the ambitious target of a 55 per cent reduction in net emissions by 2030, amongst others, through adopting the EU Climate Law, which is crucial for LEPP.

The EU Climate Law is a framework law which writes into the law the goals established by the European Green Deal to achieve climate neutrality, mainly by regulating union-wide GHG emissions.[47] Besides the long-term objective, the law also requires achieving an intermediate target.[48] The target applies collectively to the Union but not to each Member State individually. The EU Climate Law is to be read in conjunction with the Efforts Sharing Regulation, which defines the amount of emissions a Member State is allowed to emit in the main sectors which account for almost 60 per cent of total domestic EU emissions[49] and the EU Governance Regulation, which requires all Member States to adopt a national climate neutrality target and strengthen rules on national planning.

All of the 27 published 10-year national energy and climate plans (NECP) for 2021–30 include a reference to public procurement. While the scope differs between the Member States, for example, Hungary and Estonia mention public procurement just once. Croatia, amongst others, aims for 75 per cent of implemented public procurement procedures to apply GPP criteria in 2030. Slovakia's goal is for GPP to cover at least 70 per cent of the total value of public procurement. Any new procurement by De Lijn (a publicly owned Belgian transport company) will authorise only zero-emission buses in Belgium. Most NECP highlight the need for the public sector to lead the way and set a high standard. The NECP language is general and talks about promoting procurement as a means to contribute to achieving broader goals, such as established targets. These are policy documents to which it is not straightforward to attach legal nature, because it will ultimately depend on the specific details of how they are implemented.[50]

Regarding the EU Climate Law, the Commission is to monitor the progress of the Member States in adopting specific measures every five years.[51] When these measures are considered insufficient, the Commission must ask for justifications. As a cross-sectoral regulation, the EU Climate Law requires the adoption of sectoral legislation for the objective of climate neutrality to be realised. Therefore, the

[47] EU Climate Law.

[48] Tvarnø (n 32) 113ff.

[49] ie, transport, buildings, agriculture, non-ETS industry and waste.

[50] See regarding Irish National Mitigation Plan and the Irish Climate Action and Low Carbon Development Act 2015 case *Friends of the Irish Environment CLG v Government of Ireland & al, Record No2018/391 JR*.

[51] Art 7 EU Climate Law.

law must be read in conjunction with other pieces of legislation, such as discussed in section V.

The EU Climate Law does not include explicit references to public procurement. Consequently, at first glance, we cannot say that the EU Climate Law creates any mandatory requirement concerning LEPP on its own. However, the law obliges the Member States to take the next steps. Various national Climate Acts have accordingly been adopted recently. Among them are the French, Spanish and Portuguese Climate Acts, which directly refer to public procurement law.[52] These national climate acts showcase a trend shift in which public procurement matters are not only regulated in procedural Public Procurement Directives but also in a general cross-sectoral manner under climate law. The acts include, to various degrees, a combination of establishing targets (FR), a general principle (FR, SP, PT) and requirements for technical specifications and award criteria (FR, SP), and contractual clauses (FR).[53]

V. Sectoral Legislation – A Plethora of Different Solutions

Over the years, the EU legislator has adopted a range of secondary legislation where an obligation to ensure climate mitigation is established.[54] Thus, such secondary legislation will have a spillover effect and affect how public procurement is designed and carried out. Based on the Green Deal, some of these existing sectoral initiatives have been proposed to be revised.[55] Also, new initiatives have been proposed. We identified the most relevant sectoral legislation for LEPP focusing on reducing emissions. On that basis, we identified five legal sources and new legislative proposals discussed below.[56]

The first three acts are EU regulations and, thus, the most stringent regulatory tools, as there is no need for implementation in the Member States. These include the Energy Star Regulation, which mandates central government authorities to require a certain level of energy efficiency in their public contracts (Article 6).

[52] Report on Implementation and Best Practices (n 4): X Lazo-Vitoria, 'Spain: Transitioning towards Sustainable Public Procurement Mandatory Requirements', ch 13 in this volume.

[53] M Assis Raimundo, 'Climate Change Laws As Drivers of Transformation of Public Procurement and Public Contracts Law – A Comparative Overview of Recent European Experiences' (Public Procurement: Global Revolution XI, Nottingham, June 2022).

[54] A Semple, *A Practical Guide to Public Procurement* (Oxford, Oxford Publishing, 2015) 174; F Lichère and O Sulpice, 'Mandatory Requirements in Public Procurement Law: The Role of Remedies, Courts and Public Interest Litigation', ch 14 in this volume.

[55] European Green Deal (n 17).

[56] A Semple, 'Charge of the Light Brigade? The Clean Vehicles Directive and the Batteries Regulation', ch 7 in this volume; H Schebesta and MJ Plana Casado, 'Food: Mandatory EU Public Procurement Criteria for Food after the Farm to Fork Strategy', ch 8 in this volume; M Koszewska and JS Ligte, 'Textiles and Clothing: Mandatory Social Requirements As the Way Forward?', ch 9 in this volume.

Next is the EU Ecolabel Regulation, which introduced a voluntary EU Ecolabel certification scheme for products, aiming to reduce the products' negative environmental impact. Member States are urged to consider guidelines when they establish their national GPP Action Plans and consider setting targets for public purchasing of environmentally friendly products (Recital 14). In the category of regulations, the last one is the new Proposal for a Batteries Regulation which covers various aspects of the production and usage phases of batteries, such as GHG emissions.[57] It introduces minimum mandatory requirements on contracting authorities purchasing batteries or products containing them. Contracting authorities are to consider the environmental impact of batteries throughout their life cycle to minimise their impact (Article 70). They shall lay down technical specifications and award criteria based on Article 7 of the proposal to ensure that a product is chosen among those having a reduced environmental impact during its life cycle. Those specifications and criteria must be based on Article 7 on the carbon footprint of electric vehicle batteries and rechargeable industrial batteries. The Commission will adopt delegated acts supplementing the Regulation by establishing minimum mandatory GPP criteria or targets based on the requirements set out in, inter alia, Article 7.[58]

The second set of acts comprises EU Directives which leave the Member States with more discretion as they bind to the effect sought and need transposition into domestic systems. Here we have the Clean Vehicles Directive concerning the purchase or lease of vehicles intended for public transport and the purchase of the public transport service. It obliges contracting authorities to consider lifetime energy and environmental impacts, including energy consumption and emissions of CO_2, when purchasing road transport vehicles (Article 1). This obligation is to be fulfilled by complying with the minimum procurement targets for *clean duty vehicles* (Article 5). This target is a minimum percentage of clean vehicles that must be purchased out of the total. The targets are assigned for each Member State with most of them being required to reach 38.5 per cent of the whole bus fleet as 'clean'. Compliance is to be ensured by reporting on the implementation of the Directive. Second is the Energy Efficiency Directive which establishes a framework for buying energy-efficient products, vehicles and buildings.[59] It calls on the public sector to play an exemplary role in energy efficiency. It requires the Member States to ensure that three per cent of public sector buildings are renovated yearly. The Proposal for an Energy Efficiency Directive in Article 5 states that the Member States shall ensure that all public bodies' total energy consumption is reduced by at least 1.7 per cent each year. Member States shall include, in their NECP and updates thereof under Governance Regulation, a list of public bodies contributing to fulfilling the obligation. Proposed Article 6 extends the obligation to all

[57] Semple (n 56).

[58] D Gruyaert and V Pissierssens, 'Transforming the Construction Sector through Minimum Requirements', ch 10 in this volume.

[59] ibid.

public bodies instead of just the central government and increases the target from meeting minimum energy requirements to transforming buildings into net zero buildings. We can observe that some discretion is left for contracting authorities to decide how to allocate the three per cent. However, the energy efficiency requirement must be met when that is decided. Therefore, there is no discretion left in this regard when it comes to the contract design. Similarly, it is not left to the contracting authority's discretion to decide what is 'energy efficiency'. Rather, this is defined in the Directive's Annex.[60]

The third is the Energy Performance of Buildings Directive, which promotes resource-efficient public buildings. It requires Member States to adopt necessary measures to set minimum energy requirements (Article 4), ensuring that new buildings meet this minimum requirement (Article 6). When major renovations are foreseen for existing buildings, the energy performance of the building increases to meet the minimum requirements. Proposal for an Energy Performance of the Buildings Directive introduces 'minimum energy performance standards' as 'the essential regulatory tool to trigger the renovation of existing buildings on a large scale'.[61] New buildings occupied or owned by contracting authorities must be 'zero-emission' as of 1 January 2027 (Article 7(1)). The Member States shall ensure that existing buildings and building units owned by public bodies achieve, at the latest: (i) after 1 January 2027, at least energy performance class F; and (ii) after 1 January 2030, at least energy performance class E Article 9(1). Article 11(2) provides that

> Member States may set requirements related to the greenhouse gas emissions of, or to the type of fuel used by heat generators provided that such requirements do not constitute an unjustifiable market barrier.[62]

Sectoral legislation is interesting from the perspective of mandating LEPP as it affects individual contracting authorities and their procurements much faster than the distribution of targets following general climate acts would. Sectoral legislation also includes more precise indicators such as 'clean car' or 'net zero emission building'. A plethora of different obligations can be identified in the analysed sectoral legislation, ranging from procedural requirements (ie, the obligation to use climate mitigating award criteria and/or technical requirements) or substantive requirements (ie, the obligation to procure products with a set maximum amount of carbon emissions). Moreover, a mixture of targets, levels and minimum procurement requirements is visible across these discussed pieces of legislation.

VI. Targets and Public Procurement

Reducing emissions has increasingly been written into the law by establishing various targets. This suggests, particularly in the context of LEPP, moving from

[60] ibid.
[61] Proposal for an Energy Performance of the Buildings Directive (recast) COM(2021) 802.
[62] Gruyaert and Pissierssens (n 58).

procedural procurement law requirements to regulating targets. Consequently, shifting the legal discourse on where and how obligations in public procurement are created. Targets are established under EU and national climate laws, various sectoral legislations and policy/strategy documents, such as the Energy Efficiency Directive and the Proposal for a Batteries Regulation.[63] Some refer directly to public procurement, such as the Clean Vehicles Directive, and some do not, such as the EU Climate Law. Contributing to achieving the targets under LEPP can be done by establishing the minimum requirements in technical specifications, award criteria or contract performance conditions.

The analysed legal sources do not yet create an obligation to contribute to achieving the targets of economic operators. Thus, while Article 18(2) of the Classic Directive provides a basis for enforcing existing mandatory climate mitigation laws by requiring compliance with them, it focuses on the economic operators and the obligations that rest on their shoulders. So it would depend entirely if these targets are addressed to them, which, in general, they are not.

The question, though, is whether the established by law targets are binding not solely on the Member States but also on their contracting authorities. The answer will depend on the details of various acts. If one were to look at France, Spain and Portugal, it could be argued that the combined effect of the EU and their domestic climate laws creates an obligation for their contracting authorities as they expressly link the climate laws and public procurement. The combined effect is present in the EU, establishing the targets for Member States and requiring the states to act further to ensure that the target will be reached. To fulfil their obligation the Member States through their national law, distribute the target more specifically towards various areas, including public procurement and specific contracting authorities.

Similarly, sectoral legislation affecting LEPP, such as the Clean Vehicles Directive, directly addresses contracting authorities needing to contribute to various targets, ultimately leaving very little discretion to individual contracting authorities. This is important as climate protection became justiciable.[64] Besides the possibilities of the Commission pursuing infringement procedures to ensure compliance with established targets – that already happens[65] – lack of action from contracting authorities may potentially lead to them being sued for their inaction. This does not seem too far-fetched if the scale and relevance of public procurement are considered combined with the rise of climate change litigation.[66]

[63] Proposal for a Batteries Regulation (COM)2020 798, 3.

[64] J Jahn, 'Domestic Courts as Guarantors of International Climate Cooperation: Insights from the German Constitutional Court's Climate Decision' (2022) 17 *IJCL* (forthcoming) 6ff; see further Lichère and Sulpice (n 54).

[65] Regarding Italy's infringement on ambient air quality see Case C-644/18 *European Commission v Italian Republic* ECLI:EU:C:2020:895, [2020].

[66] See R Caranta, 'Opening the doors to civil society litigation in public contracts' at sapiensnetwork.eu/opening-the-doors-to-civil-society-litigation-in-public-contracts/.

VII. Conclusion

The state of climate mitigation and law in terms of procurement is scattered. Requirements regarding reducing emissions can be found in various sources of law. We are observing a trend shift where the legal discourse regarding the regulation of LEPP not only moves from facultative to mandatory but also outside of the Public Procurement Directives and domestic procurement acts to various EU sectoral regulations and directives. There is a divergence between the use of regulations and directives and the establishment of targets and minimum public procurement requirements to be addressed in technical specifications, award criteria or contract performance conditions. However, we can generally observe further development of specific requirements applicable to individual contracting authorities and their procurements. The EU and national legislators increasingly acknowledge that the current status quo of LEPP facilitation under Public Procurement Directives and even sectoral legislation is not enough. Procurement matters start to be expressly linked and addressed in general cross-sectoral national climate laws (eg, France, Spain, Portugal). Undoubtedly, this trend is connected with the scale and value of public buying and, therefore, the impact governments may achieve through their procurements.

Finally, a multidimensional yet blurred picture emerges, suggesting that the obligatory character of climate mitigation in public procurement is on the rise. The sectors where the minimum obligatory requirements are established based on the EU sectoral legislation are construction, transport and energy. Those are also some of the largest sectors procured by the public sector. Consequently, even if climate mitigation is not expressly addressed as an obligation in the procedural law (ie, Public Procurement Directives), we will de facto be dealing with minimum mandatory requirements with the majority of public procurement procedures via sectoral legislation. This means that contracting authorities will undoubtedly need basic carbon literacy to decide on methodologies, identify emissions sources and set targets to reduce their carbon footprint and other emissions. Similarly, procurement lawyers would need to broaden the scope of their expertise outside the procurement laws and become fluent in climate change laws.[67]

[67] Similarly, WA Janssen, 'On Discretion & Sustainability in EU Public Procurement Law: From Room for Diversity to Unity?' in T van den Brink and V Passalaqua (eds), *Diversity and Unity in the European Union* (Edward Elgar, forthcoming, 2023).

3

Subsidiarity Lost Along the Way? EU Public Procurement Legislation on the Road to Sustainability

TON VAN DEN BRINK

I. Introduction

The European Green Deal, adopted in 2020, contains a myriad of initiatives which have by now been crystallised inter alia in a number of legislative initiatives. Importantly, these initiatives are often not purely sectoral in that they would remain limited to the area of EU sustainability or environmental policies. Instead, they impact a broader range of fields of EU law and policy. In line with the overall purpose of this volume, this chapter focuses on the public procurement aspects of these initiatives from the perspective of subsidiarity.

Sustainability goals generally and the Green Deal objectives more specifically have been increasingly accepted and indeed viewed as urgent challenges for the EU and its Member States. In the EU's constitutional fabric, however, this itself provides no full justification for EU legislation. The subsidiarity principle (Article 5 TEU) requires that the EU legislature (and ultimately the Court) considers whether the EU is really needed to take action in light of the national possibilities to act. It requires separate consideration of whether the objectives of the proposed action 'cannot be sufficiently achieved by the Member States' and whether these objectives may be 'better achieved at the Union level'. Lower levels of governance ensure decision-making closer to the citizens and is thus preferred, also from a democratic perspective.

I will argue below that EU public procurement law, with Directive 2014/24/EU (Classic Directive) as its core legislative act, in general, has a strong 'subsidiarity salience'. Is the same true for the various Green Deal legislative initiatives that will also regulate public procurement in the future? To assess this question, I first need to take a closer look at the subsidiarity principle and its interpretation in the post-Lisbon era (section II).[1] Subsequently, the role of this principle in public procurement legislation, most notably the Classic Directive will be discussed (section III), followed by an analysis of a number of Green Deal initiatives (section IV). This will feed into the broader discussion on subsidiarity and public procurement law, a topic to which the debate on mandatory sustainability requirements has recently given new impetus.[2]

II. Subsidiarity: The Rise to Ambiguity

A. From Maastricht and Lisbon to Brussels and Strasbourg

Before assessing the impact of subsidiarity on EU public procurement law, I will first discuss its more general development as part of the EU's constitutional legal order. This is necessary to be able to understand its meaning for the specific legislation to be elaborated on in the next sections.

The Treaty of Lisbon (ToL) has marked a watershed in terms of subsidiarity's meaning and position in EU legislative processes, even though the formal introduction of the principle goes back to the Treaty of Maastricht (ToM). The principle found its way into the ToM partly as a counterbalance to the strong centralising elements of that Treaty, and partly to be able to take decisions 'as close as possible' to the citizen. Subsidiarity should contribute to a better and refined balancing of (sub-)national and EU competence at the level of concrete legislation.[3] As a general principle, it should be applied by both the legislature and the CJEU. Arguably, however, the ToL has had a much more profound effect. The ToL Subsidiarity and Proportionality Protocol[4] has given explicit powers to national parliaments to scrutinise legislative proposals on subsidiarity compliance under the Early Warning Mechanism (EWM). The EWM allows national parliaments to issue a 'yellow' or even an 'orange' card, which requires the Commission to reconsider its proposal. It does not enable them to formally block legislation. As a 'spin-off', the legislative practice equally saw the emergence of the Political Dialogue, a lighter communication channel between the Commission and national parliaments.[5] Thus, after the ToL, national parliaments gained direct access to the EU legislative

[1] The institutional and procedural aspects of the Early Warning Mechanism (EWM) have been discussed elsewhere.

[2] For a more comprehensive discussion of this debate see, W Janssen, 'Shifting towards Mandatory Sustainability Requirements in EU Public Procurement Law: Context, Relevance and a Typology', ch 1 in this volume.

[3] In contrast to the principle of conferred powers which balances EU and national competence at the level of policy areas.

[4] Protocol (No 2) on the application of the principles of subsidiarity and proportionality [2008] OJ C115/206.

[5] D Jancic, 'The Game of Cards: National Parliaments in the EU and the Future of the Early Warning Mechanism and the Political Dialogue' (2015) 52 *Common Market Law Review* 939.

procedure, whereas through the regular accountability channels, enabling them to hold ministers to account, they already had indirect access to the EU legislative procedure.

Since 2009, a vast amount of scholarly work has seen the light assessing the merits of the new system, criticising the ineffective enforcement of subsidiarity, but also the work of national parliaments that often extend scrutiny of EU legislative proposals beyond subsidiarity considerations. Such criticism fitted a general trend of critique on the principle.[6] Famously, Davies (dis-)qualified subsidiarity as 'the wrong idea, at the wrong place, at the wrong time'.[7] Particularly compelling is his argument that subsidiarity may have been introduced as a balancing mechanism between national and EU legislative authority, but it fails to deliver on that point. It is not even capable of doing so, because subsidiarity inherently implies a priority of EU policy objectives. Rather than providing a balancing mechanism between EU and national policy objectives, subsidiarity asks merely at what level of governance *EU objectives* should be pursued. From this perspective, one can understand why national parliaments have not limited themselves to subsidiarity considerations in this strict sense, but have sought to bring broader considerations of balancing national and EU interests into the decision-making.

The ToL was, however, not limited to strengthening the political-legislative dimension of subsidiarity. The Subsidiarity and Proportionality Protocol equally strengthened its judicial dimension.[8] In its turn, this has intensified the ambiguity of subsidiarity as a principle with both a political and a judicial meaning.[9] Article 8 of the Protocol provides that the CJEU has jurisdiction under Article 263 of the Treaty on the Functioning of the European Union (TFEU) in actions on grounds of infringement of subsidiarity. This may be seen as a redundant provision, because the Court would have jurisdiction to review legislative acts in any event on that ground. Still, the provision is meaningful, and has also had an impact on the Court's approach vis-à-vis subsidiarity. Before the ToL, the Court's approach was limited to a procedural check on whether the legislative institutions had duly considered the principle.[10] After the entry into force of the ToL, this has changed. The Court still attaches much weight to the legislature's discretion to apply subsidiarity, but at the same time applies a number of substantive criteria. Consequently, the case law is far from consistent. In some cases, the Court advances substantive subsidiarity arguments; in other cases, it seems to refer to its old legislative

[6] For a fairly recent overview of the literature, M Huysmans and P Van Gruisen, 'Substance and Subsidiarity: The Economic Dimension of Conflict in the Early Warning System' (2002) 44 *Journal of European Integration* 411.

[7] GT Davies, 'Subsidiarity: The Wrong Idea, in the Wrong Place, at the Wrong Time' (2006) 43 *Common Market Law Review* 63.

[8] Art 8 Protocol (No 2) (n 4).

[9] P Craig, 'Subsidiarity: A Political and Legal Analysis' (2012) 50 *Journal of Common Market Studies* 72.

[10] T van den Brink, 'The Substance of Subsidiarity. The Interpretation and Meaning of the Principle after Lisbon' in M Trybus and L Rubini (eds), *The Treaty of Lisbon and the Future of EU Law and Policy* (Cheltenham, Edward Elgar, 2012).

discretion-based approach or ignores subsidiarity-based claims altogether. In any case, the Court has thus far never annulled a legislative act on the basis of an infringement of subsidiarity.[11]

Let us return to the EU legislature. Over the years, subsidiarity has become a more visible aspect of EU legislative processes. National parliaments are indeed part of that trend, but – more importantly – EU legislative institutions themselves consider subsidiarity more explicitly now. This is the result of the EU's Better Lawmaking policies.[12] First, explanatory memoranda need to justify why the legislative act complies with the principle of subsidiarity. These justifications are at times rather generic, but in other cases, we find elaborate and substantive arguments. Second, the Commission carries a special responsibility to consider subsidiarity. This concerns not only the post-Lisbon forms of cooperation with national parliaments, but also the obligation to consider subsidiarity when carrying out Impact Assessments.

This increased procedural relevance of subsidiarity has equally increased the need to define objective criteria for the application of the principle. When can the Member States 'not sufficiently' achieve EU objectives and when is action at the EU level 'better'? The Treaty of Amsterdam Protocol on Subsidiarity and Proportionality contained a number of indicators that have not been included in the ToL Protocol.[13] However, these indicators are still relevant and have been further fleshed out in the legislative practice. The Report of the Taskforce on Subsidiarity, Proportionality and Doing Less More Efficiently contains the following indicators:[14]

With regard to whether the Member States acting alone would be sufficient:

- The cross-border aspects involved.
- Possible damage to the core objectives of the Treaty or the interests of other Member States when Member States would act alone.
- Member States' capacity to enact appropriate measures.
- Variation of the problem and its causes across levels.
- Spread of the problem (EU-wide or limited to specific Member States).
- Possible overstretching of Member States in achieving the objectives of the proposed measure.
- Variation in views of public authorities across the EU on how to best tackle the issue.

[11] See section II.B below.

[12] Interinstitutional Agreement between the European Parliament, the Council of the European Union and the European Commission on Better Law-Making [2016] OJ L123/1.

[13] Van den Brink (n 10).

[14] Task Force on Subsidiarity, Proportionality and 'Doing Less More Efficiently' Final report of 10 August 2018 at www.ec.europa.eu/info/sites/default/files/report-task-force-subsidiarity-proportionality-and-doing-less-more-efficiently_en.pdf.

With regard to whether the EU would be better suited to act the Report lists:

- Benefits; from EU level action (?).
- Economies of scale.
- Benefits from a homogenous policy approach.
- Weighing the benefits of EU-level action against the loss of competence of lower levels of governance.
- Impact on legal clarity for those having to implement the measure.

At least some of these indicators are quite broad and abstract in nature. This may not necessarily be problematic as these indicators have been designed for the political assessment to be made by the legislative institutions. Review by the Court is different, however, as will be demonstrated in the next section.

B. The CJEU's Post-Lisbon Approach to Subsidiarity

The CJEU has adopted a different approach to the operationalisation of subsidiarity. The following substantive aspects may be distilled.[15] The first is what can be called the 'connection argument'. Subsidiarity is related to the legislative act's aim, because it asks what is the most suitable level of governance *to achieve the desired aim*. Nowadays, it is common for EU legislation to pursue multiple aims. It may very well be that the EU level would be the appropriate level to pursue one of those aims, whereas the other aim(s) would be better accommodated by Member State action. In this light, the Court has had to rule on the legality of the Directive laying down accounting requirements for financial statements of undertakings.[16] The Directive pursues two objectives: (i) harmonising financial information of EU undertakings so that addressees of the financial information have comparable data; and (ii) avoiding that SMEs are faced with unreasonable burdens. Estonia challenged the legality of the Directive, claiming that the second aim could be better achieved by the Member States. The Court, however, did not accept this, using the mentioned connection argument. According to the Court, the two objectives were intricately linked,[17] and the EU legislature was, thus, better suited to regulate the issue. Accordingly, subsidiarity entails a preference for lower levels of governance, but the way in which the Court applies the connection argument results contrarily in priority for the EU level: if one legislative aim requires EU action, then connected aims shift to the EU level as well.

[15] M Huysmans, T van den Brink and P van Gruisen, 'Subsidiarity Ex-ante and Ex-post: From the Early Warning System to the Court of Justice of the European Union' (forthcoming).

[16] Case C-508/13 *Estonia v Parliament and Council* ECLI:EU:C:2015:403, [2015].

[17] ibid para 47. The argument was that if Member States would be able to alleviate burdens for SMEs, they could do so in varying ways, thereby possibly endangering the achievement of the first objective.

The second element of the CJEU's approach is to assess subsidiarity compliance only in relation to legislative acts in their entirety, rather than assessing individual parts or specific provisions thereof. This contrasts starkly with the approach of national parliaments. The latter frequently conclude that draft legislative acts in general comply with subsidiarity, but take issue with specific provisions thereof. The issue of whether individual provisions or rather the legislative act as a whole should comply with subsidiarity is closely linked to the duty to state reasons (Article 296 TFEU). In the above-mentioned case on the Directive laying down accounting requirements for financial statements of undertakings, the Court essentially brought forward two arguments why the EU legislature should not be required to bring forward arguments as to why individual provisions comply with subsidiarity. The first was that the requirement to state reasons is meant to protect addressees and enable them to understand why decisions have been adopted in the way that they are. As Estonia had been part of the decision-making, it could not legitimately claim to not know the reasons for the adoption of the directive. Second, if the legislative act 'clearly discloses the essential objective' pursued by the institution, according to the Court, it would be 'excessive to require a specific statement of reasons for each of the technical choices made by the institution'.[18] In other words, the subsidiarity justification may be of a rather general nature. This may be understandable from the Treaty definition of the subsidiarity principle, but it would at the same time be artificial to detach the subsidiarity assessment completely from the actual content of the proposal, including its individual provisions. The Court is perhaps mindful thereof when it sometimes still looks at individual aspects of EU legislation. This is indeed what can be concluded from the *Vodafone* case.[19] The Directive at stake concerned the Roaming Regulation. Complaints that the Regulation included provisions on retail prices (for which indeed EU action was more questionable in the absence of a strong cross-border element) were not accepted by the Court on the ground that these were inextricably linked to the roaming tariffs (which by definition involved cross-border aspects). Interestingly, the mentioned case was decided six months after the entry into force of the ToL and the fact that the Court engaged with substantive subsidiarity considerations may be viewed as a sign that the ToL has marked a significant change for the Court as well.[20] Indeed, the Court *did* address the individual provisions on retail prices, where it could have limited its assessment to a general one.

A third substantive element regards specific situations in the Member States. Obviously, the possibility to accommodate local circumstances and peculiarities provides a strong justification for prioritising national and subnational over EU action. At the same time, the objective of harmonisation is that national and local differences should not provide obstacles to the functioning of the internal

[18] ibid para 60.
[19] Case C-58/08 *Vodafone and Others* ECLI:EU:C:2010:321, [2010] ECR I-04999.
[20] Van den Brink (n 10).

market, or the achievement of EU objectives more broadly. This creates tension, and the CJEU seems to be siding more with the harmonisation perspective. In the Estonian case mentioned before, it considered that 'even if that Member State was more advanced' in protecting the interests at stake and indeed the level of protection could be lowered as a result of the implementation of the Directive, this provides no valid argument to conclude that the Member States are better suited to regulate the issue. In the words of the Court, subsidiarity

> is not intended to limit the EU's competence on the basis of the situation of any particular Member State taken individually, but requires only that the proposed action can, by reason of its scale or effects, be better achieved at EU level.

Here, the Court seems to follow a more consistent approach. In a decision on a Directive on airport tariffs, the Luxembourg Government took issue with some of its provisions applying to the Member States' major airports, the Luxembourg city airport being much smaller than other main airports.[21] The Court, however, decided that the EU legislature enjoys broad discretion and the exercise of that discretion was not affected by a manifest error or by a misuse of power.[22]

The last element regards the overlap with adjacent principles, most notably the principle of conferred powers and the proportionality principle. The first principle overlaps with subsidiarity when a subsidiarity consideration, such as the existence of a cross-border dimension of the regulated issue, is also a constituent element for the application of the legal basis. Article 114 TFEU, the legal basis for harmonisation of the internal market, is the most significant provision in this regard. More complicated, however, is the overlap between subsidiarity and proportionality. In a rigid interpretation of subsidiarity, the principle only regards the binary choice between regulation at the EU level and leaving the matter to (sub-) national levels. All other aspects regarding the interests of Member States would then qualify as proportionality considerations. This would, for instance, include the choice for total rather than minimum harmonisation, the choice for a directive rather than a regulation or simply the EU legislature's choice to leave discretion to the Member States. The EU's Better Lawmaking policies support the idea that such matters should indeed qualify as proportionality issues.[23] At the same time, and the legislative practice confirms this (especially national parliaments' scrutiny of legislative proposals), such elements may qualify as subsidiarity considerations as well. Lenaerts' argument that the Treaty definition of subsidiarity suggests it is not meant as a binary choice (*as far as* the Member States cannot sufficiently achieve) is a convincing one in this regard. Neither CJEU case law nor the provisions and principles the EU legislature is bound to respect (including Better Lawmaking

[21] Case C-176/09 *Luxembourg v Parliament and Council* ECLI:EU:C:2011:290, [2011] ECR I-03727.

[22] ibid para 50. It is true, however, that the Court did not dismiss the claim simply because specific local situations would not matter. It included a reasoning on substance on why the biggest airport in a Member State enjoys a privileged position, even if it is in absolute numbers rather small-sized.

[23] See T van den Brink 'Inclusief inhoud? "Beter Wetgeven" in de EU voorbij het wetgevingsproces: is er ook aandacht voor inhoudelijke kwaliteit?' (2020) 5 *RegelMaat* 330.

criteria) has settled the issue, however, which creates another aspect of ambiguity that continues to exist.

The lesson to draw from the CJEU's approach – assuming the Court will remain dedicated thereto[24] – is that individual parts of legislation matter only in a limited sense to assess overall subsidiarity compliance. Thus, individual provisions that, for example, allow or oblige the Member States to consider social and/or sustainability aspects will likely not result in separate subsidiarity assessments by the Court. In light of what has been discussed above on the distinction between subsidiarity and proportionality, such provisions may however be considered from a proportionality perspective.

III. Subsidiarity in EU Public Procurement Legislation

The centrepiece of EU public procurement legislation is Directive 2014/24/EU. Examining how subsidiarity impacted the adoption of this Directive should thus shed light on the role of subsidiarity in EU public procurement law more broadly.[25] More recently, Green Deal legislative proposals have been tabled that include public procurement aspects as well. Taken together, the current role of subsidiarity in EU public procurement law may be identified and evaluated in light of whether it meets its ambitions as laid down in the Treaties.[26]

A. Subsidiarity and Directive 2014/24/EU

Directive 2014/24/EU, the so-called Classic Directive, has not been subject to subsidiarity review by the Court. The legislative process, however, provides various insights on subsidiarity.[27]

i. The Directive and its Proposal

The considerations accompanying the Classic Directive are extremely weak and refer only to the definition of subsidiarity without giving any argument as to

[24] This is not certain. Indeed, it seems practically difficult and normatively questionable to consider subsidiarity only in such a binary and abstract (ie, detached from the concrete provisions of legislation) way. As the Court's case law on subsidiarity has evolved over time, and arguably still is developing, the Court may grow more sensitive to a specified approach to subsidiarity.

[25] The Directive 2014/23/EU on concessions and Directive 2014/25/EU on utilities will remain outside the scope of this chapter.

[26] See for such a broader approach also WA Janssen, 'On Discretion & Sustainability in EU Public Procurement Law: From Room for Diversity To Unity?' in T van den Brink and V Passalaqua (eds), *Diversity and Unity in the European Union* (Edward Elgar, forthcoming, 2023).

[27] National parliaments' positions discussed below have been consulted from www.ipex.eu unless otherwise indicated.

why the Directive would comply with the principle.[28] The ToL responsibility for EU institutions to ensure 'constant respect' for the principle was, thus, seriously neglected in this case. This seems to not be an anomaly. At the time of the adoption of the Directive, Advocate-General Kokott complained about the 'standard formulas' that the EU legislature applied and instead called for enhancing the preamble of EU legislation with 'sufficiently substantial statements' on why the legislation complies with subsidiarity.[29] In any case, the revised legislation must comply with subsidiarity too, so the EU legislature may not rely on, or refer to, subsidiarity assessments carried out in relation to earlier legislation.

The defective subsidiarity justification may be explained by political controversy. The initial Commission's Proposal[30] did include a more elaborate subsidiarity reasoning. This was mainly predicated on the internal market objective of the Directive.[31] Rather than ensuring equal access to and transparency of procurement procedures as an aim in itself, these elements would be functional to the internal market objectives in that these would ensure access for economic operators from other Member States. Interestingly, the Commission's reasoning did not stop here, but it went on to argue that this in turn is functional for the achievement of 'considerable savings and improved procurement outcomes that benefit Member States' authorities and, ultimately, the European taxpayer'. This tiered approach is remarkable as these latter objectives – which apparently sit at the apex – have not been recognised as Treaty objectives.[32] In any case, the centrality of the internal market objectives results in a convincing subsidiarity reasoning in the initial proposal. To some extent, this is inherent to internal market legal bases, because it is by definition more difficult or even outright impossible for Member States to individually prevent or remove obstacles to the proper functioning of the internal market. In this case, leaving the regulation of procurement procedures to the Member States would result in divergent requirements that would increase complexity and, thus, cause obstacles for cross-border activities. The inclusion of concrete data on the cross-border involvement in procurement procedures could have strengthened the subsidiarity justification further. Unfortunately, though, the entire subsidiarity justification got ripped out of the final Directive.

ii. National Parliaments on the Commission Proposal

National parliaments have scrutinised the initial proposal from a subsidiarity perspective. Two national parliaments, the Swedish Riksdag and the UK House of

[28] Recital 136 Classic Directive.

[29] Opinion of AG Kokott Case C-358/14 *Poland v Parliament and Council* ECLI:EU:C:2015:848, [2015]; see also Huysmans et al. (n 15) section 3.2.1.

[30] Proposal for a Directive on Public Procurement COM(2011) 896.

[31] ibid Explanatory Memorandum, section 3.

[32] See for a comprehensive discussion on the objectives of the entire 2014 Public Procurement Directives reform package, R Caranta, 'The Changes to the Public Contract Directives and the Story They Tell about How EU Law Works' (2015) 52 *Common Market Law Review* 391.

Commons, sent reasoned opinions. The Swedish Riksdag agreed with the overall purpose of the Directive, but considered that the provisions of the proposal on supervision, education, guidance and support for procurers and companies would conflict with subsidiarity. These provisions in particular aimed at requiring the Member States to set up a central body that would be entrusted with these tasks. The Riksdag brought forward that especially national diverging constitutional requirements make the Member States better suited to regulate these aspects. The UK House of Commons took issue with the same elements from the proposal. Setting up a central supervisory body would violate the UK's constitutional principle of devolution. In addition, by requiring a single supervisory body to combine administrative and judicial tasks (at least tasks that in the UK were carried out by courts), the Proposal would equally violate subsidiarity. In the final version of the Directive, a much watered-down Article 83 has been included allowing the Member States to execute the said tasks by different public bodies. This may be seen as subsidiarity directly impacting the content of legislation. In earlier research, it has already been established that constitutional, institutional and procedural aspects require – at least in the eyes of national parliaments – specific and extra justification.[33]

Apart from the two reasoned opinions, parliaments from five other Member States engaged in the political dialogue on the Proposal with the Commission: the Czech Senate, the Italian Senate and Chamber of Deputies, the Romanian Chamber of Deputies, the Danish Parliament and the German Bundesrat. These were more focused on the substantive aspects of the Proposal. The Czech Senate pointed to the risk of dividing procurements into lots to avoid meeting the thresholds and observed that favouring SMEs might not necessarily be a positive development.[34] The Italian Senate in its turn opposed the inclusion of water supply licences;[35] the Italian Chamber of Deputies asked for more room for national discretion in relation to multiple aspects of the regulatory framework, especially in light of the specificities of the Italian situation (including stricter enforcement of exclusions from participation in public tenders).[36] In a broader, non-binary interpretation of subsidiarity, such elements may be viewed as subsidiarity-based arguments. By contrast, the German Bundesrat carried out a comprehensive assessment on the full merits of the proposal, although some of its arguments may be considered to relate to subsidiarity (eg, the argument that existing German legislation already achieves the aims of the proposed legislation).[37]

All in all, the subsidiarity of the Directive as such has been hardly contested and it would indeed be difficult to argue why the Member States would be

[33] Van den Brink (n 10).
[34] Resolution of 14 June 2012, No. N 136/08, N 137/08, N 138/08.
[35] Italian Senate Scrutiny Information of 27 December 2012.
[36] Committee Opinion of 28 November 2012 at secure.ipex.eu/IPEXL-WEB/document/COM-2011-896/itcam.
[37] Bundesrat Scrutiny Information of 20 December 2011.

better suited to regulate the issue. Still, the EU legislature has seriously failed to provide a sufficient subsidiarity justification, thereby infringing not only the principle itself, but equally the duty to provide reasons under Article 296 TFEU. National parliaments have not questioned the overall subsidiarity compliance of the Proposal, perhaps as most provisions were not mandatory. They did voice subsidiarity concerns on individual elements of the Proposal. As the most powerful of these concerns have prevented the provisions concerned to make it to the Official Journal, it may safely be argued that the subsidiarity principle now indeed functions at this concrete level as well.

IV. European Green Deal Legislation Affecting Public Procurement and Subsidiarity

A. The Proposal for an Energy Efficiency Directive

The 2021 Proposal for an Energy Efficiency Directive is based on Article 194(2) TFEU, which is the specific legal basis for energy measures.[38] Its ambitions extend significantly beyond the current Directive. The overall targets for the reduction of energy consumption would become stricter, and the proposal specifically targets sectors with high energy-saving potential. The public sector will be one of these, and Article 7 of the proposal contains the obligation for contracting authorities to only purchase products, services, buildings and works with high energy-efficiency performance.

The explanatory memorandum accompanying the Proposal is quite extensive on subsidiarity.[39] The first argument relates to the *prominence of the (EU) objectives* concerned: energy efficiency as such becomes ever more urgent and the topic is at the same time closely connected to other key EU objectives such as the security of energy supply, climate change and the internal market.

The second argument is that the *problems* that prevent (further) energy savings are the *same* throughout the EU and exist everywhere: a lack of systematic information about the impacts of energy efficiency measures; insufficient incentives to drive ambition and efforts by Member States; the continued existence of barriers to energy efficient behaviour, including for investments.[40] Regarding public procurement, the IA signals that energy efficiency requirements are not systematically included in procurement procedures, with the purchase price remaining the main criterion.[41]

[38] M Andhov and F Muscaritoli, 'Climate Change and Public Procurement: Are We Shifting the Legal Discourse?', ch 2 in this volume.
[39] Proposal for an Energy Efficiency Directive (recast) COM(2021) 558.
[40] SWD Working Document Impact Assessment Report Accompanying the Proposal for Energy Efficiency Directive (recast) SWD(2021) 623, section 2.
[41] ibid section 2.2.2.

The third subsidiarity argument is that the Directive leaves the Member States considerable *discretion*. The energy efficiency target is not binding at the national level. Member States are required to define their own ambition levels, taking into account their national circumstances and contexts. The Commission also mentions the choice for a directive rather than a regulation even if this concerns primarily the proportionality principle.[42]

Fourth, the issue concerns a *transboundary problem*. The argument runs as follows: actions to increase energy efficiency and reduce energy use leads to benefits beyond national borders, such as a reduction of greenhouse gas emissions. Such external benefits may be undervalued in purely national decision-making processes.

Fifth, EU action would have *additional benefits*, according to the legislature, in that it would create trust, reliability and continuity which would stimulate investment and other involvement. Furthermore, EU action would create markets of scale for European suppliers and create certainty for investors and consumers.

The Council and the European Parliament (EP) have meanwhile assessed the Proposal. They made no significant changes to the subsidiarity justification, but did suggest changes to Article 7. The EP wished to make some of the provisions stricter. It suggested imposing on Member States the obligation to require contracting authorities to take wider sustainability goals into account and to require tenderers to disclose certain information.[43] By contrast, the Council suggested changes that would result in more discretion for the Member States by allowing them not to take into account Union GPP criteria, but instead, apply equivalent national criteria.[44] However, none of the three institutions linked these concrete procurement-related elements to the overall subsidiarity assessment. The latter thus remains quite abstract and general in nature, which is in line with the CJEU's approach as outlined above but seems nevertheless quite unsatisfactory in terms of doing justice to subsidiarity.[45]

i. National Parliaments on the Proposal

Several parliaments have analysed the proposal as part of a set of European Green Deal measures that have been assessed jointly. The Irish Joint Committee on Environment and Climate Action issued a reasoned opinion on a series of measures.[46] It concluded that the proposals, including the Proposal for an Energy

[42] Commission, 'Better Regulation Toolboxes', Tool 18: The Choice of Policy Instruments at www.commission.europa.eu.

[43] Amendments adopted by the European Parliament on 14 September 2022, A9-0221/2022 at www.europarl.europa.eu/doceo/document/TA-9-2022-0315_EN.html.

[44] Council of the European Union, 'General Approach on the Proposal for a Directive of the European Parliament and of the Council on energy efficiency (recast)', 10697/22.

[45] To be fair, the provision on 'green' public procurement is not an exception.

[46] The Irish Joint Committee on Environment and Climate Action Scrutiny Document of 28 September 2021.

Efficiency Directive, had not been sufficiently justified with quantitative and qualitative indicators. Moreover, the Committee concluded that the necessity and greater benefits of the European proposals compared to the Irish Climate Action and Low Carbon Development Bill 2021 that had just been enacted had not been demonstrated.

Similar to the Irish Joint Committee, the Czech Senate argued that the Proposal had been based on too limited empirical data.[47] Other arguments related to the specificities of the Czech situation, such as the economic dependence on industry (resulting in a different energy need) and the need for the Czech economy to rely on nuclear energy.

Some other national parliaments have scrutinised the Green Deal proposals in the context of the political dialogue. The Austrian Parliament voiced concerns about the impact on the public sector.[48] It called for flexibility and to avoid excessively strict requirements as the starting situations for public institutions can be very different. Its concerns were mainly aimed at the obligation to renovate public buildings, however, and not so much on their role as contracting authorities under Article 7 of the Proposal. The German Bundesrat was overall positive on the proposal but urged that the subsidiarity principle should be considered, especially in light of the Member State's responsibility for public housing.[49] The Bundesrat was equally positive about Article 7, stressing the potential of public procurement to contribute to the climate goals. Lastly, the Polish Sejm saw a problem with implementing the ambitious targets of the Directive in Poland and asked for a derogation and extension of the deadlines.

In sum, the Directive attracted considerable subsidiarity attention, but the public procurement aspects have been mostly ignored even though national parliaments have provided useful and relevant input thereto.

B. The Clean Vehicles Directive

The revised Clean Vehicles Directive seeks to promote clean and energy-efficient road transport vehicles.[50] Its legal basis is Article 192 (1) TFEU on the protection of the environment. The Directive is the successor of the Clean Vehicles Directive, which was seen to contribute insufficiently to a cleaner vehicle fleet in the EU. The new Directive created public procurement targets in terms of the minimum percentage of clean vehicles in relation to the total number of road transport vehicles covered by the aggregate of tendered contracts.[51] Importantly, the new

[47] Czech Senate Resolution of the Committee on EU Affairs of 3 November 2021.

[48] Austrian Federal Council Scrutiny information of 8 November 2021.

[49] Point 6 Bundesrat Scrutiny Information of 17 December 2021.

[50] A Semple, 'Charge of the Light Brigade? The Clean Vehicles Directive and the Batteries Regulation', ch 7 in this volume.

[51] Art 5 Directive amending Clean Vehicles Directive.

Directive now also defines the central concept of 'clean cars'.[52] This obviously invites an elaborate subsidiarity assessment. The preamble, however, only refers in general terms to the need for a 'common and long-term policy framework' and the scale of the issue.[53] The latter element is better explained in the Commission's Explanatory Memorandum in that climate change and air pollution warrant action at all levels of governance, even though the latter problem manifests itself at a local level. The internal market dimension allows Member State authorities to draw on the best clean technologies.

This does, unfortunately, not result in a very convincing subsidiarity justification either. The general seriousness may indeed *in general* warrant action at all levels of governance, but the subsidiarity principle requires an assessment of whether *this specific issue* should require EU action. Moreover, the internal market contribution to making 'cleaner' technology more widely available may very well be fair, but this is not promoted by the Directive as such. This is no surprise as the aim of the Directive is simply different, which is to make contracting authorities consider environmental impacts when they procure road transport vehicles.[54] The subsidiarity assessment takes this objective of the measure as a yardstick, so the element of the promotion of cross-border availability of cleaner techniques would necessarily need to fall outside the scope of such an assessment.

The explanatory memorandum also justifies the proposal by referring to its limited impact on the Member States. These remain competent to organise the provision of (public) transport and may still choose appropriate technologies. This may be viewed as a proportionality justification, but – in protecting Member State autonomy as much as possible – it has subsidiarity relevance as well.

i. National Parliaments on the Proposal[55]

No reasoned opinions have been issued in relation to the proposal, but it has given rise to political dialogues with five national parliaments. The Czech Senate called for extending the scope of the 'clean vehicle' definition[56] and, conversely, limiting the scope of application of the Directive. More importantly, the Senate wished to see the binding targets, one of the most prominent elements of the revision, deleted.[57] This point was shared by the Austrian Federal Council that argued that the targets were too strict in light of the limited availability of clean vehicles and sought furthermore to ensure a certain degree of national freedom in defining the targets of the mobility package. The wide scope of the Commission's delegated powers was another cause of concern. By contrast, the French National Assembly

[52] ibid Art 4.
[53] ibid Recital 33.
[54] ibid Art 1.
[55] Proposal for a Directive amending Clean vehicles Directive COM (2017) 653.
[56] This point was supported by the Chamber of Deputies, Resolution 34 of the 7th session of 15 February 2018, point 7 at secure.ipex.eu/IPEXL-WEB/document/COM-2017-653/czpos.
[57] Czech Chamber of Deputies Scrutiny Information of 15 February 2018.

called for more ambitious targets as well as for the introduction of an obligation to equally take environmental and energy issues into account for vehicles to be acquired outside of the obligatory percentages.[58] The effects of national parliaments' opinions have remained limited though. Especially, the hard targets still made it into the final version of the Directive.

Overall, subsidiarity played a limited role in the adoption of the Clean Vehicles Directive. Especially the substantive reasoning why the EU would need to act has been shallow.

C. Proposal for a Batteries Regulation

Unlike the Clean Vehicles Directive, the Proposal for a Batteries Regulation is based on Article 114 TFEU. The objectives, listed in the preamble, reflect this as they refer to the uneven playing field for batteries; barriers in the recycling markets; economies of scale and the need for a stable and fully harmonised regulatory framework.[59] These objectives directly feed into the subsidiarity assessment. Indeed, such objectives are almost by definition impossible for the Member State to achieve individually. Consequently, the subsidiarity justification is rather stingy.[60]

i. National Parliaments on the Proposal

No reasoned opinions have been issued on the Proposal. A small number of parliaments have completed scrutiny processes, and these have led to positive subsidiarity assessments. The French Senate pointed at the increased need for batteries and the raw materials they require;[61] the Spanish Cortes Generales supported the sustainability goals and considered the internal market route to be indispensable to achieve those (and that the pre-existing Directive achieved that goal insufficiently).[62] The German Bundesrat assessed the Directive more on substance. While equally arriving at an overall positive subsidiarity assessment, the Bundesrat included a number of more critical points relating to specific aspects of the Proposal, for example, on e-bikes, on the exclusion of nickel-cadmium batteries from the scope of application of the Directive and the proposed Commission implementing powers under Article 16. No specific issue has been raised, however, in relation to Article 70

[58] Assemblee Nationale Scrutiny Information of 7 June 2018.

[59] ibid Explanatory Memorandum, 4. During the finalisation of this chapter, the European Parliament and Council reached a provisional agreement on this Regulation on 9 December 2022, yet no final text was available at the time.

[60] See also the Impact Assessment which more by way of statements rather than by concrete evidence takes the position that the EU rather than the MS should act: SWD Impact Assessment Report Accompanying the Proposal for a Batteries Regulation SWD(2020) 335, 31.

[61] French Sénat Scrutiny Information of 8 July 2020.

[62] Cortes Generales Scrutiny Information of 10 December 2020.

of the proposal on the obligation to procure batteries in 'green' ways, even if the third paragraph of that provision delegates the power to the Commission to set the substantive standards in this regard. The only critical parliament was the Slovene National Assemblee that questioned the internal market legal basis and was also critical of the scope of secondary legislation the proposal would allow the Commission to adopt.[63] It did, however, not mention Article 70 specifically, but the point certainly applies to this provision as well. Apart from this opinion, the application of the proposed legislation to public procurement has raised no questions or concerns.

Legislative measures based on Article 114 TFEU by their very nature easily comply with subsidiarity. Yet, individual aspects of the Directive, such as the provision on public procurement, could still have given rise to a more balanced subsidiarity assessment. Here, the abstract nature of the subsidiarity justification shows its problematic sides.

D. The Proposals for the Construction Products Regulation and the European Ecodesign Regulation

The Proposal for a Revision of the Construction Products Regulation[64] and the Proposal for a Regulation on Ecodesign for Sustainable Products[65] will be discussed jointly.[66] They have raised very few subsidiarity issues. Both proposals are based on Article 114 TFEU, and the internal market rationale thus plays an important role in the subsidiarity justification. In the case of the Ecodesign Proposal, the internal market objective is combined with the aim of reducing the negative life cycle environmental impacts of products.

The explanatory memorandum of the Construction Products Proposal is rather concise on subsidiarity. Similar to the Batteries Regulation, the level playing field argument is combined with sustainability goals as well as with the need to provide legal certainty and predictability to support EU action. As a reason to include public procurement, the explanatory memorandum argues that the current regulation limits the possibilities for Member States to define national requirements for buildings or to include criteria in public procurement on sustainability objectives without putting at risk the functioning of the single market.

The explanatory memorandum of the Proposal for a Regulation on Ecodesign for Sustainable Products is more elaborate on subsidiarity.[67] The level playing

[63] Slovenian National Assembly Scrutiny Information of 10 December 2020.

[64] Proposal for a Revision of the Construction Products Regulation COM(2022) 144.

[65] Proposal for a Regulation on Ecodesign for Sustainable Products COM(2022) 142.

[66] C Backes and M Boeve, 'Regulating the Producer instead of the Procurer – The EU Sustainable Products Initiative and Extended Producer Responsibility as Ways to Foster the Transition to a Circular Economy', ch 6 in this volume.; D Gruyaert and V Pissierssens, 'Transforming the Construction Sector through Minimum Requirements', ch 10 in this volume.

[67] Proposal for a Regulation on Ecodesign for Sustainable Products (n 65) recitals 9 and 87.

field and the fragmentation of the internal market as a result of diverging national approaches appear here as well. Leaving the matter to the Member State would result in competing systems which would have detrimental effects not only for companies, but for consumers as well. The size of the internal market would, furthermore, provide leverage to promote product sustainability and influence product design and value chain management worldwide. Only a more general observation is included relating to the inclusion of public procurement, stating that the current approach has had a limited impact due to the limitations of voluntary approaches as well as a reference to the economic relevance of procurement in the EU.

i. National Parliaments on the Proposals

Based on the entries on www.ipex.eu, the Proposal for a Revision of the Construction Products Regulation has attracted very little attention. Only a few parliaments have even looked at the proposal, and none of them proceeded to scrutinise the proposal further.

The Proposal for a Regulation on Ecodesign for Sustainable Products has attracted some more parliamentary attention. The Polish Sejm joined its government's criticism of the provision that imposes a reporting obligation on Member States on the implementation and application of ecodesign requirements in relation to public procurement.[68] Equally, it voiced concerns over the wide scope of the Commission's implementing powers, the short implementation deadline and the burdens put on business. The latter points were shared by the Slovenian National Assembly which added to the concerns on the alignment of the proposal with other EU legislation. It supported the overall aims of the proposal, however, which explicitly included the mandatory criteria for green public procurement.[69]

The two proposals reveal a similar picture compared to the Batteries Regulation. The internal market legal basis silences much of the subsidiarity assessment at the EU level, which in any case remains abstract. This is all the more surprising as Article 192 TFEU (environmental protection) – which limits EU action to minimum harmonisation – could also have been considered (optionally in combination with Article 114 TFEU). This would necessarily have altered the subsidiarity assessment as well. On the other side of the spectrum we find national parliaments, but their input is of such a particular and specific nature that it has – at least thus far – no impact on the legislative decision-making processes.

[68] Sejm, 'EDL-S European Legislative Documents in the Sejm (Sejm)' at www.sejm.gov.pl.
[69] Slovenian National Assembly Scrutiny Information of 24 June 2022.

V. Conclusion

Subsidiarity is part of the EU's foundational principles that balance EU and national competence. Its political and legal dimensions are carefully distinguished in legal doctrine and, indeed, the CJEU approach is different from that of the EU's legislature. Still, the CJEU limits itself no longer to a mere procedural check but now also considers substantive aspects to some extent. A further complication is that within EU legislative procedures, the various actors approach and interpret subsidiarity differently. A prime example is national parliaments which systematically ask for specific national circumstances and peculiarities to be considered, whereas the Commission and the Court systematically dismiss such arguments. Equally, whereas national parliaments generally adhere to a wide concept of subsidiarity that includes the intensity of EU legislation and the degree of national discretion, EU institutions rather see the principle as providing only a binary choice between EU or national action.

Such downsides of subsidiarity have manifested themselves poignantly in EU public procurement legislation and the recent Green Deal proposals. The three main characteristics that have surfaced in the EU legislative and Court practice interact in a particularly negative way here: abstract versus concrete assessment; a binary approach to subsidiarity and the irrelevance of country-specific circumstances. The binary approach and the abstract assessment are intricately linked in that if the question of whether or not the EU should act is answered in a binary way, the actual way in which the EU should act – and thus the content of legislation – moves into the background and the subsidiarity assessment thus becomes abstract in nature. This is particularly troublesome for internal market-based legislation in which the objectives hardly allow Member State action as a viable alternative. Standard arguments – level playing field, the presence of a cross-border dimension; economies of scale – may easily lead to a bleak subsidiarity justification. The blind eye for specific national circumstances adds to this: it precludes that national peculiarities are considered and inform a more detailed subsidiarity justification. Thus, the Green Deal proposals analysed in this chapter have not been justified on the basis of their actual content, but rather on how the topics of these measures relate to sustainability goals more generally. Thus, the procurement provisions have not been addressed specifically at all.

This is all the more surprising in light of the 'subsidiarity sensitivity' of public procurement legislation. The adoption of the Classic Directive has led to considerable parliamentary attention; substantively the impact on the principle of national procedural and institutional autonomy has been an important concern. Nothing thereof is part of the current legislative processes. Subsidiarity generally thus fails to reach its potential as a balancing principle for EU and national competence. For the legislation assessed, a proper assessment is lacking on which elements should be regulated at the EU level and why, thereby damaging the quality of the legislative processes and the ultimate outcomes thereof. In light of the central claim of this volume, that these new legislations will amount to a paradigm shift in public procurement legislation, this is all the more problematic.

4

Mandatory Requirements in Sustainable Public Procurement: The Economic Perspective

ENRIQUE CARRERAS AND DAVIDE VANNONI*

I. Introduction

In Europe, there has been increasing attention towards the use of public procurement as a tool to reach sustainable goals, especially environmental protection (reduction of deforestation, greenhouse gas emissions, waste, air, water, and soil pollution). From simply allowing the introduction of sustainability criteria in governmental purchases, there has been a progressive shift towards a widespread recommendation to use them. Recently, due also to the fact that the diffusion of SPP practices is not satisfactory and remarkably differs across sectors and EU member countries,[1] the balance has moved forward towards imposing mandatory requirements for contracting authorities in the EU Member States.[2]

Indeed, the European Green Deal is paving the way for the above shift, intending to transform voluntary green criteria into mandatory requirements: public authorities, including the EU institutions, should lead by example and ensure that their procurement is green. The Commission will propose further legislation and guidance on green public purchasing.[3] This adds to the sector-specific mandatory

* This project has received funding from the European Union's Horizon 2020 research and innovation programme under the Marie Skłodowska-Curie grant agreement No 956696.

[1] See F Testa et al, 'What Factors Influence the Uptake of GPP Practices? New Evidence from an Italian Survey' (2012) 82 *Ecological Economics* 88; A New Circular Economy Action Plan COM(2020) 98.

[2] W Janssen, 'Shifting towards Mandatory Sustainability Requirements in EU Public Procurement Law: Context, Relevance and a Typology', ch 1 in this volume.; M Andhov and F Muscaritoli, 'Climate Change and Public Procurement: Are We Shifting the Legal Discourse?', ch 2 in this volume.; M Andhov, 'Contracting Authorities and Strategic Goals of Public Procurement – A Relationship Defined by Discretion?' in S Bogojević, X Groussot and J Hettne (eds), *Discretion in EU Public Procurement Law* (Oxford, Hart Publishing, 2019) 134; K Pouikli, 'Towards Mandatory Green Public Procurement (GPP) Requirements Under the EU Green Deal: Reconsidering the Role of Public Procurement as an Environmental Policy Tool' (2021) *ERA Forum* 699; L Mélon, 'More Than a Nudge? Arguments and Tools for Mandating Green Public Procurement in the EU' (2020) 12 *Sustainability* 988.

[3] European Green Deal COM(2019) 640.

requirements already in force in EU law, namely, the Energy Star Regulation for IT office equipment, the Clean Vehicles Directive, as well as the two Directives targeting the construction sector (the Energy Performance of Buildings Directive and the Energy Efficiency Directive).

This chapter analyses the theoretical and empirical literature, within the economics discipline, dealing with the use of rules versus discretion in designing and implementing a policy, with a specific focus on public procurement and, in particular, on policies that are aimed at reaching sustainable development goals.[4] The SPP umbrella covers both environmental and social issues, and international organisations often conduct surveys, propose guidelines and provide examples of best practices in policy reports combining both Green Public Procurement (GPP) and Socially Responsible Public Procurement (SRPP).[5] Moreover, some countries adopt an integrated approach for 'strategic' public procurement, where green and social criteria are included in the same policy packages. However, in our view, for several reasons, it is not particularly rewarding to use the same lens to analyse both GPP and SRPP.[6]

GPP is typically aimed at correcting a negative externality (pollution) or can be used to trigger a positive externality (innovation spillovers), whereas SRPP is responding to a variegated range of issues such as fairness, equity, protection of minorities and disadvantaged groups. Certain activities seem better suited for GPP (defence, energy, health, construction), while SRPP can be applied in principle to all sectors.[7] Furthermore, the theoretical and empirical literature addressing environmental policies (among which the role of governmental purchases) is much more mature, and the choice of implementing them on a voluntary versus mandatory basis is much more relevant in this context. Last, but not least, differently from SRPP, GPP has been institutionalised by most, if not all, EU countries, through the definition of a strategy, and an action plan, as well as through specific legislative (sometimes mandatory) provisions. In contrast, according to the European Commission, 'SRRP consists in a variety of different policy approaches. It has been

[4] This approach is complemented by the chapter from a public purchasing perspective, see F Schotanus and R Nicholas, 'Coercive, Memetic and Normative Influences on the Uptake of Sustainable Public Procurement: An Institutional Perspective', ch 5 in this volume.

[5] See UNEP, 'Sustainable Public Procurement. How to "Wake the Sleeping Giant"', (2021); European Commission, 'Study on 'Strategic Use of Public Procurement in Promoting Green, Social and Innovation Policies' at op.europa.eu/en/publication-detail/-/publication/6a5a4873-b542-11e7-837e-01aa75ed71a1/language-en.

[6] For a broader discussion, see C McCrudden, 'Using Public Procurement to Achieve Social Outcomes' (2004) 28 *Natural Resources Forum* 257; M Trybus, 'Social Considerations through Public Procurement: A Legal Perspective' in G Piga and T Tatrai (eds), *Public Procurement Policy* (Oxford, Routledge, 2016); K Halonen, 'Is Public Procurement Fit for Reaching Sustainability Goals? A Law and Economics Approach to Green Public Procurement' (2021) 28 *Maastricht Journal of European and Comparative Law* 535. For a partially different view, see M Andhov et al, 'Sustainability Through Public Procurement: The Way Forward Reform Proposals' (2020) 25 *SSRN Electronic Journal* 1.

[7] However, the European Commission (2019) finds that SRPP is more widespread in sectors such as maintenance of public green spaces, cleaning services, social services, and less commonly used in construction, food and catering, textiles, and transport services.

introduced more recently and is usually carried out on a voluntary basis. Only a few countries have introduced targets for SRPP.'[8]

The remainder of the chapter is organised as follows. Section II introduces the economic analysis of regulation, while sections III and IV analyse GPP and SRPP, respectively. Section V discusses a branch of the literature that studies how the different actors involved in procurement (contracting entities, procurement officials, firms, citizens) react to a specific policy. Finally, section VI draws our main conclusions about the pros and cons of using public procurement as a mandatory tool to reach sustainable development goals.

II. Regulation and the Economy

The issue of using public procurement to implement environmental policy or to achieve social goals can be fruitfully analysed by resorting to the broader concept of the role of regulation in the economy. According to the Committee for Economic Development of the Conference Board, the justifications for regulating a market economy are mainly:[9] 1) market failures (for example, the presence of externalities and asymmetric information); 2) the presence of entry barriers; 3) the desire to guarantee safety (for consumers, for workers) and fairness (inclusion, supplier diversity).[10] While GPP mainly aims at correcting market failures (for example, setting limits to the environmental pollution generated by production activities), SRPP is more linked to justifications 2 and 3 (for example, using set-asides to encourage the participation of minority businesses, or requiring that the contractor will hire a certain number of long-term unemployed or young workers).

Regulation may be more or less stringent, ranging from nudging and 'soft touch' interventions to rigid command-and-control measures. Economists generally agree that, from a theoretical standpoint, regulating by allowing for market-based adjustment of prices (for example, using taxes/subsidies[11] to discourage/encourage some practices, or issuing cap-and-trade emission permits) should be preferred to regulation that imposes changes in quantities of inputs or outputs (for example,

[8] Study on 'Strategic Use of Public Procurement' (n 5) 4. However, it has been noticed that the actual bias in favour of GPP is specific to the Global North of the world, and in particular to the EU. See T Stoffel, C Cravero, A La Chimia and G Quinot, 'Multidimensionality of Sustainable Public Procurement (SPP) – Exploring Concepts and Effects in Sub-Saharan Africa and Europe' (2019) 11 *Sustainability* 1.

[9] CED 'Regulation & the Economy. The Relationship & How to Improve It' at www.ced.org/reports/regulation-and-the-economy.

[10] Someone could argue that this distinction, while useful as a working hypothesis, is not clear-cut. For example, barriers to entry could be included in the broad category of market failures.

[11] Environmental taxes can be related to the source of emission (carbon tax) or can target the inputs/outputs used in production processes (taxes on water usage, on packages, on pesticides, fuel excises). These tools, however, are not always compliant with EU State aid rules.

setting emission standards).[12] However, the available empirical evidence on the relative merits of different types of regulation is very scant.

The first issue relates to the *effectiveness* of regulatory interventions, that is, to the actual impact of the rule in reaching the declared goal. A second issue relates to the *efficiency* of regulation, that is, to the costs of its implementation, as compared to other regulatory alternatives targeting the same final goal.

Some recent evidence shows that the fall in air pollution emissions from US manufacturing in the years 1990–2008 is mainly due to changes in environmental regulation.[13] There have also been changes in productivity (allowing more output by using fewer resources), as well as changes in trade relations (implying that some polluting activities have been delocalised abroad or substituted with imports from countries like China and Mexico). However, the econometric estimates clearly show that the main reason for the reduction of emissions leads back to environmental regulation, which implied a doubling of the implicit pollution tax that US manufacturers had to face.

Beyond investigating the effect of environmental regulation on reducing emissions or improving energy efficiency, it is important to understand the impacts on different types of firms, as well as the total impact on actual and future competition. Theoretically, regulation can create an advantage for large firms, discourage entry and raise market concentration.[14] This has important implications for interventions such as tradable permits, extended producer responsibility, and green labels.

A topic that has been highly addressed in the empirical literature is the nexus between environmental regulation and productivity. Dozens of studies tried to test the so-called Porter hypothesis, according to which environmental regulation can stimulate innovations and productivity increases that can more than compensate for the costs of complying with green policies.[15] A meta-analysis of 107 empirical studies concludes that: 'strict but flexible (i.e. market-based) environmental regulations induce innovation and over time increase country-level competitiveness'.[16] Recently, a cross-country study provided evidence in favour of the Porter hypothesis, since a more stringent environmental regulation is found to positively impact productivity, especially for highly ICT-intensive countries (Germany, France,

[12] A cap-and-trade system sets a maximum level of pollution and distributes emission permits to firms. Firms can trade emission permits, and a price on pollution is created by the usual demand and supply mechanism.

[13] JS Shapiro and R Walker, 'Why is Pollution from US Manufacturing Declining? The Roles of Environmental Regulation, Productivity and Trade' (2018) 108 *American Economic Review* 3814.

[14] A Heyes A, 'Is Environmental Regulation Bad for Competition? A Survey' (2009) 36 *Journal of Regulatory Economics* 1.

[15] M Porter and C van der Linde, 'Toward a New Conception of the Environment-Competitiveness Relationship' (1995) 9 *Journal of Economic Perspectives* 97.

[16] MA Cohen and A Tubb, 'The Impact of Environmental Regulation on Firm and Country Competitiveness: A Meta-Analysis of the Porter Hypothesis' (2018) 5 *Journal of Association of Environmental Resources Economists* 371.

the Netherlands, and Sweden).[17] Most interestingly, even if market-based policies (taxes, trading schemes, renewable certificates, energy efficiency certificates, feed-in-tariffs, deposit-refund schemes) seem to play the main role in fostering productivity improvements, a positive effect emerged also for non-market-based policies (standards, R&D subsidies).

While economists are, with some exceptions, rather sceptical about the role of mandatory regulation, especially of the command-and-control form, management scholars and business strategists are more positive about the effects of environmental regulation in shaping the environmental strategies and performance of firms. A review of the literature on the effects of both mandatory regulation (ie, the US Clean Air Act and the Clean Water Act) and voluntary programmes (ie the Sustainable Forest Initiative, the ISO certifications, the EU Eco-Management and Audit Scheme – EMAS) on firms' strategies and competitiveness concludes that mandatory regulation is generally effective in reducing pollution, increasing innovation, and spurring the adoption of greener technologies. However, the study finds that the effects of voluntary regulation are more mixed and, in general, disappointing.[18]

A key distinction between the regulation of the private sector and the regulation of the government (for example, public procurement regulation) is that the former can well empower public officials (employees of regulatory authorities, inspectors, politicians), who can extract bribes from firms in exchange of favours, while the latter typically set limits to the discretionary power of bureaucrats. This difference is crucial for understanding and evaluating the effects of mandatory versus discretionary rules. Mandatory rules are typically useful to fight corruption practices, while discretionary rules are more suitable in contexts where corruption is not the main problem and public sector capacity is high.[19]

The above discussion about the role and the impact of regulation on the economy is a useful starting point. In the next sections, we will tackle the more specific issue of the role and impact of public procurement regulation, to understand what economists have to say about the effectiveness and the efficiency of SPP policies such as GPP and SRPP. In that respect, the fact that there is a high number of alleged social, environmental, and economic benefits that the proponents of SPP simultaneously aim to reach, represents a serious barrier to a general evaluation of the pros and cons of a specific GPP or SRPP policy. Empirical economists typically perform data-intensive analysis and concentrate, at the very maximum, on two to three measurable effects (for example, the effectiveness of a policy in reducing long-term unemployment or CO_2 emissions), and leave the other potential outcomes (many of which are very hard to measure) open to qualitative speculation.

[17] R De Santis, P Esposito and CJ Lasinio, 'Environmental Regulation and Productivity Growth: Main Policy Challenges' (2021) 165 *International Economics* 264.

[18] JA Aagon-Correa, AA Marcus and D Vogel, 'The Effects of Mandatory and Voluntary Regulatory Pressures on Firms' Environmental Strategies: A Review and Recommendations for Future Research' (2020) 14 *Academy of Management Annals* 339.

[19] E Bosio et al, 'Public Procurement in Law and Practice' (2022) 112 *American Economic Review* 1091.

III. Is Green Public Procurement Supported by Theory and Empirical Evidence?

GPP is a particular instrument of environmental policy. Since the government is a big buyer[20] and a big polluter.[21] In many sectors, using environmentally friendly purchasing behaviours can accomplish several goals. On the one hand, it can reduce environmental impact directly, while on the indirect side, it can set an example to citizens and the private sector.[22] According to the OECD

> GPP policies are a reflection both of increased concern on the part of OECD governments about the effect that their purchasing decisions have on the natural environment, and a belief that the public sector should introduce practices which are consistent with those that it recommends to other actors in the economy, such as private firms and households.[23]

Environmental criteria can be introduced at various stages of the procurement process. They can be used in the design of technical specifications of products, works, or services (energy efficiency or emission standards, recyclability after use, fraction of recycled material, bio-based products, eco-labels, and certifications). They can act as selection criteria for suppliers (for example, requiring bidders to have an environmental management system). Moreover, they can enter as award criteria (contracts awarded through the most economically advantageous tender, where quality is matched with financial aspects) or as contract clauses specifying how the work or service will be performed (for example, the contractor must take care of product collection and recycling when the product becomes waste).[24]

The use of environmental criteria in public procurement is not supported by all academics and by all procurers. This is because GPP can well lead to an increase in procurement costs, can distort and restrict competition in a non-desirable way, and often implies an amount of discretion on the part of the procurer that can be abused and lead to fraud and distortions. This is especially true when there are serious monitoring and measuring problems, which make it difficult to assess

[20] Defence, construction, maintenance, transport equipment, energy, and healthcare are sectors in which the government's market share is particularly high.

[21] For an analysis of the German Government greenhouse gas footprint, see O Chiappinelli, F Gruner and G Weber, 'Green Public Procurement: Climate Provisions in Public Tenders can Help Reduce German Carbon Emissions' (2019) 51/52 *DIW Weekly Report* 433. For an estimation of Finland's carbon footprint, see A Nissinen and H Savolainen, 'Carbon Footprint and Raw Material Requirement of Public Procurement and Household Consumption in Finland' at helda.helsinki.fi/handle/10138/312377.

[22] By 'buying green', the government avoids being associated with polluting activities or other unlawful behaviour, therefore reducing the risks to incur public criticism and public outrage.

[23] N Johnstone and K Erdlenbruch, 'Introduction' in OECD, *The Environmental Performance of Public Procurement: Issues of Policy Coherence* (OECD Publishing, Paris, 2003) 9.

[24] In addition, environmental goals can be reached also by selecting the procurement model (for example, buying an external service, such as a canteen service, instead of providing in-house food for employees or school kids). Finally, for contracts below EU thresholds, it would be possible to intervene in the phase in which bids are invited (eg, only invite environmentally friendly firms).

bids and manage contracts. On the other hand, if properly designed, mandatory criteria could well reduce discretion.

However, some procurement policies can be successful in reaching environmental goals together with bringing a reduction in government purchasing costs. Providing information and training on green products, promoting greater competition between green and brown products, or the use of Life Cycle Costing (LCC) methodologies, are examples of *win-win* policies that provide revenue (cost savings) for the government similar to other market-based instruments such as taxes and trading permits.[25]

More controversial are, instead, *win-lose* policies, where environmental benefits are reached at the expense of higher overall costs. For example, price preferences for green products (ie, products with eco-labels), or programmes affecting quantity rather than price (by imposing requirements such as shares of renewable sources, shares of recycled content, shares of organic food, efficiency standards for energy-using devices, less polluting manufacturing technologies), often imply higher costs for the government. In that respect, they are similar to market-based instruments such as subsidies.

The economic theory addressing sustainable public procurement is very limited. The seminal formal analysis by Marron is a useful starting point to analyse the effectiveness[26] of *win-lose* interventions.[27] Unlike taxes, subsidies, or emission standards, that apply to all firms active in a specific market, GPP applies only to firms willing to work with the government. It is important, therefore, to go beyond the impact on public purchases only and try to understand the effect of GPP in the private market. In that respect, the green product purchased by the procurer can simply be a substitute for a brown product (substitution effect), or it also can bring a reduction in the production of the brown good and the use of less environmentally harming technologies in a specific market (transformation effect). This means that the private market could in principle reinforce or counteract the change in government purchasing. If the government policy is successful at reducing the costs of purchasing green products (eg, by encouraging innovation or by enabling scale economies)

[25] Take one example, Indian Railways saved US$7 million per annum by replacing conventional light bulbs with energy-efficient ones. Despite the high initial costs (up to 6 times the cost of incandescent bulbs), the LCC assessment revealed the economic benefits of the green purchase. See UNEP, 'Sustainable Public Procurement' (n 5).

[26] In other chapters of this book the term effectiveness means the capacity of a specific policy to increase the SPP uptake. However, in our chapter, effectiveness relates to the impact of the policy on the declared goal (for example, the reduction of pollution for a GPP policy, or the increase of the share of disadvantaged firms/workers for an SRPP policy). A policy can well be effective in increasing the share of SMEs participating in tenders, or the share of clean vehicles the government purchases, but can still be ineffective in reaching the declared goal (ie, helping SMEs to grow in the long term, or increasing the share of clean vehicles that are circulating in a country).

[27] See DB Marron, 'Buying Green: Government Procurement as an Instrument of Environmental Policy' (1997) 25 *Public Finance Review* 285; DB Marron, 'Greener Public Purchasing as an Environmental Policy Instrument' (2004) 3 *OECD Journal on Budgeting* 70.

or at increasing market acceptance of green products, there could be the desired reinforcing effect. However, GPP could also lead to private purchasing becoming browner if it results in higher prices for green products or lower prices for brown products, through supply-and-demand responses. The formal analysis by Marron shows that, for GPP to be effective in switching consumption from brown to green products, the following three requirements must be met:

1) The procurer is a big buyer in the market, ie, it buys a relevant share of the total (green and brown) production.
2) The supply is price elastic, ie, firms react intensively to changes in the price at which they can sell the product/service.
3) The private demand is price inelastic, ie, private consumers react slowly to changes in the price at which they can buy the product/service.

Marron's analysis is essentially static and does not include dynamic aspects such as the development of green technologies across time. To the extent that the government can set the example, steer the market, and accelerate the development of green technologies, it could be justified to bear higher costs in the initial years, which should be counterbalanced by lower costs in a future in which, thanks to scale economies, learning by doing and spillover effects, green products/services will become cheaper.

Other studies extended the above theoretical analysis.[28] As far as effectiveness is concerned, the arguments developed by Marron suggest that one has to evaluate case by case by including in the picture the size of government purchases, as well as the reaction of the firms and private consumers. However, the fact that GPP is indeed able to produce a positive impact on the environment (effectiveness) is only a necessary but not sufficient condition, and the costs associated with implementing the policy must be included in the picture (cost-effectiveness). In that respect, the general view is that the costs of GPP are probably higher than other alternatives, such as market-based instruments like taxes on emissions and tradable permits. Finally, GPP is often used to reach multiple environmental objectives (for example, in the case of food provision, the increase in consumption of organic food and the increase in the organic agricultural area in a specific region or, for the case of cleaning services, the use of vehicles with low emissions to reduce air pollution and the use of green chemicals to reduce water pollution). However, pursuing a series of linked objectives can well hamper the governing of the intended environmental outcome. In other words, the well-known Tinbergen rule that one instrument (ie, public procurement) should be used to reach one objective only can act as a warning for over-optimistic policymakers and procurement officers.

[28] S Lundberg and PO Marklund, 'Green Public Procurement as an Environmental Policy Instrument: Cost Effectiveness' (2013) 4 *Environmental Economics* 75; S Lundberg, PO Marklund and E Strömbäck, 'Is Environmental Policy by Public Procurement Effective?' (2016) 44 *Public Finance Review* 478.

We think that the above theoretical analysis is informative and should be duly taken into consideration in devising policies that target several goals and in evaluating the pros and cons of SPP as compared to other forms of regulation of the sector. However, in some cases, different environmental goals or a mix of green and social goals can be complementary. One example is the case of organic food catering services, which can improve the health of consumers and at the same time provide job opportunities for small (and possibly local) firms. Another is buying from firms producing low emissions, which can also create positive spillovers for the living conditions of local communities.

Moreover, the direct comparison of GPP with other environmental policies could be somehow misleading, and we believe that GPP can be better analysed as a component of a policy mix. In that respect, it can be useful in areas in which environmental regulation is absent or insufficient, and to stimulate innovation.[29] It is important also to understand if GPP policies complement or clash with other policies:

> For instance, if a GPP programme which mandates particular technological or performance standards is introduced against a regulatory background which is also based upon the application of technology-based or performance-based standards, then it is important that selection criteria in the GPP programme are consistent with these standards. In most cases they will be somewhat more stringent than standards applied in the regulatory framework. However, they should not be so ambitious as to result in a disjuncture in the market, and nor should they be so weak as to legitimate the status quo.[30]

A. Is GPP Empirically Supported?

According to the above theoretical studies, we can conclude that understanding the effectiveness and cost-effectiveness of GPP is for a large part an empirical task. Unfortunately, the empirical literature on the effects of specific GPP policies is rather scant.[31] Moreover, most studies are limited to evaluating the effect of a policy

[29] Marron is rather critical of the potential benefits of GPP. However, he suggests that it can be effective when it focuses on the development of greener products and technologies, or when a public purchase can serve as a testing ground in some pilot projects. Similarly, GPP is more likely to generate social gains when addressing issues poorly addressed by existing regulations. See DB Marron, 'Greener Public Purchasing as an Environmental Policy Instrument' (2004) 3 *OECD Journal on Budgeting* 70.

[30] Johnstone and Erdlenbruch, 'Introduction' (n 23) 13. 'Similarly, GPP programmes can be introduced against a background of economic instruments such as emission taxes or tradable permits. In some cases, this may undermine the benefits of the application of market-based instruments. For instance, if public authorities and state enterprises have to meet certain performance standards under the GPP programme, this may mean that they have lower permit holding than would otherwise be the case, thus releasing permits onto the market, driving down their price, and reducing incentives for improved environmental performance against private firms.'

[31] W Cheng et al, 'Green Public Procurement, Missing Concepts and Future Trends – A Critical Review' (2018) 176 *Journal of Cleaner Production* 770.

on the uptake of GPP practices and the behaviour of bidders.[32] Unfortunately, they rarely take a step further, most relevant from an economic point of view, to try to measure its environmental impact in terms of reduction of GHG emissions, increase in energy efficiency, reduction of pollution, etc.

Recent evidence points to a positive impact of an organic food policy implemented by Swedish procurement agencies that, by buying increasing shares of organic food, were driving the conversion of farmland towards organic agricultural practices.[33] Interestingly enough, a positive, and somewhat larger, effect is found also for a traditional market-based policy targeting the same objective, that is, giving subsidies for organic production, which applies directly to agricultural firms, and not, indirectly, through government purchases.

A positive effect of GPP is also found in the construction sector in California.[34] The municipalities that implemented green building policies for new construction, by acting as large buyers, had the effect of promoting and accelerating the diffusion of green building standards in the private sector.

Moreover, there is evidence of the estimated impact of the CO_2 Performance Ladder, a stage certification scheme for energy and CO_2 management, in reducing carbon dioxide emissions in the Netherlands.[35] The certification scheme has been developed by ProRail, a Dutch state-owned company responsible for network infrastructure management on the Dutch railway network. The firms can obtain the certification with different levels of achievement of optimal CO_2 management (from 1 to 5) and, due to the use of Most Economically Advantageous Tender (MEAT) as award criteria, a higher certificate level can help a bidder to win the contract.

Besides environmental improvements, GPP could also be beneficial to other aspects of industrial development. A recent study uses Tenders Electronic Daily to extract a sample of German firms that were awarded a governmental contract with included additional environmental award criteria.[36] The analysis shows that, as compared to firms that were not winning green procurement awards, the winners were innovating more in the subsequent years, and this suggests that GPP is effective as a demand-side innovation policy tool. The results are particularly strong

[32] S Lundberg et al, 'Using Public Procurement to Implement Environmental Policy: An Empirical Analysis' (2015) 17 *Environmental Economics and Policy Studies* 487; M Amann et al, 'Driving Sustainable Supply Chain Management in the Public Sector: The Importance of Public Procurement in the EU' (2014) 19 *Supply Chain Management: An International Journal* 351.

[33] H Lindstrom, S Lundberg and PO Marklund, 'How Green Public Procurement Can Drive Conversion of Farmland: An Empirical Analysis of an Organic Food Policy' (2020) 172 *Ecological Economics* 106622.

[34] T Simcoe and MW Toffel, 'Government Green Procurement Spillovers: Evidence from Municipal Building Policies in California' (2014) 68 *Journal of Environmental Economics and Management* 411.

[35] MG Rietbergen and C Blok, 'Assessing the Potential Impact of the CO_2 Performance Ladder on the Reduction of Carbon Dioxide Emissions in the Netherlands' (2013) 52 *Journal of Cleaner Production* 33.

[36] B Krieger and V Zipperer, 'Does Green Public Procurement Trigger Environmental Innovation?' (2022) 51 *Research Policy* 104516.

for the product (as compared to process) environmental innovations and SMEs (as compared to large firms).

The empirical studies reported above are good examples of scientifically sound public policy analysis and evaluation. However, it is difficult to generalise their results, because they refer to specific sectors (construction, food, cleaning services), different countries, and, most importantly, they analyse only one or two specific sustainability goals. There are several difficulties in evaluating the environmental effectiveness, cost-effectiveness, and dynamic incentives (for the development and diffusion of environmentally preferable products and processes), as well as the soft effects (changes in awareness and attitudes of the private market and consumers/citizens) of specific GPP policies. A study covering six programmes in six different countries, among which three are based on mandatory requirements, is a good illustrative example. The analysis was only able to evaluate, partially, the environmental performance of the projects, while the lack of data and conceptual difficulties represented serious impediments to the performance evaluation exercise.[37]

The available empirical literature is far from reaching the minimal critical mass that would allow drawing some robust conclusions about the impact of GPP. Hopefully, thanks also to the increased availability of data, more solid quantitative research will come to bridge the gap.

Our main conclusion is to treat GPP as a sector-specific policy, giving priority to the most polluting sectors. At the sectoral level, it is relatively easier to evaluate if the government is a big buyer,[38] and how suppliers and consumers would react to the policy. The OECD submitted a questionnaire to Member countries to understand their different views on improving the environmental performance of public procurement.[39] For what concerns the effectiveness of GPP, the products and services for which environmental benefits are perceived to be highest are paper and packaging, vehicles, energy services and construction, while the sectors and services in which green purchasing can be cost-effective are heating appliances, IT equipment, energy services, and vehicles. A more recent study identified as priority products for SPP (where priority was justified by several factors, such as volume of public expenditures, cost-effectiveness, the existence of eco-labels, market influence of the contracting authority) office IT, paper and stationery, vehicles, cleaning, furniture, construction.[40]

[37] R Siemens, 'A Review and Critical Evaluation of Selected Greener Public Purchasing Programmes and Policies' in OECD, *The Environmental Performance of Public Procurement: Issues of Policy Coherence* (OECD Publishing, Paris, 2003).

[38] For example, the healthcare sector is more promising than cleaning products, where the government share of purchases, typically, is not large.

[39] OECD 'Improving the Environmental Performance of Public Procurement: Report on Implementation of the Council Recommendation' (OECD Publishing, Paris, 2007); OECD, 'Improving the Environmental Performance of Public Procurement: Report on Implementation of the Council Recommendation' (2007) 7 *OECD Papers* 1.

[40] UNEP (n 5).

IV. Is Socially Responsible Public Procurement Supported by Economic Theory and Empirical Evidence?

While North-American countries, Australia and New Zealand share a long tradition of preferential public procurement policies such as affirmative action and set-aside programmes trying to promote supplier diversity and employment, in Europe preferential programmes are less popular, since they can be used to circumvent the well-established principles of efficiency (value for money), openness, non-discrimination.[41] However, there are alternative instruments to set asides that can be used to increase supplier diversity or to create jobs for categories of vulnerable workers. For example, disadvantaged firms can improve their chances of being awarded the contract if social considerations are pondered under a MEAT award criterion, if the contract is divided into reasonably small lots, or if contract clauses promote the use of subcontracting. Similar to the use of life cycle costing methods in green procurement, contracting entities can implement tendering procedures that take into account social considerations, and compute the long-run cost-benefit ratio for the whole economy. Similar to eco-labels, labels and certifications (such as the ILO convention for labour standards, or the Ethical Trading Code) that attest that the bidder is not violating ethical principles can be used at the qualification stage.

Instead of promoting SRPP, especially in its mandatory form, the government could use criminal law, labour law, tax law, or state-aids to reach its desired social goals.[42] While the same criticism emerged concerning the use of GPP, one has to recognise that, in the case of socially responsible purchases, the opponents and detractors bring arguments that are much more pregnant. For example, typical objections are the multi-faceted nature of social considerations and the fact that it is more difficult to prove the social effectiveness and the cost-effectiveness of such policies. To reduce the degree of fragmentation, some scholars suggest distinguishing *hardcore* social objectives, such as respect for human and labour rights, from the other goals of promoting inclusion and supplier diversity.[43] We agree with this operational categorisation, and we believe that mandatory requirements should mostly focus on the former group of sustainability policies. Finally, technical specifications and contract performance conditions should be the main tools to be used, as compared to other instruments such as qualification requirements

[41] However, Art 20 of the Classic Directive allows contracting authorities to reserve the right to participate in public procurement tenders to sheltered workshops favouring disabled people and other minorities and disadvantaged groups (young workers, long-term unemployed, immigrants, refugees).

[42] For reference see Trybus (n 6). For a recent example of a proposed law, see Proposal for a Corporate Sustainability Due Diligence Directive COM(2022) 71.

[43] C Cravero, 'Promoting Supplier Diversity in Public Procurement: A Further Step in Responsible Supply Chain' (2018) 2 *European Journal of Sustainable Development* 1.

and award criteria. Intervening at the early or late stages of the procurement process is reducing the risk of violating the primary goals of procurement, while the qualification and awarding stages are more likely to distort the competitive process.[44]

A. Is Socially Responsible Public Procurement Empirically Supported?

Within the field of economics, the theoretical literature that specifically investigates SRPP is practically non-existent, and often the same theoretical papers reviewed in section III, which have been developed in the context of GPP, are used to discuss the role of sustainable public procurement in general. In a similar vein, the empirical literature on the effectiveness and the efficiency of SRPP is very scant, mostly concentrates on US affirmative and set-aside programmes, and has a limited focus on evaluating the impact of specific policies on some measures of inclusion and supplier diversity.[45]

An assessment of the impact of affirmative action programmes that try to increase the utilisation of minority business enterprises (MBE) as well as women-owned enterprises (WOE) in US highway procurement pointed out the presence of a positive impact only for MBE.[46] Similarly, the impact of Women-Owned Small Business (WOSB) certification in increasing bid frequency and bid success of SMEs in US federal procurement contracts is non-significant, meaning that certified WOSB, as compared to male-owned firms and women-owned firms, were not more likely to participate in (and to win) government contracts.[47] However, there are also studies pointing out positive effects on the uptake of both GPP and SRPP. One analysis shows, for their sample of contracts awarded in Austria, Germany, the Netherlands, and the UK, that considering socially responsible goals in public procurement has a stronger influence on which firms win, compared to GPP practices.[48] In a similar vein, another study shows for Slovakia, Czech Republic, Hungary, and Poland that the inclusion of sustainability aspects in the evaluation criteria had the effect of increasing SMEs' bidding, as well as the probability for

[44] M Trybus, 'Beyond Competition and Value for Money: Corporate Social Responsibility in Public Procurement' (2020) 8 *Kilaw Journal* 217. However, sometimes, a combination of a requirement (set at such a level that there is sufficient competition) and an award criterion (to reward the most social suppliers), if properly devised, can be effective.

[45] Studies on the impact of procurement policies promoting the participation of SMEs are, instead, more common, but are not included in our selective review of empirical papers.

[46] J Marion, 'Affirmative Action and the Utilization of Minority- and Women-Owned Businesses in Highway Procurement' (2011) 49 *Economic Inquiry* 899.

[47] B Orser, A Riding and J Weeks, 'The Efficacy of Gender-based Federal Procurement Policies in the United States' (2019) 53 *Small Business Economics* 491.

[48] Amann et al (n 32).

SMEs to win the contract, but the effect was higher in the case of inclusion of social aspects.[49]

While the above papers focus on effectiveness in terms of uptake of socially responsible practices (participation of disadvantaged firms in tenders, probability of winning procurement contracts), some studies try to evaluate the impact of SRPP policies on the winning firms and, in general, on the local economy. Results are not encouraging. For instance, a study tracked a sample of more than 4,000 minority US MBEs that were awarded procurement contracts.[50] It found that the probability for them to go out of business after four years was higher as compared to similar firms that were not working with the state, especially when a significant share of their revenue was due to sales to the local government. Another study uses spending and survey data of the Metropolitan Pier and Exposition Authority in Chicago and concludes that 'preferential procurement policies often miss their objectives, achieving perverse outcomes such as minimal assistance to minority business enterprises and negligible local economic development impacts'.[51]

V. Rules versus Discretion: The Behaviour of the Different Actors

The arguments developed in the previous sections were implicitly assuming that, once a law has been enacted, procurement agencies at centralised and at different decentralised levels will duly implement it, by using competent and diligent procurement officers, with no frictions and costs associated with its enforcement.

However, to perform a complete evaluation of the pros and cons of mandatory requirements, one has to enter into the picture the presence of inefficient and corrupt public officers, and the fact that contracting authorities, especially at the local level, can suffer from a serious lack of competence. For example, there is evidence that Italian contracting entities were buying standardised goods at very different prices.[52] Higher prices were mostly due to inefficiency ('passive waste' in government spending), while corruption (active waste) was, quite surprisingly, playing a minor role.[53] Furthermore, evidence for US public works and services

[49] P Nemec, M Kubak and P Dzupka, 'The Transition of the Visegrad Countries Toward Sustainable Public Procurement' (2021) 59 *Eastern European Economics* 487.

[50] T Bates and D Williams, 'Do Preferential Procurement Programs Benefit Minority Business?' (1996) 86 *American Economic Review* 294.

[51] T Bates, 'Utilizing Affirmative Action in Public Sector Procurement as a Local Economic Development Strategy' (2009) 23 *Economic Development Quarterly* 180, 180.

[52] O Bandiera, A Prat and T Valletti, 'Active and Passive Waste in Government Spending: Evidence from a Policy Experiment' (2009) 99 *American Economic Review* 1278.

[53] While the standard solution to active waste calls for stricter rules and external controls, such strict policies are not appropriate and can instead produce a detrimental effect when inefficiency and lack of professionalism are the key problems faced by procurers.

(more complex procurements than purchasing standardised goods), shows that bureaucratic competence is a key characteristic for selecting the best contractor, and a higher competence of the contracting authority is associated with low time delays, low-cost overruns and less renegotiation.[54] An Italian study finds that facing a centralisation reform, contracting authorities, instead of being fully aligned, were trying to react in several ways. They anticipated purchases, divided contracts into smaller lots (to remain within the threshold below which centralisation was not mandatory) and aggregated into the smallest types of centralised purchasing bodies, when given the possibility to do so. Most importantly, these unintended effects and distortions partially offset the expected benefits of centralisation.[55]

A recent analysis of the link between public procurement laws, public procurement practices, and outcomes for 187 countries provides key insights into the behaviour of the different actors.[56] It finds a clear positive relationship between stricter laws (governing issues such as transparency, competition, exclusion of bidders and integrity of contracts) and procurement practices (that can be aligned to the laws or be more or less stringent), and a positive relationship between practices and outcomes (competition between bidders, time delays, cost overruns, product quality). However, a positive link between laws and outcomes emerged only for countries with the low institutional quality and low public sector capacity. The results suggest that properly motivated bureaucrats need more discretion and require fewer rules: 'Countries with weak bureaucracies need strict laws to regulate them: countries with strong bureaucracies can lay off a little.'

Finally, it is important to understand if and to what extent procurement policies such as centralisation, anti-corruption and promoting sustainable purchases are endorsed by citizens. In that respect, a study using data from a Special Eurobarometer survey conducted on more than 25,000 respondents living in 27 EU countries found that EU citizens were in general in favour of SPP practices, even when they were associated with higher purchasing costs.[57]

From the above empirical evidence, we can conclude that, in evaluating if conducting policies by using more rules or more discretion, it is not only important to look at effectiveness and efficiency. It is crucial to understand the characteristics of the public procurement environment and culture, and how different stakeholders (contracting authorities, public officials, firms working with the government, firms not working with the government and, ultimately, citizens) react to them.

[54] F De Carolis et al, 'Bureaucratic Competence and Procurement Outcomes' (2020) 36 *Journal of Law, Economics, and Organization* 537.

[55] F De Carolis, 'Procurement Centralization in the EU: The Case of Italy' (2018) *CEPR Discussion Paper* 12567.

[56] Bosio et al (n 19).

[57] S Keulemans and S Van de Walle, 'Cost-Effectiveness, Domestic Favouritism and Sustainability in Public Procurement' (2017) 30 *International Journal of Public Sector Management* 328.

VI. Conclusion

Mainstream economics relies largely on the capability of changes in prices to organise markets efficiently, so it is not surprising that there is some scepticism about the possibility to reach strategic goals using public procurement as an instrument, especially in a command-and-control form. Traditional market-based instruments, such as subsidies, taxes, and emission trading permits, apply to all firms in a market (and not only to the subset of firms that are selling, or plan to sell, to the government), and are therefore seen more favourably.

Along this line, some theoretically argue that GPP is not the most cost-effective instrument 'in terms of leading to emissions being reduced at least cost to society'.[58] Others come to the same conclusion, for both GPP and SRPP: 'Entrusting the public procurement system with the task of achieving social, environmental and innovation-related objectives is ineffective.'[59] However, this view is not univocally shared by all economists. Some proponents argue that: 'GPP holds great potential to decarbonise the economy, also relative to other decarbonization policies that are currently being implemented or discussed.'[60]

Moreover, even the opponents to the use of SPP recognise that in some circumstances (high market share of government purchases, high price elasticity of supply, and low price elasticity of private demand) GPP can be effective in reaching the desired goal. In addition, to the extent that market failures are such that the government is buying inefficiently (at a higher cost) and in a way that damages the environment, some procurement strategies (providing information and training on green products, promoting competition between brown and green products, using life-cycle costing methods) can act as *win-win* policies, to the benefit of both government expenditures and the environment. An example of 'quick win' mandatory policies that can be implemented is the use of life-cycle costing techniques, MEAT as the award criteria, and eco-labels as technical requirements.[61] Finally, GPP can be applied when the government desires to develop greener products and technologies, as well as when there is urgency, that is, an urgent need to quickly reduce hazardous pollutants.[62]

[58] Lundberg et al (n 28).

[59] S Saussier and J Tirole, 'Strengthening the Efficiency of Public Procurement' (2015) 22 *Notes du conseil danalyse economique* 1.

[60] O Chiappinelli and V Zipperer, 'Using Public Procurement as a Decarbonisation Policy: A Look at Germany' (2017) 49 *DIW Economic Bulletin* 523.

[61] The State of Berlin computed the life-cycle costs of a selected list of green products, and found for ten product categories (computers, multifunction devices, copy paper, refrigerators, indoor lighting, cleaning supplies, buildings, flooring, street lighting and vehicles) cost savings as compared to conventional products. High costs emerged, instead, for 'greener' dishwashers, textiles, electricity, waste treatment, and construction machinery.

[62] A recent example of a virtuous use of public procurement to spur innovation comes from the recent Covid-19 pandemic. The presence of a worldwide massive public demand pushed pharmaceutical companies to engage in an unprecedented innovation race and accelerated the development of various efficacious vaccines.

As to the specific issue of mandatory versus discretionary rules, again, mainstream economics is generally in favour of the latter, which is more flexible. This relies on the implicit assumption that contracting authorities can make the correct decision, implement it, undertake efficient monitoring and ex-post evaluation. However, organisations can be highly inefficient and procurement officers can lack the required competence or can be corrupted. To the extent that those distortions are widespread, mandatory rules can be more effective in reaching the desired goal. More generally, the choice between voluntary or mandatory policies should be adapted to the specific sector as well as to the local conditions (country, region, municipality): 'A voluntary system leverages on awareness-raising of practitioners as well as "peer pressure" and competition among organisations to excel, while a mandatory system relies on compliance and sanction mechanisms.'[63] We believe that, among the typologies of mandatory GPP requirements, procedural mandatory requirements, such as 'comply or explain' are particularly promising, since they leave some degree of freedom to contracting authorities.

Finally, while sustainable public procurement encompasses both GPP and SRPP, we argue that, for this analysis, they should be treated separately. In the context of SRPP, issues such as respect for human rights, health, and safety, fair working conditions, and ethical trade, should be made mandatory by law, for both private firms and procurement entities, as much as possible, using product-specific legislation to regulate the products or the producers. Conversely, other sustainability aspects such as gender inclusivity (ie, protection of women-owned businesses), minorities (immigrants, racial and ethnic groups), and other disadvantaged groups (disabled, veterans, refugees, long-term unemployed, young workers) promote social inclusion and supplier diversity and can be better tackled, in some circumstances, by setting targets (ie, using a mild form of mandatory requirement). However, we believe that intervening by giving guidelines, support, and incentives (ie, operating within a voluntary framework) could represent in most cases a better strategy.

In conclusion, as is often the case, economics can be of help in designing the optimal policy (even if it is a second-best policy according to criteria such as cost-effectiveness) and can be very useful in trying to understand, case by case, the effects of a specific procurement policy. However, the decision to go towards more stringency in GPP and/or in SRPP should be mainly a political one and should consider not only costs, but also moral, legal, and societal obligations to protect the environment and to let citizens live in a more inclusive society.

[63] European Commission, 'Study on "Strategic Use of Public Procurement"' (n 5) 99.

5

Coercive, Mimetic and Normative Influences on the Uptake of Sustainable Public Procurement: An Institutional Perspective

FREDO SCHOTANUS AND RUBEN NICOLAS[1]

I. Introduction

In recent years, public procurement has been increasingly recognised as a promising tool to contribute to a sustainability transition.[2] By leveraging its share in the economy, public procurement can drive more sustainable contract outcomes, supplier behaviour and a market transition. For example, public procurement is directly or indirectly responsible for 15 per cent of global greenhouse gas emissions and hence has the potential to significantly contribute to the decarbonisation of the market economy.[3] Nevertheless, on average, current uptake levels of Sustainable Public Procurement (SPP) remain marginal. For instance, only about nine per cent of tenders above the EU thresholds contain sustainable award criteria, mostly with low weights compared to other award criteria.[4]

While SPP may on average cost more in the short term – with different percentages suggested in different studies[5] – it could have negative market effects

[1] We thank the editors, Prof. Davide Vannoni and PhD candidate Enrique Carreras for their constructive comments and suggestions for the chapter.

[2] IPCC, 2022: *Climate Change 2022: Mitigation of Climate Change. Contribution of Working Group III to the Sixth Assessment Report of the Intergovernmental Panel on Climate Change*, PR Shukla, J Skea, R Slade, A Al Khourdajie, R van Diemen, D McCollum, M Pathak, S Some, P Vyas, R Fradera, M Belkacemi, A Hasija, G Lisboa, S Luz, J Malley, (eds) (Cambridge University Press, Cambridge, UK and New York, NY, US).

[3] WEF and BCG, 'Green Public Procurement: Catalysing the Net-Zero Economy' at www3.weforum.org/docs/WEF_Green_Public_Procurement_2022.pdf.

[4] C Yu, T Morotomi and H Yu, 'What Influences Adoption of Green Award Criteria in a Public Contract? An Empirical Analysis of 2018 European Public Procurement Contract Award Notices' (2020) 12 *Sustainability* 1261.

[5] See, eg Ekomatcentrum, 'Marknadsrapport: Ekologiskt i offentlig sektor 2019. Sigtuna: Ekomatcentrum' at www.ekomatcentrum.se/wp-content/uploads/2019/06/Rapport-Marknadsrapport-

in some situations,[6] and might be less effective than alternatives such as taxes and subsidies in certain circumstances,[7] there are multiple benefits as well. First, the long-term benefits of, for instance, phasing out fossil energy sources with renewable energy sources or by reducing energy consumption, largely outweigh the additional costs of SPP.[8] Second, the sustainability effects of SPP may reach beyond the direct supplier and shape markets.[9] Public sector suppliers that have become more sustainable may also provide sustainable supply to non-public customers.[10] Furthermore, there can even be win-win situations in the case of buying second-hand items or when higher costs in the short term are compensated by reduced costs in the long run, for instance, when a buyer purchases reusables instead of disposables. Finally, other solutions such as sustainable taxes and subsidies are not without criticism as well, are sometimes even counterproductive,[11] and might perform better when being combined with SPP. Overall, this complex relationship between costs and gains, alternatives, and direct and indirect effects on the short and long term that differ per situation calls for incentives and support for SPP, but also partial harmonisation of public procurement practices that still leaves professional contracting authorities with considerable discretionary space to procure according to their best judgement.[12]

In general, the implementation of SPP becomes challenging when environmental or social development objectives are not compatible with existing institutional structures and processes and when uncertainty exists about the outcomes of

EMC-2019-2.pdf; M Aldenius and J Khan, 'Strategic Use of Green Public Procurement in the Bus Sector: Challenges and Opportunities' (2017) 164 *Journal of Cleaner Production* 250; WEF and BCG, 'Green Public Procurement: Catalysing the Net-Zero Economy' at www3.weforum.org/docs/WEF_Green_Public_Procurement_2022.pdf.

[6] PRC Reis and S Cabral, 'Public Procurement Strategy: The Impacts of a Preference Programme for Small and Micro Businesses' (2015) 35 *Public Money & Management* 103.

[7] T van den Brink, 'Subsidiarity Lost Along the Way? EU Public Procurement Legislation on the Road to Sustainability', ch 3 in this volume.

[8] T Adrian, P Bolton and AM Kleinnijenhuis, 'The Great Carbon Arbitrage' (2022) IMF Working Paper No. 2022/107.

[9] van den Brink (n 7).

[10] H Lindström, S Lundberg and PO Marklund, 'How Green Public Procurement Can Drive Conversion of Farmland: An Empirical Analysis of an Organic Food Policy' (2020) 172 *Ecological Economics* 106622; T Simcoe and MW Toffel, 'Government Green Procurement Spillovers: Evidence from Municipal Building Policies in California' (2014) 68 *Journal of Environmental Economics and Management* 411; B Krieger and V Zipperer, 'Does Green Public Procurement Trigger Environmental Innovations?' (2022) 51 *Research Policy* 104516.

[11] See, eg, F Schotanus, 'A Better World Starts with Public Procurement. Inaugural Address Utrecht University' at www.uu.nl/medewerkers/RestApi/Public/GetFile?Employee=55038&l=EN&id=1225&t=c57c71fc8d0742249feaaf4cee511be6; European Court of Auditors, Common Agricultural Policy and Climate, Half of EU Climate Spending but Farm Emissions are not Decreasing' at www.eca.europa.eu/Lists/ECADocuments/SR21_16/SR_CAP-and-Climate_EN.pdf.

[12] See, eg, S Brammer and H Walker, 'Sustainable Procurement in the Public Sector: An International Comparative Study' (2011) 31 *International Journal of Operations and Production Management* 452; JRJ van Berkel and F Schotanus, 'The Impact of "Procurement with Impact": Measuring the Short-Term Effects of Sustainable Public Procurement Policy on the Environmental Friendliness of Tenders' (2021) 21 *Journal of Public Procurement* 300.

certain SPP practices. Accordingly, a solution for improving SPP uptake lies in creating more supportive institutional structures and processes. Supportive institutional structures and processes help the uptake of SPP directly, by offering incentives and removing red tape – although we do not expect red tape to be a substantial barrier to SPP uptake – but also indirectly, by providing security for those stakeholders facing uncertainty. This is explained in institutional theory, which describes that highly structured organisational fields, such as the public sector, cope with uncertainty by looking for institutional reference points. These reference points include the pressures on contracting authorities, such as legal mandatory requirements, policy requirements and societal expectations (ie, coercive force), the practices of their successful peers under uncertain circumstances (ie, mimetic force), and the norms and networks in their profession related to professional attitudes and approaches (ie, normative force).[13] These are important considerations in light of the sustainable transitions, in which contracting authorities will face uncertainty repeatedly, maybe even more so in the circular transition than in the energy transition.[14] Rather than making efforts to overcome uncertainty, the behaviour of contracting authorities may follow institutional structures and processes. Hence, the *pressures, practices and professional norms and networks* in the public sector can be seen as three *institutional forces* that shape the behaviour (ie, structure, culture and output) of contracting authorities and their suppliers related to SPP.

The question then arises how the forces could be used to stimulate SPP uptake. While legal mandatory requirements are part of the (coercive) force, the other forces also shape procurement and supplier behaviour. In fact, the other forces might even be more important for procurement outcomes in Member States with a high procurement capacity, as the role of procurement practice regarding tender outcomes is more important than the role of coercive forces in Member States with high procurement capacity.[15] Although the current literature *does* show specific SPP findings related to parts of each force, it does not provide an overall integrated discussion for each force nor an overall view of the three forces combined.

We, therefore, discuss in this conceptual chapter how each institutional force can be applied to stimulate effective sustainable procurement behaviour by contracting authorities, what the advantages and disadvantages of these forces are, and what can be done to try to reduce or mitigate the disadvantages. We do not discuss all possible SPP-related topics for each force, but focus on one topic for each institutional force which seems most relevant to stimulate SPP uptake.

[13] PJ DiMaggio and WW Powell, 'The Iron Cage Revisited: Institutional Isomorphism and Collective Rationality in Organizational Fields' (1983) 48 *American Sociological Review* 147; PD Jennings and PA Zandbergen, 'Ecologically Sustainable Organizations: An Institutional Approach' (1995) 20 *Academy of Management Review* 1015.

[14] J Rotmans, *Omarm de chaos* (Amsterdam, Singel Uitgeverijen, 2021).

[15] E Bosio, S Djankov, E Glaeser and A Shleifer, 'Public Procurement in Law and Practice' (2022) 112 *American Economic Review* 1091.

These are mandatory requirements (a coercive pressure), copying best practices (a mimetic topic) and the role of professional norms (a normative topic). Although copying best practices and professional norms might play an important role in shaping procurement and supplier behaviour, we focus our discussion mostly on mandatory requirements because of the aims of this book.

We categorise the method that we use in the chapter as theoretical adaptation.[16] We use an existing and established theory, institutional theory, for exploring new options for stimulating the uptake of sustainable procurement in the domain of public procurement. Using this approach, we do not aim to make an argument for, or against, mandating SPP. Rather, we aim to give insights into different forms of mandatory requirements and indicate what alternatives exist or necessary 'add-ons' in addition to mandatory requirements are required to stimulate the behaviour of contracting authorities that are challenged with implementing sustainability objectives. In the end, we argue for a mandatory approach that provides public buyers with sufficient flexibility and stimulates efforts beyond certain minimum levels of SPP. Furthermore, we argue that the combination of the three forces might be the most effective way forward. A mandatory approach with sufficient flexibility is considered to be most effective when best professional norms are changed, to correspond with the principles of sustainable development, and when the copying of best practices is stimulated by platforms and other measures.

II. Mandatory Requirements

Mandatory requirements are perhaps the most recognised institutional force that can stimulate or force contracting authorities to integrate sustainability objectives in their procurement process. In practice, mandatory requirements that affect purchasing behaviour mostly come from law and policy. Nevertheless, besides law and policy, pressures by stakeholders and societal parties, by lobbying, demonstration and litigation, can also call authorities to take societal responsibility. Examples include NGOs and citizens' initiatives such as Extinction Rebellion, a protest group active around the globe, or the Climate Emergency Fund. These initiatives – in combination with Eurobarometer outcomes, which show that European citizens think that sustainability should be more important than price or locality for public procurement[17] – highlight that the current public opinion in the EU is in support of SPP by contracting authorities.

Before we continue with a review of mandatory requirements, there is a distinction to be made between the various types, as has also been described.[18]

[16] E Jaakkola, 'Designing Conceptual Articles: Four Approaches' (2020) 10 *AMS Review* 18.

[17] S Keulemans and S van De Walle, 'Cost-Effectiveness, Domestic Favouritism and Sustainability in Public Procurement A Comparative Study of Public Preferences' (2017) 30 *International Journal of Public Sector Management* 328.

[18] W Janssen, 'Shifting towards Mandatory Sustainability Requirements in EU Public Procurement Law: Context, Relevance and a Typology', ch 1 in this volume.

Mandatory requirements can differ with respect to their source, subject and the adoptive option.

The *source* refers to the origin of the mandatory requirement. As described in the previous paragraph, we distinguish law and policy as the main sources. (For simplicity, policy also includes administrative agreements, covenants and conditional support schemes, such as the EU Structural and Investment Funds). An important difference between legal and policy requirements is that a contracting authority may not enforce or only partly enforce its policy requirements.

The *subject* of mandatory requirements refers to the type of requirement. A mandatory requirement can be substantive – such as technical specifications for the procurement of circular and zero-emission public transport – or procedural – such as the use of sustainable award criteria disregarding the substantive nature of the project. Both substantive and procedural requirements can be horizontal or sectoral. Horizontal requirements are introduced for all types of public procurement and sectoral requirements only apply to one sector.[19]

The *adoptive option* refers to whether contracting authorities have the freedom (or not) to engage in, or adopt, mandatory requirements. The adoptive option mostly differs per source. At times, mandatory requirements are part of a policy that does not apply to a contracting authority, unless it chooses to adopt it. This is the case with, for instance, the EU Structural and Investment Funds, to which contracting authorities in certain EU Member States can apply. Only once contracting authorities are awarded co-funding, are they held to SPP requirements. However, each contracting authority has the freedom to apply for co-funding or not and therefore, the adoption of these mandatory SPP requirements is a matter of choice. On the contrary, policy and legal mandatory requirements are set conditions that are handed down from the legislator to the executive. Contracting authorities have no, or limited, formal choice as to whether to adopt these requirements and must follow the conditions, or otherwise try to greenwash or social wash the public procurement documents at hand. Similarly, organisational policies are often set by top management at higher levels of contracting authorities and handed down to public buyers, who then do not have the formal option to adopt these requirements or not.

In the following sections, the advantages and disadvantages of the detailed different mandatory requirements are discussed, and how to deal with those disadvantages. We use a similar structure for sections III and IV as well.

A. Advantages of Mandating Sustainable Public Procurement by Law or Policy

In general, mandatory requirements may stimulate contracting authorities to reshape their organisational structures to achieve the prescribed SPP objectives.

[19] ibid.

For example, internal processes[20] and annual and departmental budget structures might be redesigned to better complement the long-term and external characteristics of SPP. In addition, budget holders, project leaders and contract managers lose the ability to focus on price and/or quality only and contracting authorities are more likely to assign staff to ensure that sustainability is integrated effectively into tenders. Likewise, as SPP becomes mandatory, suppliers to contracting authorities are likely to adjust their behaviour accordingly. To improve their chances of winning a contract, suppliers (proactively) include sustainability in their bids, thereby matching the requirements the buyer faces.[21]

There are some specific advantages as well for specific types of requirements. *Substantive* requirements better enable standardisation and scale, reduce uncertainty, might push innovation when the requirements are difficult to meet with existing solutions and are easier to measure.[22] It is also clear for public buyers what to do and there is less discretionary decision-making required. This makes substantive requirements particularly useful for organisations that struggle with SPP, have low procurement capacity or organisations that do not yet prioritise SPP. In addition, substantive requirements might be useful for lagging markets or markets for which it is relatively easy to develop substantive requirements.

Procedural requirements leave SPP more to the discretion of a buyer. Although procedural requirements will lead to more customised and diverse procurement behaviour, they can be applied uniformly to the very diverse set of markets in which public buyers operate. As a result, one single horizontal procedural requirement can suffice to prescribe the application of SPP for every individual tender, while effective substantive requirements need to be tailored to specific markets that would require many different specific requirements. Additionally, discretion allows public buyers to respond innovatively or creatively to new developments and unforeseen problems[23] related to SPP for a specific tender, whereas substantive requirements would limit the options of contracting authorities. Finally, procedural requirements might be especially useful to stimulate SPP for tenders in specific or small public markets, for which it might be difficult or costly to develop substantive requirements.

[20] PC Neessen, MC Caniëls, B Vos, B and JP de Jong, 'How and When Do Purchasers Successfully Contribute to the Implementation of Circular Purchasing: A Comparative Case-study' (2021) 27 *Journal of Purchasing and Supply Management.*

[21] M Amann, JK Roehrich, M Eßig and C Harland, 'Driving Sustainable Supply Chain Management in the Public Sector: The Importance of Public Procurement in the European Union' (2014) 19 *Supply Chain Management* 351.

[22] A Rainville, 'Standards in Green Public Procurement – A Framework to Enhance Innovation' (2017) 167 *Journal of Cleaner Production* 1029.

[23] J Buol and MD Vaughan, 'Rules vs. Discretion: The Wrong Choice Could Open the Floodgates' (2003) *The Regional Economist* 10.

B. Disadvantages of Mandating Sustainable Public Procurement by Law or Policy

Imposing mandatory requirements has several general disadvantages as well for all different types of mandatory requirements of SPP. First, sustainability is a broad concept which is difficult to define and measure. Accordingly, if SPP should become mandatory, the question arises how to define what SPP requirements apply to. The discussion of the Clean Vehicles Directive provides a clear example, where opportunities for environmental impact were missed due to the definitions used. The next challenge is to measure and monitor SPP.[24] On the one hand, contracting authorities might claim to apply SPP, but not really do so when monitoring and enforcement mechanisms are sparse. On the other hand, contracting authorities that are monitored might consider this to be intrusive[25] and therefore resist following the requirements or start greenwashing and social washing. Similarly, when requirements are considered burdensome and are not complementary to existing operations, contracting authorities might be resistant or simply incapable to implement them. In this regard, it is important to realise that SPP is an additional task, which complicates the procurement process, as public buyers need to make trade-offs between more different objectives that are not always compatible.[26] In addition, SPP may not (yet) be part of job requirements, assessment interviews, reporting requirements, budgets etc, which are strong drivers of behaviour by public employees.

Some specific disadvantages apply to *substantive* mandatory requirements, a specific form of mandating SPP in which the use of (product) specific standards, labels, prequalification criteria or award criteria are prescribed. Substantive mandatory requirements may be a solution when procedural SPP requirements are hard to define and measure clearly. However, this solution to the definition and measurement problem has several drawbacks.

When standards or specific prequalification criteria become mandatory, an important disadvantage could be that proactive behaviour or innovation is not stimulated. Once the standards are fulfilled there is no further incentive to pursue sustainable development. This is especially problematic when standards are set in such a way that these are acceptable and realistic for the least sustainable Member States as well. This is important as there are large differences between Member States regarding SPP uptake levels.[27] If the standard is set according to the lowest

[24] A Semple, 'Charge of the Light Brigade? The Clean Vehicles Directive and the Batteries Regulation', ch 7 in this volume.

[25] Based on JB Heide, KH Wathne and AI Rokkan, 'Interfirm Monitoring, Social Contracts, and Relationship Outcomes' (2007) 44 *Journal of Marketing Research* 425.

[26] M Igarashi, L De Boer and O Michelsen, 'Investigating the Anatomy of Supplier Selection in Green Public Procurement' (2015) 108 *Journal of Cleaner Production* 442.

[27] Yu et al (n 4).

performer, the frontrunners might lose momentum or take a step back. Similarly, if the use of certain labels or specific award criteria would become a mandatory requirement, efforts for other SPP practices such as using other procurement models (eg, buying as a service) might be scaled back.

In addition, it is possible that mistakes are made during the development of substantive requirements, resulting in ineffective or counterproductive requirements. Substantive requirements need to be kept up-to-date to avoid prioritising older and less sustainable options over the newer, more sustainable, solutions that the market has to offer. Developing and keeping substantive requirements up-to-date may in itself be complex and costly, including efforts to make sure that outdated requirements are not used anymore by contracting authorities. Especially for markets on which mainly private buyers or consumers operate, it might be more efficient to enforce sustainable product standards instead of public procurement requirements.

Furthermore, substantive mandatory requirements need not necessarily lead to the optimal use of the solutions that the market has to offer. Especially in the case of scarce resources, the mandatory use of specific sustainable specifications can lead to the selection of more sustainable supplies that are also (much) more expensive. A higher degree of (sustainable) public value might instead have been achieved if more public funds would be left over and used for tax reductions or subsidies for sustainable activities, such as renewable energy sources. The point of public welfare inefficiency is also stressed,[28] and most likely applies to the substantive requirement of SPP.

Finally, mandatory standards or other prescribed efforts for SPP might also lead to less sustainable outcomes by their indirect effect on the private market.[29] When standards become suddenly effective this can cause a sudden peak of demand for sustainability on a large scale, thereby drawing sustainable suppliers away from the private market, or increasing prices for sustainable goods. As a result, the private market, which is larger than the public market, could buy less sustainable goods, thereby decreasing the total sustainable outcome.[30] However, we do not expect such a negative effect to be very likely. First, sustainable supply possibilities are currently increasing. Second, SPP may grow a sustainable business and also stimulate the greening of unsustainable suppliers. Empirical studies show that SPP can also lead to more sustainable outcomes in the private market.[31] Finally, the implementation of new mandatory requirements takes time and is therefore unlikely to cause sudden peaks in sustainable demand.

[28] E Carreras and D Vannoni, 'Mandatory Requirements in Sustainable Public Procurement: The Economic Perspective', ch 4 in this volume.

[29] ibid.

[30] Marron (1997) described by S Lundberg and PO Marklund, 'Green Public Procurement and Multiple Environmental Objectives' (2018) 45 *Economia e Politica Industriale* 37.

[31] Simcoe and Toffel (n 10).

Procedural requirements have specific disadvantages as well. The most important one is that it does not prescribe buyers what to do, which could make it easier to make procurement mistakes or to apply social washing and greenwashing. It is also more difficult to measure to what extent SPP is applied. Similar disadvantages apply to SPP targets not set for individual organisations. Although broad targets do provide direction, individual organisations might still not feel responsible to play their part in the sustainable transition. Similarly, for Member States with low levels of procurement capacity, procedural requirements might be less effective than for Member States with high levels.

C. Reducing Disadvantages of Mandating Sustainable Public Procurement

By minimising the disadvantages of mandatory SPP, it is more likely that the targeted behavioural change among contracting authorities is achieved. First, mandatory SPP needs to be perceived as 'the right thing to do'. When mandatory SPP is perceived as just and effective, contracting authorities are more likely to endorse it.[32] To avoid greenwashing and social washing, legislators and policymakers should therefore consider the beliefs and priorities of contracting authorities when designing mandatory requirements (see also section IV). Conditional support schemes, such as voluntary green deals or the EU Structural and Investment Funds, are in that sense useful, as the engagement of contracting authorities indicates that they endorse the conditions or at least consider them as acceptable.

Second, a positive way to promote successful SPP behaviour could be by measuring and monitoring mandatory SPP practices and putting high (over) performing contracting authorities and their best practices in the spotlight (see also sections III and IV). This can be done for different types of buyers and different Member States. An example of such a spotlight approach applied on a national level can be found in Lithuania.[33]

Third, when a requirement is perceived as less burdensome, or at least proportional, contracting authorities could be more likely to endorse it, which should in turn improve both the uptake and outcomes of SPP. The perceived burden can be reduced by, for instance, offering support with the adjustments (eg, training, coaching on the job, financial support for Member States that have a less sophisticated procurement system etc), as has been done in, for instance, the Netherlands for the implementation of a new central government SPP policy.[34]

[32] J Grandia, B Steijn and B Kuipers, 'It is not Easy Being Green: Increasing Sustainable Public Procurement Behaviour' (2015) 28 *Innovation: The European Journal of Social Science Research* 243.

[33] eg Open Contracting Partnership 'Going 100% Green in Lithuania' at www.open-contracting.org/2022/10/17/going-100-green-in-lithuania.

[34] van Berkel and Schotanus (n 12).

Finally, to reduce the disadvantages of substantive and procedural requirements and to utilise their advantages, we call for a combination of both substantive and procedural requirements. Procedural requirements can overcome the perceived burden of mandatory SPP by shifting the administrative burden away from SPP to traditional procurement practice. This can be done with a so-called comply-or-explain approach, which requires the procurer to provide a public explanation in case it is not requiring or rewarding sustainable solutions that already exist in a market. If this explanation is not sufficient or correct, green or social suppliers could submit an objection to the contracting authority, or a complaints committee or file a lawsuit.[35] Note that green or social suppliers have an actual incentive to do this, as it might increase their chances to win the tender at hand, but also similar future tenders of other contracting authorities. In addition, national audit offices or accountants could play a role in monitoring SPP behaviour. Implementing a comply-or-explain approach would also lead to more data and insights under what circumstances contracting authorities do not seem able or willing to apply SPP and might need more assistance. Furthermore, being a procedural requirement, a comply-or-explain condition is customisable to every purchase and acknowledges different types of sustainability (eg, green, circular, social, inclusive etc) in different markets. It is also flexible in its use regarding specifications, award criteria and more sustainable procurement models such as buying as a service. Last but not least, a general comply-or-explain approach takes away the disadvantages related to prescribing certain labels, selection criteria, award criteria and similar mechanisms have already been effective in increasing the uptake of SPP. For instance, SPP policies successful in increasing the uptake of SPP also tend to make SPP the 'standard',[36] and so far as we know, no negative market effects have been reported about such policies.

However, a comply-or-explain approach could also lead to a very diverse SPP landscape if each contracting authority develops its own SPP approach. In addition, in the past, not all comply-or-explain approaches have been successful. In several Member States, the approach does not seem to be very successful for specific procurement techniques, such as splitting tenders into lots.[37] If buyers do not use lots, they often tend to copy-paste standard explanations as to why they do not do this (eg, because of the importance of scale or the need for an integral solution). Nevertheless, there are also successful examples of the comply-or-explain approach. For instance, it seems to have been effective in implementing the

[35] F Lichère and O Sulpice, 'Mandatory Requirements in Public Procurement Law: The Role of Remedies, Courts and Public Interest Litigation', ch 14 in this volume.

[36] See, eg van Berkel and Schotanus (n 12). We note that more is required than only changing SPP to become the standard. Several other elements are discussed in later sections about copying best practices and changing professional norms.

[37] See, eg Art 1.5 Dutch Public Procurement Act. P Heijnsbroek, 'The Netherlands: Obligations to Justify the Lowest Price and to Create as Much Societal Value as Possible' in W Janssen and R Caranta (eds), *Mandatory Sustainability Requirements in EU Public Procurement Law Reflections on a Paradigm Shift* (Oxford, Bloomsbury Publishing, 2023).

best-price-quality-ratio as an award method instead of the lowest price in the Dutch construction sector.[38] Similarly, we do not expect that copy-paste explanations will become common practice in Member States with high public procurement capacity for markets where sustainable solutions are available.

If a procedural requirement is successful in accelerating SPP, more successful best practices are likely to emerge. When any of these best practices become common in a specific market, they can be translated into substantive requirements. When such substantive requirements (eg, specific labels, selection criteria etc) are prescribed, they are relatively easy to implement for lagging organisations and might prevent a very broad landscape of SPP practices. In addition, if clear standards are set, this could create the required scale for innovative sustainable supply and prevent high administrative costs for both buyers (for developing SPP approaches) and suppliers (for developing customised sustainable solutions).

Summarising the previous sections, regardless of the mandatory tool being used, we note that taking away or reducing the disadvantages of mandatory SPP seems to be a complex task, especially for substantive requirements. Moreover, to make (mandatory) SPP effective, we argue that other forces are required as well. In the next two sections, we discuss two of these forces: copying best practices and professional norms.

III. Copying Best Practices

Copying best practices, or the mimetic institutional force, refers to the process where successful practices are copied from organisations that are considered successful and therefore legitimate. In the public sector, this happens when public management techniques, organisational structures and procurement practices of leading authorities and sources, achieving sustainable outcomes, are copied by peers. Earlier examples of copying best practices in, for instance, the Netherlands show a large uptake of social return in procurement by municipalities, while no mandatory requirements were in place.[39] This uptake could be explained due to the direct benefits for municipalities and its suitability for copy-pasting. It used to be relatively easy to copy social return requirements or award criteria as not much customisation was (perceived to be) required. This also emphasises the importance

[38] Schotanus (n 11).

[39] Although it could seem that the uptake of social return was an early example of an initiative driven by sustainable motives, the most important drivers for the uptake could also have been financially and/or locally driven. Social return for Dutch municipalities mostly means that citizens of the municipality who have a disadvantage on the labour market are employed by suppliers of the municipality. This increases local participation and it creates a positive business case for the municipality by reducing its expenses on social benefits. Based on TED data, the uptake and application of social return started earlier and is (absolutely and relatively) much higher among municipalities compared to other local authorities such as public schools and water boards that do benefit directly from social return in the Netherlands.

of specific texts for public procurement documents: these do not only explain the importance and effects of social return in a best practice, but also show the texts or spreadsheet model that has been used for the best practice tender and indicate how contract monitoring can take place.

Meanwhile, the mimetic force seems underutilised regarding SPP. Contracting authorities often simply copy their own earlier public procurement documents, at times adding a section about sustainability. While this is copying, it is not mimetic in the sense that public buyers do not draw from the best integral current SPP practices in the public sector, but from their own. In addition, in many cases, it is not likely that a simple add-on section will achieve sustainable development. For instance, circular procurement might need a drastically different procurement model (eg, buying as a service instead of buying a product). The add-on approach is therefore unlikely to lead to optimal sustainable outcomes. It is often necessary that public procurement documents and contracts are redesigned from a sustainable perspective. This requires knowledge of procurement and sustainability, the capacity to implement sustainable goals and up-to-date awareness of what different markets have to offer. If each contracting authority would have to meet these requirements independently, the chances that SPP will become common practice are lower, innovation might be scattered, and both buyers and suppliers would be encountering high transaction costs.

For best practice sharing to contribute to better SPP practice, spaces are needed where contracting authorities can access best practices that they can then copy and customise. Such spaces can be national tender platforms and the European Tenders Electronic Daily (TED) platform,[40] a separate online knowledge platform, an EC platform sharing best practices,[41] or conferences and workshops for public buyers. Examples exist of websites where up-to-date and product-specific sustainable criteria are freely accessible to public buyers to use in their public procurement documents.[42]

Finally, behind most platforms, tools and conferences there is a centralised organisation, a competence centre, an EC committee or a buyer group, which makes explicit efforts to collect and bring forth 'real' best practices that aid public buyers on their websites and via conferences and workshops. In several Member States, such organisations are already an important element in a mimetic process that furthers SPP.

[40] In which sustainable tenders are tagged or rated either as environment friendly, social, circular etc. Tagging or rating of best practices can be done by buyers and/or suppliers. Last, it can be done for the tender phase, but also for the contract realisation phase.

[41] eg European Commission, 'GPP Good Practice' at www.ec.europa.eu/environment/gpp/case_group_en.htm.

[42] eg European Commission, 'EU GPP Criteria' at www.ec.europa.eu/environment/gpp/eu_gpp_criteria_en.htm.

A. Advantages of Copying Best Practices

First and foremost, the availability of best practices lowers the barrier to engaging in SPP for contracting authorities whose procurement function is not as well developed. The value of copying best practices mostly lies in this point, that it often benefits the development of lagging organisations that struggle more with SPP to begin with. As sustainability increases the complexity of the procurement process (ie its complicatedness and uncertainty), lagging or constrained contracting authorities may not have the capacity or knowledge to apply SPP where possible. However, when best practices are established, including public procurement document texts, they may simply copy and customise the practices of their leading peers instead, thereby engaging in SPP after all. It is hard to imagine what SPP uptake levels would be without best practice sharing, but one can imagine that good SPP practices would disseminate much slower through only education and professional norms, as we discuss in section IV as well.

Furthermore, copying best practices contributes to the incremental innovation of practice. This is because leading organisations in the public sector improve upon each other's best practices and share these improvements.

Finally, copying best practices could reduce one of the problems we described earlier: it might prevent a very diverse landscape of different approaches to SPP. Instead, the mechanism could boost the best ideas and the ideas that did not work out are less likely to be copied. In addition, national or regional best practices might get more support from national or regional contracting authorities, compared to practices developed by academics or centrally by the European Commission. Nevertheless, we also see a role in initiatives funded by the EC. They can bring together frontrunners and competence centres of different Member States in, among other things, buyer groups,[43] awards[44] and networks[45] to stimulate the exchange of best practices between different Member States. Especially leading Member States could inspire other Member States.

B. Disadvantages of Copying Best Practices

A disadvantage of the mimetic process is, first, that contracting authorities copy best practices but do not necessarily understand what they copy, nor know what a best practice is. As a result, what is copied may not fit the context of the contract, or might not really be the best practice to achieve the targeted outcomes. For example, local contracting authorities may include 'travel distance' as an award criterion, that can contribute to lowering transport-related CO_2 emissions.

[43] Big Buyers for Climate and Environment at www.bigbuyers.eu.
[44] Procura+ 'Procura+ Awards' at www.procuraplus.org/awards.
[45] Procure2Innovate at procure2innovate.eu.

Though easy to measure, such a criterion may not necessarily be the best means to reduce emissions and might even raise questions of discrimination, giving local suppliers a relative advantage. Criteria that penalise emissions in a more direct manner may be more effective, as the CO_2 emissions may differ with the transport type rather than the travel distance alone. Another disadvantage of copying best practices is that certain best practices will inevitably favour certain specific solutions over others and in turn might benefit specific suppliers. This can happen when a promoted best practice is linked to a specific solution that only a limited set of suppliers offer. While that best practice then inspires contracting authorities, it leads them to write their tenders towards that specific solution and suppliers, thereby limiting the chances of other suppliers if these other suppliers do not develop their business.

C. Reducing Disadvantages of Copying Best Practices

The disadvantages mentioned above can be reduced or prevented by complementing best practices with the buyer and/or supplier ratings about their (perceived) success and background information. This can be achieved by promoting the consultation of the market and leading contracting authorities, or by organising webinars or podcasts and providing short readers on SPP, that offer insight on how to implement best practices in tenders. This will ensure that contracting authorities who find best practices are more likely to copy and implement them appropriately.

In addition, investing in quality control should ensure that the right examples disseminate. The mimetic process is an institutional force, which implies that it happens either way. Developing entities copy the practices of leaders, often by a rule of thumb (leaders are seemingly successful, so their practices are worth copying.) By first validating and then promoting best practices. Buyer groups, competence centres and others can prevent the dissemination of bad practices.

IV. Professional Norms

Professional norms can be understood as the normative professional framework in which contracting authorities operate. They generally reflect the established practices and codes of conduct and are in a sense the collective memory of the procurement profession. Professional norms are influenced by existing mandatory requirements and established best practices, but are also influenced by, among other things, education, professional journals and conferences, what is learned on the job, and what is considered a good practice and shared by knowledge networks. Some examples of networking and training organisations are CIPS in the UK, Nevi in the Netherlands and public procurement competence centres across the EU, such as PIANOo in the Netherlands or CONSIP in Italy, which offer training and education to public buyers and organise events, and therein explicitly position sustainability as an integral part of the purchasing process. These competence centres also play a role in nudging procurement behaviour to become more sustainable[46] and in the collection and dissemination of best practices, discussed before. Meanwhile, they integrate best SPP practices into education and training programmes, thereby shaping professional norms.

Professional norms generally take time to change, especially if one aims to change norms of not only procurement officers but also other persons involved with procurement decisions, such as budget holders, project leaders and contract managers. The question, thus, arises how professional norms can contribute to SPP uptake in the short term. Part of the solution is in the hands of fresh recruits who value sustainable objectives more explicitly. Especially new generation recruits often look differently at procurement-related decisions in their personal life, for instance buying second-hand goods, sharing services or eating plant-based food, and receive more education about sustainability in general. This younger generation has been entering the job market in the past years and seems to be drawn more strongly to work with a positive impact (this includes government work), compared to their predecessors.[47] Similarly, more women have found a job in public procurement and they value sustainability on average higher than men.[48] Establishing sustainability in the professional norms of the public sector can, therefore, be done by employing the younger generation, more women, and men who want to make a positive impact as well. Meanwhile, as public purchasers are educated in sustainability or SPP specifically, the norms of the profession will gradually change in support of SPP.

Another way to establish sustainable norms is through organisational policy, by leading figures and top managers, that set SPP as an important part of public operation.[49] The coercive and normative institutional forces overlap in this case. Statements from top management such as 'from now on, our key focus for public procurement is to buy sustainable' may set a professional norm, while also being coercive in effect. Though such a policy may not always have as formalised enforcement as mandatory requirements do, disregarding its norms might have negative consequences for unsustainable public buyers' positions. The extent to which norms are adopted would probably depend on how close the norm setter

[46] DU Klingler and SL Schooner, 'Promoting Sustainable Public Procurement through Economic Policy Tools: From Moral Suasion to Nudging' (2023) 4 *European Journal of Public Procurement Markets* 67.

[47] S Narayanan, 'Does Generation Z Value and Reward Corporate Social Responsibility Practices?' (2022) 38 *Journal of Marketing Management* 903.

[48] Supply Value 'Onderzoek inkooptrends' at www.supplyvalue.nl/downloads/?download-id=245210.

[49] P Sabatier and D Mazmanian, 'The Conditions of Effective Implementation: A Guide to Accomplishing Policy Objectives' (1979) 5 *Policy Analysis* 481.

and procurer are in the organisational or institutional structure (eg, vision documents by the EU are less impactful on public buyers than the organisational policy that is set within their organisation).

A. Advantages of Stimulating Sustainable Public Procurement Through Professional Norms

An important advantage of professional norms in stimulating SPP is their potential effectiveness. Training that increases awareness of sustainability among public buyers has been shown to be effective.[50] Moreover, as professional norms are also held by the public buyers and other stakeholders themselves, chances of greenwashing and social washing are lower and the quality of SPP is assumedly higher.

Once sustainability becomes established in professional norms, the effects of mandatory requirements and best practices for SPP could become stronger as well. Through professional norms, sustainability becomes a legitimate and feasible goal of public procurement and accordingly, efforts to stimulate SPP can be expected to bear more fruit.

B. Disadvantages of Stimulating Sustainable Public Procurement Through Professional Norms

There are some disadvantages to relying on professional norms only as a means to stimulate SPP. SPP can be more complicated than traditional procurement and therefore the more professional public buyers will mainly manage to do so well. These professionals meanwhile face stronger incentives to leave the public sector and become self-employed, or work for the private sector where they might be rewarded more. Such a brain drain could undermine efforts to establish SPP in the public procurement profession, slowing the process, but perhaps accelerating the uptake of SPP in the private sector.

It is the low pace that makes professional norms a less useful means to stimulate SPP uptake in the short run. Waiting for the next generation, or waiting for current public buyers to change their norms may simply take too much time, considering the urgency of the climate goals and the fast change of available sustainable solutions on the market.

Finally, efforts to change professional norms to stimulate SPP might be feasible in Member States where sustainability is valued, but less so in Member States where sustainability is valued to a lesser extent. Meanwhile, it is exactly in these Member

[50] F Testa et al, 'What Factors Influence the Uptake of GPP (Green Public Procurement) Practices? New Evidence from an Italian Survey' (2012) 82 *Ecological Economics* 88.

States where SPP uptake could be lagging behind and a push for sustainability is most needed.

C. Reducing Disadvantages of Stimulating Sustainable Public Procurement Through Professional Norms

While little can be done to speed up SPP uptake through professional norms only, it is possible to take sustainable drivers into account while employing and possibly certifying public buyers, to hold on to professionals that do well in SPP, to reward SPP behaviour in salary and promotions, and to integrate professional norms in templates and procedures. Holding on to professional sustainable public buyers can be done by rewarding them and by positioning them as so-called 'champions' in the procurement function. By also challenging them to achieve more sustainable outcomes in procurement, they might create the most public value. In addition, when the role of these 'champions' changes from solely conducting a dozen European tenders per year, to an assisting role for a tenfold number of European, national, and regional tenders, their impact could increase exponentially. Finally, it is important to note that a larger part of the public procurement volume – about two-thirds – is tendered below the European public procurement thresholds. It is therefore important to involve the most educated or experienced public buyers (in sustainability) in tenders below the thresholds as well, to ensure that professional norms improve not only above the thresholds.

V. Conclusion and Discussion

The supply side of the market currently lags behind in offering sustainable solutions, but sustainable public demand could help in driving the transition to more sustainable supply. To investigate how SPP can be stimulated, we used institutional theory, describing three topics linked to three separate institutional forces: coercive, mimetic, and normative forces. Our investigation shows that each force can be utilised to stimulate SPP, albeit with advantages and disadvantages. While some of these disadvantages can be reduced, this will require additional investments and may add to the complexity of a system which is already highly complex.

Although there are several disadvantages for each force, the most important ones seem to apply to mandatory SPP in a substantive form only. An approach of only prescribing specific standards or criteria might even have a negative effect on SPP uptake and hinder sustainable development. It could delay SPP due to implementation periods, increase costs and lead to checking the box or getting in the clear by public buyers who are less motivated for sustainability. Likewise, the more motivated public buyers may feel inclined to 'take a step back'. Substantive mandatory requirements can help standardisation and bring along lagging organisations, but it is not likely to stimulate proactive behaviour. It also does not stimulate contracting authorities to use and keep track of other non-mandatory SPP approaches, whereas there are multiple ways of making tenders sustainable, for instance through requirements, award criteria, procurement models, inviting only sustainable and social entrepreneurs to submit a bid, etc.

If mandatory requirements in the form of prescribed efforts are used, we argue this should be done carefully, in consultation with the market, and preferably focused on sectors with a high impact on sustainability themes, such as CO_2 emissions. We also argue that substantive requirements are preferably combined with an incentive that stimulates SPP beyond the minimum effort. This means that prescribed SPP efforts preferably – in most cases[51] – only become mandatory if there is another mechanism active that is flexible, can respond to changes in sustainable supply for different markets, and stimulates to do more than the minimum. A possible approach that could realise this is using a comply-or-explain approach for SPP. Public buyers have to require or reward sustainable solutions that exist in a market and if this is not possible for some reason, the buyer needs to publicly motivate this. This is a flexible approach and could be used in every Member State. On the one hand, it gives discretionary space to contracting authorities to act according to their best judgement, while on the other hand suppliers in the market and national audit offices or accountants could play a role in enforcing SPP efforts. Alongside such an approach, more standards, labels and standard criteria could be developed, possibly based on best practices that have been developed following the implementation of a comply or explain the approach for SPP.

In addition to mandatory requirements, better enabling sharing and copying best practices can improve SPP uptake in the short to middle term and also feed into professionalisation. For instance, national or European tender platforms could be used to tag and disseminate best practices, using more modern IT solutions. Professionalisation is an additional but long route to mainstream SPP, which is already taking place, but at incremental speed. Among other things, employing and certifying public buyers with a sustainable drive, rewarding SPP behaviour, organising SPP training and conferences, and sustainable policy can all be used to slowly change the norm from buying traditional to sustainable. While changing professional norms may be slow, it is important to realise that it will enhance the effectiveness of other forces as well. Contracting authorities with sustainability-oriented norms are more likely to endorse and execute SPP requirements or take up shared best practices.

This chapter has several implications for researchers, managers, buyers, and policy and lawmakers. Earlier research on stimulating the uptake of SPP mostly

[51] A possible exception is where a prescribed effort is capable of setting the bar very high. However, even if it is drastically prescribed that, for instance, all public transport buses in the EU should be zero emission buses before 2030, this could still limit social and circular efforts.

focused on topics related to one specific force (eg, with a focus on a specific aspect of the coercive force or with a focus on the behavioural side), but we argue that all three forces influence the uptake of SPP and that a combination of the three forces will most likely lead to an optimal result. As time is limited and the urgency is high, we believe parallel tracks and investments are required for all three forces, combining a top-down approach (eg, mandatory requirements) and a bottom-up approach (eg, offering SPP training). By providing strong support to all governments in the EU to develop SPP policy prescribing a 'comply or explain principle', or another *procedural* approach, it may be possible to stimulate SPP uptake in the short run, making use of the coercive force. Policy statements of individual governments could also assist in providing specific guidance[52] and practical support for contracting authorities at hand. Such activities might also help in paving the way for the implementation of SPP policies, which might be especially relevant for Member States that do not have ambitious SPP policies. However, SPP policy implementation can still be difficult[53] and may not be supported by every contracting authority in every Member State (eg, because of differences in priorities, financial possibilities, procurement capacity etc). Therefore, at the same time, new Public Procurement Directives and their national implementation in public procurement law will be important. In addition, public procurement standards and labels can be developed for those sectors that have the most impact on sustainability or when it is relatively easy to develop them. For other sectors, industry-specific product standards might be more effective.

Next to efforts in developing public procurement policy and law, copying best practices could be supported by investing in national tender platforms and the European tender announcement platform, increasing the visibility of best practices. Currently, it is difficult for buyers to find best practices while IT can help to promote them. Again, investments in conferences and best practice websites, with actual texts and tools for public procurement documents, seem useful as well. Similarly, investing in (free) education and coaching for procurement staff and staff involved with procurement (eg, budget holders, project leaders and contract managers) will assist in sharing best practices and contribute to changing the professional procurement norm to become more sustainable procurement. Likewise, investing in specific sustainable procurement courses in higher education will increase SPP awareness and help in changing the procurement norm as well. Additionally, adding sustainable (public) procurement topics to general public administration and management courses will help in reaching a broader audience than only (potential) procurement officers.

[52] Guidance could be provided regarding what sustainable focus areas are for different types of purchases. For works, the focus could be on emissions and circularity. For services, the focus could be on diversity etc.

[53] See, eg, BB Da Costa and ALT Da Motta, 'Key Factors Hindering Sustainable Procurement in the Brazilian Public Sector: A Delphi Study' (2019) 14 *International Journal of Sustainable Development and Planning* 152.

Future research could assist in better explaining the effects and challenges of (combined) SPP-related efforts for the three forces. These effects and challenges need to be studied in different contexts, as different efforts might be required in different situations, such as high versus low procurement capacity situations or central versus local authorities. In addition, more research is required on the effectiveness and possible side-effects of different types of mandatory requirements, including comply-or-explain mechanisms and substantive requirements. Finally, future research could also assist in identifying and generalising best practices and analysing success factors for influencing professional norms.

6

Regulating the Producer Instead of the Procurer – The EU Sustainable Products Initiative and Extended Producer Responsibility as Ways to Foster the Transition to a Circular Economy

CHRIS BACKES AND MARLON BOEVE

I. Introduction

The Green Deal aims to speed up the transition to a more sustainable economy and society.[1] The paradigm shift and reform towards more mandatory sustainability requirements in public procurement law, which is the topic of this book, has partially been initiated as part of the Circular Economy Action Plan[2] and within the Sustainable Products Initiative (SPI).[3] In the original communication on the New Green Deal, Green Public Procurement (GPP) and a sustainable product policy were both presented as two complementary elements of a strategy to mobilise industry for a clean and circular economy.[4] The transition to a circular economy is one of the key policies on the road to a more sustainable Europe. It wants to contribute to more sustainability by keeping the resource consumption of the EU within planetary boundaries, and therefore striving to reduce its consumption footprint and double its circular material use rate in the coming decade.[5] New legal provisions on public procurement are part of the Proposal for a Regulation on Ecodesign for Sustainable Products, the core legal instrument of what the EU calls the SPI. When defining the purpose of this new regulation, Article 1 mentions both ecodesign requirements and GPP as complementary aims. Thus,

[1] European Green Deal COM(2019) 640.
[2] A New Circular Economy Action Plan COM(2020) 98.
[3] Proposal for a Regulation on Ecodesign for Sustainable Products COM(2022) 142.
[4] The European Green Deal (n 1) 8.
[5] A New Circular Economy Action Plan (n 2) 4.

the new developments in public procurement law, in order to better serve the transition to a climate-neutral and circular economy, are embedded in a more comprehensive policy and legal framework. The SPI aims to set out a new EU policy framework for sustainable products and to help achieve the EU's climate neutrality and circular economy objectives.

We argue that the new approach to public procurement law must be evaluated as part of this broader initiative, because both do not exist in a legal vacuum. The choice to regulate the procurer, namely contracting authorities in the EU, does not limit the need to regulate the producer as well. The two can go hand in hand, and this broader context feeds into discussions about whether it is more effective to regulate both or to simply focus on one.[6] Therefore, we discuss some of the other legal instruments concerning products and producers that are essential for the shift to a more sustainable and circular economy, and to compare them to the legal initiatives of the Commission that were presented together with the proposed changes in public procurement law. For instance, the initiative will include requirements on mandatory sustainability information disclosure in the form of a digital passport, and further strengthening of consumer law. We do not discuss all proposed new rules and instruments, but concentrate on two objectives, both important though very different elements of a sustainable products policy. One of these instruments is the broadening and strengthening of ecodesign, which is extensively dealt with and further elaborated in the Sustainable Products Initiative. The other one, extended producer responsibility, is hardly mentioned. Both are important elements in regulating the producer and his products as part of the transition to a more circular economy.

II. Ecodesign

A. Purpose and Functioning

For a long time, European environmental product law in practice focused mainly on limiting energy consumption. Nowadays, it is recognised that the entire life cycle of products – from design, production to use and reuse – is important for their environmental impact.[7] The European Commission now also emphasises the importance of the design phase for the transition to sustainable and circular products. According to the Commission, 80 per cent of the environmental impact of

[6] This point is further discussed in W Janssen, 'Shifting towards Mandatory Sustainability Requirements in EU Public Procurement Law: Context, Relevance and a Typology', ch 1 in this volume and links up with the discussions about the economic effectiveness of legal obligations discussed in E Carreras and D Vannoni, 'Mandatory Requirements in Sustainable Public Procurement: The Economic Perspective', ch 4 in this volume.

[7] See, eg, R Malcolm, 'Ecodesign Laws and the Environmental Impact of Our Consumption of Products' (2011) 23 *Journal for Environmental Law* 487.

a product is determined during the design phase.[8] A significant step forward in the development of the EU sustainable product policy was the adoption of the 2005 Ecodesign Directive, establishing a framework for ecodesign requirements that products have to meet when introduced on the market or put into service. The aim of the Ecodesign Directive is to ensure the free movement of products that comply with the ecodesign requirements and to improve their overall environmental impact.[9] This Directive was originally developed in the context of the EU energy policy, which is reflected in the fact that the scope of the original 2005 Ecodesign Directive was limited to energy-using products. From the beginning, the scope of the Directive has been a point of discussion and there have been calls to broaden it. Over time, the scope has indeed been increased to include energy-related products. The Ecodesign Directive defines 'Energy-related product' as

> any good that has an impact on energy consumption during use … and includes parts intended to be incorporated into energy-related products covered by this Directive.[10]

This includes not only products such as consumer refrigerators, televisions, and external power supplies, but also products that influence energy consumption, such as insulation materials. However, the discussion on broadening the scope of the Directive has not yet been closed and has now resulted in a proposal by the European Commission to broaden it to all products (see section II.B).[11]

The Ecodesign Directive offers a framework for ecodesign requirements. The actual product-specific requirements are to be set by the European Commission, product by product, in implementing measures. In principle, all energy-related products fall within the scope of the current Directive, but implementing measures can be established only for products that meet three specific conditions: 1) the product should represent a significant volume of sale and trade, namely more than 200,000 units a year within the European Community; 2) the product must have a significant environmental impact; and 3) the product needs to have a 'significant potential for improvement in terms of its environmental impact without entailing excessive costs'.[12] Annex I of the Directive contains criteria to be taken into account when preparing ecodesign requirements in implementing

[8] A New Circular Economy Action Plan (n 2) para 2.1. See also, eg European Commission, Directorate-General for Energy, Directorate-General for Enterprise and Industry, 'Ecodesign Your Future: How Ecodesign Can Help the Environment by Making Products Smarter' at data.europa.eu/doi/10.2769/38512 3.

[9] Recital 8 and Art 1 Ecodesign Directive. According to Art 2(23) 'Ecodesign' 'means the integration of environmental aspects into product design with the aim of improving the environmental performance of the product throughout its whole life cycle.'

[10] Art 2(1) Ecodesign Directive (n 9).

[11] See, eg, TJ de Römph and JM Cramer, 'How to Improve the EU Legal Framework in View of the Circular Economy' (2020) 38 *Journal of Energy & Natural Resources Law* 245; C Backes, *Law for a Circular Economy* (The Hague, Eleven International Publishing, 2017) 42–43; Ecofys, 'Evaluation of the Energy Labelling Directive and Specific Aspects of the Ecodesign Directive' at energy.ec.europa.eu/evaluation-energy-labelling-directive-and-specific-aspects-ecodesign-directive_en.

[12] Art 15(2) Ecodesign Directive (n 9).

measures. These criteria cover all phases of a product's life cycle and, although the focus is on energy efficiency, they also cover aspects that can form the basis for a more circular design of products, such as the use of materials issued from recycling activities, the ease of reuse and recycling, and the incorporation of used products. The delegated regulations adopted so far contain mainly energy use-related requirements, but there are developments that show an increased focus on circular product design.[13] Especially in the regulations adopted in the period starting in 2019, the number of ecodesign requirements increased.[14] One example is the revised Regulation on the Ecodesign of Refrigerators that took effect on 1 March 2021 and includes not only energy efficiency requirements but also requirements for repairability, spare parts (availability, maximum delivery time), repair and maintenance information, and dismantling requirements for material recovery and recycling and pollution prevention. The integration and assessment of circular economy aspects were initially done mostly on an ad hoc basis.[15] Now, a more standard approach for the assessment is being worked on, including a more systematic incorporation of material efficiency aspects in the assessment method.[16] This may help accelerate the actual shift to more circular product design.

B. Recent Updates and Advancements

Although circular product design is gradually gaining ground in the implementing measures, the current Ecodesign Directive is still limited to energy-related products and pays little attention to keeping information about the various sustainability and circularity aspects of products up to date. After all, in order to be able to design products in a circular manner and to reuse the materials and products that are used in view of the whole product life cycle, it is essential that information is available about, among other things, the quality and properties of products, and the way they are assembled.

The second EU Circular Economy Action Plan, that was adopted in 2020, and the SPI Framework adopted in its wake, aim to bring about significant changes and accelerate the transition to a circular economy. An important part of the associated legislative package is a new Proposal for a Regulation on Ecodesign for

[13] Ecodesign Working Plan 2016–2019 COM(2016) 773. See also L van Acker, 'The New Ecodesign Package: An Important Step Towards a Circular Economy' (2020) 69 *Ars Aequi* 793, para 3.

[14] See for an overview, R Barkhausen, A Durand and K Fick, 'Review and Analysis of Ecodesign Directive Implementing Measures: Product Regulations Shifting from Energy Efficiency towards a Circular Economy' (2022) 14 *Sustainability* 10318.

[15] European Court of Auditors, 'EU Action on Ecodesign and Energy Labelling: Important Contribution to Greater Energy Efficiency Reduced by Significant Delay and Non-compliance' at www.eca.europa.eu/Lists/ECADocuments/SR20_01/SR_Ecodesign_and_energy_labels_EN.pdf 38.

[16] See European Commission, 'Product Policy Bureau on the MEErP Revision' at susproc.jrc.ec.europa.eu/product-bureau//product-groups/521/home.

Sustainable Products. On 30 March 2022, the European Commission published a proposal for this new Regulation, which aims to improve the environmental sustainability of products.[17] The Proposed Regulation will repeal the existing Ecodesign Directive discussed before. The choice for a regulation instead of a directive seems to fit into a more general trend, at least in environmental product law.[18] It shows a sense of urgency, because it reduces the risk of implementation differences between Member States and ensures that the obligations are immediately applicable once the regulation enters into force. At the same time, like the Ecodesign Directive, the Proposed Regulation provides a framework for adopting delegated acts with specific ecodesign requirements for specific products or product groups. As a result, defining ecodesign product requirements will take some time. In comparison to the Directive, the Proposal for the Regulation applies to many more products. In principle, all products fall within the scope of the proposal, with the exception of some specific products such as food, medical products for human use, and living plants and animals.[19] According to the Proposal, the (extended scope of the) Regulation will

> contribute to making products fit for a climate-neutral, resource-efficient and circular economy, reducing waste and ensuring that the performance of frontrunners in sustainability progressively becomes the norm.[20]

The European Commission will present a working plan for product categories that will be the first to be considered for specific ecodesign requirements that could be adopted in EU delegated acts.[21] The Commission reports that a preliminary assessment has shown that textiles, furniture, mattresses, tires, detergents, paints, lubricants, iron, steel and aluminium could be suitable candidates for initial action.[22] In addition to a broader scope, the Proposed Regulation allows for a wider range of ecodesign requirements that can be defined in delegated acts on specific products, such as minimum requirements for recycled content in products, a prohibition of the use of certain technical solutions that limit the reparability of products, and requirements concerning information on substances of concern used in products. Besides providing a framework for ecodesign requirements on the performance of products, the proposal will also establish information requirements aiming at making products more environmentally sustainable.[23]

[17] Proposal for a Regulation on Ecodesign for Sustainable Products COM(2022) 142 (n 3).

[18] eg Proposal for a Batteries Regulation (COM)2020 798. This Regulation is further discussed in A Semple, 'Charge of the Light Brigade? The Clean Vehicles Directive and the Batteries Regulation', ch 7 in this volume.

[19] Art 1(2) Proposal for a Regulation on Ecodesign for Sustainable Products COM(2022) 142 (n 3).

[20] ibid recital 5.

[21] ibid Art 16.

[22] European Commission, 'See Questions and Answers: Sustainable Products Initiative' at ec.europa.eu/commission/presscorner/detail/en/qanda_22_2014.

[23] See the definition of 'ecodesign requirement' in Art 2(7) and the provision on information requirements and Art 7 Proposal for a Regulation on Ecodesign for Sustainable Products COM(2022) 142 (n 3).

This means, among other things, that digital product passports will become the norm for all products that fall within the scope of the Regulation.[24] These digital product passports should ensure a more efficient transfer of information about each product and more transparency throughout its value chain. To this end, the product passports must fulfil a number of conditions, including conditions regarding the technical design and access to the information stored. The information contained in the product passports will be stored in a register that will be developed and maintained by the Commission.

It is noteworthy that the proposal also includes measures that at first glance do not fall directly within the scope of the term 'ecodesign'. For example, the proposal introduces the possibility of setting out requirements in delegated acts for mandatory GPP criteria.[25] The Proposal also provides a basis for preventing the destruction of unsold consumer products. Economic operators must publish, for instance on their website, the number of unsold consumer products they discard each year and the reasons for discarding the products. The Commission also has the power to ban the destruction of specific unused goods.

C. Limitations and Ideas for Further Improvement

Expanding the scope of the EU ecodesign approach and introducing ecodesign requirements that focus on the entire life cycle of products constitute key actions towards more circular and sustainable products. The EU Circular Economy Action Plan 2020 and the Sustainable Product Initiative have indeed paved the way for an actual shift from a linear to a circular product cycle. As the product criteria established on the basis of the current Ecodesign Directive or the future Ecodesign Regulation always are mandatory prerequisites for placing a product on the European market, this also entails a shift from encouraging appeals to mandatory rules for the circular design.

There is of course still room for improvement. For instance, the length and complexity of the process for establishing product requirements in delegated acts could well be a barrier to a speedy transition. As mentioned before, the European Commission needs to define these requirements on a product-by-product basis. According to the Commission, a standard regulatory process for a product group takes around three and a half years. A report by the European Court of Auditors, however, shows the procedure can take much longer in practice. An analysis of several product groups showed that the process took twice as long, for instance, seven years for heaters and six years for refrigerators.[26] One of the main drawbacks

[24] ibid Art 8.

[25] ibid Arts 4(3)(h); Semple (n 18); D Gruyaert and V Pissierssens, 'Transforming the Construction Sector through Minimum Requirements', ch 10 in this volume.

[26] EU Action on Ecodesign and Energy Labelling: Important Contribution to Greater Energy Efficiency Reduced by Significant Delay and Non-compliance (n 15) 18–19.

of a long delay is the risk that ecodesign requirements are already outdated before they come into force and in that way do not contribute to the necessary product innovations.[27] Although improvements in the regulatory process are possible, such as defining and applying a standard approach for review studies,[28] even the 'standard' process without delays will take about three and a half years, which is a long time. To some extent, this problem is addressed by prioritising the choice of product groups, with those with the greatest environmental impact being chosen first. However, it remains a time-consuming process. Time, of which there is very little, given the EU's circularity ambitions for 2030 and the overall ambition of achieving a circular economy by 2050.

As an alternative to legislative measures at the EU level, there is the option of self-regulation. Both the current Ecodesign Directive and the Proposed Regulation on Ecodesign for Sustainable Products allow industries to propose a voluntary agreement as an alternative to EU ecodesign requirements.[29] Self-regulation may have advantages over imposing legal requirements, the idea being that with self-imposed measures, ecodesign goals can be met more quickly and at lower costs.[30] However, self-regulation is preferable only if the sustainability and circularity goals are actually met by the self-imposed measures. The voluntary measures must be such that they serve as a driver of innovation.[31] Building on the scheme introduced in the Ecodesign Directive, the Proposed Regulation on Ecodesign for Sustainable Products provides safeguards to this end, such as laying down what the industry should submit as evidence to the European Commission and criteria for the assessment procedure. The Proposal seems to make good strides here, but what remains is the dependency on the industry's willingness to take regulatory action itself. This leaves self-regulation as a 'limited' alternative for setting ecodesign requirements in delegated acts.

With regard to product requirements, the role of national lawmakers is limited. In general, product law is a competence of the EU that ensures the free movement of products within the EU. However, there is some room left for national product-related requirements. The French Act on Circular Economy offers an interesting example. This Act requires producers to draw up and implement a five-year prevention and ecodesign plan for their products, aimed at reducing the use of non-renewable resources, increasing the use of recycled materials and increasing the recyclability of their products.[32] The plan must describe the objectives as well as the prevention and ecodesign actions that will be implemented in the next

[27] ibid 20.

[28] ibid 39.

[29] Art 17 Ecodesign Directive (n 9); Art 18 of the Proposal for a Regulation on Ecodesign for Sustainable Products COM(2022) 142 (n 3).

[30] See Recital 19 Ecodesign Directive (n 9); Commission Recommendation (EU) 2016/2125 of 30 November 2016 on guidelines for self-regulation measures concluded by industry under Directive 2009/125/EC of the European Parliament and of the Council [2016] OJ L329/109.

[31] See also Backes (n 11) 42–43.

[32] Art L. 541-10-12 Code de l'environnement.

period of five years. This French legal instrument can be seen as an innovative national tool and has added value primarily for products for which there are no ecodesign requirements at the EU level.

A further improvement of EU legislation towards circular end sustainable product design could lie in defining general principles of sustainable product design, applicable to all products, for example in the Proposal for a Regulation on Ecodesign for Sustainable Products.[33] Although these principles will be general in nature and thus provide limited guidance on sustainable product design, they could complement specific product laws, especially for products for which EU delegated acts have not (yet) been adopted. These general principles could be combined with a general requirement for producers to reduce the total environmental impact of their products, measured in easy-to-apply criteria concerning the full life cycle of the product. This would be an instrument similar to the above-mentioned French prevention and ecodesign plan.

III. Extended Producer Responsibility

A. Purpose and Functioning

Extended Producer Responsibility (EPR) is originally based on the idea that producers are responsible for the environmental impact resulting from the life cycle of a product. It builds on the 'polluter pays principle'. During the late 1990s, the instrument was adopted at the European level as a part of waste management legislation. In the Waste Framework Directive, the introduction of EPR was initially motivated as

> one of the means to support the design and production of goods, which take into full account and facilitate the efficient use of resources during their whole life cycle including their repair, re-use, disassembly and recycling without compromising the free circulation of goods on the internal market.[34]

So the purpose of this Directive was not only to make the producer responsible for the waste stemming from his product, but also to steer the design of products towards more circular use. Explicitly, the purpose was not limited to fostering recycling, but the 'higher R's' were addressed likewise. Therefore, Article 8 of the Waste Framework Directive encouraged Member States to introduce an obligation for producers to collect and accept returned post-consumer products/waste, to organise the management of the treatment of returned products/waste, and to bear the financial responsibility for all of this. This included the provision of

[33] C Backes and MN Boeve, 'Envisioning the Future of Circular Economy: a Legal Perspective' (2022) 52 *Environmental Policy and Law* 253.

[34] Recital 27 Waste Framework Directive.

information to the public about the reusability, separate collection, and recyclability of a product. However, the EU did leave ample leeway for Member States to concretize the concept of EPR. The EU itself introduced obligatory EPR schemes in four directives: for packaging waste in 1994 (Packaging and Packaging Waste Directive), for end-of-life vehicles in 2000 (End-of-Life Vehicles Directive), for waste of electrical and electronic equipment in 2003 (2003 WEEE Directive), and batteries in 2006 (Waste Batteries Directive). The EPR regulations allow individual implementation by producers as well as collective approaches. Several Member States have created collective EPR schemes for a wide variety of product groups with different characteristics and legal features. These EPR schemes often cover an entire country, but in various countries multiple (regional) systems co-exist. In the collective alternative, Producer Responsibility Organizations (PROs) are responsible for organizing the collection and treatment of recycling, under the supervision of the national governments. The national governments in turn provide the legal conditions, including targets for recycling and, theoretically, for reuse or other higher circular application.

B. Recent Updates and Advancements

The 2018 amendment to the Waste Framework Directive regulated more detailed requirements for EPR. Articles 8 and 8(a) Waste Framework Directive encourage Member States to impose potentially far-reaching requirements on, among others, producers of goods and those who import or sell materials or goods that are waste or can become waste. These powers serve to 'strengthen the reuse and the prevention, recycling and other recovery of waste', thus implementing the waste hierarchy. Article 8(a) now specifies new requirements for defining the roles of all actors, such as an obligation for companies to enable reuse, and wider stakeholder involvement, including social enterprises; for reporting on the treatment methods applied; for providing information about prevention and reuse; for control systems, auditing and transparency; and for linking the financial responsibility to recyclability.[35] Article 8(a)(1)(a) requires Member States to clearly define the roles and responsibilities of all these actors and Article 8(a)(6) urges Member States to ensure a regular dialogue between the stakeholders involved. The Member States can (or must) impose several obligations on producers and importers, among which are targets for separate collection and recycling or recovery. They can also require producers and importers to provide

[35] See in more detail K Pouikli, 'Concretising the Role of Extended Producer Responsibility in European Union Waste Law and Policy through the Lens of the Circular Economy' (2020) 20 *ERA Forum* 491; C Backes, 'Waste Framework Directive and the Circular Economy' in M Peeters and M Eliantonio (eds), *Research Handbook on EU Environmental Law* (Cheltenham, Edward Elgar Publishing, 2020) para 3.5.

information on the different components and materials used in certain products, as well as the location of dangerous substances and mixtures in these products, to be made available to centres that prepare for reuse, treatment, and recycling facilities. The Directive explicitly applies not only to Member States, as common in EU Directives, but also to the producers and importers who put goods on the EU market.

Following the reform of the Waste Framework Directive, some product-specific directives have also been amended and strengthened. The Proposal for a Batteries Regulation, which will replace the current Directive on this topic, urges Member States to significantly improve the collection and recycling of portable batteries.[36] The current collection rate of 45 per cent should rise to 65 per cent in 2025 and 70 per cent in 2030 for household batteries, and 100 per cent in 2030 for industrial, automotive, or electric vehicle batteries. However, both the revised Directive and the Proposed Regulation leave ample discretion to the Member States as to how to organise EPR. More importantly, EU law only addresses recycling or recycling and other means of recovery altogether.[37] None of the Directives defines a separate target for reuse, refurbishment or other proceedings, higher on the R-ladder. Even the Proposal for a Batteries Regulation does not separately and explicitly address the 'higher R's', except for Annex XII,[38] which now differentiates between targets for recycling and targets for material recovery as a qualitative requirement for such recycling processes. When EPR was introduced, the targets in waste law and policy mainly aimed to prevent waste disposal and waste incineration. EPR has already successfully contributed to realising these aims. However, this is not sufficient to substantially support the transition to a more circular economy.

C. Limitations and Drawbacks

Besides the fact that EPR, as designed in EU law, concentrates on the separate collection of waste and on recycling targets and not on what is needed for a transition to a circular economy, and besides the fact that it is mandatory only for a restricted number of product groups, it has some further limitations and drawbacks.

The first limitation concerns the responsibilities and the costs producers should bear. According to Article 8(a)(4) Waste Framework Directive, all operating costs of the PROs are to be covered by the producers and importers

[36] Proposal for a Batteries Regulation (COM)2020 798 (n 18).

[37] See, eg, Art 7 End-of-Life Vehicles Directive; Art 6 Packaging and Packaging Waste Directive; Annex V WEEE Directive.

[38] See in more detail Art 57 and Annex XII Proposal for a Batteries Regulation (COM) 2020 798 (n 18).

participating in the EPR schemes. However, this will not cover all costs the respective products cause once they have become waste. The responsibility of the producers is limited to realising the respective targets of an EPR scheme. The financial responsibility corresponds to this and is, therefore, also limited. If, for example, the target to separately collect batteries is set at 45 per cent or the target to recycle packaging plastic is set at 50 per cent,[39] then the producers and, if EPR has been organised collectively, the producer organisations will actually and financially only be accountable for arranging the collecting and recycling facilities that realise these targets. Hence, they will not bear full responsibility for their products after they have reached the end-of-use stage. Therefore, the idea that the 'producer's responsibility, physical and/or financial, for a product is extended to the post-consumer stage of a product's life cycle'[40] is only partly realised.

The financial responsibility with regard to products with long durability has been further limited by a judgment of the CJEU in 2022. The Court decided that producers cannot be forced to pay for the collection and recycling of products which are already on the market (here photovoltaic panels), but only for the (future) costs of the products still to be purchased. As a consequence, the Court declared Article 13(1) WEEE Directive invalid, which required producers to also cover the costs of products sold between 2005 and the entry into force of this Directive in 2012.[41] Therefore, the introduction of new EPR schemes takes time, especially for products with long durability, and can apply only to the end-of-use phase of products which are brought onto the market after the new scheme came into force.

Electronic marketplace operators and fulfilment service providers within the EU can accept producers from outside the EU without ensuring that these have complied with waste law registration and notification obligations. Such third-country free-riders take advantage of this 'legal loophole'. Consequently, they have little incentive to contribute their share of the costs for collecting and recycling the waste of their products. If such producers and distributors do not register and do not contribute to the costs of producer organisations, this can, in theory, be sanctioned by Member States authorities. However, enforcement and sanctioning in third countries are difficult and usually do not happen. According to a German report, France appears to be the only Member State to have achieved any significant results enforcing EPR on third-country producers that enter the market via electronic marketplaces.[42]

[39] See, eg, Art 6(1)(g) Waste Batteries Directive.

[40] OECD, *Extended Producer Responsibility: A Guidance Manual for Governments* (Paris, OECD Publishing, 2001) 18.

[41] Case C-181/20 *VYSOČINA WIND a.s. v Česká republika – Ministerstvo životního prostředí* ECLI:EU:C:2022:51, [2022].

[42] German Environment Agency, 'Producer Responsibility of Third-country Producers in e-commerce' at www.umweltbundesamt.de/publikationen/producer-responsibility-of-third-country-producers 43.

D. Room for Frontrunners

With regard to EPR, the role of national regulators is extensive and important. EU Directives must be transposed and all EU law needs to be operationalised, applied and enforced by national authorities. Besides that, in general, EU environmental law only provides for minimum requirements, leaving national regulators some leeway to go beyond EU requirements. While, for example, Article(8)(a)(4)(b) Waste Framework Directive encourages Member States to apply differentiated fees for producers falling under the scope of an EPR scheme, depending on the suitability of a product for circular use, the Member States themselves need to operationalise this and determine whether and to what extent differentiated fees are to be applied. Furthermore, they are allowed and encouraged to introduce EPR schemes for (groups of) products for which this is not required by EU law. The reform of the legal regime for EPR in the 2018 Waste Framework Directive amendment and the introduction of Article 8(a) Waste Framework Directive have not changed the fact that the way and extent to which this instrument is applied in the Member States may vary significantly. As far as we know, a recent and comprehensive overview of the best practices of Member States' EPR schemes and their effectiveness does not exist. Such an overview would be of much interest as the EU rules leave much leeway for different designs of EPR schemes and for introducing EPR with regard to many product categories.

E. Ideas for Further Improvement

The question is whether EPR, as elaborated in the Waste Framework Directive and the more specific directives for end-of-life vehicles, packaging waste, WEEE and batteries, is equipped to optimally foster the transition to a circular economy and society. In discussing ideas for further improvement of this instrument, the coherence with other instruments, such as product law and public procurement law, is an important issue. In the current EU sustainable products initiative, ecodesign and sustainable public procurement are further developed, but EPR is not addressed. The Circular Economy Action Plan of March 2020 mentions EPR only once. It neither promises any reforms nor announces further elaborations of the concept of EPR, but limits the ambitions to enhancing the implementation of the recently adopted requirements.[43] As EPR was introduced also to encourage producers to design their products in a more sustainable way,[44] but in practice

[43] A New Circular Economy Action Plan (n 2) 13.

[44] Recital 27 Waste Framework Directive (n 34); OECD, *Extended and Shared Producer Responsibility. Phase 2. Framework Report*, 2008 (ENV/EPOC/PPC(97)20/REV2) 8; T Lindhqvist, 'Extended Producer Responsibility in Cleaner Production: Policy Principle to Promote Environmental Improvements of Product Systems' (Doctoral Thesis/IIIEE, Lund University|2000) 56ff.

does not seem to substantially contribute to this aim,[45] discussions about the future of EPR should make clear whether this ambition still prevails and how this relates to the further development of other instruments, mainly ecodesign, which are reformed intensively by the Sustainable Products Initiative. These discussions could touch on the following issues.

i. Closing the Loophole for E-marketplaces

The difficulties in enforcing product policies with regard to third countries' producers and distributors who make use of e-marketplaces and fulfilment service providers are addressed in Articles 27 and 29 of the Proposal for a Regulation on Ecodesign for Sustainable Products. However, these proposed provisions are related to the mandatory requirements of producers and distributors stemming from the other parts of this Regulation, but not to the existing mandatory requirements under EPR schemes. It will have to be discussed how the loopholes for such operators can be closed and the enforcement of EPR requirements can be improved.

ii. Responsibility for All Products

Currently, the idea that the responsibility of producers should cover the full life cycle of their products is only partly realised. The organisational and financial responsibility is limited to what is necessary to comply with the targets of an EPR scheme. The organisational and financial accountability for the other part of the products still lies with the public authorities, in most cases the municipalities and eventually the taxpayer. If producers were to be made fully responsible for the collection and treatment of the products they put on the market, this could be an incentive to organise collection schemes in a way that minimises (expensive) losses. This, therefore, would most probably foster circular treatment. On the other hand, full responsibility would mean that producers also bear the costs of 'non-compliance' with compulsory collection schemes by consumers. Partly, they can minimise these costs by an optimal design of collection schemes, incentives for consumers and optimal information for the consumers. However, one may question whether producers in the end should be fully responsible for the (mis)behaviour of consumers.

[45] A Gottberg et al, 'Producer Responsibility, Waste Minimisation and the WEEE Directive: Case Studies in Eco Design from the European Lighting Sector' (2006) 359 *Science of The Total Environment* 38; P Kautto, 'New Instruments – Old Practices? The Implications of Environmental Management Systems and Extended Producer Responsibility for Design for the Environment' (2006) 15 *Business Strategy and the Environment* 377; OECD, *EPR Policies and Product Design: Economic Theory and Selected Case Studies* at www.oecd.org/officialdocuments/publicdisplaydocumentpdf/?doclanguage=en&cote=env/epoc/wgwpr(2005)9/final.

iii. Value Chain Organisations Determining Targets to Maximise Support for the Transition to CE

To be able to fulfil their responsibilities, producers must interact and cooperate with other stakeholders in the value chain. Traditionally, this is particularly true for actors dealing with the collection and recycling of products. How a separate collection of a product or group of products is organised depends on many factors. Sometimes, producers organise their own collection, sometimes they cooperate with retailers and in many cases public or private waste collection entities are paid by producers to do this. The Waste Framework Directive, therefore, urges Member States to 'define in a clear way the roles and responsibilities of all relevant actors involved' (Article 8(a)(1)(a)) and organise a 'regular dialogue' between all relevant stakeholders (Article 8(a)(6)). However, for EPR to contribute optimally to fostering circularity and to achieve also the higher R-applications like repair, reuse, refurbishment etc, all stakeholders in the value chain should be involved in determining the strategies for that aim, and the targets for and the design of EPR schemes should be the result of their joint effort. On the side of value retention solutions, this concerns economic actors engaged in collecting, repairing, refurbishing and reselling. While Article 8(a) encourages Member States to organise a dialogue between all stakeholders in a value chain, a more structured institutionalisation may be needed. 'Value chain management organisations' could develop and monitor circular transition strategies. Such value chain organisations could also contribute to better linking of EPR with the further development of circular product design.

IV. Concluding Remarks

To truly accelerate the transition to a circular economy as a pathway to a more sustainable Europe, a wide range of regulatory tools is needed that cover the whole life cycle of products and basically address all stakeholders, including consumers. In addition to the further development of green and social public procurement, the EU has particularly been committed to instruments that focus on products and on the producer. The analysis of the EU approach to ecodesign as well as EPR shows that these instruments each have been or are being updated to better serve the transition to a circular economy. However, they both still have limitations in their current design. The Proposal for the Regulation on Ecodesign for Sustainable Products ensures significant progress, especially by broadening the scope of the ecodesign approach, but further improvements should be discussed, such as the introduction of general principles of sustainable product design. For EPR it is important that all stakeholders in the chain are involved in setting the goals and designing the EPR Schemes which go beyond separate collection and recycling rates, and also address the 'higher R's' in circular loops. Ideas such as the introduction of 'Value chain management organisations' for this purpose should be further explored. Both instruments can complement SPP. However, attention should be paid to possible collisions,[46] such as double regulation or a lack of coordination between (life cycle) standards applied in product law and public procurement. Any evaluations of the trend towards mandatory sustainability requirements for public procurement, should be made in light of this broader picture.

[46] See also MG Faure and C Dalhammar, 'Principles for the Design of a Policy Framework to Address Product Life Cycle Impacts' in E Maitre-Ekern, C Dalhammar and H Bugge (eds), *Preventing Environmental Damage from Products: An Analysis of the Policy and Regulatory Framework in Europe* (Cambridge, Cambridge University Press, 2018) para 3.4.

PART 2

Sectoral Scrutiny – Mandatory Sustainability Requirements in Current and Future EU (Sectoral) Regulation

7

Charge of the Light Brigade? The Clean Vehicles Directive and the Batteries Regulation

ABBY SEMPLE

I. Introduction

The appeal of mandatory Sustainable Public Procurement (SPP) measures from a policymaker's perspective is clear – harness the big beast which is public procurement, and you will surely achieve significant impacts. However, the experience to date in implementing mandatory SPP measures set out in EU legislation suggests that this 'big beast' is not a dog which can be ordered to bark. It is more like an octopus, with hundreds of thousands of contracting authorities across the EU acting in ways which can be difficult to track, let alone coordinate or harmonise. Given that these contracting authorities range from tiny villages or schools to large central purchasing bodies, this is hardly surprising. The Clean Vehicles Directive[1] represents the first substantive attempt to set mandatory SPP requirements at the EU level, outside of the very limited mandatory social and environmental requirements in the Public Procurement Directives themselves.[2] The importance of targeting the road transport sector was clear – transport as a whole is responsible for around 20 per cent of the EU's total GHG emissions, of which road transport generates the largest share (72.9 per cent in 2016). Transport was the only sector

[1] Clean Vehicles Directive was amended (effectively replaced) by Directive (EU) 2019/1161 (Directive amending Clean Vehicles Directive (hereafter, the 'revised Clean Vehicles Directive').

[2] Under the 2004 Directives, the only mandatory SPP provision concerned the inclusion of accessibility criteria in technical specifications (Art 23(1) of Directive 2004/18/EC). The 2014 Public Procurement Directives added to this a requirement to ensure compliance with applicable environmental, social and labour law in the performance of public contracts (Art 18(2) of Directive 2014/24/EU/Classic Directive) and to exclude abnormally low tenders where this is due to non-compliance with applicable environmental, social or labour law (Art 69(3) of Directive 2014/24/EU/Classic Directive). All other social/environmental provisions under the Public Procurement Directives are voluntary – although in some cases they can be made mandatory under national law.

in the EU that did not record a significant decline in emissions between 1990 and 2016 – instead showing a 25 per cent increase.[3]

The question then is how, not if, the environmental impact of road transport should be addressed, and what the role of public procurement should be. As explored elsewhere in this volume, mandatory SPP measures take a variety of forms, including those which are horizontal such as the Energy Efficiency and Renewable Energy Directives, and those which focus on a particular sector, such as the Energy Performance of Buildings Directive or Clean Vehicles Directive.[4] In addition, some measures such as the Proposal for a Regulation on Ecodesign for Sustainable Products focus on setting minimum requirements which apply to the industry as a whole, rather than specifically to public procurement. On the one hand, the progressive tightening of industry-wide emissions limits on vehicles may be considered a more direct and effective way of promoting clean transport than measures targeting public procurement. On the other hand, the widespread impact of emissions limits means that they are inevitably the target of industry lobbying and, as illustrated by the Dieselgate scandal,[5] may also be subject to industry evasion. Using public contracts as a complementary measure – by mandating public authorities to choose vehicles with environmental performance better than minimum regulatory standards – has the potential to act as a carrot, increasing demand and returns to research and development (R&D) for more sustainable vehicles, rather than the stick of emissions regulations.

However, the design and implementation of such measures are not straightforward. The first myth which must be dispelled is that public procurement is a 'lever' which can be used to pull industry in a particular direction. Due to its highly dispersed nature, both the effectiveness and efficiency of mandatory SPP measures are limited, as can be seen clearly in the history of the Clean Vehicles Directive. This chapter takes a detailed look at both the original (2009) and revised (2019) Clean Vehicles Directives. Evidence regarding the impact of the original Directive gathered as part of a review carried out in 2015–17,[6] is considered. Concerns about the complexity of the requirements set out in the original Directive, and the apparent low level of implementation by contracting authorities, led the European Commission to propose a very different approach in the Revised Directive, which focuses on setting definitions and targets for the

[3] G Erbach, *European Parliament Briefing: Review of the Clean Vehicles Directive* (2019).

[4] C Backes and M Boeve, 'Regulating the Producer instead of the Procurer – The EU Sustainable Products Initiative and Extended Producer Responsibility as Ways to Foster the Transition to a Circular Economy', ch 6 in this volume; D Gruyaert and V Pissierssens, 'Transforming the Construction Sector through Minimum Requirements', ch 10 in this volume.

[5] See discussion in section II.

[6] European Commission, Directorate-General for Mobility and Transport, F Kirsch, I Skinner, S Luckhurst et al, 'Ex-post Evaluation of Directive 2009/33/EC on the Promotion of Clean and Energy Efficient Road Transport Vehicles Final Report' (2015); Proposal for a Directive amending Clean Vehicles Directive COM (2017) 653.

percentage of low and zero-emission vehicles procured in each Member State. While it is too early to evaluate the effectiveness of the Revised Directive, I identify several areas of concern and suggest ways these may be addressed at the EU, national and contracting authority levels.

As will be seen, one of the intended outcomes of the revised Clean Vehicles Directive is to accelerate the transition to battery-electric vehicles across Europe. Increasing reliance on batteries for transport, while beneficial in terms of exhaust emissions, brings a new set of environmental, social and economic risks, in particular regarding the extraction and processing of critical raw materials such as lithium, cobalt, cadmium and nickel. The Batteries Regulation,[7] proposed by the European Commission in 2020, aims to address these concerns, including by placing specific obligations on public bodies to include environmental and social considerations in the procurement process. Importantly, the Batteries Regulation also addresses end-of-life considerations, which are not addressed in the Clean Vehicles Directive but form an essential part of the EU's Circular Economy Strategy.[8] Drawing upon the lessons learned from the implementation of the Clean Vehicles Directive, I analyse the potential risks and benefits of the mandatory procurement measures included in the Batteries Regulation (which at the time of writing has not yet been adopted.) The chapter concludes with some observations regarding the design and implementation of mandatory SPP measures which may be relevant to other sectors.

II. Profile and Impact of Public Procurement of Road Transport Vehicles

Public procurement was estimated to account for up to 3.4 per cent of new car registrations in 2012–20, 2.8 per cent of new vans, 6.4 per cent of new trucks and 75 per cent of new buses.[9] Public sector vehicles are used for a wide range of purposes, from emergency response and specialised defence vehicles to ordinary passenger cars and vans, as well as buses[10] and coaches. Vehicles may be procured

[7] Proposal for a Batteries Regulation (COM)2020 798. During the finalisation of this chapter, the European Parliament and Council reached a provisional agreement on this Regulation, the text of which is available at: www.europarl.europa.eu/RegData/commissions/envi/inag/2023/01-18/ENVI_AG (2023) 740776_EN.pdf.

[8] A New Circular Economy Action Plan COM(2020) 98.

[9] Erbach (n 3). Note that the figures are the upper estimates provided in the Ex-post Evaluation of Directive 2009/33/EC on the Promotion of Clean and Energy Efficient Road Transport Vehicles Final Report (n 6) – and that considerable uncertainty exists regarding the actual number of vehicles procured by the public sector.

[10] Procurement of buses is largely carried out by contracting entities within the scope of the Utilities Directive – whether at the national, regional or local level.

directly through purchase or leasing arrangements, or indirectly through service contracts relating to the transport of people or goods. The direct purchase of vehicles accounts for approximately 75 per cent of public procurement of vehicles (65 per cent for buses), with the remainder accounted for by leasing and service contracts.[11] The size of public fleets has been reduced in most Member States in recent years, both as a result of privatisation and the shift to outsourced services. Significant differences between Member States can be observed in terms of preferred vehicle technologies, charging/refuelling infrastructure and the cost and availability of alternative-fuelled vehicles. For example, in 2021 56 per cent of new buses registered in the Netherlands were fully electric, whereas 100 per cent of new buses registered in Cyprus, Greece and Slovenia were diesel-powered.[12] In Italy, Spain and France, compressed natural gas (CNG) is used in the vast majority of buses, whereas in Germany, Finland and Denmark battery electric is now the dominant technology.[13] While an overall trend towards electrification can be observed in public sector fleets, for some vehicle types (such as coaches, ambulances and fire engines) or applications (such as long-distance rural driving or haulage) internal combustion engines are still strongly preferred.

Road transport was responsible for 78 per cent of EU oil consumption in 2015 – and the share of diesel used in road transport grew from 51 per cent in 2000 to more than 66 per cent in 2015.[14] From the late 1990s until 2015, diesel vehicles were promoted as a greener alternative to petrol, due to their lower average emissions of carbon dioxide (CO_2). However, diesel engines emit more nitrogen oxides (NOx) and fine particulate matter – both of which have severe impacts on air quality and human health. Tight emission limits were set in the US and EU to control these dangerous substances, however, in 2015 it emerged that Volkswagen (and, latterly, several other major vehicle manufacturers) had evaded these limits by installing software in vehicles which detected when tests were being carried out (defeat devices). Real emissions in normal driving conditions exceeded the tested levels by as much as 40 times in some cases.[15] This scandal, which came to light at the time when the original Clean Vehicles Directive was being evaluated, provides several salutary lessons regarding environmental legislation in the transport sector. The first is that favouring a particular technology due to its apparent

[11] European Commission, Directorate-General for Mobility and Transport, S Winne, A Tsamis, M Biedka et al, 'Impact Assessment Study for the Review of Directive 2009/33 on the Promotion of Clean and Energy: Efficient Road Transport Vehicles Final Report' (2020).

[12] European Automobile Manufacturers' Association (ACEA), 'New Medium and Heavy Bus Registrations by Fuel Type, European Union' at www.acea.auto/figure/buses-eu-fuel-type.

[13] European Alternative Fuels Observatory, 'Figures for Total number of alternative fuelled (BEV, PHEV, H2, LPG, CNG, LNG) buses (M2&M3) for Italy, Spain and France' at www.alternative-fuels-observatory.ec.europa.eu/transport-mode/road.

[14] Erbach (n 3).

[15] United States Environmental Protection Agency, 'Notice of Violation of the Clean Air Act to Volkswagen AG, Audi AG, and Volkswagen Group of America' at www.epa.gov/sites/default/files/2015-10/documents/vw-nov-caa-09-18-15.pdf.

environmental benefits must be undertaken with caution, and attention paid to other detriments which may be associated with the technology. The second is that the automotive industry cannot be trusted to comply with legislation, especially where this creates technical and/or financial challenges. The third is that a lack of strong enforcement powers at the EU level, together with a lack of political will both at the EU and national level, means large-scale evasion of environmental regulation can go unpunished for extended periods.[16]

All of this means that individual contracting authorities who attempt to identify truly green vehicles and verify their performance in practice may have the odds stacked against them. While cost and other performance considerations still dominate many public procurement decisions, environmental impacts can no longer be ignored. As progressively tighter emissions limits for vehicles come into effect, more focus is likely to be placed on the total life-cycle impact of vehicles: including the embodied impacts from production as well as those associated with maintenance and end-of-life treatment. Comparing and verifying these effects is complex, and despite the automotive industry embracing electrification, its overall objective is still to increase the number and value of vehicles sold, which runs directly contrary to the public sector objectives of reducing emissions, road congestion and costs. Mandatory SPP measures, such as those set out in the revised Clean Vehicles Directive and Batteries Regulation, therefore have an important role to play in supporting contracting authorities to make environmentally responsible procurement decisions. Going further, many contracting authorities are also aware of the negative social impacts of vehicles and batteries, for example, due to poor labour conditions and human rights violations in supply chains, or the impacts on human health (in particular for children and vulnerable adults) associated with air pollution, road congestion and inactive travel.[17]

III. The Original Clean Vehicles Directive

The original Clean Vehicles Directive applied to the purchase of road transport vehicles in contracts covered by the Public Procurement Directives or awarded by public service obligation operators.[18] It set a requirement in terms of 'how to buy'

[16] In 2011, the European Commission's own Joint Research Centre published a report regarding the use of defeat devices to evade emissions limits for diesel vehicles, however, no action was taken until after the US Environmental Protection Agency issued notices of violation to Volkswagen.

[17] See K Krawiec, S Markusik and G Sierpińsk *Electric Mobility in Public Transport–Driving Towards Cleaner Air* (Cham, Springer, 2021).

[18] Public service obligations relate to transport routes which are in the general interest, but which cannot be run commercially. Rules regarding the award of such contracts are set out in Art 14 and Protocol No 26 of the Treaty on the Functioning of the European Union (TFEU).

(ie environmental impacts had to be taken into account in procurement decisions) instead of 'what to buy' (ie minimum environmental performance levels or specified fuel or vehicle technologies). Contracting authorities, entities and public service obligation operators were required to take the operational lifetime energy and environmental impacts of vehicles into account, including:

- Energy consumption.
- Emissions of carbon dioxide (CO_2).
- Emissions of oxides of nitrogen (NOx), non-methane hydrocarbons (NMHC) and particulate matter (PM).

Two main options were provided for how to take these factors into account: either in the technical specifications (ie by setting minimum performance requirements) or in the award criteria. If award criteria were used, there was an option to monetise the impacts (as part of life-cycle or whole-life costing), in which case a standard methodology and reference values were provided.[19] It was also possible to combine the use of technical specifications and award criteria. Transposition into national law was slow – only three Member States (Denmark, Czech Republic and Portugal) notified the Commission of transposition by the deadline. Eleven others received a Reasoned Opinion regarding transposition and one (Finland) was referred to the Court of Justice. The majority of Member States opted to implement all of the options outlined above, with only Slovenia, Estonia and the Czech Republic applying a more restrictive approach.[20] Some unexpected effects were observed in the way contracting authorities applied the options in practice:

- where technical specifications were used, these often only required compliance with the current emissions standards, meaning no additional environmental benefits were achieved beyond minimum legal requirements;
- where award criteria were used, the weighting assigned to environmental considerations was typically quite low, meaning they had minimal effect on the outcome of procedures; and
- where the monetisation methodology was applied (which was rare), this tended to favour diesel vehicles over other types, due to the relative costs assigned to fuel, CO_2 and pollutant emissions.[21]

The 2015 evaluation report frankly acknowledges the lack of evidence regarding the implementation of the Directive and its associated impacts, noting that there

[19] Art 6 and Annex to Clean Vehicles Directive.

[20] Ex-post Evaluation of Directive 2009/33/EC on the Promotion of Clean and Energy Efficient Road Transport Vehicles Final Report (n 6) 21.

[21] ibid 25. Further discussion and analysis of the monetisation method is given in Annex 9 of the Report.

were no reporting requirements for Member States, and few had undertaken any monitoring. There was also no EU-level monitoring mechanism in place other than the production of consultancy reports. To evaluate the Directive, the report draws upon analysis of data from Tenders Electronic Daily (TED) – which often contains incomplete details of contracts[22] – together with a stakeholder survey, workshops and interviews. The costs and benefits of the Clean Vehicles Directive were estimated using the available data and comparison with a baseline, suggesting it was responsible for a modest 5.5 per cent reduction in CO_2 emissions for passenger cars and 2.2 per cent for vans.[23] The impact on air pollution was even more marginal and may have been cancelled out by the bias towards diesel in the monetisation methodology. For heavy-duty vehicles (such as buses), no effect from the implementation of the Clean Vehicles Directive was observed, due to the difficulty associated with verifying emissions for these vehicles. In analysing the reasons for this underwhelming impact, the report stated that:

> A key underlying reason for limited effectiveness of the Directive is the absence of a definition of what a 'clean vehicle' is and of relevant provisions for minimum requirements (e.g. limit values in terms of fuel/energy consumption, CO_2 and air pollutant emissions) that contracting authorities should meet when setting their requirements. In their absence, it is very often the case that contracting authorities set requirements that can be met by the majority, if not all, vehicles on the market.[24]

Drawing on the report's findings, the Commission evaluated several options for strengthening the Clean Vehicles Directive in the impact assessment published in 2017. These included repealing the Clean Vehicles Directive without setting any new requirements; incremental changes such as updating the monetisation methodology and providing a definition of a clean vehicle; adopting a regulation requiring the application of an amended monetisation methodology; and several options for increasing the scope of the Directive to include service contracts while adopting definitions of clean vehicles based on emissions limits and/or fuel types. The possibility of extending the scope to include all contracts with a 'major transport element' was also considered, but rejected on the grounds that this would be too difficult to define and apply.[25] The impact assessment also did not take

[22] A particular data gap exists in relation to contracts awarded under framework agreements, as there is no obligation to publish individual contract award notices which would indicate the volume or value of actual purchases (as opposed to the often inaccurate/overly generous estimates of overall framework value or volume). In many Member States, vehicles are typically purchased through centralised frameworks.

[23] Ex-post Evaluation of Directive 2009/33/EC on the Promotion of Clean and Energy Efficient Road Transport Vehicles Final Report (n 6) 42. These are significantly lower than the predictions set out in the 2007 Impact Assessment, however as noted impact assessment did not evaluate the policy option eventually adopted in the Directive.

[24] ibid 3.

[25] Commission Staff Working Document Impact Assessment Accompanying the Proposal for A Directive of the European Parliament and of the Council amending Directive 2009/33/EC on the promotion of clean and energy-efficient road transport vehicles 34.

forward options which would have addressed the life-cycle emissions of vehicles, or other environmental impacts such as those covered in the EU GPP criteria for road transport vehicles (eg, materials and production processes, extension of vehicle life, noise emissions, end-of-life considerations). The rationale for this was that such approaches were not appropriate to apply as mandatory requirements, given their complexity and the additional effort required to apply them in practice.[26] Under the heading 'Analysis of social impacts' the only considerations taken into account were job creation and accessibility of public transport (due to possible price increases linked to the procurement of clean vehicles) – omitting any reference to supply chain human or labour rights or the broader social and health impacts of vehicles.

IV. The Revised Clean Vehicles Directive

The general objective for the revision of the Clean Vehicles Directive was to 'accelerate the procurement of clean vehicles in the EU' – notably *not* to reduce the overall environmental impact of vehicle procurement. It follows a very different approach to the original Clean Vehicles Directive, by setting binding targets for each Member State in terms of the number of low and zero-emission vehicles procured as a percentage of overall vehicle procurement (including indirect procurement through service contracts).[27] The Directive provides for two reporting periods, with higher targets coming into effect from 1 January 2026. Definitions are provided for 'low and zero-emission vehicles' for different categories, based on exhaust CO_2 emissions and, for light-duty vehicles, real driving emissions (RDE) of pollutants. For cars and vans, the permissible emissions drop from 50g CO_2/km up to the end of 2025, to zero for vehicles procured from 1 January 2026. For heavy-duty vehicles, given the lack of EU legislation enabling verification of emissions, a number of alternative fuel types are listed with no maximum emission levels set – except for buses, where a certain percentage of zero-emission vehicles must be procured.

The relevant values are shown in Table 1, along with the alternative fuel technologies which meet the standards.[28] The targets set for Member States range from 17.6 to 38.5 per cent for light-duty vehicles, 6–15 per cent for trucks and 24–65 per cent for buses. In terms of scope, the Revised Directive applies to a much wider range of contracts, including refuse collection, courier services

[26] ibid 38.

[27] For a discussion of the revised approach, see O Blazo 'Reform of the Clean Vehicles Directive: From Performance Criteria to Target Values' (2019) 63 *Strani pravni zivot* 59.

[28] The requirements for light-duty vehicles are aligned with the CO_2 emission performance standards for cars and vans set out in Passenger Car Regulation, whereas the permissible fuel technologies for trucks and buses are those set out in Alternative Fuels Directive.

and other transport services. The revised Directive thus significantly broadens the application of the Clean Vehicles Directive, while also deepening its environmental ambition by setting clear emissions requirements which exceed general legislative standards. However, a number of vehicles are either automatically exempt (coaches, agricultural and forestry vehicles, mobile machinery) or can be exempted by Member States (armoured vehicles, emergency services, construction and other specialised vehicles.)

Table 1 Summary of vehicle requirements under the revised Clean Vehicles Directive

Vehicle type	Up to 31 December 2025	From 1 Jan 2026
Cars and vans	Max **50 g CO2/km**; Max **80% of emission limits** for air pollutants based on RDE	**0 g CO2/km**
Trucks and buses*	Hydrogen, battery electric, plug-in hybrids, natural gas (CNG/LNG, biomethane), liquid biofuels**, synthetic and paraffinic fuels, LPG.	

Notes

* For buses, half of the target for each period must be met by procuring zero-emission vehicles (or one-quarter of the target if more than 80% of the buses procured are double-decker).

** Restrictions apply to prevent the use of biofuels associated with land use change as specified in Directive 2018/2001, and to prevent the blending of liquid biofuels, synthetic and paraffinic fuels with conventional fossil fuels.

A risk with this approach is that some public authorities may invest in a relatively small number of green (low or zero-emission) vehicles, while still operating a sizeable grey (petrol or diesel) fleet. In areas where charging infrastructure is lacking or other barriers to use apply, electric vehicles may be underused where a residual grey fleet is still available. Given that most battery-electric vehicles have a higher carbon footprint than an equivalent fossil-fuel vehicle at the point that they leave the factory,[29] procurement of electric vehicles which do not actually serve to reduce the use of fossil-fuel vehicles is counterproductive. Removal of the requirement to evaluate the environmental impact of all vehicle purchases also opens the door to heavily polluting vehicles being purchased (albeit in smaller numbers)

[29] The embodied emissions in an electric vehicle (EV) compared to an internal combustion engine vehicle (ICEV) depend upon both the location and method of production – and in particular the carbon intensity of electricity in the place(s) of manufacture. For example, an EV produced in China will have a considerably higher carbon footprint than an equivalent ICEV, due to the high proportion of coal and oil in China's energy mix. One study found that an EV produced in Germany generates 10 t CO_2eq, compared to 6.6 t CO_2eq for an equivalent ICEV – 50% higher (A Regett, W Mauch, and U Wagner, 'Carbon Footprint of Electric Vehicles – A Plea for More Objectivity' (2019) *Forschungsstelle für Energiewirtschaft* (FfE) e.V. Research Center for Energy Economics) The 'payback period' for these higher embodied emissions depends upon: i) the mileage driven; and ii) the emissions associated with electricity production in the place(s) where the vehicle is charged.

without any consideration of their environmental impact. The Revised Directive is not technology-neutral – which seems risky given the prior experience of a particular vehicle technology (diesel) being favoured by policymakers on environmental grounds. It also omits any concrete obligation[30] to address the environmental impacts of vehicles beyond emissions – for example, material usage, production techniques, measures to extend vehicle lifetime, or end-of-life considerations. It thus represents a missed opportunity to promote circular economy models in the automotive sector.

Importantly, the Revised Clean Vehicles Directive does introduce reporting requirements at the Member State level, as well as requiring the European Commission to report on the implementation of the Directive. Member States were required to report on transposition, including how the targets have been allocated at the national level, by August 2022.[31] In April 2026, and every three years thereafter, they must report on the numbers and categories of vehicles procured in line with the Directive. The question of enforcement is less clear. The initial targets cover a period of over four years, and any non-compliance would only become evident after April 2026, when the first reports from Member States are due. While overall responsibility for meeting the targets is at the national level, some Member States may choose to put in place enforcement measures vis-à-vis contracting authorities or entities. Unlike the Public Procurement Directives themselves, which may be enforced by economic operators with an interest in a procurement procedure under the Remedies Directives, there is no provision for economic operators to seek to enforce the Clean Vehicles Directive or indeed other mandatory SPP measures set out in EU legislation.[32] Given the underlying logic and stated objective of the Clean Vehicles Directive, which is to increase sales of clean vehicles, (some) vehicle manufacturers might be considered to have the greatest interest in enforcement. However, the way in which the targets are expressed, and the retrospective nature of compliance, would make it difficult for an economic operator to enforce the provisions in any individual procurement procedure, even if this was provided for in the Clean Vehicles Directive.

[30] Article 1 of the Revised Directive states: 'This Directive requires Member States to ensure that contracting authorities and contracting entities take into account lifetime energy and environmental impacts, including energy consumption and emissions of CO_2 and of certain pollutants, when procuring certain road transport vehicles', however, the concrete obligations relate to the operational impacts (exhaust emissions/fuel type) only.

[31] In April 2022, the Commission sent reasoned opinions to Bulgaria, Cyprus, Hungary and Sweden for failing to communicate their national measures to transpose the Revised Clean Vehicles Directive. See European Commission, 'April Infringements Package: Key Decisions' at ec.europa.eu/commission/presscorner/detail/EN/INF_22_1769.

[32] F Lichère and O Oriane Sulpice, 'Mandatory Requirements in Public Procurement Law: The Role of Remedies, Courts and Public Interest Litigation', ch 14 in this volume; M Andhov and F Muscaritoli, 'Climate Change and Public Procurement: Are We Shifting the Legal Discourse?', ch 2 in this volume.

V. Proposal for a Batteries Regulation

In December 2020, the Commission published its Proposal for a Batteries Regulation. The Regulation has the twin aims of reducing the environmental impact of battery production, use and disposal, and boosting Europe's market share for battery production. The scope of the Proposed Regulation includes not only batteries used for transport purposes, but also those used in portable devices and for industrial purposes. Unlike the Clean Vehicles Directive, the Batteries Regulation takes a whole life-cycle approach, and is thus aligned with the EU's circular economy strategy. Key obligations on firms placing batteries on the EU market include supply chain due diligence; restrictions on hazardous substances; recycled content labelling with minimum recycled content for lead, cobalt, nickel and lithium being phased in; carbon footprint labelling with a maximum carbon footprint being phased in; minimum electrochemical performance and durability; extended producer responsibility for collection and recycling used batteries; recycling efficiency requirements; and a QR code/digital battery 'passport' to record key information.

The proposed supply chain due diligence clause would require third-party certification in relation to a number of environmental and social risks in battery supply chains. In terms of public procurement, the Proposed Regulation requires life-cycle environmental impacts of all types of batteries and accumulators to be addressed in technical specifications and award criteria for all contracts covered by the current set of Public Procurement Directives 'to ensure that a product is chosen among products with significantly lower environmental impacts over their lifecycle'.[33] The specifications and award criteria must address the carbon footprint, recycled content and performance and durability requirements for the batteries purchased. The requirement to apply award criteria is interesting, given that recent data suggests that non-cost award criteria are still only used in a minority of public procurement procedures.[34] The provision is accompanied by a power granted to the Commission to adopt delegated regulations regarding public procurement of batteries, which could for example require the application of specific GPP/SPP criteria. This approach raises interesting questions regarding subsidiarity and the most effective means of applying harmonised SPP requirements, given the wide diversity in the size and nature of contracts which include batteries.[35]

[33] ibid Art 70.

[34] European Commission, 'Single Market Scoreboard: Public Procurement' at single-market-scoreboard.ec.europa.eu/policy_areas/public-procurement_en, figures relate to 2021. Indicator 5 on Award Criteria shows that in 19 out of 27 Member States, more than half of contracts were awarded based on the lowest price/cost only – and in several Member States the percentage was over 90%.

[35] For further discussion, see M Andhov, R Caranta, WA Janssen, O Martin-Ortega, *Shaping Sustainable Public Procurement Laws in the European Union, EP Greens Report, November 2022* (forthcoming, 2023); K Pouikli, 'Towards Mandatory Green Public Procurement (GPP) Requirements under the EU Green Deal: Reconsidering the Role of Public Procurement as an Environmental Policy Tool' (2021) 21 *ERA Forum* 699.

After a significant delay, both the European Parliament and the Council adopted their positions on the Regulation in March 2022. The Parliament sought to extend the scope of the Regulation, expanding the list of materials subject to supply chain due diligence and inserting liability provisions.[36] The Council, under the French presidency, also proposed increasing the scope of batteries covered and strengthening the limitations on hazardous substances, while extending the timelines for the implementation of several provisions.[37] In terms of public procurement, the Parliament proposed to slightly strengthen the language in Article 70 so that contracting authorities would be required to 'give preference to the most environmentally friendly batteries based on their entire life cycle' (rather than just taking account of the life-cycle environmental impacts). This wording suggests that award criteria would have to be used as part of the mandatory GPP criteria. The Council for its part did not table any substantive amendments to the public procurement article, but proposed a timeline of five years from the date of adoption for the Commission to develop criteria, with the criteria becoming mandatory for contracting authorities after six years.

At the time of writing, interinstitutional negotiations are underway, with the final Regulation expected to be adopted in the second quarter of 2023. At this stage, what can be observed is that the Proposal for a Batteries Regulation takes both a broader and deeper approach than the Clean Vehicles Directive in terms of the environmental and social considerations addressed. Keeping in mind that one of the key expected impacts of the Clean Vehicles Directive will be to increase the procurement of battery electric vehicles, the Regulation has the potential to act as a complementary force, filling in some of the gaps left by the Clean Vehicles Directive. However, much will rest upon the approach taken by the Commission to the delegated regulations. Detailed GPP/SPP criteria covering the full range of battery types covered by the Regulation do not currently exist at the EU level, although some of the key environmental impacts of batteries are addressed in other criteria sets.[38] Drawing on the lessons learnt from the original Clean Vehicles Directive implementation, close involvement of contracting authorities in the development of the criteria, as well as piloting them in practice, is highly recommended.

VI. Discussion and Appraisal

Unfortunately, the Clean Vehicles Directive in its original form was not effective in achieving its environmental objectives. While a number of reasons can be

[36] European Parliament, 'Amendments adopted by the European Parliament on 10 March 2022 on the proposal for a regulation of the European Parliament and of the Council concerning batteries and waste batteries' COM(2020)0798 – C9-0400/2020–2020/0353(COD).

[37] Council of the European Union, 'Proposal for a Regulation of the European Parliament and of the Council concerning batteries and waste batteries, repealing Directive 2006/66/EC and amending Regulation (EU) No 2019/1020 – General approach' 2020/0353(COD).

[38] For example, EU GPP criteria on computers SWD(2021) 57; EU GPP criteria on road transport vehicles SWD(2021) 296.

(and have been) identified for this, a fundamental problem is that the Directive did not adequately reflect the practical realities of public procurement, including the variety of ways in which vehicles are procured and used by the public sector. A second problem was that it did not provide a clear definition of a clean vehicle, or require contracting authorities to go beyond the minimum emission standards already in place. While the revised Clean Vehicles Directive addresses some of the key concerns about the original version by presenting a clearer and simpler mandate for contracting authorities to purchase a certain percentage of low or zero-emission vehicles, this approach is not without its own risks. Chief amongst these is the risk that many contracting authorities will not be able to comply with the Directive, due to its inflexibility. A second risk is that in focusing on a relatively narrow definition of clean vehicles, the Directive ignores broader life-cycle impacts such as those arising during the production and end-of-life phases. This second defect appears to have been avoided in the Proposal for a Batteries Regulation, which does clearly address embodied emissions and end-of-life treatment. The Proposal for a Batteries Regulation also goes further than the Revised Clean Vehicles Directive in addressing social impacts as part of supply chain due diligence. However, it does not detail the criteria to be applied by contracting authorities, leaving this to delegated legislation.

As can be seen from the example of the Clean Vehicles Directive, careful consideration needs to be given to whether expanding the scope of contracts covered by mandatory SPP measures means that the comprehensiveness of the measures is adversely affected. While the revised Clean Vehicles Directive captures a greater proportion of public contracts related to road transport, by setting targets which only apply to some of the vehicles procured under these contracts, it allows emissions and other environmental impacts to go unaddressed for a sizeable portion of vehicles procured by the public sector. It also ignores broader life-cycle impacts by focusing solely on exhaust emissions. The underlying idea seems to be that purchasing low or zero-emission vehicles is always a good thing, regardless of how much they are used or whether they are replacing fossil fuel vehicles. Such vehicles are already subsidised and receive preferential tax treatment in most Member States. To achieve real environmental gains, the impact of electric or other alternative fuelled vehicles needs to be assessed on a fleet-wide basis, taking account of usage patterns for different vehicles, total fleet size and substitutability. While the problems affecting the original Clean Vehicles Directive mean that the 2019 reform was a step in the right direction, it may have created a different set of problems which in turn will need to be addressed. In part, this seems to stem from the view that the original Clean Vehicles Directive was too complex, making it difficult to implement and monitor compliance. The desire for simplicity is a recurring theme in policy and legislation concerning public procurement – however, the promise of simple policy measures to address complex problems should always be treated with caution.

A second fundamental problem affecting the original Clean Vehicles Directive is that it did not sufficiently consider the way in which its provisions would be applied in practice by contracting authorities. For example, several of the findings from the 2015 evaluation report could have been predicted if more input had been sought from those directly involved in public procurement during the development of the Directive. The use of technical specifications merely to reiterate the current legally binding emissions standards (meaning no added environmental benefit arose from the Clean Vehicles Directive) and the fact that the monetisation methodology favoured diesel vehicles, became apparent when contracting authorities applied the Clean Vehicles Directive in real procurement procedures. These defects could probably have been avoided by running even a small-scale pilot of the proposed approach. Unfortunately, those directly involved in public procurement seldom have time to respond to legislative consultations, and so the practical perspective is often missing from well-intentioned legislation. This shortcoming does not appear to have been addressed in the development of the revised Clean Vehicles Directive or in the Batteries Regulation, despite their laudable attempts to increase the environmental and social ambition of public procurement. This is a problem not only because it is likely to diminish the effectiveness of these measures, but also because it limits the credibility of EU environmental legislation, which is sometimes seen as being divorced from day-to-day reality. Finally, the social impact of transport and vehicles, notably supply-chain human and labour rights and impacts on the health of those using or exposed to vehicles, is not addressed in the revised Clean Vehicles Directive.[39]

Tennyson's poem 'The Charge of the Light Brigade' commemorates an event during the Crimean War (1853–56), when a British cavalry brigade was ordered to attack the wrong position and suffered extreme casualties. The blunder was due to a misunderstanding between commanding officers. As the war on climate change intensifies, so does the appeal of simple technical fixes – however such fixes are almost always illusory. This is particularly true in areas such as transport which involve complex global supply chains and multifaceted environmental and social impacts. While the appeal of relatively simple mandatory SPP measures is clear, legislation which effectively instructs contracting authorities to choose particular technologies carries a number of risks: from non-compliance to unintended consequences such as the more intensive use of older, more polluting fossil-fuel vehicles (which still account for a significant portion of many public sector fleets.) Tennyson's poem should serve as a cautionary tale for those who would order the public procurement brigades in a particular direction: to ensure that the position is correct and that adequate lines of communication are in place to resolve problems on the ground.

[39] The situation is similar with textiles; see M Koszewska and JS Ligte, 'Textiles and Clothing: Mandatory Social Requirements as the Way Forward?', ch 9 in this volume.

8

Food: Mandatory EU Public Procurement Criteria for Food after the Farm to Fork Strategy

HANNA SCHEBESTA AND MARIA JOSÉ PLANA CASADO

I. Public Procurement and Food Sustainability: The Farm to Fork Strategy and the Green Deal

Up until 2019, the European Commission consistently underlined the value of Green Public Procurement (GPP) of food and catering services as a *voluntary* instrument, that is, 'meaning that Member States and public authorities can determine the extent to which they implement it'.[1] This vision has seen a drastic turn under the Green Deal and the connected policy actions, in which the Commission emphasises the opportunities of *mandatory* criteria.

The Green Deal Communication firmly framed procurement as a strategic instrument to stimulate demand for sustainable products and services, indicating that the Commission would 'propose further legislation and guidance on green public purchasing'.[2] This proposal, which was not specifically made for food and catering services, was neither reflected in a specific 'key action' in the Annex of the Green Deal Communication, nor did the policy text further give any indication of the type of measures (legislative or not, horizontal or sector-based) that the Commission intended to discuss. The mandatory approach was further elaborated in the 2020 Circular Economy Strategy,[3] which indicated that the Commission will propose minimum mandatory GPP criteria and targets in sectoral legislation and phase in mandatory reporting.[4] Indeed, a sectoral approach to minimum mandatory public procurement requirements was included in the Green Deal action on the food domain, that is, the Farm to Fork (F2F) Strategy, which aims to create a

[1] EU GPP criteria on food SWD(2019) 366.
[2] European Green Deal COM(2019) 640, 8.
[3] A New Circular Economy Action Plan COM(2020) 98.
[4] ibid 2.2.

'fair, healthy and environmentally friendly food system'.[5] The Strategy proposes an Action Plan with 27 initiatives,[6] and also brings, for the first time, the topic of public procurement into the realm of EU food law.

The FTF Strategy proposes the use of procurement in order to achieve 'sustainability' goals for the EU food system.

The topic of sustainable food procurement and execution of catering services is covered twice in the policy part of the F2F Strategy. First, when discussing how to ensure sustainable food production (section 2.1 of the Communication), the Commission proposes to use 'green' public procurement to boost demand for organic foods to help support the shift to organic farming.[7] Second, when discussing how to promote sustainable food consumption and facilitate the shift to healthy, sustainable diets (section 2.4), it indicates that the best way of setting minimum mandatory public procurement requirements for sustainable food procurement should be determined, as a tool to help realise that shift in consumption. Additionally, it vows to 'lead by example and reinforce sustainability standards in the catering contract for its canteens'.[8]

The proposal to discuss mandatory requirements for sustainable food procurement and catering services is reflected in Action 22 of the Draft Action Plan included in the Annex to the Communication. Action 22, originally planned for the third quarter of 2021, is to

> [d]etermine the best modalities for setting minimum mandatory criteria for sustainable food procurement to promote healthy and sustainable diets, including organic products, in schools and public institutions.

The possibility of adopting mandatory requirements for sustainable food procurement is now discussed in connection with the proposed Framework for a Sustainable Food System (FSFS, expected end 2023), which also covers the sustainability labelling of food. The scope of this proposal thus goes beyond 'green' public procurement, and targets 'sustainable' public procurement instead. Note that in this particular wording 'health' is mentioned separately from sustainability, although arguably this is rather for emphasis than conceptual distinction.

In addition, the Communication on Organic Production[9] proposes to integrate organic products into the minimum mandatory criteria for sustainable food public procurement to be developed as part of the legislative framework for sustainable food systems by 2023 and use the national action plans on organic farming to monitor and encourage the application of GPP by public authorities.

In this chapter, we analyse and address the challenges involved in operationalising the F2F Strategy's proposal to define minimum mandatory public

[5] Farm to Fork Strategy, COM(2020) 381.

[6] H Schebesta and JJL Candel, 'Game-changing Potential of the EU's Farm to Fork Strategy' (2020) 1 *Nature Food* 586.

[7] Farm to Fork Strategy COM(2020) 381 (n 5) 8.

[8] ibid 13.

[9] Organic Production Action Plan COM(2021) 141.

procurement criteria for food at the EU level. We first outline the state of the art of food procurement (section II). We trace back how EU law and policy slowly moved away from a strict cost-efficiency rationale to embrace GPP, and finally strategic procurement more broadly. For food, the current *voluntary* GPP criteria for food, catering services and vending machines play a crucial role in defining GPP options. Next, we highlight the contentious issue of how exactly 'sustainable' food can be defined and operationalised (section III), and analyse the current GPP criteria for food in light of environmental, nutritional and social sustainability. Next, we propose and debate the legal modalities with which mandatory 'sustainable' procurement criteria could be implemented at the EU level (section IV). In the conclusions, we argue in favour of sharply defined EU SPP criteria, which must be applied by Member States in a flexible way by setting targets.

II. Food Procurement: Voluntary GPP Criteria as the State of the Art

The sector-specific approach to public procurement is a new phase in the evolution of EU public procurement law.[10] Implicitly, it is a recognition that different rationales of procurement may need a sector-specific balance.

A. The Formulation of EU Voluntary Green Public Procurement Criteria

Public procurement rules traditionally ensure efficient spending of taxpayers' money (often referred to as 'best value for money') at the national level. Before the Public Procurement Directives were introduced, many jurisdictions considered public procurement law also as a steering instrument for the economy, in which the 'power of the public purse' was used as a tool to tie public money to so-called 'secondary considerations' in the public interest.[11]

The initial EU public procurement framework implemented a 'nationality neutral' lowest price rationale that largely banned the inclusion of secondary considerations. Over time, the inclusion of social considerations was recognised as a subject of concern and emerged as one of the more frequently voiced critiques.[12]

[10] Apart from the utilities sectors which always had a specific regime in EU law. W Janssen, 'Shifting towards Mandatory Sustainability Requirements in EU Public Procurement Law: Context, Relevance and a Typology', ch 1 in this volume; M Andhov and F Muscaritoli, 'Climate Change and Public Procurement: Are We Shifting the Legal Discourse?', ch 2 in this volume.

[11] H Schebesta, *Damages in EU Public Procurement Law, Studies in European Economic Law and Regulation 1* (Cham, Springer, 2016).

[12] C McCrudden, 'Buying Social Justice: Equality, Government Procurement & Legal Change' (2007) 7 *Oxford Legal Studies Research* 505.

In response, the EU legal framework moved from pure cost (lowest price) considerations to the more open MEAT criteria; which with the introduction of the 2014 regime change included a stronger emphasis on LCC. The current public procurement rules seek to accommodate greater inclusion of common societal goals in the procurement process. These goals include environmental protection, social responsibility, innovation, combating climate change, employment, public health and other social and environmental considerations.

Historically, the European Commission largely worked on GPP[13] with other secondary considerations being side-lined. These 'green origins' have led to the development of common and voluntary GPP criteria,[14] and Member State action plans to report on the greening of their procurement.[15] The Commission in 2017 opened for a wider debate beyond the greening of procurement,[16] recognising it as a 'powerful tool for spending public money in an efficient, *sustainable* and strategic manner'. In this line, the Commission called for a wider uptake of *strategic* procurement and a targeted approach for priority sectors. At the time, food was not mentioned among the priority sectors in 2017, and the prioritisation of food as a sector under the Green Deal actions reflects the increased political saliency of food system governance.

B. GPP Criteria for Food, Catering Services and Vending Machines

The Commission had, however, formulated GPP criteria[17] specifically for food, catering services and vending machines (hereafter in short: 'GPP criteria for Food') already in 2008; their latest revision was published in 2019.

The EU GPP criteria are voluntary tools that address the four 'leverage points' in a public procurement procedure – namely the technical specifications, selection criteria, award criteria and contract performance criteria. The GPP criteria collect green sample clauses that can be 'safely' used by contracting authorities

[13] Public Procurement for a Better Environment COM(2008) 400. This was the culmination of several political initiatives starting from the Decision No 1600/2002/EC of the European Parliament and of the Council of 22 July 2002 laying down the Sixth Community Environment Action Programme OJ L242/1 identifying green procurement as important. See also Lisbon Strategy; Buying Green 1st edn; Europe 2020: A Strategy for Smart, Sustainable and Inclusive Growth COM(2010) 2020; Buying Green 2nd edn; Buying Green 3rd edn.

[14] As had been proposed by the Public Procurement for a Better Environment COM(2008) 400 (n 13) GPP for different product groups are available at www.ec.europa.eu/environment/gpp/eu_gpp_criteria_en.htm.

[15] Integrated Product Policy Building on Environmental Life-Cycle Thinking COM(2003) 302.

[16] Making Public Procurement Work in and for Europe COM(2017) 572.

[17] The GPP criteria are developed by the European Commission's Joint Research Centre's Institute for Prospective Technological Studies (JRC-IPTS) and adopted in consultation with an informal GPP Advisory Group.

when drafting public procurement documents. The GPP criteria are a soft law tool without a dedicated binding legal act (ie, unlike the EU Ecolabel); they are therefore non-binding.

By their very nature, the GPP criteria focus on environmental aspects. Particularly in the area of food, however, the reformulation process leading to the 2019 revision excavated demands transcending environmental considerations, notably the wish to include fair trade (social considerations), and to some extent health. However, the European Commission, being institutionally tied to a green mandate, proved itself reluctant to move into ethical considerations going beyond the environment. While the environmental approach may have impacts on health and nutrition, as well as on elements belonging to the social or economic dimensions of sustainability, these impacts are purely incidental, and come in the guise of environmental considerations only. For instance, while the GPP criteria are advocating plant-based menus, the reason is linked to the beneficial emission and energy used rather than a consideration that plant-based food is healthier for humans, or safeguards animal welfare.[18]

Although the criteria address all the leverage points identified (ie, selection criteria/qualification of the tenderer, technical specifications, award criteria, and contract performance clauses), most of the recommendations relate to the drafting of technical specifications and award criteria. Thresholds in technical specifications are included as minimum values and thresholds in award criteria are included as the starting point to get points awarded. The following example illustrates how the main core criteria recommended as a technical specification for food supply are drafted:

Table 2 Technical Specifications[19]

Option A: The following food and drink products [to be inserted by the contracting authority] must comply with Regulation (EC) No 2018/8481 [on organic production]. Option B: At least once a week, the main ingredients of the menus served will be food and drinks that comply with Regulation (EC) No 2018/8481. Option C: At least X per cent of the total purchases of food and drink products must comply with Regulation (EC) No 2018/8481.

This example brings out one of the complexities around the drafting of food procurement clauses: measurement and a green and/or sustainable reference standard. The criteria aim to measure the quantity of foods supplied by either using a ban on certain foods, a frequency, or a percentage value of either in units, weight/volume or value (price) of food purchased. As elaborated in the explanatory notes of the 2019 GPP criteria, the contracting authority has to specify the option chosen for measurement and how it will be verified.

[18] EU GPP criteria on food SWD(2019) 366 (n 1) 49.
[19] ibid.

Except for contract performance clauses, which largely relate to management,[20] EU food GPP criteria mostly focus on what type of foods to procure, particularly covering the sourcing of fruits and vegetables, dairy products, fish and seafood and meat.[21] Here again, the rationale behind the design of the food criteria is to minimise environmental impacts by means of choosing which – more environmentally friendly – foods to procure. For instance, negative environmental impacts resulting from the use of pesticides and fertilisers in agriculture are to be minimised by sourcing more organic products, which are grown with no (or less) chemical input than those from conventional agriculture under the Organic Production Regulation.

It must be noted that there are relevant differences between the 2016 and 2019 versions of the EU criteria. In the 2016 EU GPP criteria, core criteria included not only the supply of organic foods, but also, amongst others, of foods from 'integrated production', seasonal foods and packaging with a high content of recyclable materials. Those three elements are removed from the list of recommendations in the 2019 version of the report, which instead includes plant-based menus, vegetable fats from sustainable sources, fair trade foods and procedures for the prevention of food waste as recommended core criteria. Those changes do not only illustrate the struggle to move into considerations other than purely environmental, but also, as discussed in the next section, the complexity of identifying criteria that really bring more sustainability to food procurement.

One of the main critiques of the EU GPP criteria is their exclusive focus on *green* criteria – this stems in part from their origin in an environmental policy context.[22] The green approach works less successfully in food than for other product categories, because:

> [o]ther GPP criteria that were developed for goods and services have much purer environmental considerations; in comparison, food is a particularly complex product, in which environmental concerns co-exist with other concerns such as animal welfare, organic production, or social fairness. This complexity already stood in the way of the formulation of EU Ecolabel criteria for food, which became an abandoned endeavour.[23]

The reasons why the idea to create an EU Ecolabel for food generally and fishery and aquaculture products particularly failed, are on one hand the realisation that 'green food' is not enough, and on the other hand the challenge of facing trade-offs

[20] Such as those relating to the training of staff, the replacement of vehicles and equipment or food and beverages redistribution to prevent food waste.

[21] B Neto and M Gama Caldas, 'The Use of Green Criteria in the Public Procurement of Food Products and Catering Services: A Review of EU Schemes' (2018) 20 *Environment, Development and Sustainability* 1905.

[22] H Schebesta, 'Revision of the EU Green Public Procurement Criteria for Food Procurement and Catering Services – Certification Schemes as the Main Determinant for Public Sustainable Food Purchases?' (2018) 9 *European Journal of Risk Regulation* 316.

[23] ibid.

between different policy dimensions that foodstuffs combine. The GPP criteria for food and their formulation processes above all illustrate the challenge of finding consensus on what constitutes sustainable, or even merely ecologically sustainable, food. However, the GPP criteria for food provide important indications on the future design of minimum criteria – the choice of 'leverage point' (ie, selection criteria, technical specifications, award criteria, or contract performance clauses), the measurement, and a relevant standard or sustainability indicator (such as 'organic').

III. What are Sustainable Foods?

The inability to define what sustainable food is, constitutes a barring issue for mandating sustainable food procurement in the first place. Molin, Martin and Björklund reported in 2022 that 'despite an abundance of literature on transforming the food system through more sustainable food choices, few studies addressed certain types of foods to procure'.[24]

A. Sustainability as a Multidimensional Concept

Sustainability is a multidimensional and elusive concept, which (according to the Food and Agricultural Organisation of the United Nations [FAO] definition) generates a positive value along economic, social, and environmental dimensions simultaneously.[25] As a result of such complexity, there is no consensus about what 'sustainable food' is.[26]

The F2F Strategy does not provide a definition of the concept of 'sustainable food'. Instead, the policy refers to sustainability in certain dimensions, mainly relating to environmental, nutritional/healthy and social sustainability. However, it is clear from the policy document that a conceptualisation of food sustainability will be provided only within the context of the Framework for Sustainable Food Systems, which is expected in 2023. While 'fuzzy concepts' can be useful in achieving political consensus, they are of little use in public procurement, which requires sharply defined criteria to be operational. In the formulation of the GPP criteria, we witnessed a harsh struggle to identify certain foods or practices as sustainable, with arguably limited results along some of the sustainability dimensions. The next sections illustrate the trade-offs that have to be made when defining some of the

[24] E Molin, M Martin and A Björklund, 'Addressing Sustainability within Public Procurement of Food: A Systematic Literature Review' (2022) 13 *Sustainability* 13395.

[25] FAO, 'Sustainable Food Systems: Concept and Framework' at www.fao.org/3/ca2079en/CA2079EN.pdf.

[26] Molin et al (n 24).

criteria that are used the most in food procurement, in the dimensions of environmental, nutritionally/healthy and socially sustainable foods.

i. What is Environmentally Sustainable Food?

Given that environmental concerns have been the starting point for drafting the *green* criteria, one might assume this to be the 'easiest' dimension of sustainability, where operationalisation has been largely completed. The GPP criteria for food operationalise the 'pure' environmental dimension of food sustainability for instance by reference to organic food, seasonal produce, or local or short food supply chain production. We discuss these concepts below and show why they remain contentious when it comes to sustainability.

a. Organic Foods

Organic production is governed by the Organic Production Regulation on organic production and labelling of organic products. This Regulation codifies what organic food is in the EU. In other words, there is a legal definition of what is organic (or bio) and what is not. In a nutshell, organic foods cannot include GMO ingredients or components, be processed using ionising radiation, and have strict limits regarding the use of chemically synthesised inputs. Both the GPP criteria and scientific literature often use organic production as a shortcut to environmental sustainability, because of its codification in EU law. Additionally, research shows that organic production can play an important role in improving biodiversity and as having reduced GHG emissions, particularly when compared to conventional agriculture. However, those two elements are not explicit requirements of organic production in EU law. Also, the Organic Production Regulation does not consider the amount of water or electricity necessary to obtain the food, nor does it consider the environmental impact of its packaging. Furthermore, EU rules actually facilitate international agreements that entail that an organic product manufactured on another continent can be legally labelled as organic in Europe, despite the carbon footprint associated with its transport. Organic foods, therefore, do not by definition have a lower environmental impact than regular foodstuffs. This is in fact acknowledged in the EU GPP criteria for food, which despite strongly recommending increasing the purchase of organic foods in public contracts indicate that although

> [t]he inclusion of a criterion on organic food products is proposed based on studies that demonstrate that the possibility of achieving some environmental benefits can be brought under certain conditions, (…) it is not yet possible to draw a general conclusion on the environmental benefits for all the conditions that are currently present across Europe.[27]

[27] EU GPP criteria on food SWD(2019) 366 (n 1) 20.

The use of organic production as 'the' shortcut for environmental sustainability also was said to work against the integration of small primary producers in public procurement (at least until the adoption of the Regulation). The argument being that the mandatory certification required for organic products was a barrier to entry for those unable to cover certification costs/burdens. Taking this last concern into account, the 2016 version of the EU GPP criteria opted for using 'integrated production' as a complementary shortcut to operationalise environmental (and, to some degree, social) sustainability.

Integrated production is defined by the International organisation of biological and integrated control (IOBIC) as a 'farming system that produces high-quality feed and other products by using natural resources and regulating mechanisms to replace pollution inputs to secure sustainable farming'.[28] EU law does, however, not include a (legal) definition of the concept. Instead, some Member States have adopted their own rules to define, govern and certify such methods of farming within their territory. In the absence of an EU standard (and therefore of a homogeneous understanding of which practices characterise integrated production and how to validate them), the 2019 GPP criteria report removes the criterion on integrated production from the list of recommended core and comprehensive criteria for food procurement. In the 2019 report, an explanatory note however indicates that, although integrated production is no longer a recommended core or comprehensive criteria, contracting authorities may decide to include an integrated production criterion, on an individual basis, 'by indicating the percentage of total purchases not complying with organic food products criterion that must comply with the rules in place where the food products are produced or a specific private scheme'[29] such as those for integrated production.

b. Seasonal Produce

Seasonal produce as a 'green' GPP criterion has a longstanding history: it was already present in the original 2008 criteria, which recommended the purchase of seasonal produce to reduce the total cost of catering services from a life-cycle costing perspective.[30]

Purchasing of seasonal foods is generally considered to refer to the practice of only purchasing products grown within that season in a specific territory. The assumption that seasonal products are grown within reach, and therefore minimise food miles and the environmental effects of transport is not valid across the board.[31] Typically, production effects are more significant than logistics. Further,

[28] IOBC, 'Integrated Production IOBC-WPRS Objectives And Principles' at www.iobc-wprs.org/ip_integrated_production/IOBC-WPRS_IP_objectives_and_principles_4th_edition_2018_EN.pdf.

[29] EU GPP criteria on food SWD(2019) 366 (n 1) 18.

[30] ICLEI – Local Governments for Sustainability & Ecoinstitut Barcelona, 'GPP Training Toolkit Background Product Report Food and Catering services' (2008) 27.

[31] AM Vargas et al, 'The Role of Local Seasonal Foods in Enhancing Sustainable Food Consumption: A Systematic Literature Review' (2021) 10 *Foods* 2206.

there is no legal definition of what constitutes seasonal foods. In absence of such a definition, the public procurement rules require that the contracting authority includes a working definition of this concept in the public procurement documents, potentially even including a calendar of which foods are considered seasonal every time of the year. These problems around seasonality were already echoed in the 2016 revision of the GPP criteria: the 2016 JRC technical report indicated that, even if many institutions and studies recommend the purchase of seasonal produce based on the potential of such purchases to limit GHG emissions, such conceptualisation was flawed because, among other reasons, it did not differentiate between imported and homegrown products, and therefore

> in some cases, it is better to import a product in season in another country, rather than boosting domestic production (extend season), as for instance through heated greenhouses or by keeping harvested crops (e.g. potatoes) in cold storages for months (Webb et al., 2013).[32]

Still, the 2016 GPP criteria kept seasonal products as a criterion (probably because seasonal produce as a technical specification was the second most used criterion in catering services, right after organic production, in 2016).[33] The 2019 edition of the Food GPP criteria no longer includes seasonal produce as a recommendation. Only an 'explanatory note' warns contracting authorities about the complexity of using this criterion, and underlining the fact that documents must include 'at what time of the year which food and drink products are to be delivered/offered'.[34]

c. Short/Local Supply Chains

Foods produced in short or local supply chains are another related 'shorthand' for sustainable food, that combines environmental and social sustainability.[35] Contracting authorities try to promote local food sourcing in order to integrate small producers in public procurement. However, this is often problematic. The principle of non-discrimination enshrined in EU public procurement law prevents contracting authorities from requesting the supply of products of a specific origin or locality (except for EU-protected designations of origin or geographical indications). In this regard, already the 2016 technical report indicated that 'buying local is not something the EU GPP can propose due to discriminatory purposes related to trading within and outside the EU'.[36]

[32] European Commission, 'JRC Science for Policy Report Revision of the EU Green Public Procurement Criteria for Food and Catering Services', JRC102669 230.

[33] ibid 27.

[34] EU GPP criteria on food SWD(2019) 366 (n 1) 17.

[35] A Farm to Fork Strategy COM(2020) 381 (n 5) 2.

[36] JRC Science for Policy Report Revision of the EU Green Public Procurement Criteria for Food and Catering Services (n 32) 230.

Contracting authorities use different strategies to get suppliers and caterers to buy local to realign food security and sustainability objectives with public procurement legislation. One of the most popular ones is to switch focus from local products or suppliers to short supply chains. There is no generally valid definition of 'short supply chain' in EU law,[37] and therefore Member States use different concepts. A recurring concept is that of 'proximity' products, for instance by the Catalan Government in Spain. Proximate foods are then defined in Catalan law as those offered either in direct sales, or with a maximum of one intermediary between primary production and the final consumer.[38]

The issue of 'short supply chains' once more illustrates the complexity of defining sustainable food. Next to the social considerations inherent to the call for more local production, environmental considerations may play a role, assuming that local food will have a smaller carbon footprint in terms of transportation costs than imported foods. Next to these rationales, the localisation of food production also speaks to the issue of food security.

ii. What is Nutritionally Sustainable and Healthy Food?

The F2F Strategy, in its wording, emphasises the importance of creating mandatory public procurement criteria for the provision of healthy and nutritional food, presumably as a dimension of sustainability. The Commission seems to assume that better health and nutrition come (at least to some degree) from switching from (among other) meat to (specifically) plant-based diets.[39]

The 2019 GPP criteria for food recommend plant-based as a core, comprehensive and award criteria for food procurement. For instance, it identifies that, when drafting the technical specification for catering services, contracting authorities should request bidders to ensure that their service includes at least one vegetarian or plant-based menu one day per week, that half of the dishes offered daily should be vegetarian or plant-based, or that 'meat dishes should be bulked up (40 per cent) with beans, grains or vegetables'.[40]

Additionally, the Communication implies that organic food could also be used as a shortcut for better health and nutrition. This is also frequently done in

[37] The so-called Rural Development Regulation includes a definition of the term 'short supply chain', but it should be regarded as directly valid only in the context of the specific legal framework. The concept is defined in Art (2)(m) of Rural Development Regulation, in the following terms: 'short supply chain: means a supply chain involving a limited number of economic operators, committed to co-operation, local economic development, and close geographical and social relations between producers, processors and consumers'.

[38] Decreto 24/2013, de 8 de enero, sobre la acreditación de la venta de proximidad de productos agroalimentarios, DOGC núm. 6290, of 10 January 2013.

[39] A Farm to Fork Strategy COM(2020) 381 (n 5) 2.4.

[40] This criteria is made for circumstances where there are no other relevant recommendations on nutritional intake based on the type of clients they are contracting the catering service and set the thresholds accordingly (for instance, the nutritional intake needs of the elderly in a public retirement home). EU GPP criteria on food SWD(2019) 366 (n 1).

the literature.[41] However, the fact remains that processed plant-based and organic foods do not have to follow any specific nutrition requirements; therefore, they can still be high in fat, sugar or other nutrients/substances known to cause non-communicable diseases.

Other sustainability dimensions are not addressed in the GPP criteria: health is arguably an important component of 'sustainable food'. However, health effects are hardly addressed, for instance, there are no criteria relating to healthy products in vending machines.[42]

The general question of how to determine which foods are nutritious (or healthy foods) remains an unanswered question at the EU level. The 2006 Nutrition and Health Claims Regulation set the legal basis for the development of EU-wide nutrition profiles, a tool that should make such categorisation easier, but this initiative has been on hold ever since. Some work on the nutrition aspects is now being conducted under the F2F Strategy, although it is unclear how and what type of EU-wide nutrition label will ultimately be mandated.

Finally, legal certainty requires that individual public procurement documents do not request bidders to offer 'nutritious' or 'healthy' food products or menus, but define specific parameters that supply must meet (for instance, prohibiting fried foods or desserts with a sugar content that goes above a certain threshold).

iii. What is Socially Sustainable Food?

Social sustainability clusters a wide and diffuse category of issues, combining 'issues such as fair trade, fair wages, safe working conditions, ethical purchasing, and healthy diets for consumers are addressed'.[43] Especially in EU policies 'social' considerations tend to constitute a very large umbrella category that may be understood to comprise social, ethical and sometimes even health considerations. In the current EU GPP criteria for food, 'social sustainability' mainly refers to two areas: animal welfare and fair trade. The original mandate for drawing up *green* procurement criteria is reflected in the limited consideration given to these categories. For instance, animal welfare is only considered regarding the sourcing of eggs and fish products. In terms of mechanism, social sustainability is incorporated either by compliance with a voluntary EU legislative standard, by reference to international standards, or by reference to private certification schemes.

The 2019 GPP criteria for food propose technical specifications that prohibit eggs from hens raised in cages (ie, eggs coming from conventional farming labelled with code 3 Regulation 589/2008).[44] The marking of eggs stands out as one of the

[41] Molin et al (n 24).
[42] Schebesta (n 22).
[43] Molin et al (n 24) 14.
[44] EU GPP criteria on food SWD(2019) 366 (n 1) 9. The code translates an indication about whether the egg being purchased was from a chicken raised in a cage, on soil, outdoors or completely organically (3, 2, 1 and 0 respectively).

few pieces of EU legislation requiring the mandatory labelling of animal welfare, and more generally, ethical and social concerns.

For other aspects, public procurement documents are to rely on private standard certification schemes. This is the case, for instance, regarding animal welfare. Criteria can be set by reference to certification schemes, which must be based on multi-stakeholder organisations with a broad membership and address general aspects such as 'low stress, minimum use of necessary antibiotics, stunned slaughter, minimum transportation times, and addresses particular aspects such as the grazing season for milk cows or no-tail docking on pigs'. The GPP criteria for food further mention that product compliance could be shown through third-party certified, widely accepted, and recognised standards such as, for example, Label Rouge, Globalgap with the add-on of Animal welfare, or RSPCA Assured.

Socially fair requirements can also be set by reference to international fair and ethical trade standards, including working conditions for production in accordance with the core conventions of the International Labour Organisation (ILO), or certification schemes on sustainable trade and pricing. The GPP criteria specify that these do not need to be part of the Fair Trade movement, and that schemes such as Fairtrade®, UTZ, Bonsucro, etc, or other schemes at the country level can be considered.

Fishery and aquaculture products, by contrast, are not governed by reference to the Marine Stewardship Council (MSC) certification scheme but should be addressed by reference to a list of species at risk. One requirement is that 'No fish or fish products are to be used from species and stocks identified in a "fish to avoid" list.' Valid reference lists are, for instance, the Marine Conservation Society 'fish to avoid', WWF's sustainable seafood guides, IUCN, Seaweb Europe, CITES, FAO, NOAA, Monterey Bay Aquarium, Seafood Watch, Greenpeace, or national seafood guides. This effectively focuses the GPP seafood criteria on the environmental dimension, cutting out broader objectives of MSC-type certification schemes that additionally cover other sustainability dimensions such as ecological effects of fishing or socially responsible work and pricing conditions.

Overall, the GPP criteria refer to standards set elsewhere (in legislation, international standards, or certification schemes), but they add a layer of relatively detailed requirements on the minimum criteria or principles that such standards have to respect. This comes closest to a GPP-based definition of minimum standards, rather than purely references to external standards.

B. Certification Schemes as a Metric to Define 'Sustainability'

The discussion above shows that 'sustainable food' does not exist. It can be only more or less performative in different sustainability dimensions (eg, social, economic). Food is an area in which many standards[45] exist that operationalise one or several dimensions of sustainability. These can be issue-based standards, such as fair trade, multidimensional standards, such as MSC, or unidimensional standards such as 'dolphin-free'. In terms of measuring the dimensions of sustainability, private standards already have a more advanced metric to operationalise sustainability in food products (see, eg, standardsmap.org). Certification schemes therefore could indeed be part of the solution in defining parameters of sustainability, as they may provide a pragmatic and readily deployable instrument to govern 'sustainable food procurement'. However, two challenges for using certification schemes to identify sustainable foods need to be addressed.

First, the current public procurement rules place restrictions on the use of private standards as a tool in public tenders where the use of labels in public procurement procedures has been contested.[46] In the *Dutch Coffee* case,[47] the Commission argued that the use of EKO and MAX HAVELAAR labels in a public procurement notice for the supply of coffee machines and ingredients was a breach of Article 23(6) and Article 23(8) of (the old) Directive 2004/18 concerning the technical specifications and additionally that they did not constitute a permissible award criterion. A part of the question of the validity of labels is now codified in Article 43 of the 'Classic' Directive. Accordingly, contracting authorities may require specific (eco) labels or equivalent under specific circumstances only. The conditions of a required label must be linked to the subject matter of the contract. If not all conditions of a given label are actual requirements in a procurement procedure, authorities must identify the required criteria, and may define technical specifications by reference to particular aspects of the label only. Equivalent labels must be accepted. In addition, and relatively remarkably, the Article also contains requirements on the governance of labels, notably they must be formulated in an open and transparent procedure in which all relevant stakeholders may participate; accessible; set by a third party (economic operator applying for the label cannot exercise a decisive influence). Labels are a useful short-hand for sustainability, but under current public procurement law, their use remains a challenge.

[45] We use the word 'standard' here loosely, although a more technical distinction between standard third-party certification schemes and accredited schemes is certainly valid, see H Schebesta, 'Control in the Label: Self-declared, Certified, Accredited? On-pack Consumer Communication about Compliance Control in Voluntary Food Schemes from a Legal Perspective' in P Rott (ed), *Certification – Trust, Accountability, Liability* (Cham, Springer, 2019).

[46] On the potential role of eco-labels in GPP, see H Schebesta, 'EU Green Public Procurement Policy Modernisation Package, Eco-Labelling and Framing Measures' in S Schoenmakers, W Devroe and N Philipsen (eds), *State Aid and Public Procurement in the European Union* (Cambridge, Intersentia, 2014); R Caranta, 'Labels as Enablers of Sustainable Public Procurement' in B Sjafjell and A Wiesbrock (eds), *Sustainable Public Procurement Under EU Law* (Cambridge, Cambridge University Press, 2016).

[47] Case C-368/10 *Commission v Kingdom of the Netherlands* ECLI:EU:C:2012:284, [2012] ECR I-284.

Second, from a legal regulatory point of view, private standards are highly, if not almost entirely, unregulated in terms of their validity and quality. Therefore, while private standards may be a practicable way within public procurement, this in turn necessitates better *governance* of private standards. Under the umbrella of the European Green Deal and the F2F Strategy, there are a number of legal actions pending to improve the control of food labelling, green labelling and labelling in general.

IV. How to Operationalise EU-Mandatory Sustainability Public Procurement Criteria for Food?

The European Commission is steadily setting courses on mandatory minimum public procurement requirements for food. The search for *what* practises precisely sustainable food procurement requires and *how* this can be done (legal modalities) are to be defined further along in the legislative process.

There are certain inconsistencies in the political mandates under the European Green Deal umbrella, notably the Circular Economy and Farm to Fork Strategies. Mandatory criteria were put forward on one hand under the Circular Economy Strategy, which is very GPP oriented – it proposed the extension of how GPP is defined and aimed to strengthen monitoring of GPP. Under this 'transversal' non-sector specific mandate, mandatory criteria would be limited to the green/environmental dimension. By contrast, the F2F Strategy clearly envisaged much broader 'sustainable' mandatory criteria. Setting minimum mandatory public procurement requirements can be considered one of the actions 'dedicated to creating an enabling framework'[48] for sustainable food systems. This is matched by the idea that the umbrella Sustainable Food System Framework (FSFS) law could incorporate sector-specific rules.

Minimum mandatory public procurement requirements for food are one of the few knowns of the otherwise relatively vague outlines of the future FSFS proposal. Still, the Commission has to date not given away any significant indication about what this initiative could look like. The F2F Communication 'is ambitious but also vague' and to date, the only official document other than the F2F Communication referring to this initiative is the inception impact assessment report for the FSFS, which does not provide much detail, apart from confirming that the minimum public procurement criteria will be legislated in the framework of the FSFS instrument.[49]

[48] H Schebesta, N Bernaz, and C Macchi, 'The European Union Farm to Fork Strategy: Sustainability and Responsible Business in the Food Supply Chain' (2020) 15 *European Food and Feed Law Review* 420, 423.

[49] ibid 426.

There is, however, a forthcoming JRC report that should provide clarity on this initiative, but there is no public information about the status or content of the report yet. Therefore, for now, the uncertainties outweigh what we know about this initiative.

Two main modalities for mandatory sustainable public procurement are discussed, namely mandatory criteria and targets. In this sense, either certain requirements would be set at the EU level when purchasing (specific) food products or in catering services, perhaps on the basis of an evolution of the GPP criteria for food, or the proposal could establish minimum mandatory targets that must be met.

A. Sector-Specific Mandatory Public Procurement Requirements

The idea of imposing mandatory public procurement criteria is already a reality in other sectors. For instance, the Energy Star Regulation requires contracting authorities to buy energy-efficient IT office equipment;[50] the Clean Vehicles Directive bans the purchase of vehicles that are not considered 'clean' as defined in the Directive, and sets national targets[51] for their public procurement; the Energy Performance of Buildings Directive establishes that all new buildings owned and occupied by public authorities comply with a 'nearly zero-energy' standard. Also, the Energy Efficiency Directive includes a 'soft' obligation to purchase energy-efficient buildings and equipment of the highest energy labelling class available.[52] Similar obligations could be stipulated in a sector-specific food instrument, and then notably the FSFS.

In light of the current impossibility of defining sustainable foods, the question is what requirements the minimum criteria would prescribe in terms of content.

In formulating minimum mandatory sustainability requirements, the work on the GPP criteria for food will prove most illuminating. The criteria have undergone several rounds of reformulation, presumably greening slightly with each iteration. It would be a low-hanging fruit to adapt their scope, leading to an evolution from GPP towards SPP criteria.

On the other hand, while pragmatically convincing and practicable, the GPP criteria approach for food is also crude. Only the organic scheme is close to a public 'sustainability' food scheme, and it is lacking the social dimension and has some weaknesses in the environmental dimension relating to packaging, CO_2 emissions, and energy input. Since there are only very few public schemes (such as organic), the GPP for a large part is forced to rely on private standards for the

[50] See Art 6 of the Energy Star Regulation.
[51] See Art 5 of the Directive amending Clean Vehicles Directive.
[52] See Art 5 of Energy Efficiency Directive.

metrification of sustainability performances. The same would happen for future SPP criteria. In order for this system to work, private standard governance would need to be subject to greater regulatory scrutiny and require more ambitious, complete and holistic sustainability ambitions in order to avoid greenwashing. A key initiative in this regard is the proposal to adopt a Sustainability Labelling Framework, which would govern the provision of information on the sustainable performance of the foods. At the time of writing this chapter, nothing is yet known about the proposed content of this initiative, other than that the new framework should ensure 'consistency with other relevant EU labels (eg, organic) and taking into account other relevant ongoing Union initiatives'.[53]

B. Mandatory Targets

With that in mind, as an alternative to mandatory criteria, the European Commission could enshrine mandatory minimum targets for public procurement in EU law, directed at the Member States, but leaving the national legislator (or even regional contracting authorities) the power to decide how to best meet such targets.

This could be done by adopting the spirit of the Clean Vehicles Directive, which requires Member States to ensure that at least a certain amount of the vehicles they procure are 'clean' by setting national targets (expressed as minimum percentages of clean vehicles in the total number of road transport vehicles covered by the aggregate of all contracts across that Member State[54]), thus providing flexibility for each Member State to decide on how to meet the target.[55]

A target-based strategy would in fact also align with what is already happening at the Member State level. Since 2003, the European Commission in its Communication on Integrated Product Policy (IPP) encourages Member States to draw up National Action Plans (NAPs) for greening their public procurement. Currently, some countries recommend or mandate the use of GPP criteria for food and catering services, or a nationally adapted version thereof.[56]

If the EU is serious about meeting its organic production goals, a baseline core legal minimum requirement should involve the commitment to a certain percentage of organic food in public procurement procedures. This could have a meaningful effect also on the production of organic food. Since organic

[53] European Commission, 'Inception Impact Assessment – Sustainable Food System Framework Initiative' at www.eur-lex.europa.eu/legal-content/EN/TXT/HTML/?uri=PI_COM:Ares(2021)5902055.

[54] See Art 5(1) of the Directive amending Clean Vehicles Directive (n 51).

[55] A Semple, 'Charge of the Light Brigade? The Clean Vehicles Directive and the Batteries Regulation', ch 7 in this volume.

[56] European Commission, 'National GPP Action Plans' at www.ec.europa.eu/environment/gpp/pdf/GPP%20NAPs_April%202022.pdf.

production only certifies some characteristics, such as limited pesticide use, other criteria are needed in order to cover additional dimensions. For these, a combination would be the formulation of EU-based SPP criteria, which Member States authorities can choose from in order to meet EU-defined targets of sustainable food procurement.

V. Conclusion

In this chapter we identified two main issues about mandatory minimum public procurement criteria for food, namely: (1) how to define what sustainable food is and measure it; and (2) which legal modalities can operationalise mandatory public procurement criteria.

One of the obvious bottlenecks in food sustainability is the contentious question of what sustainable food really is. The competing dimensions of sustainability make it very complex for individual contracting authorities to draft specifications that will actually meet policy objectives relating to sustainability. Furthermore, it is impossible to define 'sustainable food', only different sustainability dimensions along which foods perform. The first goal is, therefore, to make the sustainability performance of foods measurable (the metrification of sustainability performance). The definition of the sustainability dimension is far from complete in the GPP criteria for food, and when evolving towards wider SPP criteria, the question of the other dimensions arises: how should public procurement determine what is sustainable in terms of nutrition and social considerations? How can the three dimensions be computed? And how can the trade-off between different dimensions, for instance, social and environmental, be incorporated? These issues are far from being settled. We are therefore likely facing a protracted operationalisation process whereby the metrification of the sustainability performance of different foods – and thereby our understanding of how to define 'sustainable food' – will grow increasingly accurate.

In the meantime, public and private label governance (if improved) can serve as an (initial) credence mechanism for these dimensions, before more sophisticated sustainability metrics, and possibly a public EU sustainability food label, have been developed. We conclude that under better regulatory preconditions public and private food standards could serve as a meaningful shorthand in public procurement procedures. The fact that standards are multidimensional, one-dimensional or mono-issue-based may provide room for adapting sustainable procurement to local conditions.

Virtually infinite options exist when it comes to drafting public procurement criteria with sustainability criteria: should all purchases require certain organic products? Fair trade coffee? Ban all vegetable fats not considered to be sourced sustainably? Limit the supply of animal protein in favour of more plant-based menus? Individual contracting authorities struggle when deciding what criteria to prioritise, and within this context, mandatory minimum public procurement requirements would partly solve the problem of inclusion, because they would set a minimum threshold that all public procurement documents must comply with.

However, there are negative sides to such a 'sustainability standardisation'. The type of tender affects the number and variety of criteria that it is advisable to include in the same procedure, insofar as these criteria can often have repercussions both on the cost of the provision and on the real possibilities of the bidders in a specific community to comply with all specifications. As expressed in the 2019 EU GPP criteria, the decision to require certain products or practices 'must take into account the market situation (e.g. availability of products fulfilling the criteria, required number of likely suppliers, etc)'.[57] The background report accompanying the (original) 2008 GPP criteria also acknowledged that the 'varying market conditions in different EU countries [made it] not possible to recommend a specific minimum percentage for different organic food types'.[58] In order to make a serious commitment to sustainability, and in order to trigger a change in the market structure, the future minimum criteria for public procurement need to be more courageous than that.

In light of these considerations, mandatory sustainable food public procurement is likely to be undertaken by a 'phasing in' of obligations, that is, obligations becoming gradually restraining over time. In the first instance, it still remains difficult to determine what sustainable foods are, which in our view makes it more likely that mandatory procurement will be implemented by setting targets rather than mandating specific contract clauses. This leaves some discretionary policy space for the prioritisation of policy and the importance of food sustainability dimensions to be done at the local level.

[57] EU GPP criteria on food SWD(2019) 366 (n 1) 15.
[58] ICLEI – Local Governments for Sustainability & Ecoinstitut Barcelona (n 30).

9

Textiles and Clothing: Mandatory Social Requirements as the Way Forward?

MAŁGORZATA KOSZEWSKA AND
JEANNE SVENSKY LIGTE*

I. Introduction

It is estimated that in 2017 more than €1.9 trillion was spent by public authorities annually at the EU level, which amounted to 14 per cent of the EU total GDP.[1] The textile and clothing (TC) industries contribute a share of up to 6 per cent of the total manufacturing industry in the EU, thereby having a significant impact on EU GDP as well. It is estimated that €8.6 billion was spent on textiles and workwear by the public sector and around 93,000 tonnes of workwear were purchased across Europe in 2015.[2] The main TC product categories for public procurement are clothing and accessories (occupational, corporate, workwear and accessories, and protective clothing), interior textiles (curtains, drapes, valances and textile blinds, linens, carpets), followed by medical textiles (dressings; clip, suture, ligature supplies).[3] The main contracting authorities of TC are represented by the

* This project has received funding from the European Union's Horizon 2020 research and innovation programme under the Marie Skłodowska-Curie grant agreement No 956696.

[1] European Semester Thematic Factsheet Public Procurement at www.policycommons.net/artifacts/2035650/european-semester-thematic-factsheet/2788093/. The percentage is not including the spending on utilities. With utility procurement, the estimated percentage is 19% or equal to €2.3 trillion.

[2] European Textiles & Workwear Market, 'The Role of Public Procurement in Making Textiles Circular (ECAP)' at www.ecap.eu.com/wp-content/uploads/2016/09/ECAP-Workwear-Report-Pt-1-def-final.pdf.

[3] M Koszewska, 'The Role of Ecolabels in Creation of Life-Cycle Criteria: The Case of Textile and Clothing Products' in M Andhov, R Caranta and A Wiesbrock (eds), *Cost and EU Public Procurement Law: Life-Cycle Costing for Sustainability* (London, Routledge, 2019).

health sector followed by general public services, defence, public order and safety, and education.[4]

TC is considered to be one of the major product groups in global trade according to the World Trade Organization Report.[5] At the same time, the TC industries are confronted with sustainability issues and the generation of many environmental as well as social problems. The TC industries are considered among the most complex supply chains, involving a series of transformation activities, for example, from cotton farming, cotton being the most commonly used natural fibre from virgin material, to clothes as the finished product. Their production models significantly link upstream and downstream markets and involve a multiplicity of actors and a myriad of labourers who work almost invisibly in long production chains.[6]

The different production stages in the TC industries take place in different countries connected with one another into a complex chain, including not only producers but also distributors, retailers, and end customers. This trans-continental supply chain, with several tiers of subcontracting, makes the control and monitoring of the working conditions ever so challenging. To this day, when global competition forces companies to lower the sales price of their product, procurement as a supply chain function continuously searches for alternatives to remedy the situation, mostly through global sourcing for cost reduction of raw materials, facilities, and labour, leaving the sources to travel along the supply chains until their end when the finished products reach end-customers.[7] Consequently, a large part of the production had been transferred to emerging and developing countries that provide low labour costs and are geographically closer to the producers of raw materials, mostly in China and the region of South and Southeast Asia. With a value of up to US$125 billion, the EU is the world's second-largest importer of TC after the US, with the sources coming mainly from China, Bangladesh, Turkey, India, Cambodia, and Vietnam.[8]

The intense pressure from the market for mass and fast production at a low cost causes garment labourers to work extra hours, mostly without overtime wages and other benefits such as paid holidays or health insurance. That led

[4] ibid.

[5] SG Annapoorani, 'Social Sustainability in Textile Industry' in SS Muthu (ed), *Sustainability in the Textile Industry* (Singapore, Springer, 2017).

[6] P Guarnieri and F Trojan, 'Decision Making on Supplier Selection Based on Social, Ethical, and Environmental Criteria: A Study in the Textile Industry' (2019) 141 *Resource, Conservation, and Recycling* 347, 348.

[7] A Rushton, P Croucher and P Baker, *The Handbook of Logistics and Distribution Management*, 7th edn (London, Kogan Page Publishers, 2022).

[8] Koszewska (n 3); N Sajn, 'Environmental Impact of the Textile and Clothing Industry: What Consumers Need to Know' [2019] *European Parliamentary Research Service* 2.

to a situation in which the labourers experience violence, harassment, intimidation, and abusive conditions at the workplace.[9] It is estimated that there are over 750 million people employed in TC production around the world, with 350 million people working specifically in the cotton sector.,[10] What is more, with around 75 per cent of the total labourers in these industries being women, it is also known as a female-dominated field. Public awareness of social issues in TC production has been growing. Over the years, one of the most tragically salient events was the collapse of Rana Plaza in 2013, which killed at least 1,132 garment labourers in Dhaka, Bangladesh.[11]

Two years later, the United Nations introduced the 17 Sustainable Development Goals that are intended to be achieved by 2030. Given that TC are industries where the issues of poverty, gender-based violence and inequality, forced and bonded labour, as well as child slavery, are raised very often, they have great potential for significant contributions to the success of the SDGs, particularly through Goal 1 (No Poverty), Goal 5 (Gender Equality), and in relation to the economic aspect of Goal 8 (Decent Work and Economic Growth).[12]

Despite the growing interest in social problems in the TC industries, they remain much less recognised and addressed compared to environmental ones. One of the reasons for this is the fact that they are more difficult to measure. Most of the guidelines as well as certification schemes and labels refer mostly to environmental aspects.[13] Also, the tools aimed at helping to assess and compare different products objectively, for example, Life Cycle Assessment (LCA), refer to environmental issues, while the social life cycle assessment (S-LCA) is much less developed.

This chapter has the following aims: first, to assess the current status of social regulations for the TC industries with reference to minimum mandatory public procurement requirements, targets, as well as product-specific legislation; second,

[9] NA Gnanaselvam and B Joseph, 'Depression and Behavioural Problems Among Adolescent Girls and Young Women Employees of the Textile Industry in India' (2018) 66 *Workplace Health & Safety* 24, 30.

[10] United Nations Economic Commission for Europe (UNECE), 'UN Alliance Aims to Put Fashion on Path to Sustainability' at www.unece.org/forestry/press/un-alliance-aims-put-fashion-path-sustainability.

[11] ILO, 'The Rana Plaza Accident and Its Aftermath' at www.ilo.org/global/topics/geip/WCMS_614394/lang--en/index.htm.

[12] Textile Exchange, 'Threading the Needle: Weaving the Sustainable Development Goals into the Textile, Retail, and Apparel Industry' at www.textileexchange.org/wp-content/uploads/2022/03/Textile-Exchange-kpmg-threading-needle-report.pdf.

[13] In the case of public procurement, the crucial document is the Green Public Procurement Textiles Technical Background Report at www.ec.europa.eu/environment/gpp/pdf/tbr/textiles_tbr.pdf; the environmental challenges in the context of TC public have been discussed in detail in Koszewska (n 3).

to investigate if and how progress towards mandatory social requirements is being made in these industries. Some examples implemented in the EU countries will also be provided for reference as to how social aspects have so far been considered in terms of mandatory criteria in public procurement procedures. Finally, some recommendations for social considerations to be included as mandatory criteria for the supplier selection process in public procurement for TC products are presented.

II. Social Challenges in Public Procurement of Textiles and Clothing Products

A. Social Challenges in Textile and Clothing Industries

The social aspects of the TC supply chain can be seen from the different perspectives of the actors involved and can be specified for the make phase, also known as the production phase (farming/chemical fibre production and manufacturing), and in the use phase (see Figure 1 below). As for the make phase, the social challenges experienced by the garment labourers include issues that are mainly addressed in the UN 2030 SDGs such as a low living wage, gender inequality, high poverty rate, weak social protection system, and other issues that are commonly found in the labour market of the developing countries. In the use phase on the other hand, the social aspects are addressed through the lens of the safety of the users wearing the products, for example, uniforms and protective clothing, including the quality of the product as well as how effective they are in protecting the users from accidents and hazardous materials such as chemicals and gases.

More details about social problems and impacts in all stages of the TC supply chain are presented in Figure 1.

Social challenges in the TC industries may also be organised into the following main categories:[14]

- human/worker rights (main issues: low wages, restricted worker rights, excessive working hours, and child labour) – relevant mostly to the make phase;
- healthy and safe working conditions: (labourers' exposure to health and safety hazards due to toxic chemicals used in fibre production/cultivation as well as

[14] S Moschitz, F Crippa, P Defranceschi and AO Vidal, *RESPIRO Guide on Socially Responsible Procurement of Textiles and Clothing* (Belgium, EUROCITIES, 2007).

in further production processes; ensuring a high level of labourers' protection by the textile product itself in the use phase);

- quality of employment and equal opportunity;
- adverse impact on the living conditions and quality of life of a large number of chemical and toxic substances used in the production, as well as issues related to the end-of-life.

Figure 1 Social problems and impacts on the TC supply chain

Life-cycle Aspect	Activity	Problem	Social Impact
Production	Farming Cotton planting Harvesting	Under-age workers Migrant-labour discrimination Money lending with high interest High suicide rate due to debt Illnesses from chemicals used in plantation	Child labour Modern slavery Human trafficking Debt bondage Health diseases
	Manufacturing Ginning Spinning Knitting Weaving Dyeing Trimming Printing Finishing	Low living wage Unpaid overtime work No benefit, such as insurance, sick leave, or holiday No restroom break Verbal and sexual abuses Gender wage gaps Gender-based discrimination for promotion at the supervisory level No opportunity for training and promotion Unsafe and unhealthy working environment No formal contract High urbanisation rate	High poverty Forced labour Exploitation Gender inequality Harrassment Low education level Low transparency of human rights
Transport	Distribution of goods at all stages	Improper treatment from suppliers Emissions from fossil fuels	Low quality of life due to pollution and climate change
Use	Wearing protective clothing	Low quality of the material Low durability Improper design Gender-based discrimination due to design and size Uncertified products (without) Ecolabels or CE marking)	Low safety level Discomfort during use High vulnerability to injuries
End-of-life	Disposal	TC waste is sent to developing countries to reuse, recycled, or incinerated Purchasing new products to spend the allocated annual budget, even though the ones already purchased are still in good condition	Land degradation and unhealthy living conditions due to waste pollution

B. Social Public Procurement Criteria for Textiles and Clothing

Social aspects of public procurement are increasingly attracting public attention. However, still little is known about the actual application of social requirements to public procurement. Currently, no research is conducted that would consider different sectors and different countries and that would enable an assessment of the level of implementation of Socially Responsible Public Procurement (SRPP). There were some studies done, however, for specific countries like Nigeria[15] or Portugal,[16] as well as with reference to a selected group of EU countries.[17] Generally, they showed that the use of social criteria in public procurement is very limited.[18] The findings from Nigeria suggest that public procurement was used mostly to promote a range of government policies and programmes like occupational pension, worker compensation, industrial training and corporate tax compliance. Thus, the aim was to look out for the government self-interest rather than for social good. In the case of Portugal, it can be concluded that social criteria have not so far achieved the same success as environmental ones. Similar conclusions come from the broader European study mentioned above. As regards the sectoral approach, an analysis was done specifically for the construction industry.[19] However, none of the reviewed studies focused on nor referred to the TC industries. Therefore, while assessing the application of social criteria to public procurement for TC products, one can only make some assumptions and hypotheses based on the results of the research findings for other sectors and, generally, to public procurement practices, as well as on the research that focused on TC but only considered the environmental aspects.[20]

[15] TO Akenroye, 'An Appraisal of the Use of Social Criteria in Public Procurement in Nigeria' (2013) 13 *Journal of Public Procurement* 364, 365.

[16] M da Silva Gomes, 'Sustainable Public Procurement in Portugal-State of the Art and Future Prospects' (2013) 8 *European Procurement and Public Private Partnership Law Review* 60, 60.

[17] European Commission, 'Study on Strategic Use of Public Procurement in Promoting Green, Social and Innovation Policies' at op.europa.eu/en/publication-detail/-/publication/6a5a4873-b542-11e7-837e-01aa75ed71a1/language-en.

[18] See also W Janssen, 'Shifting towards Mandatory Sustainability Requirements in EU Public Procurement Law: Context, Relevance and a Typology', ch 1 in this volume, section IV.

[19] L Montalbán-Domingo, T García-Segura, MA Sanz and E Pellicer, 'Social Sustainability Criteria in Public-Work Procurement: An International Perspective' (2018) 198 *Journal of Cleaner Production* 1355, 1355; JL Fuentes-Bargues, MJ Bastante-Ceca, PS Ferrer-Gisbert and MC González-Cruz, 'Analysis of the Situation of Social Public Procurement of Works at the Valencian Region (Spain)' (2020) 13 *Sustainability* 175.

[20] A Renda, J Pelkmans, C Egenhofer, L Schrefler, G Luchetta, C Selçuki, J Ballesteros and AC Zirnhelt, *The Uptake of Green Public Procurement in the EU27* (Brussels, European Union, 2012). PwC Sustainability, *Collection of Statistical Information on Green Public Procurement in the EU: Report on Data Collection Results* (Pricewaterhouse Coopers, Significant and Ecofys, (2009) at www.ec.europa.eu/environment/gpp/pdf/statistical_information.pdf; see Koszewska (n 3).

In this context, the results of the available research show that the implementation of 'social' criteria in public procurement practices has still a long way to go.[21] The general conclusion is that social aspects are far behind the environmental ones, as much more progress has been made on the latter through the implementation of the GPP policy and guidelines.[22] Other research has shown that there are cross-country differences in the way social aspects of procurement are considered, which indicates that in-depth cross-country analyses are needed.[23]

On the other hand, the studies on the environmental aspects of TC public procurement revealed that compared to other product groups, TC still has a long way to go when it comes to implementing environmental criteria in the public procurement process.[24] Nonetheless, it is worth stressing that the environmental criteria are still more recognised, better defined, and much easier to measure, compared to the social ones. Additionally, contracting authorities have concrete guidelines to help them implement those criteria in the public procurement process.[25]

Therefore, one can assume that the extent to which the social considerations are implemented in public procurement for TC is even more limited than is the case for the environmental requirements. However, to verify this conclusion, more in-depth empirical analyses are required that would identify and explore differences that hold between sectors, countries, and regions. Finally, we should not think that all is doom and gloom in this area and stress that positive signs can also be observed. The European Commission has recently taken some initiatives to facilitate the uptake of social considerations in public procurement and to promote their use in the EU.[26] Unfortunately, at the EU level, there is still a lack of guidance and documents that would refer to specific product groups or industries. At the same time, such initiatives can be observed at the Member State level as well as local levels. They will be discussed further in this chapter.[27]

[21] Akenroye (n 15) 364–97; da Silva Gomes (n 16) 60; Montalbán-Domingo et al (n 19) 1355; Fuentes-Bargues et al (n 19) 18.

[22] da Silva Gomes (n 16).

[23] Montalbán-Domingo et al (n 19); Study on 'Strategic Use of Public Procurement in Promoting Green, Social and Innovation Policies (n 17).

[24] Koszewska (n 3).

[25] The European Commission offers sets of GPP criteria for different product groups, including textiles. The GPP aims to facilitate the inclusion of environmental criteria into public tenders. The GPP criteria for textile products and services were established in 2012 and were updated in 2017. The last version of the EU GPP Criteria for Textile Products and Services Guidance Document form 2020 is available online at www.ec.europa.eu/environment/gpp/pdf/200406_JRC120265_eu_green_public_procurement_criteria_for_textile_products_and_services_guidance_document.pdf.

[26] A series of workshops on the use of social clauses were organised and 'buying social' guide was updated in 2021 at www.ec.europa.eu/info/policies/public-procurement/tools-public-buyers/social-procurement_en#european-accessibility-act.

[27] Below, section III.A. At the beginning of 2021, the Federal Government in Germany published the 'Guide for Sustainable Textile Procurement'. The document for the first time clearly defines not only environmental but also social criteria for textile public procurement along the entire supply chain, available at www.bmz.de/de/aktuelles/55960-55960.

III. Requirements for Textiles and Clothing in the Context of Sustainability and Public Procurement

A. Mandatory Requirements for Textiles and Clothing

The existing mandatory requirements that refer directly to TC products are not public procurement-specific provisions in the sense that they apply independently from whether the procurer is a private company or a contracting authority. One of the fundamental mandatory regulations referring to TC is Textile Regulation on fibre names and related labelling and marking of the fibre composition of textile products. It was adopted to ensure that citizens, businesses, and public authorities can identify their rights and obligations, and to protect consumer interests as well as to ensure the proper functioning of the EU internal market. The regulation introduces a mandatory requirement to indicate the product fibre composition at all stages of the industrial processing and commercial distribution of that product. All products containing at least 80 per cent of the weight of textile fibres, including raw, semi-worked, worked, semi-manufactured, semi-made, and made-up products are covered by the Regulation and must be labelled or marked whenever they are available on the market.[28]

The problem is, however, that this regulation does not cover important aspects like size, country of origin, or wash/care labelling. This can be viewed as a shortcoming in the context of sustainability and circularity, where product durability, life span extension, energy and water conservation during use, as well as maintenance, take-back, and recycling systems, are of particular importance. Lack of mandatory requirements in this area results in a lack of homogeneity in labelling requirements for clothing products across the Member States. For example, in the case of care labels, although there are no required harmonised mandatory care instructions at the EU level, some Member States require them to comply with the GINETEX system as specified in ISO 3758.[29] Unification of the mandatory requirements for a care labelling system at the EU level could be very beneficial for circular business models, where the use phase of clothing is crucial.

More specifically, those requirements could also be developed further, beyond ISO 3758, to include recommendations on washing temperature, alternative

[28] Textiles and Clothing Legislation at www.ec.europa.eu/growth/sectors/fashion/textiles-and-clothing-industries/legislation_en#textile_legislation_background.

[29] GINETEX, the International Association for Textile Care Labelling, has devised an internationally applicable care labelling system for textiles based on symbols. More information is available online at www.ginetex.net/; see also M Koszewska, 'Clothing Labels: Why are They Important for Sustainable Consumer Behaviour?' (2021) 16 *Journal of Consumer Protection and Food Safety* 1, 2.

detergents, that is, low-temperature detergents, precautions against the use of fabric conditioners, reduced washing frequency, and precautions against tumble-drying. H&M and GINETEX have already introduced a CleverCare symbol which is included on product labels and provides a link that users can follow to find tips on environmentally advantageous care and maintenance.[30]

Another important piece of legislation with mandatory requirements that applies directly to TC products and is also addressed to the public sector is the Regulation on Personal Protective Equipment. Personal Protective Equipment (PPE) is designed to protect workers or employees from injuries or illness from contact with hazardous materials such as chemical, radiological, physical, electrical, or mechanical, at the workplace.[31] TC for several public services, such as firefighter and military uniforms, or medical protective gowns, use PPE extensively, with an increased demand observed since the COVID outbreak.

The regulation defines legal obligations to ensure that PPE on the EU internal market provides the highest level of protection against risks/hazards for the user. The CE marking attached to PPE attests to this protection.[32] The producer has an obligation to put the CE marking on the PPE product as a visible indication of conformity with the fundamental requirements. The CE marking signifies that products sold in the EEA meet high safety, health, and environmental protection requirements.

Unfortunately, there is no guarantee that the products with the CE marking are safe since counterfeiting and misuse are widespread.[33] The monitoring system that had been in operation until recently, turned out to be not effective enough, due to limited resources and capacity. For this reason, a new EU Regulation (Regulation 2019/1020) has been introduced to strengthen the monitoring of the European internal market.[34]

It is also worth stressing that the CE marking is obligatory only for those products that fall under one of the EU directives/regulations, such as the PPE Regulation, that require this marking. Otherwise, affixing markings to a product is forbidden.[35]

[30] ibid.

[31] J Se, 'Standards for Protective Textiles' in RA Scott (ed), *Textiles for Protection*, Woodhead Publishing in Textiles 1 (Cambridge, Woodhead Publishing Limited, 2005).

[32] The term CE is an abbreviation of the French '*Conformité Européene*' which means 'European Conformity' and was initially introduced as 'EC Mark' based on the EU Directive 93/68/EEC in 199310. The symbol indicates that the products have been assessed and meet the requirement of the EU product directive and are able to meet the safety standards.

[33] EU Consumers at www.ec.europa.eu/growth/single-market/ce-marking/eu-consumers_en.

[34] Products that fall under the so-called harmonisation rules (including PPE) are better monitored since 16 July at www./eur-lex.europa.eu/legal-content/EN/TXT/?uri=CELLAR:903d90ee-9712-11e9-9369-01aa75ed71a1.

[35] CE Marking at www.europa.eu/youreurope/business/product-requirements/labels-markings/ce-marking/index_en.htm.

In the context of a broader focus on sustainability, it is also worth mentioning the Registration, Evaluation, Authorisation, and Restriction of Chemicals (REACH) Regulation. It addresses the restricted chemicals (including certain azo dyes, flame retardants, waterproofing and stain-repellent chemicals, and nickel) in products sold on the EU internal market. The Regulation aims to enhance the level of protection in the area of human health and the environment. In that sense, it refers both to social and environmental aspects. It applies to all products that contain chemical substances, so in fact, to almost all TC product groups purchased by public authorities.[36]

The regulations discussed in this section refer to some extent to social aspects, for example, human health, and safety requirements, as well as environmental ones, for example, the elimination of prohibited chemicals and proper information on fibre composition (these are especially important in the context of effective recycling and circular economy). Many of the covered issues relate both to environmental and social aspects (REACH restrictions to chemicals or sustainable use of pesticides are aimed at the protection of human health as well as the environment). Some of them have a more general character, and refer to many different product groups, whereas some are textile specific.

Table 3 EU Legislation related to Textile and Clothing Products

Relevant Instruments	**Policy Area**	**Release Date**	**General**	**Textile specific**	**Social dimension**	**Environmental dimension**
Directive 2001/95/EC (Product Safety Directive)	General product safety	3 December 2021	+		+	
Directive 2009/128/EC (Pesticides Directive)	Framework for Community action to achieve the sustainable use of pesticides, relevant for cotton fibres used in textiles	21 October 2009		+	+	+

(continued)

[36] More about REACH is available online: www.ec.europa.eu/environment/chemicals/reach/reach_en.htm.

Table 3 ***(Continued)***

Relevant Instruments	**Policy Area**	**Release Date**	**General**	**Textile specific**	**Social dimension**	**Environmental dimension**
Regulation (EU) 1007/2011 (Textiles Regulation)	Textile Fibre Names and Related Labelling and Marking of the Fibre Composition of Textile	27 September 2011		+	+	+
Regulation (EU) 2016/425 (Regulation on Personal Protective Equipment)	Personal Protective Equipment (PPE)	9 March 2016		+	+	
Regulation (EC) 1907/2006 (REACH Regulation)	Registration, Evaluation, Authorisation and Restriction of Chemicals (REACH)	18 December 2006	+		+	+
Regulation (EU) 2018/848 (Organic Production Regulation)	Organic production and labelling of organic products, relevant for cotton fibres used in textiles	30 May 2018		+	+	+

Based on the above, we conclude that, at the moment, mandatory requirements related to TC products are addressed to the producers rather than contracting authorities. In fact, there are no mandatory public procurement requirements (minimum or targets) that would refer directly to this product group. As previously stated, there are only product-specific legislative instruments that regulate the product or the producer from an environmental and/or social perspective, rather than the conduct of national, regional, or local public authorities or their public procurement process. This could be one of the reasons why the level of implementation of environmental and social criteria for public procurement of TC products is rather low compared to other product groups.

However, there is a clear indication of the need for such regulations since trade unions and employer organisations operating in the catering, private security, and industrial cleaning services undertook it to produce sectoral guidelines on procuring the best value for contracts.[37] Such initiatives were also undertaken by local authorities for TC products. In 2014, the city of Ghent with the Association of Flemish Cities created *Toolbox for Socially Sustainable Workwear – A guide for public buyers* to support contracting authorities in procuring workwear produced in a more socially responsible way.[38] The challenge was to increase transparency throughout the textile supply chain.

As for the future, the recently released EU Strategy for Sustainable and Circular Textiles seems very promising.[39] One of its main objectives is that:

> all textile products placed on the EU market are durable, repairable and recyclable, to a great extent made of recycled fibres, free of hazardous substances, produced in respect of social rights and the environment.

Especially high hopes are put on its Annex.[40] The Annex specifies 24 key actions stating the date of their implementation. However, the vast majority of them still refer to environmental issues with significant stress on the circular economy and only one referring directly to social aspects, that is, enforcing the Proposal for a Corporate Sustainability Due Diligence Directive in the textile sector as of 2023.[41]

In the context of public procurement, of special importance seems to be also the key action requiring that mandatory requirements concerning GPP and Member State incentives be introduced by 2024.[42] It is, however, crucial that the mandatory requirements are not limited to green requirements alone. This issue was raised in the 'Joint position on the EU strategy for sustainable textiles' prepared by the Fair Wear, Solidaridad, Ethical Trading Initiative, and Fairtrade International.[43] These organisations point to such issues as giving equal weight to human and environmental rights in new and/or circular business models, better inclusion of social criteria in public procurement as part of the strategy, as well

[37] Buying Social Guide, 2nd edn, 16; Choosing Best Value in Contracting Food Services at www.contract-catering-guide.org/wp-content/uploads/2019/09/Catering-Services_Best-Value-Guide_EN_Web.pdf; Buying Quality Private Security Services at www.securebestvalue.org/wp-content/uploads/2014/11/Best-Value-Manual_Final.pdf; How to Derive MEAT Criteria – Introducing Quality Criteria into Public Procurement at www.efcanet.org/sites/default/files/2020-01/MEAT%20booklet_final.pdf.

[38] Toolbox Socially Responsible Workwear A Guide for Public Purchasers at www.stad.gent/sites/default/files/article/documents/ToolboxSocResWorkwear_1406.pd.

[39] EU Strategy for Sustainable and Circular Textiles COM(2022) 141.

[40] ibid Annex.

[41] See sections III.B and IV.

[42] Although the GPP is still a voluntary instrument at the moment, many of the EU Member States have been developing their own national criteria and are committed to even more ambitious targets. It is also worth mentioning that in the case of other product groups like IT office equipment, vehicles, or buildings, the specific mandatory GPP rules have been sporadically included in various legal acts.

[43] Joint Position on the EU Strategy for Sustainable Textiles at www.api.fairwear.org/wp-content/uploads/2021/08/Joint-position-paper-EU-Strategy-for-Sustainable-Textiles.pdf.

as the integration of socially responsible business conduct with special attention for new business models with a positive impact on the whole supply chain and sector dialogue.

B. Social Requirements for TC in the Context of Public Procurement

The issue of including social criteria in public procurement refers directly to SRPP. It aims to ensure that public procurement achieves social benefits and that the impact on society of the goods, services, and works purchased by public authorities is addressed in the procurement process.[44]

The Public Procurement Directives are binding for contracting authorities in all Member States and they are believed to have created a flexible legal framework to achieve social objectives like job creation, inclusion opportunities for different groups of people, fair treatment of workers regardless of gender, race, ethnicity, religion or disability, promoting human rights due diligence in global supply chains, facilitating the access of social businesses to procurement opportunities, and providing inclusive, efficient social services. The Public Procurement Directives brought about a lot of changes, including an extension of the set of provisions relating to the SRPP.[45] These changes have also been incorporated in the second edition of 'Buying Social: A Guide to Taking Account of Social Considerations in Public Procurement'. This Guide is a tool that provides practical examples and suggestions for public authorities to consider the social impact in the purchasing process.

More broadly speaking, one of the central issues discussed in the context of SRPP is labour rights, where the basic reference point is the Conventions of the International Labour Organisation (ILO). The conventions are of special importance for the TC sector, due to the labour-intensive character of TC products. Once adopted by the ILO and ratified by the signatory countries, they are binding in nature.[46]

Article 18(2) of Directive 2014/24/EU provides that

> Member States shall take appropriate measures to ensure that in the performance of public contracts economic operators comply with applicable obligations in the fields of environmental, social and labour law established by Union law, national law, collective agreements or by the international environmental, social and labour law provisions listed in Annex X.[47]

[44] REACH Regulation.

[45] A Semple, 'Socially Responsible Public Procurement (SRPP) under EU Law and International Agreements' (2017) 12 *European Procurement and Public Private Partnership Law Review* 293, 293.

[46] Moschitz (n 14).

[47] See M Andhov, 'Article 18(2) Public Procurement Principles' in R Caranta and A Sanchez-Graells (eds), *European Public Procurement: Commentary on Directive 2014/24/EU* (Cheltenham, Elgar Publishing, 2021) 204.

The applicable social, and labour laws, other than those at the international level, are not further specified. However, they do include the EU social laws, on the condition that they are relevant to the subject matter.[48] These EU legislative instruments mostly discuss the social aspects that are generally similar to what has been stated in the ILO Conventions, although some instruments also regulate work ethics. For example, the Posted Workers Directive stresses equal opportunity for transnational hiring and posting locations for the employees, and the Asbestos Directive which also relates to safety and environmental aspects of human protection from excessive exposure to asbestos.

A very apt summary of the role of Directive 2014/24/EU in improving the use of social criteria in public contracts was made by Semple who noted that

> Article 18(2) thus appears to underwrite the ability of contracting authorities to insist on the application of equality legislation, for example, both by rejecting tenders which do not comply with it and by taking action against subcontractors who do not comply.

Although the new Public Procurement Directives bring some clear objectives regarding social considerations, they still leave a lot of aspects unsaid and almost all the social provisions remain optional for contracting authorities.[49] Accordingly, we should look at them as the first and a small step towards increasing the implementation of social criteria in public procurement procedures. However, there is still a need for more clear-cut legislative measures that would also consider sector-specific challenges. One of the latest documents with very high expectations for positive changes in the obligatory inclusion of social aspects in business operations throughout global value chains is a Proposal for a Corporate Sustainability Due Diligence Directive. The Proposal aims to enforce a business obligation to avoid negative human rights impacts, such as child labour and labour exploitation as well as adverse impacts on the environment. The rules on Corporate Sustainability Due Diligence are enforced through administrative supervision as well as civil liability.[50]

The assessment of the proposal is not straightforward. On the one hand, we have generally positive voices stressing that it is an important step forward in the legal regulation of corporate human rights and environmental due diligence, as it contains several ambitious aspects like provisions on enforcement and civil liability, the establishment of binding legal due diligence duties for companies, provisions regarding prevention, monitoring, enforcement, remediation, and

[48] The list of EU legislations that related to social aspects in working conditions are including Transfer of Undertakings Directive; Working Time Directive; Posted Workers Directive; Equal Treatment Directive; Race Directive; Equality Framework Directive; Directive 89/391/EEC about Health and Safety of Workers; Asbestos Directive.

[49] A Semple, *Practical Guide to Public Procurement* (Oxford, Oxford University Press, 2015).

[50] The Member State will be obliged to designate an authority to supervise and impose effective, proportionate, and dissuasive sanctions, including fines and compliance orders and will have to ensure that victims get compensation for damages resulting from the business activities.

as it covers the full value chain.[51] Therefore, in this sense, the proposal is seen as the most ambitious of its kind.[52] On the other hand, the shortcomings of the draft are stressed as well. Those most frequently mentioned are limitations towards the number of companies covered in the scope as well as provisions limiting the extent of the due diligence obligation.[53] According to some, the draft fails the expectations of the UN Guiding Principles (UNGPs) and existing EU legal obligations as well as policy commitments, which ultimately may result in a decade-long reduction in established social responsibilities for companies.[54] Still, the Proposal is especially important for the TC industries as they were regarded in the draft as one of the high-impact industries, and enforcing the Corporate Sustainability Due Diligence Directive in the textile sector as of 2023 is one of the key actions presented in the Annex of the EU Strategy for Sustainable and Circular Textile.[55]

All in all, at present we have neither mandatory requirements that would allow for more effective enforcement of the inclusion of social criteria for TC products in public procurement on the EU level, nor additional supportive instruments that would guide public buyers in this process. Those exist only as good practices appearing at the local level or they refer mostly to environmental criteria.[56] A good example of a document referring to the EU GPP criteria for TC products is the Guidance Document: EU GPP Criteria for Textile Products and Services.[57] The GPP award criteria recommended in that document focus on the environmental impact of production such as a minimum percentage of organic fibre, energy conservation, as well as treatment during the use and end-of-life cycle. The social requirements play a marginal role and only appear as a social consequence of an environmental problem. For example, social impacts of the use of resources, water, land, chemicals, GHG emissions and pollutants. There is a clear need for similar documents/guidelines that would concentrate directly

[51] CM O'Brien and O Martin-Ortega, 'Sustainable Corporate Governance: Submission to Consultation on European Commission's Proposal for a Directive on Corporate Sustainability Due Diligence COM (2022)71 Final', (2022).

[52] C Patz, 'The EU's Draft Corporate Sustainability Due Diligence Directive: A First Assessment' (2022) 7 *Business and Human Rights Journal* 291, 291.

[53] The Danish Institute for Human Rights, 'Legislating for Impact Analysis of the Proposed EU Corporate Sustainability Due Diligence Directive' at www.humanrights.dk/publications/legislating-impact-analysis-proposed-eu-corporate-sustainability-due-diligence. See also R Caranta, 'Towards Socially Responsible Public Procurement' (2022) 23 *ERA Forum* 149.

[54] O'Brien and Martin-Ortega (n 51); Patz (n 52).

[55] See EU Strategy for Sustainable and Circular Textiles (n 39).

[56] Buying Quality Private Security Services (n 37).

[57] There are three basic documents that refer to GPP for TC, see EU GPP criteria for textiles SWD(2017) 231; European Commission, 'JRC Science for Policy Report Revision of the EU Green Public Procurement (GPP) Criteria for Textile Products and Services Technical report with final criteria', JRC107241; European Commission, 'JRC Technical Report EU Green Public Procurement (GPP) Criteria for Textile Products and Services Guidance Document', JRC120265.

on the social requirements and that would at the same time consider the specific challenges faced by the TC industries.

In summary, the Proposal for a Corporate Sustainability Due Diligence Directive is promising but requires further dialogue to consider how the shortcomings identified can be overcome.

C. Best Practices in Implementing Social Criteria for Public Procurement of Textiles

In 2020, the EC released 71 good practice cases through more than nine diverse products and services from 22 Member States and five non-EU countries showing good implementations of SRPP aimed to achieve positive outcomes by integrating social aspects in public contracts.[58]

A good example can be taken from the Ministry of Labour and Social Affairs (MoLSA) in Czechia. MoLSA drew from the core of the ILO Conventions and established a requirement for bidders to ensure that the textile products they purchased were made by workers whose rights are protected. In addition, the bidders had to prove that they were a member of the Fair Wear Foundation (FWF) and were committed to implementing the eight labour standards in their supply chain. It is a familiar concept since the standards were derived from the ILO Convention and the UN's Declaration on Human Rights.[59]

In another example, the City of Bonn in Germany collaborated with the African Women's Development and Communication Network (FEMNET) to develop the Social Criteria Questionnaire, an assessment tool to verify the tenders for the uniforms of green space maintenance employees. In this assessment, the social criteria were assigned a worth of 30 per cent of the total award criteria, while another 30 per cent were awarded for the quality and durability of the products.

When discussing good practice, it is worth mentioning that the EU Member States have introduced some measurable targets. For example, mandatory criteria are included in the tender contract with proportional weighting expressed as percent of the total score. Some examples are presented in Table 4.

[58] European Commission, 'Making Socially Responsible Public Procurement Work: 71 Good Practices' (2020).

[59] Those eight cores of the ILO Conventions are: Forced Labour Convention, 1930 (No. 29); Abolition of Forced Labour Convention, 1957 (No. 105); Freedom of Association and Protection of the Right to Organize Convention, 1948 (No. 87); Right to Organize and Collective Bargaining Convention, 1949 (No. 98); Equal Remuneration Convention, 1951 (No. 100); Discrimination (Employment and Occupation) Convention, 1958 (No. 111); Minimum Age Convention, 1973 (No. 138); and Worst Forms of Child Labour Convention, 1999 (No. 182).

Table 4 Examples of mandatory requirements/targets in the National Action Plans

Country	Specific criteria for textiles	Environmental criteria	Circular Criteria	Social Criteria	Mandatory rules
Croatia National Procurement Plan https://sudovi.hr/en/oszd/public-procurement/public-procurement	yes	yes	yes	–	Adopting GPP at least 50% in 2020 with high energy performance
Cyprus National Action Plan	yes*	yes	–	no	Adopt the national criteria of at least 50%
Denmark The Responsible Procurer https://csr-indkob.dk/products/tekstiler/	yes*	yes	yes**	yes	Adopt 50% of GPP
Estonia Estonian Action Plan for Green Public Procurement (but not in force) https://ringmajandus.envir.ee/en/green-public-procurement	no	yes	yes	no	Implementing 30% of all GPP by 2023

(continued)

Table 4 ***(Continued)***

Country	Specific criteria for textiles	Environmental criteria	Circular Criteria	Social Criteria	Mandatory rules
France National Action Plan on Sustainable Procurement 2022–2025*** https://www.ecologie.gouv.fr/sites/default/files/PNAD-PAGEAPAGE-SCREEN%283%29.pdf Responsible Public Procurement https://www.economie.gouv.fr/daj/achats-publics-responsables	yes	yes	yes	yes	Textile products purchased by central and local authorities must be from reuse and recycled materials (AGEC law).
Greece National Action Plan for the Promotion of Green Public Procurement (2021–2023) https://www.mindev.gov.gr/	yes*	yes	yes	no	Adopt at least one core criterion in the Annex of GPP
Lithuania Lithuanian National Progress Plan https://www.e-tar.lt/portal/lt/legalAct/17da9120942c11e5a6f4e928c954d72b/asr	yes	yes	no	no	Implementing GPP by 50% in 2025

(continued)

Table 4 ***(Continued)***

Country	Specific criteria for textiles	Environmental criteria	Circular Criteria	Social Criteria	Mandatory rules
Poland National Action Plan on Sustainable Public Procurement for 2022–2025*** https://www.uzp.gov.pl/baza-wiedzy/zrownowazone-zamowienia-publiczne	no	yes	yes	yes	Increasing the value of GPP up to 7% by 2025
Portugal The National Strategy for GPP (ENCPE 2020) https://www.apambiente.pt/index.php?ref=17&subref=154&sub2ref=242	yes*	yes	–	–	The tendering process has to include environmental criteria by 60% (direct & indirect administration)
Slovakia National Action Plan for GPP for 2016–2020 https://rokovania.gov.sk/RVL/Material/21622/1	yes*	yes	yes	no	The total value of GPP is up to 70% by 2030

*recommended/not yet developed/.
**implementation at the municipality level.
***GPP not developed at the national level.

However, it needs to be stressed that, at present, most of the presented good practices refer to environmental criteria and are based on GPP guidelines.

IV. Conclusions and Future Trends

The review of the current state of mandatory requirements for TC procurement showed that presently they are very limited and dispersed. They are also much less developed than the environmental ones. A majority of them only indirectly refer to social criteria such as, for example, the Textiles Regulation which covers the general obligation to provide a complete fibre composition of the textile product. In this sense, it does contribute to the protection of consumer interests.

Mandatory regulations that more directly address social aspects are the Personal Protective Equipment and REACH Regulations, both with a strong influence on human health due to provisions aimed at the protection of the user and/or the production worker against hazardous risks (chemical, radiological, physical, electrical, or mechanical). However, their enforcement is extremely difficult due to the costs of controlling and monitoring long and globally scattered textile value chains. For this reason, the need for more effective enforcement of the EU chemicals safety and environmental legislation was stressed by the members of the high-level roundtable on the implementation of the chemical strategy for sustainability.[60] The joint statement highlighted that even the most ambitious legislation will never ensure an adequate level of protection for consumers and workers if it is not properly enforced. Furthermore, it pointed to the urgent need for harmonised and standardised control test methods, lab capacity, as well as the budget and resources to effectively control whether representative samples contain restricted chemicals or not.[61]

The analysis of the existing requirements showed that those related to TC products occur only in a form of product-specific legislation that regulates the product or the producer, not the purchasers (ie, contracting authorities). If mentioned, most of the social requirements refer to such issues as human/worker rights or the quality of employment and equal opportunity. Although referred to in the Public Procurement Directives, these considerations still form part of a voluntary legal framework. Setting objectives with social provisions remaining optional for contracting authorities seems to be insufficient for significant changes towards more socially responsible public procurement. Consequently, there is a strong need for measurable, obligatory targets in this area with specific instruments addressing particular product groups. The national or local examples show

[60] Joint Statement on Enforcement of EU Chemical Legislation Ahead of the 2nd Meeting of the High-Level Roundtable at www.euratex.eu/news/joint-statement-on-enforcement-of-eu-chemical-legislation-ahead-of-the-2nd-meeting-of-the-high-level-roundtable/.

[61] ibid.

that such instruments can be very effective. Some examples are presented in the table in section III.C.

It is also worth emphasising that even the most sophisticated legal clauses will not work effectively without the dialogue and cooperation of all parties involved in the procurement process.[62] All solutions, to be effective, must consider the complexity of the relationships occurring in the value chains of the textile industry. Cooperation between all parties is essential as is the involvement of all stakeholders in the product purchasing process across global networks. The most substantial challenge which is to ensure full transparency throughout the textile value chain can only be overcome through cooperation. These chains are too complex for suppliers to tackle by themselves, and it is difficult to provide guarantees whether the social conditions have been met throughout the chain. Furthermore, contracting authorities do not have effective verification instruments. This brings us to the conclusion that even though social aspects seem to be more universal than environmental ones (the latter involve a great deal of technical aspects), still it would not be sufficient to introduce only general mandatory requirements. Also, it is a risky limitation to focus only on selected, high-impact sectors.[63] In the future, it could indeed be beneficial to introduce mandatory social requirements for all sectors and companies and, at the same time, also support them with sector-specific guidelines and toolboxes that would help fulfil those requirements in practice.

The future in the case of TC products looks very promising with the recently released EU Strategy for Sustainable and Circular Textiles, especially with the high hopes concerning its Annex.[64] In the context of public procurement, it seems of special importance that mandatory requirements concerning GPP and Member State incentives were introduced by 2024 and, as for social aspects, the action enforcing the Proposal for a Corporate Sustainability Due Diligence Directive in the textile sector as of 2023. Nonetheless, it is crucial that the mandatory requirements are not limited to the green requirements and that the Proposal for a Corporate Sustainability Due Diligence Directive will be further discussed to eliminate its existing shortcomings, and that both will be supplemented with additional sector-specific guidelines mentioned above.

[62] Buying Quality Private Security Services (n 37).

[63] It is pointed out as one of the shortcomings of the Proposal for a Corporate Sustainability Due Diligence Directive.

[64] How to Derive MEAT Criteria (n 37).

10

Transforming the Construction Sector Through Minimum Requirements

DOROTHY GRUYAERT AND VEERLE PISSIERSSENS

I. Introduction

Public procurement has been considered an effective method for environment protection for a while.[1] It can be used as a tool for achieving various 'secondary' or 'horizontal' objectives, including social and environmental objectives, which go beyond the mere act of purchasing the required goods, services and works.[2] Sustainable Public Procurement (SPP) in general is not only important because of its positive environmental, economic and social effects, but also because, in principle, it is expected that the public sector should lead by example, being the driver for sustainable development. Moreover, public procurement is seen as an important tool to support innovations.[3] Contracting authorities have the (buying) power to truly affect economic operators in their role as 'clients' or employer/supervisor of the works. These three considerations make public procurement a key area for reaching sustainability goals, not in the least with regard to the construction sector.[4]

[1] See more extensively, F de Leonardis, 'Green Public Procurement: From Recommendation to Obligation', (2011) 34 *International Journal of Public Administration* 110; A Wiesbrock and B Sjåfjell, 'Public Procurement's Potential for Sustainability' in B Sjåfjell and A Wiesbrock (eds), *Sustainable Public Procurement Under EU Law: New Perspectives on the State as Stakeholder* (Cambridge, Cambridge University Press, 2015).

[2] The concept of 'secondary' or 'horizontal' objectives is used to describe policy objectives other than the primary purpose of maximising the best value for money. See S Williams-Elegbe, 'Public Procurement as an Instrument to Pursue Human Rights Protection' in A Marx, G Van Calster, J Wouters with K Otteburn and D Lica (eds), *Research Handbook on Global Governance, Business and Human Rights* (Cheltenham, Edward Elgar, 2022) 143.

[3] A Wiesbrock, 'An Obligation for Sustainable Procurement? Gauging the Potential Impact of Article 11 TFEU on Public Contracting in the EU' (2013) 40 *Legal Issues of Economic Integration* 105, 108. See for a more critical approach KM Halonen, 'Is Public Procurement Fit for Reaching Sustainability Goals? A Law and Economics Approach to Green Public Procurement' (2021) 28 *Maastricht Journal of European and Comparative Law* 535, 541.

[4] W Janssen, 'Shifting towards Mandatory Sustainability Requirements in EU Public Procurement Law: Context, Relevance and a Typology', ch 1 in this volume.

This chapter discusses how public procurement law can be used as a tool to transform the construction sector and the (public) building stock towards more sustainable immovable property at the lowest possible environmental impact. In addition, SPP has the potential to elevate the construction sector itself to a higher environmental standard. It is well-known that the construction sector is a resource-intensive industry that uses a lot of raw materials and generates huge amounts of demolition waste.[5] The construction industry has the most significant impacts on the environment and climate. Therefore, it is a market where there is much to gain in terms of sustainable development. That is the case not only because of its substantial economic size and the significant amount of investments in real estate, but also because the construction sector must continue to meet growing demands for housing, facilities, etc. Moreover, the construction sector is known for its innovative products and pioneering spirit. Circular building projects and the so-called product-service systems (PSS) in the construction sector are powerful examples of this.[6]

This chapter is structured as follows. Section II will illustrate how the construction sector is affected by EU policy and legislative instruments on SPP. Until now, EU regulatory action has been rather soft-touch, with the exception of (the rise of) some mandatory requirements in secondary legislation that will also be analysed in that paragraph. Section III examines the common ways in which green and social requirements are being integrated into contracting authorities' construction contracts and real estate projects and discusses the room for improvement in the execution phase. Section IV shifts the perspective and explores how specific requirements in the construction industry as a whole may impact the transformation of sustainable public procurement beyond possibilities and towards obligations. Finally, Section V provides concluding thoughts.

[5] Eurostat, 'Generation of Waste by Economic Activity' at ec.europa.eu/eurostat/databrowser/view/ten00106/default/line?lang=en.

[6] In PSS, there is a focus on the use and access of a product instead of its ownership. A user pays for the service a product can provide instead of paying to own the product. See amongst others M Farooque, A Zhang, M Thürer, T Qu and D Huisingh, 'Circular Supply Chain Management: A Definition and Structured Literature Review' (2019) 228 *Journal of Cleaner Production* 882, 896; J Hojnik, 'Ecological Modernization through Servitisation: EU Regulatory Support for Sustainable Product-service Systems' (2018) 27 *RECIEL* 162, 165; B Keirsbilck and S Rousseau, 'The Marketing Stage: Fostering Sustainable Consumption Choices in a "Circular" and "Functional" Economy' in B Keirsbilck and E Terryn (eds), *Consumer Protection in a Circular Economy*, (Antwerp, Intersentia, 2019) 96; V Mak and E Terryn, 'Circular Economy and Consumer Protection: The Consumer as a Citizen and the Limits of Empowerment Through Consumer Law' (2020) 43 *Journal of Consumer Policy* 227, 246.

II. Development of SPP Rules in the Construction Sector

A. Current Status: Encouraging rather than Obliging SPP

The relevance of the construction sector for the achievement of the EU sustainable agenda (being the first climate-neutral continent by 2050) has been acknowledged in a number of EU policy and legislative documents.[7]

The first edition of the Handbook on Green Public Procurement of the European Commission contained guidelines on the purchasing of environmentally friendly construction services when procuring a product or tendering for a construction, building maintenance or renovation project.[8] Similarly, the Communication on public procurement for a better environment noted that for most public authorities, construction and renovation works and running costs of buildings represent a major share of annual expenditure, in some cases over 50 per cent.[9] Therefore, the construction sector was listed as a priority sector for GPP.

However, these EU initiatives did not contain mandatory requirements to pursue sustainability through public procurement, thus leaving the discretionary power of contracting authorities unaffected. The same is true for the general Article 18(2) of the Classic Directive, the scope of which has been highly debated in legal scholarship.[10] It appears that this provision does not impose an obligation on the contracting authorities, but rather an obligation on the Member States to ensure compliance.[11]

The debate about how to move towards green public procurement and towards a more sustainable public building stock continued to grow. On 20 May 2016, the European Commission published general guidelines for office buildings

[7] See also P Nowicki, 'Article 4 Threshold amounts' in R Caranta and A Sanchez-Graells (eds), *European Public Procurement: Commentary on Directive 2014/24/EU* (Cheltenham, Edward Elgar, 2022) 44; K Pouilki, 'Towards Mandatory Green Public Procurement (GPP) Requirements under the EU Green Deal: Reconsidering the Role of Public Procurement as an Environmental Policy Tool' (2021) 21 *ERA Forum* 699.

[8] Buying Green, 1st edn.

[9] Public Procurement for a Better Environment COM(2008) 400.

[10] M Andhov, 'Article 18(2) Principles of Procurement' in R Caranta and A Sanchez-Graells (eds), *European Public Procurement: Commentary on Directive 2014/24/EU* (Cheltenham, Edward Elgar Publishing, 2021) 199; P Kunzlik, 'The 2014 Public Procurement Package – One-step Forward and Two Back for Green and Social Procurement?' in Y Maurique and K Wauters (eds), *EU Directive 2014/24 on Public Procurement: A New Turn for Competition in Public Markets?* (Brussels, Larcier, 2021) 170; Pouilki, 'Towards Mandatory Green Public Procurement (GPP) Requirements' (n 7) 713; D Renders, C Delforge and K Polet, *Principes Élémentaires du Droit des Marches Publics* (Brussels, Larcier, 2021) 33; M Steinicke and PL Vesterdorf (eds), *EU Public Procurement Law: Brussels Commentary* (Baden-Baden, Nomos, 2018) 331.

[11] See the extensive analysis in Janssen (n 4).

in particular: the EU GPP criteria for office building design, construction and management.[12] These GPP criteria offer a supporting framework on how to procure environmentally improved office buildings. The Commission is currently working on a proposal to revise these GPP criteria. A consultation was launched on 4 May 2022.[13] The revision process will consider expanding the scope to other types of buildings purchased and/or maintained by public authorities, in particular schools and social housing. The Commission looks into the possibility to develop green public procurement criteria for public buildings related to life cycle and climate resilience. The use of these GPP criteria remains again, however, voluntary. The criteria are broad in scope, but have a limited impact in practice due to the voluntary approach.[14]

Similarly, the European Green Deal paid considerable attention to the construction sector as one of the resource-intensive sectors where a transition is pursued by the Commission, inter alia by proposing 'further legislation and guidance on green public purchasing'.[15] With regard to the construction sector, the following section of the European Green Deal is particularly relevant: 'The Commission will consider legal requirements to boost the market of secondary raw materials with mandatory recycled content (for instance for packaging, vehicles, construction materials and batteries).'[16]

Subsequently, on 14 October 2020, the European Commission presented its strategy to trigger a renovation wave for Europe's building stock.[17] The Renovation Wave priorities are: (i) tackling energy poverty and worst-performing buildings; (ii) renovation of public buildings; and (iii) decarbonisation of heating and cooling. Again, GPP is considered as a tool for those who voluntarily opt for it.

Moving towards SPP in the construction sector, or any sector, cannot be achieved through 'simply' adding green or sustainability clauses to the public procurement documents or by adding an additional check in the public procurement process; for example, through the mandatory exclusion grounds, contracting authorities ensure that they do not contract with an entity (or individual) that has been convicted for fraud or human trafficking. Green or social characteristics of the goods, services or works that are being procured do (unfortunately) not allow for such a tick-the-box approach.[18] Although one could argue that the mandatory

[12] EU GPP criteria for Office building design SWD(2016) 180. Another sector-specific voluntary guidance exists for road design, construction and maintenance, see European Commission, 'JRC Science for Policy Report Revision of Green Public Procurement Criteria for Road Design, Procurement Practice Guidance Document', JRC102168.

[13] Consultation on the first draft of the revised EU Green Public Procurement criteria for buildings at circulareconomy.europa.eu/platform/en/news-and-events/all-news/consultation-first-draft-revised-eu-green-public-procurement-criteria-buildings.

[14] A New Circular Economy Action Plan, COM(2020) 98, para 2.1.

[15] EU Climate Law; European Green Deal, 8.

[16] ibid.

[17] Renovation Wave for Europe COM(2020) 662.

[18] Article 57 Classic Directive.

exclusion ground related to a conviction by a final judgment for child labour and other forms of trafficking in human beings is related to Socially Responsible Public Procurement (SRPP), this is setting the bar for SRPP rather low – as a lack of conviction for this type of horrendous crime does not in itself guarantee any actual SRPP standards.[19]

Until now, existing (primary and secondary) EU law still encourages rather than obliges SPP.[20] That is also the case for the construction sector-specific secondary law that complements the Public Procurement Directives. SPP remains (both in general and in the construction sector) a voluntary instrument and it is up to the Member States and their contracting authorities to implement it.

However, it seems that development towards the introduction of sectoral mandatory requirements is under construction. Hereinafter, we will discuss the three main topics that we have detected in the construction sector-specific secondary law as being illustrative of how mandatory requirements in the construction sector may take shape.

B. Renewable Energy, Energy Efficiency and Mandatory Minimum Energy Performance Standards (MEPs) for (Public) Buildings

EU regulatory action has been rather soft-touch with regard to its approach to the energy performance of buildings (Energy Performance of Buildings Directive), the promotion of renewable energy use and the call to promote resource-efficient public buildings (Old Renewable Energy Directive).[21] In a small number of sectors, EU energy legislation has introduced mandatory minimum standards for the environmental performance of certain products, imposing on contracting authorities the obligation to require a certain level of energy efficiency for these products, such as office equipment or vehicles. Such measures help align public sector demand behind environmentally highly performing and/or innovative products.[22] However, when it comes to buildings, the public sector was merely called on to lead by example by adopting a minimum number of energy efficiency measures and by promoting resource-efficient buildings.[23]

[19] See also Kunzlik (n 10) 170; D Segall, 'Human Rights and the Global Construction Sector: Deconstructing the Challenges Faced by Low Wage-workers' in A Marx, G Van Calster, J Wouters with K Otteburn and D Lica (eds), *Research Handbook on Global Governance, Business and Human Rights* (Cheltenham, Edward Elgar Publishing, 2022).

[20] See also Janssen (n 4); T van den Brink, 'Subsidiarity Lost Along the Way? EU Public Procurement Legislation on the Road to Sustainability', ch 3 in this volume.

[21] For what preceded, see P Kunzlik, 'The Procurement of "Green" Energy' in S Arrowsmith and P Kunzlik (eds), *Social and Environmental Policies in EC Procurement Law* (Cambridge, Cambridge University Press, 2009) 369.

[22] See also Kunzlik (n 10) 168–69.

[23] Green Paper on the Modernisation of EU Public Procurement Policy COM(2011) 15, 41.

Article 9 Energy Performance of Buildings Directive calls for the Member State to ensure that all new buildings are 'nearly zero-energy buildings'. This may, at first sight, look like a mandatory environmental requirement, but since it is not further specified what is meant by 'nearly', this (rather weak and open-ended) target for the public building stock calls on Member States' responsibility without formulating clear legal obligations for contracting authorities.[24] Indeed, it is one thing to say that a public authority should 'green up' its procurement contracts, but it is another to say that, if the contract is not green, it is illegitimate.[25]

Old Renewable Energy Directive stipulates in Article 13(5) that:

> Member States shall ensure that new public buildings, and existing public buildings that are subject to major renovation, at national, regional and local level fulfil an exemplary role in the context of this Directive from 1 January 2012 onwards. Member States may, inter alia, allow that obligation to be fulfilled by complying with standards for zero energy housing, or by providing that the roofs of public or mixed private-public buildings are used by third parties for installations that produce energy from renewable sources.

This exemplary role was repeated in the Renewable Energy Directive (Article 15(5)). Subsequently, the Energy Efficiency Directive[26] again stressed (at Recital 19) the main consideration that central governments should lead by example, although this should not affect the rules on public procurement:

> With regard to the purchase of certain products and services and the purchase and rent of buildings, central governments which conclude public works, supply or service contracts should lead by example and make energy-efficient purchasing decisions. (…) The provisions of the Union's public procurement directives should not however be affected. For products other than those covered by the energy efficiency requirements for purchasing in this Directive, Member States should encourage public bodies to take into account the energy efficiency of purchase.

This in a way weakens the mandatory requirement of leading by example, turning it into an empty box.

Article 5 of the Energy Efficiency Directive further explained the exemplary role of public bodies' buildings and provided that Member States shall ensure that, as of 1 January 2014, three per cent of the buildings owned and occupied by its central government is renovated each year to meet at least the minimum

[24] A definition of 'nearly zero-energy building' has recently been introduced in Art 2 of the Proposal for an Energy Performance of the Buildings Directive: 'a building with a very high energy performance, as determined in accordance with Annex I, which cannot be lower than the 2023 cost-optimal level reported by Member States in accordance with Article 6(2) and where the nearly zero or very low amount of energy required is covered to a very significant extent by energy from renewable sources, including energy from renewable sources produced on-site or nearby'. See below section II.B.

[25] F de Leonardis, 'Green Public Procurement: From Recommendation to Obligation' (2011) 34 *International Journal of Public Administration* 113.

[26] The Energy Efficiency Directive was amended in 2018 by the Directive (EU) 2018/2002 amending Directive 2012/27/EU on energy efficiency.

energy performance standards that the Member State has set in the application of Article 4 Energy Performance of Buildings Directive. This is coming closer to a specific minimum mandatory public procurement target being inserted in EU legislation. Article 24(1) Energy Efficiency Directive provides that Member States must report on the progress made. The Energy Efficiency Directive also introduced an obligation to purchase energy-efficient buildings and equipment of the highest energy labelling class, but only insofar as this is consistent with cost-effectiveness, economical feasibility, wider sustainability, technical suitability, as well as sufficient competition.[27]

Both the Energy Performance of Buildings Directive and the Energy Efficiency Directive were revised by Directive 2018/844/EU. On 14 July 2021, the Commission published a new Proposal for an Energy Efficiency Directive, as part of the 'Fit for 55' package to reduce greenhouse gas emissions by at least 55 per cent by 2030, and achieve a climate-neutral Europe by 2050.[28] This Proposal emphasises that the public sector is an important economic actor in its own right and is responsible for around five to ten per cent of the total Union final energy consumption.[29] Public buildings are estimated to use around two per cent of the Union's final energy consumption. The Commission explains that cost-effective savings potentials still exist in the entire public sector both in the renovation and energy management of existing buildings as well as the future procurement of energy-efficient buildings, products and services. The Proposal acknowledges that the indicative nature of the current Energy Efficiency Directive does not achieve its objective.[30]

The necessary horizontal framework for action is provided in Article 5 and Article 6 (public buildings) and Article 7 (public procurement) of the Proposal. Article 7 strengthens the public procurement provisions by extending the obligation to take into account the energy efficiency requirements by all public administration levels, and by removing conditionalities with regard to cost-effectiveness, technical and economic feasibility. Member States shall ensure that all public (procurement) contracts and concessions with a value equal to or greater than the thresholds laid down in Article 8 of the Concessions Directive, Article 4 of the Classic Directive and Article 15 of the Utilities Directive meet: (i) the high energy-efficiency performance standard as well as; (ii) the energy efficiency first principle. This 'energy efficiency first' principle is added in the new Article 3 and entails that Member States shall ensure that energy efficiency solutions are taken into account in the planning, policy and major investment decisions related to the following sectors: (a) energy systems; and (b) non-energy sectors, where those sectors have an impact on energy consumption and energy efficiency. The construction sector falls under the latter category.

[27] Annex VIII Energy Efficiency Directive.
[28] Proposal for an Energy Efficiency Directive (recast) COM(2021) 558.
[29] ibid 3.
[30] ibid 15.

According to Article 7(5) of the Proposal, Member States *may require* again that contracting authorities and contracting entities take into account, *where appropriate*, wider sustainability, social, environmental and circular economy aspects in procurement practices with a view to achieving the Union's decarbonisation and zero pollution objectives. *Where appropriate*, and in accordance with the requirements laid down in Annex IV, Member States shall require contracting authorities and contracting entities to take into account Union GPP criteria. According to the proposed Annex IV(c), where a product or a service is covered by the Union GPP criteria, with relevance to the energy efficiency of the product or service, contracting authorities *make the best efforts to* purchase only products and services that respect at least the technical specifications set at 'core' level in the relevant Union GPP criteria.

Furthermore, Member States will be required to support public bodies by providing guidelines and methodologies on the assessment of lifecycle costs, and by putting in place competence support centres and encouraging using aggregated procurement and digital procurement. Member States would also be required to publish information on winning tenders (in line with the thresholds set out in the Public Procurement Directives).[31] However, the current publication rules do not include an obligation to include technical/SPP-related information in the publication.

Article 7(5) of the Proposal also includes a provision that contracting authorities *may* require that tenders disclose a Global Warming Potential[32] of new buildings, in particular for new buildings above 2,000 square metres. The aim is again *to increase awareness* of the circular economy and the whole life-cycle of carbon emissions in public procurement practices. Article 5(5) of the Proposal stipulates that Member States *shall encourage* public bodies to consider life cycle carbon emissions of their public bodies' investment and policy activities. In conclusion, except for the general statement that Member States shall ensure that tenders purchase only products, services, buildings and works with high energy-efficiency performance included in Article 7(1) and the requirements referred to in Annex IV, this Proposal leaves us again with voluntary sustainability targets. The question arises whether this will suffice to truly transform the public building stock and to constrain the impact of the construction sector on the environment.

On 15 December 2021, the European Commission adopted its Proposal to revise the Energy Performance of Buildings Directive.[33] It follows up on the three main

[31] ibid 21.

[32] Numeric indicator in $kgCO_2e/m^2$ (of useful internal floor area) for each life cycle stage averaged for one year of a reference study period of 50 years.

[33] Proposal for an Energy Performance of the Buildings Directive.

goals of the Renovation Wave (see above section II.A), including the intention to propose mandatory minimum energy performance standards ('MEPs'). Article 9 of the Proposal for an Energy Performance of Buildings Directive sets the following minimum energy performance standards:

1. Member States shall ensure that

(a) buildings and building units owned by public bodies achieve at the latest

   (i) after 1 January 2027, at least energy performance class F; and
   (ii) after 1 January 2030, at least energy performance class E;

(b) non-residential buildings and building units, other than those owned by public bodies, achieve at the latest

   (i) after 1 January 2027, at least energy performance class F; and
   (ii) after 1 January 2030, at least energy performance class E;

(c) residential buildings and building units achieve at the latest

   (i) after 1 January 2030, at least energy performance class F; and
   (ii) after 1 January 2033, at least energy performance class E;

Moreover, Article 7 of the Proposal for an Energy Performance of Buildings Directive specifies that as of 2030, new buildings must be zero-emission buildings; new public buildings must be zero-emission as of 2027.

Member States shall take the measures necessary to ensure the implementation of minimum energy performance standards, including appropriate monitoring mechanisms and penalties (see Article 9(6) of the Proposal for an Energy Performance of Buildings Directive). In Article 11(3) of the Proposal for an Energy Performance of Buildings Directive, the Commission also introduces an obligation for Member States to require zero-emission buildings to be equipped with measuring and control devices for the monitoring and regulation of indoor air quality. Also, in existing buildings, the installation of such devices shall be required, where technically and economically feasible, when a building undergoes a major renovation.

These MEPs are illustrative of the sector-specific transformation and the building stock as a whole (public and private buildings) (see below section IV), while the public authorities still fulfil an exemplary role by achieving the same energetic classes sooner. This will automatically lead to energy-related GPP criteria for public buildings. The obligation for Member States to lay down minimum requirements on the energy performance of new buildings and of large existing buildings that are subject to major renovation will affect the definition of the subject matter and technical specifications of the works contract.

Regarding this transition in the construction sector, the Flemish region in Belgium also provides an example worth mentioning. On 9 July 2021, the Flemish Government decided to impose an obligation to renovate non-residential (public and private) buildings on all new owners and holders of a long lease right or right of superficies who acquired their right as of 1 January 2022.[34] If the buildings do not meet certain specific energy requirements, the necessary works should be carried out within five years after the real estate transaction. Moreover, users of (non-residential) public buildings with a usable area of at least 250 m² must display the cover sheet of a valid energy performance certificate for non-residential buildings visible to the public (Article 19 of the decision of 9 July 2021).

C. The Sustainable Products Initiative

A second topic of secondary law that is relevant to the construction sector, is the European Commission's Sustainable Products Initiative. This Proposal for a Regulation on Ecodesign for Sustainable Products[35] is extensively discussed in chapter six.[36] Final construction products[37] also fall within the scope of this proposed Ecodesign Regulation, but given the need to manage the strong inter-linkages between their environmental and structural performance, including their health and safety, ecodesign requirements will be laid down under the Proposal for a Revision of the Construction Products Regulation (see below section II.D), except for energy-related construction products, which are already regulated under the existing Ecodesign Directive.

With regard to GPP, the Commission here again acknowledges that more mandatory criteria may be needed.[38] In order to contribute to the objective of reaching climate neutrality, improving energy and resource efficiency and transitioning to a circular economy that protects public health and biodiversity, the Commission should have the power to require, where appropriate, contracting authorities to align their procurement with specific GPP criteria or targets, to be set out in the delegated acts adopted pursuant to the Proposal for a Regulation on Ecodesign for Sustainable Products. Although it is still unclear when it will be deemed 'appropriate', it is clearly stated that the Commission may *require* public authorities to use GPP.

[34] Decision of 9 July 2021 of the Flemish Government to revise the Energy Decision of 19 November 2010, concerning the implementation of a renovation obligation for non-residential buildings and provisions on the energy performance certificate for non-residential buildings, *Official Gazette* 10 August 2021. A similar obligation for residential buildings will enter into force on 1 January 2023.

[35] Proposal for a Regulation on Ecodesign for Sustainable Products COM(2022) 142.

[36] C Backes and M Boeve, 'Regulating the Producer Instead of the Procurer – The EU Sustainable Products Initiative and Extended Producer Responsibilty as Ways to Foster the Transition to Circular Economy', ch 6 in this volume.

[37] The Proposal lists some examples at Recital 43: heaters, boilers, heat pumps, water and space heating appliances, fans, cooling and ventilating systems and photovoltaic products (excluding building-integrated photovoltaic panels).

[38] Recital 19 of the Proposal for a Regulation on Ecodesign for Sustainable Products: 'New approaches may also be needed for the preparation of mandatory public procurement criteria and for bans on the destruction of unsold consumer products.'

The Commission continues (at Recital 87 of the Proposal for a Regulation on Ecodesign for Sustainable Products) that the criteria or targets set by delegated acts for specific product groups should be complied with not only when directly procuring those products in public supply contracts, but also in public works or public services contracts where those products will be used for activities constituting the subject matter of those contracts. It is thus clear that this also applies to the construction sector. The Proposal for a Regulation on Ecodesign for Sustainable Products continues (at Recital 87):

> Compared to a voluntary approach, mandatory criteria or targets will ensure that the leverage of public spending to boost demand for better performing products is maximised. The criteria should be transparent, objective and non-discriminatory.

The same ambition can be found in the Proposal for a Revision of the Construction Products Regulation (see below section II.D).[39]

As promising as this sounds in terms of mandatory SPP in general, and for public buildings in particular, Article 58 of the Proposal for a Regulation on Ecodesign for Sustainable Products again lowers the expectations, describing green public procurement as an incentive (sub chapter six). Article 58(1) states that the requirements 'may' take the form of mandatory technical specifications, selection criteria, award criteria, contract performance clauses, or targets, as appropriate. Article 58(2) continues that:

> When establishing requirements pursuant to Article 4, third subparagraph, point (h), for public contracts, the Commission shall take into account the following criteria:
>
> (a) the value and volume of public contracts awarded for that given product group or for the services or works using the given product group;
> (b) the need to ensure sufficient demand for more environmentally sustainable products;
> (c) the economic feasibility for contracting authorities or contracting entities to buy more environmentally sustainable products, without entailing disproportionate costs.

D. The Construction Products Regulation

The Construction Products Regulation lays down harmonised conditions for the marketing of construction products in the EU. It ensures that construction products that are placed on the single market are accompanied by information that provides insight into the performance of the construction products. The Construction Products Regulation provides that CE marking is applied to products

[39] See Recital 90 and 91 of the Proposal for a Revision of the Construction Products Regulation COM(2022) 144.

in the framework of harmonised standards and that a declaration of performance is required to accompany products. An evaluation of the Construction Products Regulation was launched in 2016 and on 30 March 2022 the Proposal for a Revision of the Construction Products Regulation was adopted (the Revised Construction Products Regulation). Both the Construction Products Regulation and the Revised Construction Products Regulation ensure that construction works be designed and executed so as not to endanger the safety of persons, domestic animals or property nor damage the environment. It remains to be seen if the distinction between what is regulated in the Revised Construction Products Regulation and the Proposed Ecodesign Regulation (see above section II.C) will be clear.

One of the advantages of the Construction Products Regulation and Revised Construction Products Regulation in a public procurement context is that, through its harmonisation of essential characteristics of construction products (eg, reaction to fire, insulation of sound, etc), it allows for an objective standard against which various construction products can be compared. However, under the Construction Products Regulation, the Member State remained responsible for safety, environmental and energy requirements applicable to buildings and civil engineering works, meaning that these elements are still subject to local flavour and ambitions (or lack thereof).

The Revised Construction Products Regulation aims, amongst other things, to: (i) address the sustainability performance of construction products; and (ii) enable the construction ecosystem's contribution to meeting climate and sustainability goals. In order to achieve this, the Revised Construction Products Regulation requires the manufacturers to deliver environmental information about the life cycle of their products. Again this could be an element that allows contracting authorities to take life-cycle elements into account in a, hopefully, standardised manner.

In addition, the Revised Construction Products Regulation will require manufacturers to:

- design and manufacture a product and its packaging in such a way that its overall environmental sustainability reaches the 'state of the art level';[40]
- give preference to recyclable materials and materials gained from recycling;
- respect the minimum recycled content obligations and other limit values regarding aspects of environmental sustainability;

[40] Article 3(32) provides that '"state of the art" means a way to achieve a certain goal which is either the most effective and advanced or close to it and thus above the average of ways which can be chosen.'

- make available, in product databases, instructions for the use and repair of the products;
- design products in such a way that re-use, remanufacturing and recycling are facilitated.[41]

To prove that the construction product meets these requirements, the manufacturer shall draw up a declaration of performance and a declaration of conformity and affix the CE marking. The manufacturer shall draw up technical documentation describing the intended use and all the elements necessary to demonstrate performance and conformity. This technical documentation shall include the mandatory or facultative calculation of environmental sustainability assessed in accordance with harmonised technical specifications, except in the case of used, remanufactured or surplus products.

Particularly relevant for the topic of this chapter is Article 84 of the Revised Construction Products Regulation which is titled 'Green public procurement'. This article allows the Commission to adopt 'sustainability requirements applicable to public contracts, including implementation, monitoring and reporting of those requirements by the Member States'. This illustrates and confirms our view that GPP requires an added emphasis on the contract execution phase, while the current Public Procurement Directives lack focus on that phase and this provides for a pitfall for actual GPP (see below section III.B).

Paragraph 2 of Article 84 states that if the Commission imposes these 'sustainability requirements' they *may* take the form of mandatory technical specifications, selection criteria, contract performance clauses, or targets, for contracting authorities. The final paragraph of Article 84 provides that when setting these requirements, the Commission shall take the following criteria into account:

(a) the value and volume of public contracts awarded for that given product family or category or for the services or works using the given product family or category;
(b) the need to ensure sufficient demand for more environmentally sustainable products;
(c) the economic feasibility for contracting authorities or contracting entities to buy more environmentally sustainable products, without entailing disproportionate costs.

This Proposal again considers green public procurement in the construction sector as an option, not an obligation. The Commission is empowered to supplement the Construction Products Regulation by delegated acts establishing sustainability

[41] European Commission, 'The European Commission's Questions & Answers: Revision of the Construction Product Regulation' at ec.europa.eu/commission/presscorner/detail/en/QANDA_22_2121.

requirements. Similar to the Ecodesign Regulation, such requirements *may* take the form of mandatory technical specifications, selection criteria, award criteria, contract performance clauses, or targets, *as appropriate* (see Article 87 of the Revised Construction Products Regulation). Whether there will be mandatory requirements is up to the Commission. However, it is promising that the Commission may do so through delegated acts.

III. Implementation of Mandatory SPP Rules Throughout Different Public Procurement Phases

True SPP can only be achieved if it is genuinely included throughout the public procurement and contract execution process, meaning in the preparation, selection and award phase and the implementation phase. If SPP is not included throughout the various stages of the public procurement procedure and subsequent execution of the contract for works, a contracting authority may end up with SPP only on paper, but not in reality. In addition, the offers that were unsuccessful during the award phase (eg, deemed not green or sustainable enough) could in practice have resulted in a greener or more sustainable solution than the winning bid that was implemented with weak monitoring and contract management. If for example, a contractor's bid was successful because amongst others its proposed construction has the lowest energy consumption, this low energy consumption should be monitored, reported, and reviewed throughout the lifespan of the building. Otherwise, what are both tenderers and contracting authorities 'fighting' for in the award phase?

A. Current Status: Focus on the 'Award' of Public Procurement Contracts

In relation to contracts for works, there are various options for a contracting authority to include sustainable aspects, whether it is within the construction process itself (eg, amount of water used during the construction), the materials used (eg, use of re-usable modular bricks) and/or the energy efficiency of the building itself. The current rules provided in the Public Procurement Directives allow contracting authorities to take GPP requirements into consideration or to set these types of standards.[42] Article 70 of the Classic Directive explicitly states that contracting

[42] For a more detailed insight on this please see: A Semple, 'Article 62 Quality Assurance Standards and Environmental Management Standards' in R Caranta and A Sanchez-Graells (eds), *European Public Procurement: Commentary on Directive 2014/24/EU* (Cheltenham, Edward Elgar Publishing, 2021) 673.

authorities 'may lay down special conditions relating to the performance of a contract' and that these may include environmental and social considerations.

However, in our opinion, when preparing the public procurement documents, contracting authorities should review to what extent they are (going to be) able to, both from a technical and capacity point of view, review whether the SPP requirements are actually met, both in the offer and in the ultimate works provided.[43]

B. Room for Improvement: Enforcement in the Execution Phase

Currently, the 2014 Public Procurement Directives are almost exclusively focused on the *award* of public contracts, with a few exceptions such as Article 70 'conditions for performance of contracts', Article 72 'modification of contracts during their term' and Article 73 'termination of contracts' of the Classic Directive, which also relate to the contract execution.[44] However, as sustainable public procurement moves to the forefront, the focus moves from 'the price paid to the contractor' to the 'value of the work (good or service) throughout its lifespan'.[45] One could argue that the 2014 Public Procurement Directives may also need to switch gears, beyond allowing for life-cycle costs to be taken into account.[46] SPP not only requires that a contracting authority correctly selects tenderers, fairly evaluates offers and subsequently awards contracts, it also requires that certain standards are upheld during and after the execution of the contract. Even more so, in principle, sustainable public procurement selection (eg, environmental management systems and/or supply chain management systems) and award criteria (eg, minimum level of performance in the technical specifications) will have an increased focus on the construction and/or use of the work after the initial works have been carried out.[47]

One could argue that under the current rules, an economic operator is already required to execute a public contract in line with their submitted offer and that this is therefore sufficiently covered. This reasoning however increases the risk of greenwashed public procurement, meaning that a contracting authority may have set very high standards in its tender documents and (very) critically assessed the various offers, but finds that certain standards (however robustly written into the

[43] Buying Green, 3rd edn, 40.

[44] See also P Telles and G Skovgaard Ølykke, 'Sustainable Procurement: A Compliance Perspective of EU Public Procurement Law' (2017) 3 *European Procurement and Public Private Partnership Law Review* 249.

[45] The 2014 Public Procurement Directives allow to take life cycle costs into account, see also Semple (n 42) 673.

[46] Article 68 Classic Directive.

[47] Buying Green (n 43) 46–54.

tender documents and however harsh the offers were judged in relation to these standards during the award phase) are not met during contract execution.[48]

The current public procurement rules provide little to no guidance on this topic. For example: if the tender documents stated that a building needs to be constructed in line with a specific type of sustainable certification (eg, BREEAM certificate), whether or not the building will meet this requirement will only be known once the building is constructed. Even though Article 72 of the Classic Directive provides that in some cases modifications to a public procurement contract must be published through a notice in the *Official Journal of the European Union*, there is no real sanction if contracting authorities fail to do so. In addition, not all modification grounds are covered by this notification requirement.

Naturally, these types of 'non-compliances' may amount to an unlawful modification of the contract during its term, as provided for in Article 72 of the Classic Directive, which may lead to the termination of the contract, as provided in Article 73 of the Classic Directive. However, the mechanism related to unlawful 'contract modifications' does not provide an adequate tool to really assist contracting authorities in actually achieving SPP. A breach of the rules as codified in Article 72 of the Classic Directive is often only invoked by a third party, for example, the contractor that was ranked second or a supervisory authority.[49] However, it is very hard for a third party to know the intimate details of contract execution, especially in relation to very technical SPP requirements and/or the performance of some of the materials used or of the building itself. This is illustrated by the fact that the total number of CJEU judgments regarding contract modifications is relatively low.[50]

In addition, it does not provide for a 'show of ambition' to have compliance with contract execution to be (almost fully) dependent on other vigilant third parties. Moreover, in case of a breach, the only solution offered by Article 72 of the Classic Directive is the retendering of the contract, which from a sustainability point of view may be a very unappealing option. Also, the tools provided in the Remedies Directives such as ineffectiveness (which has a time limit of six months), imposition of penalties and/or shortening of the duration of the contract may be equally inadequate to meet sustainability concerns.

This leads to our conviction that there should be an increased focus on the monitoring and management of public procurement contracts during the contract execution phase.

[48] ibid 66.

[49] P Bogdanowicz 'The EU Rules on Contract Modifications in the Context of the Insolvency of Economic Operators: Advania Sverige and Kammarkollegiet (C–461/20)' (2022) 31 *PPLR*.

[50] Joined Cases C-721/19 and C-722/19 *Sisal SpA and Others v Agenzia delle Dogane e dei Monopoli and Ministero dell'Economia e delle Finanze* ECLI:EU:C:2021:672, [2021]; Case C-549/14 *Finn Frogne A/S v Rigspolitiet ved Center for Beredskabskommunikation* EU:C:2016:634, [2016]; Joined Cases C-496/18 and C-497/18 *HUNGEOD Közlekedésfejlesztési, Földmérési, Út- és Vasúttervezési Kft. and Others v Közbeszerzési Hatóság Közbeszerzési Döntőbizottság* ECLI:EU:C:2020:240, [2020]; Case C-263/19 *T-Systems Magyarország Zrt. and BKK Budapesti Közlekedési Központ v Közbeszerzési Hatóság Közbeszerzési Döntőbizottságand* ECLI: EU: C: 2020:373, [2020].

IV. Transforming the Construction Industry as a Whole: The Benefits of a Sector-Specific Approach

When considering the possibility of mandatory public procurement requirements, the idea arises that more can be achieved by transforming a sector as a whole instead of imposing constraints on the public authorities who act within that particular sector. If green and/or social requirements apply solely to public procurement, their potential effects on private consumption can have a downside effect. Therefore, it is better to treat SPP as a sector-specific policy.[51] As also stated by Halonen:

> Sectoral legislation that would set a higher, industry-wide environmental standard for all suppliers, and not only those supplying the public sector, would be the most effective way forward because it would not leave room for demand substitution.

Setting specific standards on what to buy, is the task of EU sectoral legislation.[52] Article 11 TFEU stipulates in this respect that:

> environmental protection requirements must be integrated into the definition and implementation of the Union's policies and activities, in particular with a view to promoting sustainable development

Although the literal text seems to create a clear legal obligation ('must be integrated'), this article's scope and practical implication remain uncertain and debated.[53]

It seems that the real estate and construction sector constitutes a good example of such sectoral legislation that enhances sustainable development. Not only the public procurement related to the construction sector, but that sector as a whole should align with green and social goals. If mandatory requirements for the public building stock are pursued through the rules on public procurement, this would create a strange situation where more stringent rules apply to immovable property for which a contracting authority concludes a building contract compared to the immovable property for which real rights are vested by the contracting authority.

General green building standards (for all types of buildings) would naturally lead to a greener public procurement. GPP is then no longer a matter of focusing on green *alternatives*. This implies a sector-specific transition from voluntary

[51] E Carreras and D Vannoni, 'Mandatory Requirements in Sustainable Public Procurement: The Economic Perspective', ch 4 in this volume.

[52] See also M Andhov et al, 'Sustainability Through Public Procurement: The Way Forward Reform Proposals' (2020) *25 SSRN Electronic Journal* 1.

[53] Janssen (n 4); M Andhov and F Muscaritoli, 'Climate Change and Public Procurement: Are We Shifting the Legal Discourse?', ch 2 in this volume.

regulations towards mandatory requirements. And this is exactly what is happening with the MEPs for (public and private) buildings. Following the examples in the real estate and energy sector, such as the Energy Performance of Buildings Directive and Energy Efficiency Directive, may lead to new minimum environmental and social standards in other legislation.[54]

V. Concluding Remarks

For many years, contracting authorities were 'invited' to bear in mind environmental principles as much as possible in procuring construction projects. Although governments have a significant opportunity to promote sustainable buildings through public procurement, in practice this has not been done in a consistent way since SPP have been mainly non-obligatory. This chapter aimed to provide an understanding of whether the adoption of mandatory rules for public procurement contributes to turning the public building sector into a more sustainable and social environment.

We analysed the common ways and the future legislative proposals of how SPP is/should be integrated to create a more sustainable (public) building stock. Arguably, it might be a more direct and appealing way to pursue sustainability goals sector-wide instead of through mandatory SPPs. This is particularly true for the building stock.

However, we do believe that the public procurement rules would benefit from mandatory SPP as long as this is supported by clear contract management and enforcement during the execution phase. A framework of rules without considering the enforcement issues would make it an empty shell. Article 58 of the Proposal for a Regulation on Ecodesign for Sustainable Products and Article 87 of the Revised Construction Products Regulation already hints towards 'contract performance clauses', but as discussed above, it remains open-ended and non-obligatory.

If we are to use public procurement as an effective tool towards a more sustainable economy, contracting authorities should be handed the effective tools to do so. Providing legal certainty and clarification on contract monitoring/management and on how to handle changing situations, beyond 'in case of changes please re-tender', should empower contracting authorities in their search for more sustainable public procurement.

[54] See also Andhov et al (n 52).

PART 3

Member State Experiences – Mandatory Sustainability Requirements on the Member State Level

11

Italy: Leading the Way Towards Mandatory Sustainable Public Procurement through Minimum Environmental Criteria

GIULIA BOTTA

I. Introduction

Public authorities' purchasing power across all EU Member States represents an important share of overall public spending, serving as a potential tool for societal change and strategic regulation. In Italy, public procurement accounts for 10 per cent of the GDP and 22 per cent of total public expenditure.[1] It is increasingly recognised as a driver for sustainable production and consumption through sustainability criteria.[2] Despite the potential, EU Sustainable Public Procurement (SPP) rules provide *legal possibilities*[3] rather than obligations, creating implementation challenges and risks of a limited and fragmented uptake.[4]

When considering a possible gradual shift from voluntary to mandatory SPP requirements, Italy is the most prominent example in the EU of requiring

[1] OECD, *Government at a Glance* (OECD Publishing, Paris, 2021) 162.

[2] R Caranta 'Public Procurement for the SDGs – Rethinking the Basics' in L Mélon (ed), *Sustainability in Public Procurement, Corporate Law and Higher Education* (Routledge, forthcoming, 2023); B Sjafjell and A Wiesbrock (eds), *Sustainable Public Procurement under EU Law: New Perspectives on the State as Stakeholder* (Cambridge, Cambridge University Press, 2016).

[3] M Andhov 'Contracting Authorities and Strategic Goals of Public Procurement – A Relationship Defined by Discretion?' in S Bogojevic, X Groussot and J Hettne (eds) *Discretion in EU Public Procurement Law* (Oxford, Hart Publishing, 2020); M Andhov, 'Article 18(2) Public Procurement Principles' in R Caranta and A Sanchez-Graells (eds), *European Public Procurement Commentary on Directive 2014/24/EU* (Cheltenham, Edward Elgar Publishing, 2021).

[4] W Janssen, 'Shifting towards Mandatory Sustainability Requirements in EU Public Procurement Law: Context, Relevance and a Typology' ch 1 in this volume; A Renda, 'GPP Uptake in the EU27: Still a very Fragmented Picture' in Renda et al, *The uptake of GPP in the EU27* (DG Environment, CEPS, College d'Europe, 2012); K Pouikli, 'Towards Mandatory GPP Requirements under the EU Green Deal: Reconsidering the Role of Public Procurement as an Environmental Policy Tool' (2021) 21 *ERA Forum* 699.

mandatory minimum sustainability criteria in public procurement law. Substantive Minimum Environmental Requirements (Criteri Ambientali Minimi-CAMs) have been adopted since 2011, becoming mandatory for all contracting authorities in 2017 under Article 34 of the Italian Public Contracts Code (Codice dei Contratti Pubblici).[5] The criteria now exist for 18 procurement categories, regularly updated and currently being expanded. Notwithstanding a well-developed normative framework, public authorities face challenges and obstacles in practice, hindering their effective implementation which would require further legal adaptation and transformation.

As the first EU country to include legally binding SPP requirements for all contracting authorities,[6] the Italian case may inspire other Member States on the transition towards mandatory SPP requirements. This chapter provides insights into the Italian public procurement framework, shedding light on both opportunities and challenges. The public procurement legal system is briefly presented (section II), followed by an overview of key national legislative steps towards mandatory SPP with a focus on environmental considerations (section III). Further, the core features, structure and the argument for the adoption of the CAMs are unpacked, exploring key implementation obstacles (section IV). To make sense of their practical application, selected rulings in Italian case law are scrutinised (section V). To conclude, the attention is on the way forward, reflecting on the choice between voluntary and mandatory in the Italian context (section VI).

II. A Brief Overview of the Italian Public Procurement Legal System

Public procurement in Italy represents an important share of GDP. Data from the Italian Anti Corruption Authority[7] (ANAC) shows that €169.9 trillion is spent yearly by over 22,000 public agencies at the central, regional and local levels. From 2015 to 2018, the public contracts' market value has increased by 23 per cent, representing a significant amount that should be leveraged to orientate the market towards more sustainable consumption and production.[8]

[5] D. Lgs. 18.04.2016 n. 50, Codice dei Contratti Pubblici. From the 1st of July 2023 a new Code is expected to enter into force (D.Lgs. 31.03.2023, n. 36, Codice dei Contratti Pubblici). The provisions discussed in this article have been inserted into Article 57 of the new Code.

[6] G Giannattasio 'Le fasi più critiche nelle procedure di gara: l'e-procurement può migliorare l'efficienza e la qualità nel ciclo degli acquisti?' [2022] *Riv. amministrazione in cammino* 35.

[7] ANAC, *Relazione Annuale 2020*, (2020).

[8] G Mazzantini, 'Analisi economica della spesa pubblica italiana' in L Fiorentino and A La Chimia (eds), *Il procurement delle pubbliche amministrazioni, tra innovazione e sostenibilità* (Napoli, Astrid, 2021).

Graph 1 Total market value of public tenders (superior to EUR40,000) 2015–2019, ANAC (2020)[9]

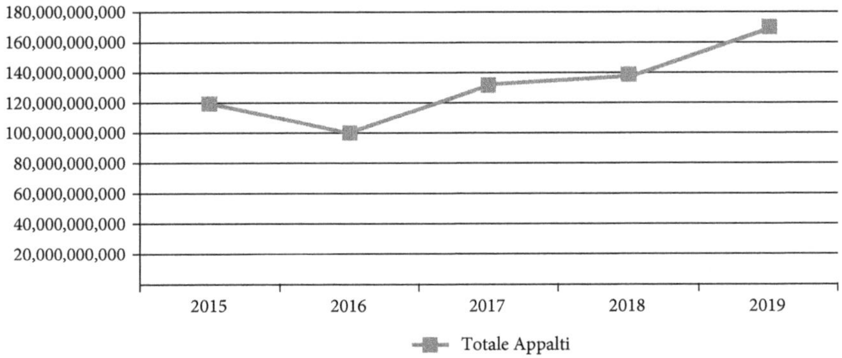

Pursuant to Article 117 of the Constitution, the state has exclusive competence to regulate competition in public procurement markets.[10] The law governing public contracts is provided by the Italian Public Contract Code (Codice dei Contratti Pubblici), adopted with Legislative Decree 50/2016, transposing the 2014 Public Procurement Directives. The Code was modified by Legislative Decree 57/2017 (Decreto Correttivo) and updated by Legislative Decree 76/2020 (Decreto Semplificazioni) and Legislative Decree 77/2021 (Decreto Semplificazioni PNRR). The Code applies to all types of public procurement and concession contracts related to goods, works, and services, both above and below the EU threshold. It lays down a number of procurement principles. Under Article 4, the award of public contracts must respect cost-effectiveness, efficacy, impartiality, equal treatment, transparency, proportionality, publicity, safeguard the environment and pursue energy efficiency.[11] Under Article 30, in designing the procurement economic consideration may take a backseat when conflicting with social, health, environmental and heritage protection considerations and the promotion of sustainable development.[12]

Although the applicable law is the same all over Italy, the actual management of procurement procedures is mostly decentralised. National and sub-national authorities and their sub-entities, including local healthcare authorities, are competent to award public contracts. The legislator has progressively introduced

[9] ANAC, Relazione Annuale 2019 (Camera dei Deputati Roma, 2 luglio 2020) 154, available at: www.anticorruzione.it/documents/91439/171942/Anac+Relazione+annuale+2020+su+attivit%C3%A0+2019+-+Relazione.pdf/587ffcc4-fc34-7f49-747f-2b248868d429?t=1652188932693.

[10] See also Codice dei Contratti Pubblici (2016), Art 2 *State, Regions and Autonomous Provinces legislative competences.*

[11] Codice dei Contratti Pubblici (2016), Art 4 *Principles relating to the award of excluded public contracts.*

[12] Codice dei Contratti Pubblici (2016), Art 30 *Principles for the award and execution of procurements and concessions.*

measures of centralisation.[13] All contracting authorities may award public works contracts (under €150,000) and supply and services contracts (under €40,000) but above those thresholds can do so only when holding a specific qualification. Alternatively, they can have recourse to central purchasing bodies. Amongst the 32 qualified central purchasing entities, Consip S.p.A. is the most relevant at the national level, acting as a national central purchasing body for frequently purchased supplies and services via framework agreements.[14]

III. The Road Towards Sustainable Public Procurement in the Italian Legal System

Following the 2014 Public Procurement Directives, the current Italian legislative framework contains multiple *possibilities* to include sustainability considerations.[15] Focusing specifically on the environmental dimension of Sustainable Public Procurement (SPP), also referred to as Green Public Procurement (GPP), the European Commission has referred to public procurement as a process whereby public authorities may seek to procure goods, services and works with a reduced environmental impact throughout their life cycle.[16] Such a definition has been gradually endorsed in Italy, first as a voluntary process and later becoming a mandatory legal requirement.[17] However, the path towards mandatory minimum social requirements is still ongoing, and so far only voluntary social criteria are included in the law.

A. Early-stage Developments in the EU and in the 2006 Public Contracts Code

Some developments towards progressive implementation of SPP in the EU, particularly with a focus on environmental protection, date back to the early 2000s. The EU Green Paper on Integrated Product Policy and Communication 302/2003[18] invited the Member States to adopt National Action Plans on Green Public

[13] G Racca 'Central Purchasing Bodies in Italy: Reluctance and Challenges' in C Risvig Hamer and M Comba (eds), *Centralising Public Procurement: The Approach of EU Member States* (Cheltenham, Edward Elgar, 2021).

[14] V Guerrieri 'Centralizzazione e sostenibilità: CONSIP e altri soggetti aggregatori' in L Fiorentino and A La Chimia (eds), *Il procurement delle pubbliche amministrazioni, tra innovazione e sostenibilità* (Napoli, Astrid, 2021).

[15] M Magri, 'La sostenibilità degli appalti pubblici come problema di coerenza' in A Maltoni (ed), *I contratti pubblici: La difficile stabilizzazione delle regole e la dinamica degli interessi* (Editoriale Scientifica, Napoli, 2020).

[16] Public Procurement for a Better Environment COM(2008) 400.

[17] R Caranta and S Marroncelli, 'Gli appalti pubblici tra mitigazione e resilienza: Il contributo del GPP alla lotta contro i cambiamenti climatici' [2021] *Riv. giuridica dell'ambiente* 23.i; Apolloni et al 'Is Public Procurement Going Green? Experiences and Open Issues' in G Piga and S Treumer (eds) *The Applied Law and Economics of Public Procurement* (Oxford, Routledge, 2014).

[18] Integrated Product Policy Building on Environmental Life-Cycle Thinking COM(2003) 302.

Procurement. The Directives in 2004 started the process of clarifying the legal possibilities to include sustainability considerations in procurement.[19]

At the national level, the Italian Code of Public Contracts (2006), implementing Directive 2004/18/EC, allowed for the use of sustainable considerations in specific provisions.[20] The Italian legislature did not stop at this, but paid specific attention to social and sustainable procurement in additional provisions,[21] such as in Article 2 on procurement principles. The Code introduced the possibility to link the Most Economically Advantageous Tender (MEAT) criterion to considerations inspired by social demands, environmental, health protection and the promotion of sustainable development (Article 83). Article 68 explicitly required that, wherever possible, technical specifications have to be defined in such a way as to take into account the criteria of environmental protection. Finally, embryonal environmental criteria were being developed by proactive public authorities. For instance, some Regional Environmental Authorities (ARPA) developed advanced criteria for specific procurements.

B. The National Action Plan on GPP

The National Action Plan on Green Public Procurement (NAP-GPP)[22] was adopted by the Ministry of the Environment in 2008. It marked a fundamental step to give effect to Communication 302/2003. Three objectives shape this plan: (1) the reduction of greenhouse gas emissions; (ii) the efficient use and preservation of natural resources; and (iii) the reduction of waste and hazardous substances, aiming to reach 30 per cent of green purchasing by 2009. In this regard, the Ministry committed to defining non-mandatory minimum environmental requirements applicable to purchasing procedures above and below the EU threshold for eleven product categories, identified by the Finance Act (2007).[23] Such requirements were inspired by the EU GPP criteria.[24]

The NAP-GPP was revised in 2013, emphasising the need to reinforce commitment not only to green requirements but also to social considerations,[25] and leading to the adoption of the Italian Guide on the Integration of Social Aspects in

[19] A Appolloni 'GPP in Italy: As an Environmental Policy Toll: Innovation Design Issues' (2012).

[20] Recitals 1, 5, 6, 27, 29, 33, 43, 44 and 46 and Arts 23, 26, 27, 48, 53.

[21] Art 42.1.f Technical and professional ability of suppliers; Art 44 Labels and environmental management systems; Art 69 Contract performance conditions; Art 83.1.e MEAT.

[22] Ministry of the Environment, National Action Plan on Green Public Procurement at www.mase.gov.it/pagina/piano-dazione-nazionale-sul-gpp.

[23] Art 1(1127) Law 296/2006: 1) furniture; 2) construction materials; 3) road maintenance; 4) green areas; 5) lighting and heating; 6) electronics; 7) textiles; 8) stationery; 9) catering and food; 10) sanitation; 11) transports.

[24] Public Procurement for a Better Environment (n 16); Sustainable Consumption and Production and Sustainable Industrial Policy Action Plan COM(2008) 397.

[25] L Cellura, T Cellura and G Galluzzo, *Manuale per l'applicazione dei criteri sociali negli appalti pubblici* (Milano, Appalti & Contratti Maggioli Editore, 2022).

Public Procurement.[26] This anticipated the EU Strategy Europe 2020: A strategy for smart, sustainable and inclusive growth, outlined the urgency for an ecological transition but also a socially inclusive revolution, further emphasised in the EU publication, Buying Social – A Guide to Taking Account of Social Considerations in Public Procurement (2021).

Law 221/2015 on Environmental provisions to promote green economy measures and to limit the excessive use of natural resources (Collegato Ambientale) marked a turning point. It introduced a new provision in the 2006 Public Contracts Code (Article 68-bis), laying down an obligation for *all* public administrations to include mandatory environmental requirements under specific procurement categories. Paragraph 1 of this provision obliged the contracting authorities to fully comply with CAMs in a few specific sectors,[27] while paragraph 2 provided for other categories[28] where CAMs had to be applied to at least 50 per cent of the value of the tender-both below and above the EU threshold.

C. The 2016 Public Contracts Code

The fundamental shift towards binding SPP criteria for broader categories was the adoption of the new Public Contracts Code (Code) in 2016, which transposed the 2014 Public Procurement Directives.[29] The Code emphasises the role of public procurement in protecting the environment. As anticipated, Article 4 lists environmental protection and energy transition as general principles related to the award of public contracts. Other provisions in the Code further strengthen the focus on environmental considerations in procurement: Article 34 on energy and environmental sustainability criteria, as amended by Article 23 of Legislative Decree 56/2017, is central when discussing mandatory requirements in public procurement law.[30] Paragraph 1 mandates that contracting entities shall contribute to the achievement of environmental goals provided for in the NAP-GPP, by including CAMs *at least* as technical specifications and contract performance clauses in public procurement documents. Furthermore, paragraph 2 makes it possible to include CAMs as award criteria when adopting MEAT, thereby fostering quality, innovation and sustainable development.[31] Finally, paragraph 3 contains an important feature when it comes to mandatory requirements. It provides that the

[26] Ministry of the Environment, D.M. 6.06.2012, Guida per l'integrazione degli aspetti sociali negli appalti publicci.

[27] Public lighting, electronics, energy services for buildings.

[28] Waste management, toner cartridges, green spaces, paper, catering and food, cleanings, textiles, office furniture.

[29] SPP in the Classic Directive: Arts 18.2, 20, 42, 43, 47, 67, 68 and 69.

[30] Technical specifications (Art 68.5); labels (Art 69); exclusion grounds (Art 80); means of proof (Arts 85(f) and 86); quality assurance (Art 93); MEAT (Art 95.2); LCC (Art 96.3).

[31] S Arrowsmith and P Kunzlik, 'Public Procurement and Horizontal Policies in EC Law: General Principles' in S Arrowsmith and P Kunzlik (eds), *Social and Environmental Policies in EC Procurement Law: New Directives and New Directions* (Cambridge, Cambridge University Press, 2009).

CAMs must be applied to all public contracts of any value. Accordingly, it specifies that the obligations of paragraphs 1 and 2 shall apply to the award of any contract, whatever its value, in relation to the categories of supplies, services or works falling within the defined subject matter of the CAMs.

IV. Unpacking the CAMs: Potential Transformation and Current Barriers

A detailed step-by-step procedure is envisaged under the NAP-GPP to design and review the CAMs.[32] The Ministry of the Environment has a key role in the coordination of this process through the GPP Management Committee, which is responsible for follow-up on the NAP-GPP implementation with planning duties and operational coordination functions between working groups and a GPP Standing Panel.[33] Specific working groups are appointed for each category, composed of technical experts, public administrators, and representatives from research centres, universities, trade unions, and business associations to conduct technical and scientific evaluations and develop the criteria after technical consultation with qualified experts. The final package of technical criteria, integrated with methodological and operational instructions on purchasing procedures and environmental targets, is shared with the GPP Management Committee and the Standing Panel for evaluation and review. After having heard comments from the Ministry of Development and the Ministry of Economics and Finance feedback, the Ministry of the Environment enacts the CAM through an ad hoc Ministerial Decree.

Each set of mandatory criteria applies to a specific procurement category, constituting substantive minimum mandatory requirements, designed taking into account the EU GPP criteria. As substantive requirements, CAMs are regulated by the law and required by the public procurement procedure, differently from procedural requirements which are preferred in other EU countries, as in the case of the Dutch law.[34]

Today, the CAMs apply to 18 categories: office furniture; urban furniture; nappies; working shoes and leatherware; paper; ink cartridges; public works; street lighting (maintenance and management); street lighting (services); indoor lighting, heating and air-conditioning; cleaning services and rental and cleaning of linen; urban waste; food and catering; sanitisation of hospitals; printers; textiles; vehicles; green spaces. Despite their technical nature, these criteria are to be seen as flexible instruments.[35] The criteria are, indeed, updated periodically based on the

[32] NAP-GPP, s 4.4.

[33] NAP-GPP, s 6: composed of the Ministry of Environment, Ministry of Economic Development, Ministry of Economy and Finance, Consip, ENEA, ARPA, ISPRA, Regions.

[34] P Heijnsbroek, 'The Netherlands: Obligations to Justify the Lowest Price and to Create as Much Societal Value as Possible', ch 12 in this volume.

[35] L Cioni, 'Criteri ambientali minimi – L'inosservanza dei criteri ambientali minimi é una causa di esclusione?' (2020) 10 *Giur. It.* 2237.

maturity of the market segment, the public expenditures volume and the potential environmental impacts. A number of additional CAMs are under revision[36] and currently waiting for final approval by the Ministry of the Environment, whereas new categories have been proposed for additional sectors.[37]

In technical terms, each set of requirements displays peculiarities adapted to specific characteristics of the relevant product or service category, nonetheless, they all share a common structure. The first section of each CAM contains general references to the relevant environmental and, if applicable social,[38] legal sources. Guidance on how to include environmental considerations from the start of the procurement process is provided as well, whilst also acknowledging the importance of a careful assessment of the purchasing need and market analysis as a crucial reality check.[39] In the second section, the specific criteria are unpacked in substantive terms, envisaging 'basic criteria' – applicable to the contract subject matter, the selection of bidders, technical specifications, contract performance conditions – and 'award criteria'.

Throughout the public procurement cycle, six phases can be identified as general entry points[40] for the application of CAMs: environmental considerations can be included in the *procurement planning* by conducting environmental impact assessments, taking into consideration life-cycle costs and organising preliminary market consultations to understand the required sustainability levels. When designing the *subject matter of the contract*, the next phase is to outline the intention to purchase environmentally-friendly products by requiring a reference to environmental considerations in the title and the subject matter of the contract. Furthermore, precise mandatory *technical specifications* are provided by CAMs, which even go as far as providing model clauses to be included in public procurement documents. Specific *selection criteria*, which prove a candidate's technical capacity to perform the contract and aim to avoid any possible damage to the environment, are also an option. However, as opposed to technical specifications, these selection criteria are not mandatory. Subsequently, contracting authorities are encouraged to adopt quality-based award criteria and to allocate additional points for environmental and social considerations.[41] Finally, specific *contract performance conditions* and contract clauses constitute mandatory requirements for the contracting authorities in the execution of the contract.[42]

[36] Waste management; interior furniture.

[37] Under current definition: urban furniture, PC and server, design services and construction work, public transport services. Newly proposed CAMs: cultural events; food and beverage sales services (indoor bars and vending machines); construction and maintenance of roads, energy services for buildings.

[38] Social criteria and human rights recommended under CAMs: Office Furniture, Workshoes and Leatherware, Food and Catering, Textiles, Green Spaces.

[39] W Janssen, 'Regulating the Pre-procurement Phase: Context and Perspectives', in KV Thai (ed), *International Public Procurement – Innovation and Knowledge Sharing* (Cham, Springer, 2015).

[40] T Cellura, *L'applicazione dei criteri ambientali minimi negli appalti pubblici – Gli acquisti verdi dopo il correttivo al nuovo codice degli appalti* (Milano, Appalti & Contratti Maggioli Editore, 2018).

[41] S Colombari, 'Le considerazioni ambientali nell'aggiudicazione delle concessioni e degli appalti pubblici' (2019) 1 *Urbanistica e appalti* 5.

[42] M Cozzio, 'Appalti pubblici e sostenibilità: Orientamenti UE e il modello Italiano' (2021) 6 *Giornale dir. amm.* 721.

In conclusion, the CAMs contain substantive minimum mandatory requirements for technical specifications and contract performance clauses. They are powerful steering tools for the contracting authorities, as they shape public procurement procedures in the direction of sustainable development. Notwithstanding their potential, barriers are also faced by contracting authorities which hinders their effective application. Quantitative and qualitative studies on SPP and more specifically on GPP uptake in Italy have shown the mismatch between the potential benefits of the CAMs and the practical barriers in implementation, showing lights and shadows of their effective application.

In 2018, for the first time, the Italian GPP Observatory[43] which tracks GPP implementation at the local level,[44] conducted a quantitative study showing that only €40 billion out of €170 billion was spent by the public administration for SPP, namely less than one-fourth. The survey, collecting 1,048 responses from provincial main cities (Comuni Capoluogo) and municipalities with more than 15,000 inhabitants, revealed that 29.38 per cent of them had not applied CAMs in any procurement category, despite the recently introduced legal obligation. The 2021 survey showed slightly improved results.[45] Nonetheless, a scarce capacity to monitor the adoption of CAMs has emerged: more than 60 per cent of municipalities with more than 15,000 inhabitants out of 238 respondents replied that they do not have any monitoring system in place.

The survey also monitored the implementation of individual CAMs categories, revealing unequal application. The most adopted requirements are: printers (66 per cent), paper (73 per cent) and cleaning services (61 per cent). The least applied: building (39 per cent rarely, 29 per cent never), furniture (22 per cent rarely, 28 per cent never), textiles (31 per cent rarely, 27 per cent never), workshoes and leatherware (32 per cent rarely, 31 per cent never). These data need to be contextualised. A lower rate may be explained by the more recent adoption of a specific CAM. For instance, the criteria on workshoes entered into force late in 2018 and the data refers to public contracts 'awarded' in 2019. Recourse to framework agreement possibly set up by central purchasing bodies might also entail delays in adopting the CAMs as a framework agreement will set the rules for contracts to be awarded for the next three to four years.

The national survey also highlighted that key challenges hindering a smooth application of CAMs are linked to three critical aspects: (1) lack of training and technical expertise; (2) difficulties in designing and managing 'green tenders'; and (3) the lack of potential economic operators available on the (local) market.

[43] Osservatorio Appalti Verdi at www.appaltiverdi.net/category/monitoraggio/.

[44] S Falocco, M Mancini per Osservatorio Appalti Verdi, 2021. *I Numeri Del Green Public Procurement In Italia. Legambiente e Fondazione Ecosistemi.*

[45] Respondents: 89 chief municipalities, 238 minor municipalities, 99 environmental protected areas, 40 public healthcare agencies.

Graph 2 Obstacles in CAMs application (%): Italian GPP Observatory (2021)[46]

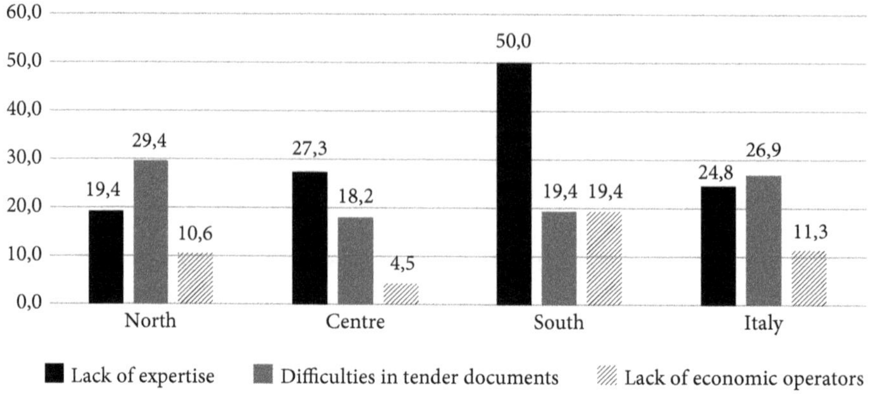

Other qualitative studies have revealed further challenges. Semi-structured interviews were conducted by the author with regional and national contracting authorities for a 2022 transnational project on SPP of the Chair of Public Contracts Law and Sustainable Development of the University of Lyon.[47] The results showed additional barriers starting from the fact that limited resources and organisational capacity are allocated to SPP within each contracting authority, even in central and regional purchasing bodies.[48] Further difficulties are related to monitoring and verification of sustainability considerations, requiring additional burdens, time, and costs for these authorities. Nonetheless, an increasing number of contracting authorities gradually recognise the benefits of life-cycle costs. Including considerations on environmental and social externalities is a key to change from business-as-usual and perceiving SPP costs as investments. A final critical aspect relates to a lack of enforcement leaving leeway to illicit practices. This is linked to marginal official national monitoring and supervision by the ANAC on the application of Article 34 – although the Public Contracts Code explicitly provides for it (Article 213.9). The Article explicitly provides that the ANAC Observatory of Public Works, Services and Supplies Contracts, supervises compliance with the Code and monitors the application of CAMs and the achievement of the objectives set out in the NAP-GPP. In case of non-compliance, sanctions may be applied as provided by Article 213.13, which are discussed in paragraph 5.2. ANAC has

[46] S Falocco et al, *I numeri del green public procurement in Italia* (n 44) 51. Available at: www.legambiente.it/wp-content/uploads/2020/10/I-numeridel-Green-Public-Procurement-in-Italia_rapporto2020.pdf.

[47] CEPDD Project, Chair of Public Contracts Law, University of Lyon 3, France, funded research project by Agence Universitaire de la Francophonie (2022). Countries involved: Canada, Quebec; Netherlands; France; Italy; Portugal; Switzerland.

[48] R Vluggen et al 'Sustainable Public Procurement External Forces and Accountability' (2019) 11 *Sustainability* 5696; O Chiappinelli, F Gruner and G Weber, 'Green Public Procurement: Climate Provisions in Public Tenders Can Help Reduce German Carbon Emissions' (2019) 9 *DIW Weekly Report* 433.

set up a monitoring platform to collect data on CAMs, which, however, is closed for maintenance, postponing the official monitoring and creating a space for legal uncertainty.

V. Making Sense of the Application of the CAMs: The Role of the Italian Case Law

Six years after the entry into force of the Code, the administrative case law has shed light on important interpretative principles related to the concrete application of CAMs. The litigation took place both at the regional (Regional Administrative Tribunals, TAR) and national level (Consiglio di Stato). Case law plays a relevant role in consolidating substantive SPP practices.[49] The courts have scrutinised the legal value and potentially controversial aspects of CAMs, thereby supporting the conclusion that it is a dynamic and evolving regulatory framework that can be conceived as a living law.[50]

The Annual Monitoring Report on Administrative Justice[51] collects quantitative data on case law litigated by Consiglio di Stato and TARs between 2016 and 2020. On average around 10,000 cases per year (with a peak of more than 12,000 in 2019) have been decided at the second instance. A National Study of the Impacts of Administrative Case Law on Public Procurement highlighted that public procurement-related rulings in 2017 amounted to 3,457, whereas the total amount of public tenders was 255,151 (totalling at 1.4 per cent).[52] In 2018, 3,603 cases were litigated following 238,101 procedures (1.5 per cent). The overall number of rulings by both Consiglio di Stato and TARs explicitly mentioning the 'Minimum Environmental Requirements' (CAMs) is relatively low: only 33 in 2017 and 46 in 2018. Most recently, the number has only slightly increased, even considering the expansion of CAMs: 79 in 2019, 56 in 2020, and 84 in 2021.[53] Such data suggests a relatively peaceful implementation of CAMs in practice.

Amongst others, particular attention in the case law has been focussed on clarifying CAM's legal value, and on the possible consequences of non-compliance by both the contracting authorities and the economic operators.[54]

[49] G Montedoro, 'Appalti e diritto comunitario nella giurisprudenza del Consiglio di Stato' in A Maltoni (ed), *I contratti pubblici* (Napoli, Editoriale Scientifica, 2020).

[50] T Murphy, 'Living Law, Normative Pluralism, and Analytic Jurisprudence' (2012) 3 *Jurisprudence* 177.

[51] Consiglio di Stato, *Relazione sull'attività della Giustizia Amministrativa 2020* (2021).

[52] G Veltri, Analisi di Impatto del Contenzioso Amministrativo in Materia di Appalti – Biennio 2017/2018 (2019).

[53] Giustizia Amministrativa Consiglio di Stato Tribunali Amministrativi Regionali at www.giustizia-amministrativa.it/web/guest/dcsnprr?p_p_id=GaSearch_INSTANCE_2NDgCF3zWBwk&p_p_lifecycle=1&p_p_state=normal&p_p_mode=view&_GaSearch_INSTANCE_2NDgCF3zWBwk_javax.portlet.action=searchProvvedimenti&p_auth=ImqnCisL.

[54] Creiamo PA, 'Il percorso tecnico-specialistico per L'attuazione del green public procurement nelle pubbliche amministrazioni – Sintesi dei risultati ottenuti' [2020] *La giurisprudenza Italiana* 45.

A. Uncovering Article 34's Content: Mandatory or Voluntary in Nature?

Since 2017, the courts have interpreted Article 34, thereby elucidating its core content and the legal value of CAMs. The case law has clarified that CAMs are a secondary source of law (lex specialis) set up by Ministerial Decrees and, accordingly, hierarchically subordinate to the Code.[55] Other acts of a different nature cannot modify or supplement the provisions contained in the Ministerial Decree.[56] Furthermore, considering the specific subject matters of the requirements, the CAMs are mandatory for the peculiar procurement category provided for by the Ministerial Decree.[57] Nonetheless, contracting authorities can freely decide to adapt such requirements *by analogy* to other procurement categories. This discretion is not unlimited but must be assessed on a case-by-case basis given possible limitations to competition.[58]

The mandatory nature of CAMs has been confirmed by multiple cases. TAR-Veneto referred to CAM as an 'imperative and cogent rule'.[59] Consiglio di Stato, on a dispute related to energy services procurement, has clarified Article 34(1) conditions of application: contracting authorities are not only obliged to pursue *general* environmental sustainability objectives, but they must do so in accordance with the procedures and minimum criteria set out in the Ministerial Decree introducing the specific CAM at stake.[60] Furthermore, on the discretionary margins of CAMs, the Court highlighted that it is absolutely correct and appropriate for the contracting authority to pursue its own needs, but it is not within its discretion to decide whether and how to pursue environmental objectives, given that the law requires it to comply with the CAM.

The voluntary nature of Article 34(2) may create ambiguity on the specific legal value of award criteria. Both TAR-Abruzzo and the Consiglio di Stato in a dispute on food and drink vending machines have recognised that *at least* technical specifications and contract performance clauses in the CAMs are binding.[61] The mandatory value of Article 34(1) is, however, distinct from the voluntary nature of Article 34(2) recommending that award criteria are 'taken into account' in the evaluation of MEAT. The Court also clarified that the selection criteria suggested in the CAMs are not binding. Another ruling of the Consiglio di Stato clarified that there is no obligation to adopt the award criteria listed in the Ministerial Decree, nor does it require strict correspondence between them and the evaluation criteria of the technical offer contained

[55] NAP-GPP 13.
[56] Cons. Stato, sec. VI, 27.03.2019, n. 2036.
[57] TAR Toscana, sec. II, 27.11.2018, n. 1531.
[58] Cons. Stato, sec. V, 29.012018, n. 604.
[59] TAR Veneto, sec. III, 20.02.2019, n. 142.
[60] Cons.Stato, sec. V, 3.02.2021, n. 972.
[61] TAR-Abruzzo–Pescara, sec. I, 20.11.2017, n. 330; Cons. Stato, sec. III, 17.04.2018, n. 2317.

in the lex specialis.[62] Thus, the requirements have a certain flexibility in their structure by mixing mandatory and voluntary requirements.

B. Contracting Authorities and Non-Compliance with CAMs

Non-compliance with the CAMs, such as incorrect application or total/partial absence of mandatory requirements means that the decision taken in the public procurement procedure may be annulled and the same contract may be declared ineffective.

Non-compliance may relate to the incorrect application of a specific CAM by the contracting authority. For instance, TAR-Lombardia and the Consiglio di Stato have ruled on an incorrect procedure related to energy performance contracts for municipality buildings.[63] The call for tender was considered unlawful and, therefore, annulled as in breach of the relevant CAM it did not include the requirement of energy certification of the building.

TAR-Toscana ruled on the award of a public lightning contract contested by the applicant who ranked second.[64] The appellant complained that the winning tenderer should have been excluded, or at least penalised in the award scores because it did not comply with technical specifications requiring 'luminous intensity class G3', pursuant to the specific CAM. The Court concluded that the technical specifications complied with Article 34, but the contracting authority failed to check that the bid did not comply with the technical specifications.

An incorrect application and non-compliance may also be found in connection with the distortion of competition. TAR-Lombardia expressly outlined the need for the contracting authority to carry out a prior in-depth investigation – especially through preliminary market surveys (Article 66) – to verify the availability of the products on the market and the appropriateness of the tender price to avoid 'unreasonable and impossible requests, with possible consequent distortion of competition'.[65]

C. The CAMs as Minimum Requirements of the Technical Offer

The case law has clarified that technical offers that do not comply with the minimum environmental criteria must be excluded pursuant to Article 94 of the Code. The provision, transposing Article 56 of the Classic Directive on general principles of selection and award,[66] mandates that a contract shall be awarded after having

[62] Cons. Stato, sec. VI, 4.04.2019, n. 2344.
[63] TAR Lombardia–Milano, sec. I, 24.04.2020, n. 685 and Cons. Stato, sec. V, 3.02.2021, n. 972.
[64] TAR Toscana, sec. I, 14.05.2018, n. 645.
[65] TAR Lombardia-Milano, sec. IV, 12.02.2018, n. 403.
[66] TAR Veneto, Sec. III, 29.05.2020, n. 481.

verified that: a) the tender complies with the requirements and conditions set out in the call for tender, in the invitation to bid and in the public procurement documents; and b) the tender comes from a tenderer not excluded (Article 80) and fulfilling the selection criteria set by the contracting authority (Article 83).

The case law and the literature have investigated the interconnection between CAMs, non-compliant-tenders and possible exclusion from the procedure. TRGA Trentino Alto-Adige considered whether CAMs are the minimum essential requirements of the technical offer and at which stage their means of proof must be required.[67] Referring to specific provisions of the lex specialis, it was not clear whether the contracting authority could exclude tenders that did not comply with the specific CAM. To provide a concrete answer to the appellant's claims, the panel had to resolve a classification problem. The law does not offer clear indications on the question of whether technical information in the Ministerial Decrees must be considered *essential* requirements of the technical offer or if they can also be a corollary. In its ruling, the Court answered in the affirmative: non-compliance with the CAMs would result in the exclusion of the tenderer offer, since CAMs are considered as minimum requirements to participate in the tender. Consequently, non-compliance with the Ministerial Decree would cause the exclusion of the offer,[68] even in the absence of an explicit provision that regulates this.[69]

Building on these precedents and adhering to a pattern of using ineffectiveness well beyond what is required by the EU Remedies Directives, a recent judgment of the Consiglio di Stato has declared ineffective a contract concluded following an award procedure which had not incorporated the relevant CAMs.[70]

Still related to the verification of minimum environmental requirements, another dispute has clarified that proof of compliance with the CAM may also be required before the final award, as it does not relate to either subjective requirements of participation to the tender, or the evaluation criteria to be used for the award of the contract; the contracting authority, indeed, is required to carry out the necessary checks in the preparatory phase of the execution of the contract.[71]

In conclusion, although the general rate of litigation seems limited and this aspect could be explained by the rather short period of time since the Corrective Decree[72] has been adopted, it could also suggest a positive trend. Including sustainability considerations in the procurement process, thus, is not creating excessive litigation. This could be a sign of an ongoing paradigm shift towards more sustainable production and consumption from both public buyers and suppliers thanks to the introduction of mandatory requirements.

[67] T.R.G.A. Trentino-Alto Adige, Sez. Trento, 14.05.2020, n. 66.

[68] Cons. Stato, sec. V, 2.08.2019, n. 5505.

[69] R De Nictolis, *I nuovi appalti pubblici* (Bologna, Zanichelli, 2017) 1054.

[70] Cons. Stato, Sez. III, 14 Ottobre 2022, n. 8773; see A Iurascu, 'How Will the Adoption of Mandatory GPP Criteria Change the Game? Lessons from the Italian Experience' EPPPL 1/2023, 1.

[71] Cons. Stato, sec. VI 27.03.2019, n. 2036.

[72] Consiglio Nazionale della Green Economy, 'L'applicazione del GPP a un anno dal nuovo codice degli appalti' (2017).

VI. Conclusion

Having explored the journey towards SPP in the Italian legal ecosystem, the focus has been on clarifying the content, legal value and application of the CAMs. Their adoption inspired by the EU GPP criteria represents an innovative development in the EU scenario characterised by fragmented and diversified approaches in the EU Member States. Exploring the gradual shift from voluntary to mandatory requirements, Italy leads the way in this transformation, as the first country in the EU to have required the mandatory application of substantive minimum sustainability requirements under national public procurement law. Particularly, Article 34 is the core provision in this process, requiring contracting authorities to introduce *at least* technical specifications and contract clauses related to minimum environmental requirements.

Despite the advanced normative approach, Italy faces challenges in the effective implementation of CAMs. The Italian GPP Observatory has monitored the CAMs uptake, showing difficulties in implementation by municipalities, related to lack of expertise, training and capacity, together with obstacles in engaging the market and in effective monitoring. Further ambiguities and margins of discretion have been raised by the case law, playing a pivotal role in consolidating Article 34's legal value. Despite the challenges, a peculiar mutual dynamic process is helping to gradually root down a method for contracting authorities: on one side, embryonal environmental criteria developed internally by single organisations and the EU GPP criteria have fed a process of higher standardisation led by the Ministry of Environment through CAMs. On the other hand, this process has inspired the adoption of a similar method also for specific tenders of procurement categories falling outside CAMs, showing that CAMs can function as drivers of transformation.

What is the way forward then? The future seems promising, considering recent constitutional developments and the potential of the National Recovery and Resilience Plan (PNRR), which suggests a way ahead for sustainable development. The recent amendment to the Constitution, by Constitutional Law n. 44/2022,[73] has elevated the 'protection of the environment, biodiversity and ecosystems, even in the interest of future generations' to primary constitutional value. Furthermore, Article 41 on constitutional economic rights and duties now states that economic initiatives shall not be carried out 'in such a way as to damage health and the environment' suggesting a stronger commitment to shift to a sustainable consumption and production paradigm.[74] Finally, the Italian PNRR, under the Green Revolution and Ecological Transition mission, has outlined the relevance of SPP. Reforms are envisaged to rationalise public contracts regulations and to

[73] Constitutional Law 22.02.2022, n. 44 'Modifiche agli Articoli 9 e 41 della Costituzione in Materia di Tutela dell'ambiente'.

[74] L Fontanesi, 'Modification of Italian Constitution: Environment Elevated to Protected Primary Value' (2022) XII *National Law Review*.

streamline the implementation of the CAMs,[75] providing more technical support to contracting authorities and expanding requirements to new sectors, such as the field of cultural events.

Despite the present barriers and challenges, a shift from voluntary to mandatory is gradually happening thanks to CAMs, encouraging contracting authorities to *lead by example* and to *purchase by example* and this could inspire other Member States or relevant EU proposals. Nonetheless, to ensure a truly transformational process, further legal interpretation, continual updates and expansion to new sectors and mandatory social considerations will be necessary, taking into constant account obstacles encountered by contracting authorities.

[75] Osservatorio Appalti Verdi, 'GPP ai tempi del PNRR. Gli acquisti verdi per promuovere la sostenibilità ambientale e sociale' (2021).

12

The Netherlands: Obligations to Justify the Lowest Price and to Create as Much Societal Value as Possible

PAUL HEIJNSBROEK

I. Introduction

Sustainable Public Procurement (SPP) has been a relevant topic in Dutch public procurement practice for several years. The activity in this context has mainly been focused on stimulating SPP within the current legal framework, but discussions on mandatory requirements have surfaced as well. This is not surprising given the approximate €86 billion that is spent annually by Dutch contracting authorities.[1]

At the core of the legal framework lies the Dutch Procurement Act 2012 (Aanbestedingswet 2012; DPA 2012). This is the first 'mature' public procurement legislation in the Netherlands since the introduction of the Public Procurement Directives in the 1970s. Before the DPA 2012, Dutch procurement legislation consisted of a relatively short reference to those Directives, followed by – nearly identical – copies of the 2004 Classic and Utilities Directives in separate decrees, as well as a separate Act for the Remedies Directives. The DPA 2012 aimed to end this 'patchwork' of different laws and implement the Classic Directive, Concession Directive, Utilities Directive and Remedies Directives – each in their own chapter of the DPA 2012.

In addition, the DPA 2012 contains a first chapter with general principles and rules, which also applies below the EU thresholds. This chapter includes the principle of proportionality. More concrete rules on proportionality are included in the so-called Proportionality Guide.[2] The DPA 2012 prescribes that any deviations from those rules have to be justified, which is commonly referred to as the legislative 'comply or explain' approach. The Proportionality Guide also contains

[1] Monitor of Procurement Procedures in the Netherlands, 2017–2019 at www.pianoo.nl/nl/document/19201/monitor-aanbestedingen-nederland-2017-2019.

[2] An English version of the Proportionality Guide is available at www.pianoo.nl/en/legal-framework/proportionality-guide.

many examples and explanations of what is to be considered proportionate. The guide looks at proportionality from both an effectiveness ('best value for taxpayers' money') and a legitimacy point of view.

In the original proposal for the DPA 2012, innovation and sustainability were acknowledged as goals of public procurement. However, stimulating innovation and sustainability was seen as a matter of professionalising public procurement rather than something that required new rules.[3] In other words, the current rules could be used for innovation and sustainability and did not need to be altered or extended.[4]

There have been various voluntary initiatives to stimulate SPP. For example, the paragraph on sustainability in the Proportionality Guide. This paragraph contains guidelines on how to set proportionate requirements and criteria relating to sustainability if a contracting authority wishes to use them. Another example is the so-called Sustainable Procurement Manifesto (Manifest Maatschappelijk Verantwoord Opdrachtgeven en Inkopen), which is a voluntary policy document that enables contracting authorities to set ambitions and goals relating to SPP.[5] Furthermore, noteworthy are the guidance on the website of the Dutch Public Procurement Expertise Centre (PIANOo) with regard to SPP, the development of a uniform social return policy as part of a broad action plan to professionalise the public procurement sector,[6] and a 'national plan for sustainable procurement 2021–2025' that contains various policy goals.[7] This national plan refers to an evaluation by the Ministry of Foreign Affairs that has shown that the lack of a mandatory system of action plans, measurable goals and monitoring based on a solid overarching strategy is the largest obstacle to SPP's success in the Netherlands.[8]

The DPA 2012 also contains mandatory public procurement requirements relating to SPP, which is contrary to many of the other Member States in which only legal possibilities for SPP exist.[9] There are two relevant provisions that both concern horizontal procedural mandatory requirements. The first is Article 2.114(4), that states that if contracting authorities choose the lowest price or cost (eg, life-cycle costing) as the award criterion, they need to justify that choice

[3] Kamerstukken II 2009/10, 32 440, nr. 3, para 3.5.

[4] For an overview of the possibilities within the legal framework at that time, see P Heijnsbroek, 'Aanbesteding bij gebiedsontwikkeling en duurzaamheid' in N Teesing (ed), *Duurzame gebiedsontwikkeling: Over vormen van regulering en de rol van aanbesteding* (Den Haag, Boom Juridische Uitgevers, 2013).

[5] The previous version of the manifesto is available in English at www.pianoo.nl/en/sustainable-public-procurement/developments/sustainable-procurement-manifesto-2016–2020-text; See also M Houweling and B Tonino, 'Maatschappelijk verantwoord inkopen: van MVI naar MVOI' (2022) 4 *VGR* 131.

[6] Actieagenda Beter Aanbesteden; available on at www.rijksoverheid.nl/onderwerpen/aanbesteden/documenten/kamerstukken/2019/09/04/overzicht-acties-beter-aanbesteden.

[7] Nationaal Plan MVI 2021–2025 at www.pianoo.nl/sites/default/files/media/documents/2021-02/plan_mvi_opdrachtgeven_met_ambitie_inkopen_met_impact_2021–2025-jan2021.pdf.

[8] ibid 19.

[9] G Botta, 'Italy: Leading the Way towards Mandatory Sustainable Public Procurement through Minimum Environmental Criteria', ch 11 in this volume; X Lazo-Vitoria, 'Spain: Transitioning towards Sustainable Public Procurement Mandatory Requirements', ch 13 in this volume.

in the public procurement documents. The second provision is Article 1.4(2), that requires contracting authorities to ensure that as much societal value as possible is created for public resources.

This chapter examines both provisions in detail, in theory as well as in practice (sections II and III), to see whether they can be effectively used to mandate SPP (section IV).[10] As will be concluded below, this appears to be possible in theory, but there are various obstacles in practice. This potentially also offers lessons learnt for the EU and other countries aiming to mandate SPP in the future.

II. Obligation to Justify the Lowest Price or Cost as the Award Criterion (Article 2.114(4))

Originally, the proposal for the DPA 2012 followed the 2004 Public Procurement Directives and gave contracting authorities a free choice between: (a) the lowest price; and (b) the best price-quality ratio. This was however amended by the Dutch House of Representatives (Tweede Kamer) into a preference for the latter: if contracting authorities choose the lowest price as the award criterion, they need to justify that choice in the public procurement documents.[11] The obligation only applies above the EU thresholds.

The obligation was introduced with a view to increasing sustainable public procurement. According to the explanatory note, the government needs to make a change with regard to sustainable and innovative public procurement. This change would include more consideration for the use phase of a product, 'real' sustainability and less energy consumption. The note states that the government should challenge the market to propose the most optimal solutions by providing room for innovation and sustainability. This should be done by a focus on the best price-quality ratio, including the total cost of ownership and a life cycle analysis of products instead of the purchase price or the lowest price.

Following the 2014 Public Procurement Directives, the possibility of using the lowest cost as the award criterion was added to the DPA 2012 (eg, life-cycle costing). As a result of another amendment by the House of Representatives, the choice for that award criterion also needs to be justified (ie, the same applies to

[10] See on this subject also: WA Janssen and G Bouwman, 'Legislating Societal Value in Dutch Public Procurement Law: From Symbolism to Substance' (2020) 2 *Public Procurement Law Review* 91. In Dutch: E Verweij, 'Attero zuid / Gemeente tynaarlo' (note) (2014) 13 *JAAN*; AJ van Heeswijck, 'De verplichting tot het creëren van zoveel mogelijk "Maatschappelijke waarde" voor de publieke middelen' (2015) 22 *TBR* 130; CEC Jansen, 'De inschrijver als hoeder van het algemeen belang?' (2015) 80 *TBR* 463; WA Janssen, 'Verplicht maatschappelijk verantwoord aanbestedesn. Een eerste verkenning van een paradigmaverandering' (2020) 3 *TA* 19; WA Janssen and N van Wijk-Gilst, 'Maatschappelijk verantwoord aanbesteden: Van mogelijkheden naar verplichtingen in een veranderende maatschappelijke context' (2021) 13 *TBR*; WA Janssen and EE Neele, 'De (in)effectiviteit van open en concrete aanbestedingsrechtelijke verplichtingen in de strijd tegen klimaatverandering' (2021) 16 *TBR*; AJ van Heeswijck, 'Handhaving van duurzaamheidsverplichtingen bij aanbestedingen' (2021) 20 *TBR* 161.

[11] Kamerstukken II 2011/12, 32 440, nr. 25.

the lowest cost as to the lowest price).[12] The respective Members of Parliament felt that the lowest cost as an award criterion is in its essence the lowest price of a product during its entire life cycle – and should therefore be treated the same as the lowest price award criterion.[13] As a result, the best price-quality ratio is the general rule, from which any deviation – that is, lowest price or cost – has to be justified ('comply or explain').

The provision in the DPA 2012 is only procedural and lacks a concrete, substantive norm to assess in which circumstances a contracting authority may decide to use the lowest price. This has made it difficult to challenge and review a contracting authority's decision to opt for the lowest price or cost. To fill this gap, the Proportionality Guide states that the lowest price or cost is the wiser choice if there really are not sufficient distinguishing criteria on which tenderers can provide added value.[14] The Committee of Public Procurement Experts (Commissie van Aanbestedingsexperts, CPPE) has tried to provide more guidance on this subject. The CPPE was introduced by the DPA 2012[15] and publishes non-binding advisory opinions which are intended as an accessible remedy for complaints in public procurement procedures under the DPA 2012. Although the opinions are non-binding, they are authoritative. A recent judgment confirmed that a contracting authority cannot simply disregard a CPPE opinion.[16] A tenderer can choose to submit a complaint to the CPPE instead of legal proceedings in court, or – in some circumstances – as a first step, before going to court.[17]

According to the CPPE, the lowest price or cost is allowed only when the choice for the best price-quality ratio would be 'inefficient'.[18] This situation occurs when it can reasonably not be expected that the best price-quality ratio as the award criterion would create enough room for tenderers to feel sufficiently challenged to offer 'innovative and sustainable solutions'. Whether such circumstances exist needs to be determined on a case-by-case basis and in view of all the relevant facts. The following circumstances can especially be relevant, according to the CPPE and case law: the subject matter of the public procurement procedure, the relevant market, and the extent to which awarding the contract based on the best price-quality ratio is useful with a view to the aim of more innovative and sustainable public procurement.[19] The contracting authority needs to explain its assessment in the public procurement documents. This assessment and explanation can be challenged before the CPPE (or the court).

[12] Kamerstukken II 2015/16, 34 329, nr. 11.

[13] This approach has been criticised; see D Versteeg, 'Levenscycluskosten: De sleutel naar circulair werk?' in R Koolhoven (ed), *Preadviezen: Circulair bouwen* (Den Haag, Instituut voor Bouwrecht, 2018) para 4.5.

[14] Proportionality Guide (n 2) para 3.5.5.

[15] Art 4.27 DPA 2012.

[16] District Court Den Haag 7 December 2021, ECLI:NL:RBDHA:2021:13815.

[17] In practice there is usually only time to go to court after a CPPE advice if the complaint is lodged well before the tender submission deadline.

[18] As laid down for the first time in Opinion 224. See also Opinions 348, 421, 432 and 568.

[19] CPPE opinion 224; District Court Gelderland 3 June 2014, ECLI:NL:RBGEL:2014:3493.

A similar reasoning has been applied by the courts. In various cases, the District Court Midden-Nederland has given the 'inefficiency' of the best price-quality ratio as an example of a sufficient justification.[20] It is, however, not clear in what other situations the lowest price/cost may be a justified award criterion. In 2018, the Court explained that it is not relevant whether tenderers can distinguish themselves on the market in general, but that the question is whether there is a sufficient distinctiveness with regard to the specific contract concerned, on top of the minimum requirements in that public procurement procedure.[21] In a 2019 case, the Court stated that the contracting authority did not sufficiently explain that no value could be attributed to the quality of the tenderers' service, while the claimant had shown that a distinction based on service level was possible.[22] In a recent case from 2021, the contracting authority successfully argued that all the quality requirements were already incorporated into the terms of reference, which left no room for tenderers to distinguish themselves on quality aspects.[23] These cases show that a contracting authority cannot suffice with a general justification of the lowest price or cost, but needs to specify why – in the specific circumstances of the public procurement procedure concerned – the best price-quality ratio would not be efficient.

III. Obligation to Procure as Much Societal Value as Possible (Article 1.4(2))

The second relevant provision in the DPA 2012 is Article 1.4(2):

> The contracting authority or contracting entity ensures that as much societal value as possible is created for public resources when entering a [public contract].[24]

This provision applies both below and above the EU thresholds. As will be explained in detail, practice proves that it is difficult to enforce this provision, including for SPP purposes. An important reason for that arguably lies in the origin of the provision, that is, its wording and the explanation of its purpose/contents provided in the legislative process.

Article 1.4(2) is – again – the result of an amendment by the House of Representatives.[25] Contrary to the original proposal for the DPA 2012 by the

[20] District Court Midden-Nederland 4 May 2018, ECLI:NL:RBMNE:2018:1963; District Court Midden-Nederland 30 January 2019, ECLI:NL:RBMNE:2019:312; District Court Midden-Nederland 8 September 2021, ECLI:NL:RBMNE:2021:4356.

[21] District Court Midden-Nederland 4 May 2018, ECLI:NL:RBMNE:2018:1963.

[22] District Court Midden-Nederland 30 January 2019, ECLI:NL:RBMNE:2019:312. A similar outcome can be found in District Court Midden-Nederland 4 May 2018, ECLI:NL:RBMNE:2018:1963.

[23] District Court Midden-Nederland 8 September 2021, ECLI:NL:RBMNE:2021:4356.

[24] Translated from Dutch.

[25] Kamerstukken II 2011/12, 32 440, nr. 46.

government, such amendments usually do not contain an extensive explanatory note and are not part of the legal review of the proposal by the Dutch Council of State (Raad van State). This amendment was no exception: there is only a very short explanatory note to the amendment, which does not deal with the legal consequences of the provision. The explanatory note states that there is a large general interest to spend public resources as well as possible, thereby creating societal value. According to the note, examples in other countries have shown that procurement policies in this context can result in important savings for the government.

In the following discussions and additional explanation to the amended proposal, two aspects of the provision can be distinguished. First, the focus was mainly on achieving the best value for taxpayers' money.[26] The initiator of the amendment emphasised the need to procure the best price-quality ratio. This aspect is very closely linked to Article 2.114(4) in the DPA 2012, that, as discussed, urges contracting authorities to choose the best price-quality ratio as the award criterion ('comply or explain'). The price-quality ratio does, however, not require the inclusion of more societal objectives, but usually concerns the price and quality of the goods, works or services for the contracting authority as a client (eg, technical merit, aesthetic and functional characteristics).

Second, achieving the best price-quality ratio (in a strict sense) was not the only aim of the obligation to achieve as much societal value as possible. This is not apparent from the legislative history, but references were made to 'social return' (ie, an obligation to involve persons with a distance to the labour market) and the inclusion of sustainability, innovation and 'external policy goals' into the consideration of what is the best quality for the best price in a specific case.[27] The initiator of the amendment stated that 'societal value cannot always be expressed in euros'.[28] Unfortunately, no examples are given of what these external policy goals could be.

In view of the above, a contracting authority is arguably obliged by Article 1.4(2) DPA 2012 to make an assessment of the societal value when organising a public procurement procedure. This assessment should result in the choice for the maximum societal value in that specific context, which can include not only the best price-quality ratio instead of the lowest price, but also other elements, such as sustainability, innovation, social return and external policy goals.

In practice, the assessment of what would create the most societal value is usually not an explicit element of Dutch public procurement documents. Unlike Article 2.114(4), the provision on societal value does not require contracting authorities to include their assessment in the public procurement documents. It is not unlikely that contracting authorities consider societal value as a concept when drafting public procurement documents, but it is not common to include such

[26] Handelingen 2011/12, nr. 48, item 4.
[27] Handelingen 2011/12, nr. 48, item 4 and Kamerstukken II 2011/12, 32 440, nr. C.
[28] Handelingen 2011/12, nr. 48, item 4.

considerations explicitly in those documents. This makes it difficult for tenderers to understand the contracting authority's reasoning and to challenge that assessment if needed.

A. Court Cases

The provision on societal value has, nevertheless, been invoked in a number of court cases.[29] There are a relatively small number of cases, that is, approximately ten published cases in total since 2012, whereas the total number of public procurement court cases lies around 130 per year in the Netherlands.[30] Furthermore, all the cases on societal value are preliminary relief proceedings (kort geding) at first instance. Although this applies to most cases in Dutch procurement law practice, it puts the importance of these cases in perspective. For example, they have been decided on by a single judge and they do not constitute binding precedents for future cases.

In the cases regarding the societal value provision, the substantive review by the courts is limited. They stress that contracting authorities have a broad discretionary power when determining the award criteria and that the court therefore should take a cautious approach in its review of the admissibility of the applied award criteria. This results in little more than a marginal review by the court, consisting of the test whether the contracting authority made a decision that is 'incomprehensible, unreasonable or unacceptable'.[31] Such an approach is not new in Dutch public procurement law and is generally applied when a tenderer challenges the reasoning in a contract award decision.[32] Clearly, it raises the bar for tenderers who are challenging the contracting authority and might explain why only a few challenges are successful.

Most of the relevant court cases deal with award criteria and the question of whether the applied award (sub)criteria result in the actual best price-quality ratio. These cases concern the points that were granted to different separation methods for waste processing,[33] the relative weight attributed to price versus quality,[34] an award mechanism that could favour a more expensive bid with a similar level of quality,[35] the alleged non-distinctiveness of the award criteria[36] and an award mechanism that would result in a decision by lot instead of a decision based on

[29] A more detailed description of several of these cases is included in Janssen and Bouwman, 'Legislating Societal Value in Dutch Public Procurement Law' (n 10).

[30] 'Aanbestedingsrechtspraak in Nederland 2016–2018', annex to Kamerstukken II 2018/19, 34 252, nr. 13.

[31] District Court Noord-Nederland 25 October 2013, ECLI:NL:RBNNE:2013:7100.

[32] See, eg, District Court Den Haag 11 December 2018, ECLI:NL:RBDHA:2018:14593.

[33] District Court Noord-Nederland 25 October 2013, ECLI:NL:RBNNE:2013:7100 and District Court Noord-Nederland 29 November 2013, ECLI:NL:RBNNE:2013:7367.

[34] District Court Overijssel 30 September 2016, ECLI:NL:RBOVE:2016:3761.

[35] District Court Den Haag 25 February 2014, ECLI:NL:RBDHA:2014:2965.

[36] District Court Den Haag 12 January 2017, ECLI:NL:RBDHA:2017:4854.

the best price-quality ratio.[37] In these cases, the application of the societal value provision is very closely linked to Article 2.114 DPA 2012 on the choice of the award criterion. When a contracting authority chooses the best price-quality ratio as the award criterion, it is obliged under Article 2.114 and earlier case law to ensure that the award mechanism lets the best offer win.[38] The courts stated that in this context, the societal value provision 'corresponds' to Article 2.114 DPA 2012. It appears that the courts saw no real added value in the societal value provision and that, in substance, an assessment based on Article 2.114 sufficed.[39] The cases did not concern societal aspects, but merely the proper functioning of the award mechanism (ie, is the mechanism actually able to identify the best offer based on the chosen award criteria?).

Not all court cases on the societal value provision concern award criteria. Three of those cases are relevant to discuss here. In a 2016 case, the tenderer claimed that the start date of the tender procedure was too early, because there were relevant initiatives that needed to be concluded first, including the creation of a database management system.[40] The Court dismissed this claim, stating that the tenderer did not put forward any facts or circumstances that indicate that the public procurement procedure would not create savings.

In 2017, a tenderer claimed that the contracting authority infringed the societal value provision because the price of the winning tender was low to such an extent that it would result in a default by the winning tenderer during the execution of the contract.[41] However, the Court dismissed this claim because it already concluded – in the context of a claim based on the provision on abnormally low tenders – that it was not plausible that the price offered would result in problems during the execution of the contract. In the view of the court, it was farfetched to invoke the societal value provision in this context.

The third and final case dates from 2018 and concerns the supply of school books.[42] Two tenderers claimed that the contracting authority infringed the principles of procurement law and did not ensure a level playing field because of differences between publishers and distributors of school books (both of which

[37] District Court Den Haag 3 September 2015, ECLI:NL:RBDHA:2015:10440.

[38] See Case C-31/87 *Gebroeders Beentjes BV v State of the Netherlands* ECLI:EU:C:1988:422, [1988] ECR 4635 para 19; District Court Leeuwarden 22 April 2004, ECLI:NL:RBLEE:2004:AT2756; District Court Leeuwarden 21 January 2005, ECLI:NL:RBLEE:2005:AS3521.

[39] See also Janssen and Bouwman, 'Legislating Societal Value in Dutch Public Procurement Law: From Symbolism to Substance' (n 10) who conclude that the societal value provision concerns 'symbolic legislation'. A similar conclusion can be found in Janssen, 'Verplicht maatschappelijk verantwoord aanbestedesn. Een eerste verkenning van een paradigmaverandering' (n 10) 29; Janssen and Neele, 'De (in)effectiviteit van open en concrete aanbestedingsrechtelijke verplichtingen in de strijd tegen klimaatverandering' (n 10) 132; Van Heeswijck, 'De verplichting tot het creëren van zoveel mogelijk "Maatschappelijke waarde" voor de publieke middelen' (n 10) 164–65.

[40] District Court Midden-Nederland 8 January 2016, ECLI:NL:RBMNE:2016:104.

[41] District Court Amsterdam 8 March 2017, ECLI:NL:RBAMS:2017:1504.

[42] District Court Den Haag 27 November 2018, ECLI:NL:RBDHA:2018:13949. The societal value provision was also invoked with regard to the level playing field in a more recent case; the Court however did not explicitly mention that provision in its reasoning. District Court Rotterdam 4 May 2021, ECLI:NL:RBROT:2021:4205.

participated in the public procurement procedure). Those claims were dismissed by the Court. The Court seems to use that conclusion to 'automatically' also dismiss the claim based on the societal value provision. In other words, because the procurement principles were not infringed, the contracting authority did also not infringe the societal value provision.

In short, the claims were dismissed in all three cases. This should not come as a surprise, because it seems that little was put forward to substantiate the alleged lack of societal value and that the argument was in fact used merely to support other claims. So far, the societal value provision has therefore not played a significant role in the case law.

B. Committee of Public Procurement Experts (CPPE)

The CPPE has shown that it is willing to take a less 'cautious' approach than the courts and provide a more in-depth review of substantive complaints regarding the societal value provision. Over the years, more than 15 opinions have been published. A part of these opinions concern award criteria and the question of whether the award mechanism results in the award to the best offer.[43] These opinions are in line with the case law described earlier.

The CPPE has also dealt with procedural matters and other substantive aspects. In terms of procedure, the CPPE has used on multiple occasions a two-step approach towards the burden of proof for infringements of the societal value provision.[44] The first step is that the tenderer (ie, the complainant) needs to elaborate on its claim that the contracting authority infringes the societal value provision. Claiming such an infringement is not enough, but the CPPE does not seem to require proof by the tenderer. If the tenderer passes this bar, the second step is that it is up to the contracting authority to prove that it has fulfilled its obligation under the societal value provision. This approach seems to indicate that the actual burden of proof is on the contracting authority rather than the tenderer, provided that the latter can substantiate its claim to a certain extent. Such an approach is likely to give tenderers a much better chance of succeeding compared to the cautious approach by the courts that was described above.

The CPPE two-step approach is somewhat similar to the CJEU's reasoning in the *eVigilo* case from 2015.[45] This reasoning also fits within the importance the CJEU attributes to the contracting authorities' obligation to state reasons for their decisions, since it puts their addressee in a position to defend its rights and decide

[43] Opinions 421, 449, 499, 512, 602 and 659.

[44] The approach is laid down for the first time in Opinion 48.

[45] Case C-538/13 *eVigilo Ltd v Priešgaisrinės apsaugos ir gelbėjimo departamentas prie Vidaus reikalų ministerijos* ECLI:EU:C:2015:166, [2015] para 44.

in full knowledge of the circumstances whether it is worthwhile to bring an action against those decisions.[46]

With regard to other substantive aspects than achieving the best price-quality ratio, four examples are relevant to discuss. The first is a case where the contracting authority imposed a social return obligation on the contractor.[47] The tenderer claimed that this obligation infringed the societal value provision because it would be ineffective, would not result in sustainable jobs, would result in displacement in the labour market and would create a threshold for SMEs. The CPPE dismissed this claim, because the tenderer did not elaborate its claim enough and therefore failed the first step of the two-step approach.

The second example concerns access for SMEs.[48] The CPPE recommended keeping the public procurement procedure as clear and simple as possible and asking for as little effort from the tenderers as possible, in order to let small enterprises compete (if it is likely that they would be interested). According to the CPPE, this would increase the possibility that as much societal value as possible is created.

The third example, or actually a category of examples, relates to the scope of the contract. The CPPE stated that the societal value provision not only applies to the way that the most economically advantageous offer is determined, but also to the choice for a certain product and the exclusion of other products,[49] as well as the choice for a certain working method and the exclusion of other working methods.[50] The first case concerned the choice for on-premise installation of a software solution, which excluded SaaS solutions (Software as a Service). The CPPE concluded that the tenderer did not sufficiently substantiate its claims (as required in the first step), which resulted in the dismissal of the claims. The second case was about the choice of a traditional tunnel building method (open excavation), which excluded other, allegedly more innovative working methods. The tenderer proposed an alternative method with a tunnel boring machine, which he believed would result in less CO_2 emission and less impact on traffic. He claimed that his method, therefore, had more societal value. The contracting authority however stated that the alternative method would take too much time. In view of the time pressure on the project, the contracting authority had chosen to prescribe the traditional working method and not allow any variants. The CPPE stated that, in view of the contracting authority's reply, the tenderer did not sufficiently substantiate its claims. This reasoning appears to be somewhat of a mix of both steps. Although the CPPE's conclusion is part of the first step, the CPPE reaches that

[46] Case C-927/19 *'Klaipėdos regiono atliekų tvarkymo centras' v UAB* ECLI:EU:C:2021:700, [2021]. See also R Caranta, 'Procurement Transparency as a Gateway for Procurement Remedies' in KM Halonen, R Caranta and A Sanchez-Graells (eds), *Transparency in EU Procurements* (Cheltenham, Edward Elgar, 2019).

[47] Opinion 375.

[48] Opinion 410.

[49] Opinion 476.

[50] Opinion 522.

conclusion after taking the contracting authority's arguments into account, which would normally only be relevant in the second step.

The fourth and last category of examples consist of two opinions in which the CPPE concluded that the contracting authority infringed principles of procurement law (ie, equal treatment, transparency and proportionality).[51] In addition, and superfluously, the CPPE stated that it is doubtful whether the contracting authority ensures as much societal value as possible, in view of the infringement of those principles. This is the mirror image of the court case on the school books: in that case, the societal value provision was not infringed because the procurement principles were not infringed, whereas in these CPPE cases, those principles were infringed, which could also result in an infringement of the societal value provision.

As with the court cases, the CPPE cases show that the societal value provision is used to challenge other aspects than the choice for the award criterion and the suitability of the award mechanism. None of these claims did however result in the establishment of an infringement of that provision, mostly because the tenderer did not substantiate its claim sufficiently.

IV. Relevance of Both Obligations for Sustainable Public Procurement

Article 2.114(4) DPA 2012 limits the possibility to award a public contract on the basis of the lowest price or cost. In that context, sustainability plays a role: using the lowest price as the award criterion is arguably only allowed if there is no room for tenderers to offer more innovative and sustainable solutions. The preference for the best price-quality ratio as the award criterion is therefore meant to stimulate competition on sustainability aspects.

Once the contracting authority has chosen the best price-quality ratio as the award criterion, Articles 2.114 and 1.4 DPA 2012 require the use of an award mechanism that ensures that the actual best offer wins. This is, however, very much linked to how the points will be given and the weighting of quality versus price. These obligations do not stimulate or force a contracting authority to let sustainability (including social aspects) play an explicit role in the public procurement procedure. In other words, the contracting authority is free to use requirements or criteria relating to SPP, but is not required to do so.

Although the societal value provision could provide such a requirement, practice shows that this has not (or not yet) been the case. The provision allows to include aspects that 'cannot be expressed in euros' and 'external policy goals' into the public procurement process, that is, aspects that go beyond the traditional best price-quality ratio. SPP is likely to fit those descriptions and could therefore create

[51] Opinions 502 and 526.

more 'quality' and 'societal value'. The cases before the CPPE have shown that this may include social return obligations or an exclusive choice for a certain type of product or working method (which choice could be based on environmental and social considerations). However, practice so far has shown that the provision has not been able to function as a legal basis to make SPP mandatory. There are several factors that might explain this outcome.

First, the societal value provision in the DPA 2012 contains an open, rather vague norm. It does not explain what 'societal value' is. The legislative history contains some explanation, but refers to 'other aspects' as *possibilities* to be included in the procurement process rather than as mandatory aspects that need to be taken into consideration. In that sense, the provision seems to be without real obligations. It might be very difficult to provide a clear definition of 'societal value' in the DPA 2012. An alternative to such a definition could be that contracting authorities adopt own policy rules in which they give an interpretation of or guidelines on 'societal value'. This could perhaps be done in the context of the Sustainable Procurement Manifesto that was referred to in the introduction. However, it is potentially not very attractive to contracting authorities to limit themselves voluntarily by their own interpretation of the law.

Second, the lack of a definition of 'societal value' or even an explicit objective of that provision would make it very difficult to assess what aspects may be included in the contracting authority's assessment of the societal value and how much weight should be contributed to each of those aspects. For example, how should a contracting authority determine which type of solution creates the most societal value and should therefore be favoured? This has been referred to as a 'priority problem' in the design of the provision.[52]

Third, the societal value provision does not require the contracting authority to describe or explain its assessment of the societal value in a specific public procurement procedure. As a result, even when there has been such an assessment, it is not apparent to the tenderers. Without such transparency, it is very difficult for tenderers to enforce the societal value provision. By comparison, the choice for the award criterion has to take place according to the 'comply or explain' principle: the contracting authority either 'complies' by choosing the best price-quality ratio or 'explains' its choice for the lowest price or cost in the public procurement documents. That explanation can then be reviewed in light of a concrete norm, which is the required 'efficiency'. This factor is linked to the previous two, because it is difficult to describe the societal value assessment when it is not clear how that assessment should be made and what concrete norm applies. A 'comply or explain' regime might be an interesting way to work out the societal value provision. Perhaps certain SPP aspects can be defined (by law or policy) that should be taken into account, unless the contracting authority can explain that it would not be 'efficient' in the specific circumstances of the public contract concerned.

[52] Janssen and Neele, 'De (in)effectiviteit van open en concrete aanbestedingsrechtelijke verplichtingen in de strijd tegen Klimaatverandering' (n 10) 133.

Fourth, the societal value provision gives contracting authorities broad discretionary power. This has led courts to take a cautious approach, that in practice limits the chance of success for a tenderer that challenges the compliance of this provision. The two-step approach by the CPPE might solve this issue and seems to be in line with the CJEU's case law on other, somewhat comparable aspects of public procurement law. If courts would remain to take a cautious approach, a 'comply or explain' regime would probably not make a significant difference in practice.[53]

Fifth, the question is *who* should enforce the societal value provision. Tenderers might not always be the most obvious party to ensure compliance. The provision aims to achieve a goal in the *general* interest, which does not necessarily also have to be in the interest of a specific tenderer. This has been labelled a problem of 'ownership' of the general interest that the provision pursues.[54] There is also a legal component to this factor, because the law requires a tenderer to have sufficient interest for its claim, which could be missing if the claim is only in the general interest.[55] In the court case on the alleged abnormally low tender, the District Court Amsterdam wondered whether the societal value provision is not only in the interest of the contracting authority, which would preclude a tenderer to invoke that provision.[56] A similar reasoning is used in Dutch case law in relation to the provision on abnormally low tenders, which – according to that case law – provides a *possibility* but not an *obligation* for contracting authorities to investigate and reject potential abnormally low tenders.[57] This interpretation is based on the wording of the DPA 2012, which states that in most cases the contracting authority 'can' (instead of 'must') reject an abnormally low tender.[58] The wording of the societal value provision does however not contain such discretion: the contracting authority must ensure that as much societal value as possible is created for the public resources. The District Court of Amsterdam seems to have overlooked this difference in the above-mentioned case.[59]

V. Conclusion

Within the context of the trend towards mandatory sustainability requirements in public procurement law, this chapter discussed the Dutch context in order to also potentially provide learnings for other Member States or the EU legislature.

[53] *cf* earlier criticism on the 'comply or explain' regime with regard to the scope of the contract in the annex to Kamerstukken II 2017/18, 34 252, nr. 8.

[54] Jansen, 'De inschrijver als hoeder van het algemeen belang?' (n 10) 464; Verweij, 'Attero zuid / Gemeente tynaarlo' (n 10).

[55] Articles 3:303 BW and 6:163 BW (Dutch Civil Code).

[56] District Court Amsterdam 8 March 2017, ECLI:NL:RBAMS:2017:1504. See also Van Heeswijck, 'De verplichting tot het creëren van zoveel mogelijk "Maatschappelijke waarde" voor de publieke middelen' (n 10).

[57] See, eg, District Court Amsterdam 21 September 2021, ECLI:NL:RBAMS:2021:6209.

[58] Article 2.116 DPA 2012.

[59] District Court Amsterdam 8 March 2017, ECLI:NL:RBAMS:2017:1504.

The preference in the DPA 2012 for the best price-quality ratio instead of the lowest price or cost can stimulate SPP. Moreover, the 'comply or explain' regime requires contracting authorities to explain any choice for the lowest price or cost. This mechanism has ensured that in practice contracting authorities choose the award criterion more deliberately and that tenderers can successfully challenge a choice for the lowest price or cost. This provision in the DPA 2012 does however not require the inclusion of SPP aspects to determine the quality (as part of the best price-quality ratio).

The societal value provision could entail such a requirement, because that provision demands to create as much societal value as possible and including SPP aspects could result in more societal value. As discussed, this provision has however not led to the mandatory inclusion of SPP. Several factors have been distinguished that seem to stand in the way of more extensive and mandatory use of the societal value provision with a view to SPP. These factors include both substantive issues (ie, unclarity of the norm, its priorities and the 'ownership' of the general interest that it serves) and procedural issues (ie, no obligation to describe the assessment of the societal value in the public procurement documents and a cautious approach by the courts as a result of the contracting authorities' broad discretionary power). It is likely that these obstacles can be overcome, perhaps partly by adopting a 'comply or explain' regime and using the CPPE's two-step approach. But this will require further action from the legislator and/or contracting authorities themselves.

13

Spain: Transitioning Towards Sustainable Public Procurement Mandatory Requirements

XIMENA LAZO VITORIA[1]

I. Introduction

The purpose of this chapter is to describe the status of Sustainable Public Procurement (SPP) in Spain. In particular, it aims to explore the transformation which public procurement is undergoing as it transitions from a voluntary to a mandatory model. This change of focus is based on the European Green Deal, as well as on the successive technical documents, plans, regulations and strategies that have subsequently been approved.[2] However, this transition towards mandatory SPP has also arisen out of new domestic rules (at both the state and regional levels) approved in recent years in Spain. Climate laws have had a particularly significant impact and are driving the renewal of public procurement against a backdrop of decarbonisation of the economy, the energy transition and the creation of a fairer and more inclusive model of society.

This chapter begins by outlining the regulatory framework governing public procurement in Spain. It goes on to describe and evaluate the development of SPP in general legislation, in the aforementioned climate change legislation, in the special rules for EU Next Generation funds and in sector-specific legislation. Finally, it ends with an analysis of lessons learned and obstacles, which continue to prevent SPP from unleashing its full transformational power.

[1] This chapter is part of the Research Project '*Green Public Procurement: a strategic tool for tackling climate change. An analysis of the food, building and sustainable transport sectors, as well as in the context of rural depopulation*', *Reference: PID2021-122131OB-I00*, financed by the Spanish Ministry of Science and Innovation.

[2] W Janssen, 'Shifting towards Mandatory Sustainability Requirements in EU Public Procurement Law: Context, Relevance and a Typology', ch 1 in this volume.

II. An Overview of the Regulatory Framework Governing Public Procurement and the Development of SPP in Spain

The key legislation in Spain is Law 9/2017 of 8 November on Public Sector Contracts (Ley 9/2017, de 8 de noviembre, de Contratos del Sector Público, hereinafter LCSP).[3] This law is based on earlier Spanish legislation of 2011 and motivated by the need to transpose the Classic Directive and Concessions Directive into Spanish national law. In turn, the Utilities Directive was incorporated into Spanish law through emergency legislation in 2020 (hereinafter RD-L 3/2020).[4]

The LCSP is extensive (it has 347 Articles, 55 additional provisions, 5 transitional provisions and 16 final provisions), its regulation is exhaustive and applying it is far from straightforward.[5] Under the framework of the division of legislative competencies between the state and the Autonomous Regions (*Comunidades Autónomas* in Spanish), most of the content of the LCSP is 'basic' in nature[6] meaning it applies to the entire public sector including the Autonomous Regions and local authorities. A few Autonomous Regions have approved legislation that implements it, such as Aragon in 2011 and the Basque Country in 2016. Furthermore, Navarre, as the only Region with exclusive competence in the field of public contracts, has its own regional law of 2018.[7]

The approval of the LCSP and RD-L 3/2020 undoubtedly marks a turning point in achieving strategic objectives through public procurement, in line with the provisions of the 2014 Public Procurement Directives.[8] Moreover, sustainability emerges as a central feature of the LCSP as its first Article establishes that

> social and environmental criteria must be incorporated into all public procurement processes in an overarching manner (…) in the belief that their inclusion will provide

[3] See JM Gimeno Feliú (ed), *Estudio sistemático de la ley de contratos del sector público* (Navarra, Aranzadi Thomson Reuters, 2018).

[4] See Spanish Royal Decree-Law 3/2020 of 4 February.

[5] See especially J Tejedor Bielsa, *La contratación pública en España, ¿sobrerregulación o estrategia? Causas y consecuencias de su problemática aplicación* (Navarra, Aranzadi, 2018).

[6] The Spanish Constitution of 1978 assigns exclusive competence to the state to establish basic legislation on contracts and administrative concessions. The Autonomous Regions are responsible for developing this basic legislation, provided that this is allowed for in their respective Statutes of Autonomy. However, in the case of the LCSP, such regulatory development has been rather limited, probably due to the particularly exhaustive nature of this Law.

[7] See V Aguado I Cudolà, *La contratación pública responsable. Funciones, límites y régimen jurídico* (Navarre, Aranzandi Thomson Reuters, 2021) especially 139–70; JM Pérez Fernández, 'La cuestión competencial en el ámbito de la contratación del sector público: la delimitación de lo básico en la doctrina constitucional (STC 68/2021, de 18 de marzo)' (2021) 216 *Revista de administración pública* 189.

[8] See M Razquin Lizarraga (ed), *Nueva contratación pública: Mercado y medio ambiente* (Navarre, Aranzadi Thomson Reuters, 2017); X Lazo Vitoria (ed), *Compra pública verde* (Barcelona, Atelier, 2018); R Galán Vioque (ed), *Las cláusulas ambientales en la contratación pública* (Seville, Editorial Universidad de Sevilla, 2018); T Quintana López (ed), *La contratación pública estratégica* (Valencia, Tirant lo Blanch, 2020).

greater value for money of the goods or services delivered under the contract, as well as increased and improved efficiency in the use of public funds.[9]

This strategic vision is a cornerstone of the legislation. Gimeno Feliu pointed out that the LCSP reinforces the idea of procurement as an investment rather than as an expense, which is more typical of a bureaucratic, economic vision of bidding processes.[10] Indeed, the legislator now declares public procurement to be one of the instruments based on the internal market that should be used to achieve smart, sustainable and inclusive growth (preamble to the LCSP).

To complete the regulatory map, it should be noted that, in addition to the LCSP and RD-L 3/2020, three other areas of regulation are of relevance to this work. First, the increasingly significant role of sectoral legislation in strategic purchasing. Second, extensive rules on climate change, promote the mandatory inclusion of environmental clauses into procurement proceedings, but which are not formally integrated into the LCSP. And third, the new rules approved for managing EU Next Generation Funds, which have become an ad hoc procurement framework with significant provisions for SPP. The main features of all the rules mentioned here are outlined in the following section.

Beyond the regulatory sphere, various instruments and guides have been approved to facilitate strategic purchasing. In particular, at the state level, the Inter-ministerial Commission for the incorporation of ecological criteria into public procurement was created in 2018 (although it did not come into effect until 2021). And 2019 saw the approval of the Plan for the promotion of socially responsible public procurement and the Ecological Public Procurement Plan, followed by the approval of the Guide on Innovative Public Procurement two years later. It should be noted that, despite their non-regulatory nature, some of these instruments include *SPP mandatory requirements as a target*.[11]

III. SPP Mandatory Requirements in the LCSP and RD-L 3/2020

The LCSP and RD-L 3/2020 contain a wide variety of SPP mandatory requirements. A substantial proportion of these may be classified as *procedural and horizontal SPP mandatory requirements*.[12] This group includes, for example:

[9] Art 27.2 of RD-L 3/2020 uses practically identical wording.

[10] JM Gimeno Feliu, 'La visión estratégica en la contratación pública en la LCSP: Hacia una contratación socialmente responsable y de calidad' (2020) 415 *Revista economía industrial* 89.

[11] This is the case of the Public Ecological Procurement Plan of the General State Administration (2018–25). This Plan provides a timetable for the adoption of its provisions in such a way that, by 2025, 50% of the contracts put up for tender in the 20 sectors included in its scope of application should incorporate carbon footprint as an award criterion.

[12] This broad horizontal and procedural approach is also visible in the Netherlands. See P Heijnsbroek, 'The Netherlands: Obligations to Justify the Lowest Price and to Create as Much Societal Value as Possible', ch 12 in this volume.

a) the need to incorporate the environmental or social requirements mentioned in the previous section;[13] b) the obligation to take 'social, environmental and innovation considerations' into account in the definition of the contractual subject matter (Articles 35.1.c of the LCSP and 53.1.c of RD-L 3/2020);[14] c) the mandate to include social, labour and environmental considerations in public procurement documents in the form of selection criteria or award criteria, or as conditions relating to the performance of a contract (Article 122.2 of the LCSP), as well as the environmental and social aspects of the technical specifications (Article 124 of the LCSP); d) with regards to award criteria, the obligation to use multiple criteria based on the best quality-price ratio and that the use of price as the sole criterion must be duly justified (Article 145.1 of the LCSP and 66.1 of RD-L 3/2020).[15]

A further substantial set of rules may be categorised as *substantive SPP mandatory requirements*: for example, in contracts with the subject of 'services to the person',[16] the Law requires that the criteria related to quality account for at least 51 per cent of the score (Articles 145.4 of the LCSP 9/2017 and 66.4 of RD-L 3/2020). Two additional examples are the preferential use of established methods of life-cycle cost (Articles 148.4 of the LCSP and 67.3 of RD-L 3/2020) and rules supporting SMEs.[17] Within this same set of rules, but with its own special characteristics, it is worth mentioning the inclusion of at least one environmental, social or innovation condition relating to performance in each public contract.[18] This is

[13] Regional Navarre Law 2/2018, of 13 April, on public contracts contains a similar rule in its Art 2 'to be incorporated into public procurement in a cross-cutting, mandatory manner', but adds that to put this principle into effect, public contracts 'must include mandatory award criteria, as well as social or environmental implementation requirements'.

[14] Moreover, the Regulation expressly allows the subject matter of the contract to be defined based on specific needs or functionalities particularly when it is possible to incorporate technological, social or environmental innovations which improve the efficiency and sustainability of the assets, works or services being contracted. (Arts 99.1 LCSP and 52.1 RD-L 3/2020). See M Pardo López 'Mención de criterios sociales y medioambientales en la definición del objeto del contrato' in M Pardo López and A Sánchez García (eds), *Inclusión de cláusulas sociales y medioambientales en los pliegos de contratos públicos* (Navarre, Aranzadi, 2019) 49–6; A Román Márquez, 'Contratación pública ecológica y objeto del contrato: El diseño "verde" de las prestaciones contractuales en el derecho comunitario e interno' (2018) 39 *Revista aranzadi de derecho ambiental* 22.

[15] It should be noted that the use of price as the sole award criterion is extremely limited because the legislator has established a list of those contracts which must apply a range of criteria in order to be awarded. For example, works and service concessions, the majority of service contracts, etc. However, the new scheme (d) may be distorted if, for example, as is often the case, the economic factor is given a high or very high weighting compared to the other criteria. Or if economic aspects are concealed as quality criteria. See especially R Fernández Acevedo, 'Los criterios de adjudicación al servicio de la calidad ambiental y de la lucha contra el cambio climático: En precio en Jaque' in X Lazo Vitoria (ed), *Compra pública verde y cambio climático* (Barcelona, Atelier, 2022).

[16] The Spanish legislator uses the wording of the recital 114 Classic Directive.

[17] For example, the Spanish legislator has established the division into lots as mandatory (Art 99.3 LCSP), going beyond what is established by the European legislator (the 'explain or divide' rule). See J Miranzo, 'Pymes y compra pública verde: Derribando barreras' in X Lazo Vitoria (ed), *Compra pública verde y cambio climático* (Atelier, Barcelona, 2022).

[18] See C de Guerrero Manso, 'La inclusión de condiciones especiales de ejecución como medida efectiva para la defensa del medio ambiente a través de la contratación pública' (2018) 19 *Revista aragonesa de administración pública* 141.

the first time that Spanish legislation has made this compulsory and, moreover, applied it across the board, that is, whatever the type of contract or its economic threshold. It should be stressed that the Regulation itself offers a long list of environmental and social requirements to be incorporated into contracts[19] and also that infringement may even be cause for rescinding a contract (Articles 202 of the LCSP and 105 of RD-L 3/2020). This obligation has been criticised for being too broad and for not introducing any differentiation depending on the type of contract in question or its purpose.[20] It is clear that the legislator appears to have opted for real 'shock therapy' here to accelerate the sustainability of tenders in Spain. To this end, a phase has been selected that avoids the problems which selection criteria can typically present (entry barrier, proportionality)[21] and which does not leave compliance with these up to companies (award criterion). Nonetheless, this does not mean its introduction has been free of problems and it is also true that there is still considerable room for improvement in the application of these provisions. It is common to see merely formal compliance with the law, the introduction of generic clauses and non-specific obligations or, to give another example, that a clause is limited to reiterating a requirement already included in a previous regulation.[22]

In general terms, the framework outlined above appears to go beyond what is established by the 2014 Public Procurement Directives. As indicated, the mandatory focus of SPP is intensified in general procurement and concession contract law.[23] This drive is promoting sustainable public procurement in Spain. Indeed, according to official data from the Government of Spain (2021), there was a clear increase in SPP both for contracts subject to harmonised regulation and for contracts below the EU economic thresholds during the period 2018 to 2020. This increase was especially notable for social aspects, which rose to 18.09 per cent in 2020 compared to 11.30 per cent in 2018. Furthermore, the incorporation of ecological criteria, although at a lower value of 11.52 per cent in 2020, practically doubled in the first year of the series, from 5.80 per cent in 2018.[24]

The following table outlines mandatory SPP content in the LCSP and RD-L 3/2020.

[19] For example, recruiting a greater number of people with disabilities than that required by national legislation, encouraging training in the workplace, delivery of bulk products or organic production.

[20] For example, see M Sánchez Morón, *Derecho administrativo. Parte general* (Tecnos, Madrid, 2021).

[21] For example, the requirement for 100% of the energy marketed to be of renewable origin, which was rejected by Supreme Court Judgment 376/2022, of 25 March, since it was considered disproportionate.

[22] See M Giménez Baldazo 'Nivel de concurrencia en licitaciones de comedores escolares: ¿éxito o fracaso de la inclusión de criterios de sostenibilidad?' (2022) 181 *Contratación administrativa práctica* 119.

[23] European law has traditionally opted for a *voluntary* approach to the incorporation of SPP requirements (Recital 95 Classic Directive), complemented by specific obligations included in the sector directives (eg, building, energy efficiency, promotion of clean energy-efficient road transport vehicles).

[24] See Government of Spain, Triennial Report on public procurement in Spain in 2018, 2019 and 2020 at www.hacienda.gob.es.

Table 5 SPP mandatory requirements in the LCSP and RD-L 3/2020[25]

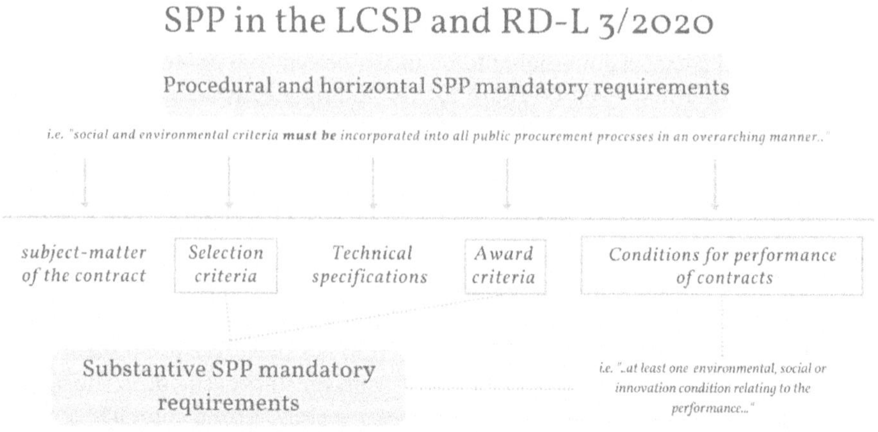

IV. The Consolidation of Mandatory SPP in Climate Change Legislation

Copious climate change legislation has been adopted in Spain over the last five years. These rules are of particular interest in this work, because they extend the use of mandatory SPP. Indeed, it could well be said that a 'climatic shift' has occurred in procurement regulations given the widespread use of this key instrument in the fight against climate change.[26] As outlined below, most of these rules could be classified as *procedural and horizontal SPP mandatory requirements* since they apply to a broad range of public contracts and define general obligations within public procurement procedures.

State legislation on climate change has been in force since May 2021, namely Law 7/2021 of 21 May 2021 on climate change and energy transition (LCCTE for its initials in Spanish), and there are also several regional laws on the matter.[27] Catalonia was the first region to legislate on climate change in 2017. It was followed by Andalusia (2018), the Balearic Islands (2019) and the Autonomous Region of Navarre (2022).[28] Other Autonomous Regions are also in the process of approving

[25] Royal Decree-Law 36/2020.

[26] See X Lazo Vitoria, 'Compra pública verde: Una herramienta estratégica de lucha contra el cambio climático' in X Lazo Vitoria (ed), *Compra pública verde y cambio climático* (Atelier, Barcelona, 2022).

[27] See F Hernández González, 'La compra pública verde en la legislación autonómica sobre cambio climático' in X Lazo Vitoria (ed), *Compra pública verde y cambio climático* (Atelier, Barcelona, 2022).

[28] The recent Navarre Law of March 2022 includes clauses which are identical to those found in the state Law of May 2021. These clauses relating to technical specifications and award criteria are analysed in the following two paragraphs.

similar regulations (Canary Islands, Autonomous Region of Valencia, Aragon and the Basque Country), so each autonomous territory is likely to have its own climate legislation in the near future.

As a novel feature, the LCCTE establishes the mandatory inclusion of technical specifications related to reducing emissions and carbon footprint specifically aimed at fighting climate change. This requirement applies to a wide variety of public contracts. To facilitate this task, the Law charges the Ministry for Ecological Transition and Demographic Challenge and the Ministry of Finance with the task of jointly preparing a catalogue of contractual subject matter which specifies such emission reduction and carbon footprint requirements. This provision aims to facilitate and accelerate the incorporation of these types of clauses on a mass scale, especially in strategic sectors such as the food sector, which is explicitly mentioned in the state Law. The LCCTE established a timeframe of one year from its entry into force to prepare the aforementioned catalogue. Unfortunately, this deadline has already passed without the document including substantive requirements having been prepared and published. Thus, this first instrument has, so to speak, 'withered on the vine', as its effectiveness is linked to a technical regulation (catalogue of subject matter) that has not been brought to fruition even though the legal deadline for it has passed.

A second novel feature of the LCCTE is the establishment of award criteria which must be included in works contracts, works concessions and project plans. In contrast to what happens with technical specifications, the legislator does not defer this requirement until a technical document has been approved. Rather these criteria are understood to be mandatory from the time the Law came into force in May 2021. Furthermore, the LCCTE itself sets out what these award criteria are through the inclusion of six categories in Article 31.2: for example, it mentions that the cited contracts must include 'maximum energy rating requirements for buildings which are the subject of tenders' or 'use of sustainable construction materials, taking their useful life into account'. Other award criteria included in Article 31.2 of the LCCTE are worded so generically that their mandatory content is blurred. This is the case with the criteria referring to the 'minimisation of waste generation' and especially to 'measures for adaptation to climate change'.

It should be noted that the state legislator has decided that the two rules set out above shall apply only to contracts opened for tender by the State Public Administration. This decision has led to a great deal of perplexity and unease since the Autonomous Regions, local authorities and the rest of the (non-state) public sector have been left out. It is indeed difficult to understand why these provisions for fighting climate change were not made applicable to all public sector procurement given that the decision-making power lies at the national level.

Regional climate change legislation also delivers significant innovations for the consolidation of mandatory sustainable procurement. For example, Catalan Law 16/2017 of 1 August on climate change mandates the inclusion of specific technical specifications and award criteria relating to the efficient use of resources and the minimisation of greenhouse gas emissions in all public procurement procedures. More importantly, Article 29.1 d) of this Law states that quantification of the use of resources and gas emissions 'must be included in the calculation of the cost of investment, operation and maintenance of the contract's subject matter'. However, Article 35 of the aforementioned legal text entitled 'Green procurement' merits a different assessment given its highly programmatic nature. Its content is as follows:

> in the procurement regime of the entire Catalan public sector, objective criteria must be established which, within the framework of the principles of freedom of access, transparency, equality, objectivity and efficiency, promote green procurement.

A valuable statement of principles, but it logically needs fleshing out with content in the form of additional regulations (eg, green procurement instructions) and specific programmes to turn this ideal into a reality.

In contrast, the Balearic Islands Law of 2019 merely refers to 'promoting' sustainability in public procurement. However, where relevant, it does require the contracting authority to explain why sustainable clauses have not been included. With regards to energy, it should be noted that Balearic Islands legislation establishes that public contracts for electricity supply must deliver certified energy of 100 per cent renewable origin. It also includes a series of mandatory technical specifications for works contracts or works concessions such as those materials with a low environmental impact must be incorporated into buildings or that new buildings or facilities must have zero energy consumption.

V. Sustainable Public Procurement in the Framework of the Next Generation Funds

The legislation on Next Generation EU Funds is worthy of special attention since it makes widespread use of public procurement as a strategic tool to achieve fair recovery in accordance with a more sustainable and resilient production model.[29] The Next Generation EU (NGEU) initiative is an instrument for economic recovery designed by the EU to help repair the immediate economic and social damage caused by the COVID-19 pandemic.[30] To manage the substantial resources allocated to Spain, the Spanish Government has approved a set of measures (2020) and various Autonomous Regions have also begun to draw up rules for the

[29] JJ Pernas García, 'Comprar "Rápido" y "estratégicamente" en la ejecución de los fondos Next Generation' (2021) 20 *Revista aragonesa de administración pública* 155; T Moreo Marroig, 'La paradoja de ejecutar los fondos Next Generation EU y no causar daño al medioambiente' in X Lazo Vitoria (ed), *Compra Pública Verde y Cambio Climático* (Barcelona, Atelier, 2022). The importance of this Fund is also recognised in the Italian context, see G Botta, 'Italy: Leading the Way towards Mandatory Sustainable Public Procurement through Minimum Environmental Criteria', ch 11 in this volume.

[30] The funds, a total of €750 billion, were agreed by the European Council on 21 July 2020. Around €140 billion of this amount are allocated to Spain.

administration and implementation of these resources.[31] These rules feature a section devoted specifically to public procurement since the latter is one of the channels that will have the greatest impact on the use of these funds.

Regulations issued by both the state and Autonomous Regions establish as a preferential instrument the preparation of model procurement documents that incorporate SPP considerations. In this regard, RD-Law 36/2020 emphasises the benefits of standardising procurement processes so/to ensure these always include 'all the green, digital, innovation, SME-empowerment and social responsibility criteria deemed necessary and which are covered by the corresponding legal regulation'. (Article 50). Likewise, the legislation of some Autonomous Regions such as Catalonia and Andalusia sets out a similar regulation. This is undoubtedly the right decision given that such model procurement documents promote the inclusion of social, environmental and innovation considerations/criteria across the board in all procurement processes, thereby avoiding fragmentation of this task.

It is worth noting that while Andalusia has opted to reiterate the state regulation for its own region, Catalonia, in contrast, establishes more specific obligations. It specifies that the award criteria and special conditions for the performance of contracts 'must include' one or more of the following:

> improvements in salary or working conditions; employment stability; incorporation of people at risk of social exclusion (including the long-term unemployed); subcontracting with a specialised work centre or reintegration enterprise; calculation of life cycle; fair trade; locally-sourced products; environmental criteria; digitalisation, innovation and knowledge criteria; promotion of SMEs and tertiary sector organisations; and gender equality.

Besides model procurement documents, a major portion of the regulations approved by the Autonomous Regions includes specific SPP provisions. The below table shows how these SPP clauses appear, for example, as selection criteria, technical specifications, award criteria or special conditions for the performance of contracts. A clear preference for including SPP requirements in the form of award criteria can be detected. Furthermore, in order to promote quality as opposed to an approach focused primarily on price, some rules have been introduced to limit the weight of the latter as an award criterion. This is the case for the Canary Islands, which states emphatically that 'the selection of the award criteria must be clearly aligned with the best quality-price ratio, *with the idea of value rather than price*' (emphasis added) and that the price will represent a maximum of 30 per cent of the total points that can be awarded (Article 41).

[31] See Royal Decree-Law 36/2020, of 30 December, which establishes urgent measures for the modernisation of the Public Administration and for implementation of the Recovery, Transformation and Resilience Plan. This state Regulation was subsequently developed in two Ministerial Orders, both dated 29 September 2021. For the autonomous regions, 12 out of the 17 had approved specific Regulations on this matter at the time of completing this work. All legislation on Next Generation Funds approved in Spain has been systematised in a document that is updated regularly. See the Independent Office for the Regulation and Supervision of Public Procurement (OIReScon), Guía Básica Plan de Recuperación, Transformación y Resiliencia at www.hacienda.gob.es/es-ES/Oirescon/Paginas/HomeOirescon.aspx.

Table 6 Overview of SPP requirements in Next Generation EU[32]

	Autonomous Regions						
SUSTAINABLE PROCUREMENT	ANDALUSIA	BALEARIC ISLANDS	CANARY ISLANDS	CASTILE-LA MANCHA	CATALONIA	EXTREMADURA	AUTONOMOUS REGION OF VALENCIA
MODEL PROCUREMENT DOCUMENT	✓	✓	⊗	✓	✓	⊗	⊗
SELECTION CRITERIA	⊗	⊗	✓	⊗	⊗	⊗	⊗
AWARD CRITERIA	✓	⊗	✓	✓	⊗	✓	✓
TECHNICAL SPECIFICATIONS	⊗	⊗	⊗	⊗	⊗	⊗	⊗
CONDITIONS FOR PERFORMANCE OF CONTRACTS	⊗	⊗	⊗	⊗	⊗	⊗	⊗
GENERAL CRITERIA	⊗	⊗	⊗	⊗	✓	⊗	⊗

[32] Royal Decree-Law 36/2020.

VI. SPP Mandatory Requirements in Sector-Specific Legislation

This analysis of Spanish legislation would not be complete without reference to sectoral/sector-specific legislation that has progressively established a broad range of SPP mandatory requirements.[33] Given the limited length of this chapter, we are able to offer only a few examples here. Some Autonomous Regions have adopted specific laws on food and food wastage. These contain procedural SPP mandatory requirements, for example, Catalonia's Law 3/2020, of 11 March, on the prevention of food loss and wastage, which requires the inclusion of clauses aimed at targeting food loss and wastage in public contracts. In Castile-La Mancha, Decree 19/2019, of 26 March, promotes measures to prevent food wastage and to facilitate the redistribution of food. This orders the incorporation of requirements concerning food redistribution in procurement documents, especially in the form of award criteria.[34]

A second area is the waste sector. For example, the recent Spanish Law 7/2022, of 8 April, on contaminated waste and soils for a circular economy, requires public contracts to include the use of products that are highly durable, reusable, repairable or made of recyclable materials, as well as products made with waste materials or by-products.[35] And finally, it is important to mention the highly progressive Basque Country legislation (Law 10/2021 of December 9 on the Environmental Administration of the Basque Country) which, among many other innovations, stipulates the inclusion of a minimum percentage of 40 per cent of by-products, secondary raw materials and recycled materials in works and supply contracts.[36]

[33] For an analysis of the obligation of incorporating SPP through sector legislation, see P Válcarcel, 'Impulso decisivo en la consolidación de una contratación pública responsable. Contratos verdes: De la posibilidad a la obligación' (2011) 1 *Actualidad jurídica ambiental* 16; I Sanz Rubiales, 'La protección del ambiente en la nueva ley de contratos: Del estado meramente "comprador" al estado "ordenador"' (2018) 205 *Revista de administración pública* 57.

[34] For an overview of Spanish law, see L Salamero, 'El desperdicio de alimentos' in L Salamero (ed), *Manual Básico de Derecho Alimentario* (Tirant lo Blanch, Valencia, 2019). Additionally, note that a State Bill on the Prevention of Food Losses and Waste is being debated, but this adopts a non-mandatory approach.

[35] See F Sanz Larruga, 'Comentario al título I de la ley de residuos y suelos contaminados para una economía circular: Instrumentos de la política de residuos (Arts. 14-16)' (2022) 21 *Revista aragonesa de administración pública*, 139.

[36] See X Lazo Vitoria, 'Una nota a la futura ley de administración ambiental de euskadi: Compra verde obligatoria y eco innovación' (2021) *Observatorio de contratación pública* at www.obcp.es/opiniones/una-nota-la-futura-ley-de-administracion-ambiental-de-euskadi-compra-verde-obligatoria-y.

VII. Lessons Learned and Challenges of SPP in Spain

Spain is progressing towards consolidating a mandatory model of sustainable public procurement.[37] The legislative landscape described above is very extensive, is evolving rapidly[38] and accounts for a very wide range of SPP mandatory requirements. In spite of this, this tool has not yet unleashed its full transformational power.

This stems first from the complexity of the legal framework itself and the lack of readiness of the contracting authorities for a sustainable approach in the preparation of tenders. Therefore, increased professionalism is key to consolidating SPP. Providing contracting authorities with resources and comprehensive training is still the great 'remaining challenge'.[39] This lack of professionalism is exacerbated by the highly fragmented nature of public procurement in Spain, that is, there is a multitude of small public buyers 'without expertise or the necessary means'.[40] It is, therefore, necessary to accompany progress in the legal framework with strong governance[41] to drive and facilitate sustainable public procurement for both contracting authorities and tendering companies.

The preparation of catalogues, guidelines and other tools is essential to provide legal certainty and minimise the margin of error. These catalogues offer clear benefits: standardised, up-to-date clauses which have undergone a technical and legal review to enable their incorporation directly or with minimal adaptation. These catalogues are particularly important where contracting authorities have a greater margin of discretion (procedural SPP mandatory requirements).

On the other hand, a report by the Government of Spain (2021) indicates that the introduction of SPP has been hampered by difficulties in complying with the requirement to link to the contract subject matter when trying to adapt to specific procurement procedures the open worded SPP criteria laid down by the LCSP or the RD-L 3/2020.[42] This is directly related to the restrictive interpretation of the incorporation of social and environmental clauses maintained by some courts annulling buying decisions taken on the basis of the rather vague mandates in the

[37] The mandate to include social, environmental and innovation clauses (LCSP and RD-L 3/2020) has played a fundamental role in this process. Note that many of the laws cited in this work reproduce this mandate for their own scope of application.

[38] Proof of this is, eg, the Draft Bill on the Organisation and Strategic Use of Public Procurement in Aragon.

[39] MA Sanmartín Mora, 'La profesionalización de la contratación pública' in JM Gimeno (ed), *Observatorio de contratos públicos 2011* (Navarra, Aranzadi, 2012).

[40] See Government of Spain, Triennial Report on public procurement in Spain in 2018, 2019 and 2020 at www.hacienda.gob.es.

[41] This is what has taken place in the Basque Country, where the level of green public procurement is around 26% of total tenders and presents a degree of implementation of 3.7 (out of 5) on SDG indicator 12.7.1.

[42] The report states that there exist even greater difficulties in the case of award criteria of a social nature, given the need to measure the performance of bids, something which is particularly complex in the social field.

LCSP and RD-L 3/2020,[43] something which has been strongly criticised in the literature.[44] In this regard, there is substantial room for improvement and clarification of the legal requirements.[45] This might lead some economic operators to challenge procurement documents for rather than against sustainability.

Finally, the establishment of mechanisms for monitoring, controlling and evaluating SPP requirements (eg, through performance indicators) remains essential. This often-overlooked aspect is undoubtedly vital for assessing not only the suitability of the clauses incorporated into each contract, but also for evaluating progress in sustainable public procurement in an objective way.

[43] Above section IIff.

[44] See JA Moreno Molina, 'Criterios sociales de adjudicación en el marco de la contratación pública estratégica y sostenible Post-Covid 19' (2021) 210 *Revista Española de derecho administrativo* 45. For example, an award criterion is not considered to be related to the subject matter of the contract when it consists of the following: a) a rise in salary above that stipulated in the sector agreement (cleaning services); b) work-life balance measures; c) the requirement of a gender equality plan; d) measures for integrating people with disabilities and/or at risk of exclusion from the labour market. This is because 'it does not improve the quality of the services delivered under the contract, or the performance or characteristics of the contract'.

[45] The aforementioned report states that the European Commission should make a pronouncement on this requirement, which would simplify the task of contracting authorities, 12.

PART 4

Future Perspectives – The Future of Sustainable Public Procurement

14

Mandatory Requirements in Public Procurement Law: The Role of Remedies, Courts and Public Interest Litigation

FRANÇOIS LICHÈRE AND ORIANE SULPICE[1]

I. Introduction

The use of public procurement to promote sustainability is a growing concern in several EU Member States. While so far most EU public procurement law, as written in Directive 2014/24/EU, is simply enabling Sustainable Public Procurement (SPP), some Member States have taken more ambitious measures by imposing obligations upon contracting authorities. Italy, Spain and the Netherlands may be mentioned here, but also more recently France with Article 35 of the law of 22 August 2021, which will come into force in 2026.[2] Moreover, the European Green Deal advocates minimum mandatory green criteria, targets, and product regulation for public procurement are foreseen in sectoral initiatives.[3] Thus, SPP is enforced by a growing number of hard and soft law measures that contracting authorities are encouraged to apply. Several research reports have suggested

[1] The authors are most grateful to Giulia Botta for her inputs in explaining the Italian cases quoted in this chapter.

[2] G Botta, 'Italy: Leading the Way towards Mandatory Sustainable Public Procurement through Minimum Environmental Criteria', ch 11 in this volume; P Heijnsbroek, 'The Netherlands: Obligations to Justify the Lowest Price and to Create as Much Societal Value as Possible', ch 12 in this volume; X Lazo-Vitoria, 'Spain: Transitioning towards Sustainable Public Procurement Mandatory Requirements', ch 13 in this volume.

[3] T Tátrai and O Diófási-Kovács, 'European Green Deal – the Way to Circular Public Procurement' (2021) 22 *ERA Forum* 523; A Sapir, T Schraepen and S Tagliapietra, 'Green Public Procurement: A Neglected Tool in the European Green Deal Toolbox?' (2022) 57 *Intereconomics* 175; W Janssen, 'Shifting towards Mandatory Sustainability Requirements in EU Public Procurement Law: Context, Relevance and a Typology', ch 1 in this volume; R Caranta and W Janssen, 'Collective Reflections on the Future of Mandatory Sustainable Public Procurement', ch 15 in this volume.

reforms to reinforce sustainability through public procurement.[4] This will inevitably have consequences for the system of remedies as well.

From the outset, it must be recalled that the principle of procedural autonomy of the EU Member States still plays an important role and that it is unlikely that the Remedies Directive will be amended in the near future. This Directive states in Article 1 that

> Member States shall take the measures necessary to ensure that (…) decisions taken by the contracting authorities may be reviewed effectively and, in particular, as rapidly as possible

but has few details on how to implement this objective.[5] Therefore, the following reflections rely more on the Member States' system of remedies with a specific emphasis on French and Italian law, as both systems present a lot of case law that is interesting in terms of public procurement law and remedies.

Given that the legal framework on environmental and social considerations for public procurement is recent, one cannot really take a retrospective look at litigation patterns. Nevertheless, with the help of some older and recent case law, we can try to imagine the role that economic operators or other types of litigants could play when mandatory sustainable requirements come into effect. Despite the broader focus of the European Green Deal mentioned before, the focus here will mainly be on the environmental category, because minimum mandatory GPP requirements have been applied in Italy since 2017 through technical specifications and contract performance conditions imposed for a specific purchase, whereas in France they will take the form of mandatory award criteria and environmental clauses from 2026 onwards.

In France, the inclusion of sustainable development objectives in the definition of a contracting authority's needs is a legal obligation but the courts have taken a restrictive approach towards it (section II.A below). At present, 'environmental' contract clauses are present in 13.47 per cent of all public contracts of French national authorities and in 17.61 per cent of those of local authorities.[6] Comparatively, Italy is more advanced. Under Article 34, 'energy and environmental sustainability criteria' of the Italian Public Contracts Code, which was recast in 2017, all public authorities must include minimum environmental criteria (CAM) in their public procurement procedures (technical specifications and contract performance clauses) for 18 specific categories of public procurement.[7]

[4] M Andhov et al, 'Sustainability Through Public Procurement: The Way Forward Reform Proposals' (2020) 25 *SSRN Electronic Journal* 1; World Bank, *Green Public Procurement: An Overview of Green Reforms in Country Procurement Systems, Climate Governance Papers* (Washington DC, World Bank, 2021).

[5] R Caranta, 'The Interplay between EU Legislation and Effectiveness, Effective Judicial Protection and the Right to an Effective Remedy in EU Public Procurement Law' (2019) 12 *REALaw* 63.

[6] Ministère de l'économie, des finances et de la relance, 'Recensement économique de la commande publique Chiffres 2020' at www.economie.gouv.fr/files/files/directions_services/daj/marches_publics/oecp/recensement/recensement_chiffres2020_20211012.pdf/.

[7] Botta (n 2).

The possible introduction of mandatory requirements at the EU level is likely to change the role of remedies as set out by the EU Remedies Directive and by Member States' statutory law or case law. This poses novel and numerous questions: what role should economic operators play in upholding these requirements before the national courts, particularly when – as it is often the case – national enforcement agencies are not present? Can these participants indeed challenge the set-up of procurement or even 'what' is being procured? Is this a new form of public interest litigation? To try to answer these questions, we will investigate what measures can be challenged (section II) and who can challenge them, which leads to the question of civil society litigations (section III).

II. What Measures can be Challenged When SPP Mandatory Requirements are at Stake?

The following paragraphs deal with legal arguments that competitors may put forward in challenging either the award process or the lawfulness of the contract itself in case mandatory requirements are in place, like in Italy from 2017 or in France from 2026 onwards. There can be two different situations: either the contracting authority has not demanded enough with regard to mandatory sustainable requirements set by law, which could lead to the risk of non-compliance with these requirements (eg, in the case of a very low weighting for the ecological criterion) or has gone too far regarding the latter, which in turn could lead to the risk of discrimination or the absence of a link with the subject matter of the contract (eg, setting Corporate Social Responsibility policies as an award criterion). In the third section of this subchapter, we will consider specific legal arguments for third parties other than economic operators, which could extend the availability of standing before the courts.

A. General Provisions and Targets

Some legal texts tend to set up obligations in such general terms that one may wonder if they are enforceable. For instance, under the former French Code on public procurement (*Code des marches publics*, replaced in 2018 by the *Code de la commande publique* in order to include provisions on concession contracts and which reiterated the formula),

> The nature and extent of the needs to be met shall be precisely determined before any call for competition or any negotiation not preceded by a call for competition, taking into account sustainable development objectives.[8]

[8] Authors' translation.

This appears to be a similar legislative provision to the one that currently exists in the Netherlands, where contracting authorities are procedurally asked to procure 'as much societal value as possible for their public expenditures'.[9] Similarly, such a broad approach also exists in Spain where there is an obligation to take 'social, environmental and innovation considerations' into account in the definition of the contractual subject matter.[10] In a 2011 judgment, the *Conseil d'Etat*, the Supreme Administrative Court in France, held that the French provision quoted above requires contracting authorities to balance different objectives, but not the inclusion of a specific environmental criterion, as long as the award is based on Most Economically Advantageous Tender (MEAT) criteria, which was indeed the case as the price was combined with technical criteria.[11] Furthermore, the *Conseil d'Etat* noted that the technical criteria indeed included one environmental aspect but, unlike in Spain, this does not seem to have been decisive in the reasoning.[12] In applying the same provision in another case, the *Conseil d'Etat* dismissed the argument that the objective of sustainable development must lead a contracting authority to admit a variant that is more favourable to it despite variants not being allowed by the contract notice.[13] The lesson from these French judgments is that to produce any binding legal effect, precise sustainability requirements must be embedded in provisions dealing with technical specifications and award criteria rather than just being enshrined in general objectives. This appears to align with the approach taken by the Dutch Courts in enforcing the obligation mentioned before.[14]

The enforceability of general provisions may also be questioned concerning targets set in sectoral EU legislation and addressed to the Member States rather than to contracting authorities. For instance, Article 5 of revised Clean Vehicles Directive provides that

> Member States shall ensure that the procurement of vehicles and services referred to in Article 3 complies with the minimum procurement targets for clean light-duty vehicles set out in Table 3 of the Annex and for clean heavy-duty vehicles set out in Table 4 of the Annex. Those targets are expressed as minimum percentages of clean vehicles in the total number of road transport vehicles covered by the aggregate of all contracts referred to in Article 3, awarded between 2 August 2021 and 31 December 2025, for the first reference period, and between 1 January 2026 and 31 December 2030, for the second reference period.

As also discussed by Andhov and Muscaritoli, it is very unlikely that a court would overturn a specific award procedure on the basis that it would not secure the attainment of a general objective set for a given Member State, even if the contracting

[9] Heijnsbroek (n 2).
[10] Lazo-Vitoria (n 2).
[11] CE, 23 November 2011, *Communauté urbaine de Nice-Côte d'Azur*, n° 351570.
[12] Lazo-Vitoria (n 2).
[13] CE 31 March 2010, *Syndicat mixte de la région d'Auray Belz Quiberon*, n° 333970.
[14] WA Janssen and G Bouwman, 'Legislating Societal Value in Dutch Public Procurement Law: From Symbolism to Substance' (2020) 2 *Public Procurement Law Review* 91.

authority were part of the government, that is, not independent from the authority that must enforce this obligation, because it still lacks the specific responsibility under the law to meet the general objective.[15] Indeed, if the Member State did not transpose the EU targets into measurable and enforceable duties for contracting authorities, courts facing a challenge to a specific public procurement procedure would not have the full picture. In other words, a macroeconomic objective cannot be enforced at the microeconomic level. This is probably the reason why, when transposing this Directive, the French Government mirrored the obligations of the Member States to each contracting authority or entity. However, it remains uncertain whether a third party could challenge a given award procedure if there is only a general requirement to buy a certain percentage of clean vehicles since the challenger would face difficulties to prove that the given award procedure breaches the general objective set for a given contracting authority.

B. Minimum (Threshold) Mandatory Requirements/Criteria

The issue of setting a minimum sustainability weighting is regularly raised in academic spheres,[16] courtrooms and public debates. As an example of the latter, in 2021, the French Government rejected a member of Parliament's proposal to set a 20 per cent minimum weighting for environmental criteria, stating that it was not suitable for intellectual services, without even considering its adoption for works and supply contracts only.

In the absence of such a precise weighting in the public procurement legislation, can the courts set a minimum weighting if a statute requires that sustainability is considered in the award criteria? In theory, the separation of powers between the executive and the judiciary may restrain courts from being proactive in this regard, unless the law clearly encourages it.[17] However, the presence of general obligations in the law may set this question aside since they could be interpreted by courts as encouraging them to be more proactive even without explicitly requiring it. It may all depend on whether the courts are inclined to make a teleological interpretation of the law but it is not yet clear whether it will be the case.

Some indications as to the probable answer may be drawn from the case law concerning a requirement to include an award criterion on sub-contracting to SMEs that was foreseen by a 2004 law regarding public-private partnerships. A French ministry put the weighting of this criterion at two per cent, which clearly implied that this criterion had no substantial effect, but it was not challenged.

[15] M Andhov and F Muscaritoli, 'Climate Change and Public Procurement: Are We Shifting the Legal Discourse?', ch 2 in this volume.

[16] F Lichère, 'La Loi Climat et Résilience et la Commande Publique: Lutte Contre le Réchauffement Climatique ou Renforcement de la Résilience Face à ses Effets ?' [2022] *AJDA January* 31.

[17] Indeed, one can imagine a specific law adopted by parliament which would insist that contracting authorities – ie, part of the executive – should favour green procurement: a teleological interpretation of the law may be sufficient to impose a minimum of weighting.

However, it is not clear whether any court, if asked the question, would have been inclined to adopt a proactive approach by imposing a minimum weighting as this might affect the discretionary power of contracting authorities to procure as they see fit.[18] A French law clearly making price a mandatory award criterion did not lead to a very demanding position from the French *Conseil d'Etat*. It refused to overturn an award procedure for a service contract for civil servant training that had set the price at only 10 per cent and the quality at 90 per cent in the award criteria.[19] Nonetheless, it is true that one of the arguments put forward by the French *rapporteur public* (a position similar to an advocate general before the CJEU) in that case relied on the risk of side effects if the *Conseil d'Etat* had annulled the decision.[20] Contracting authorities would have interpreted the case law as implying that the price criterion should be given an important weighting, something which is already often done in practice and regularly denounced as the cause of difficulties or even litigations during the execution phase.[21] In addition, the conclusions of the *rapporteur public* did not exclude that a lower weighting could be treated as being equivalent to no criterion, which would then be unlawful if the criterion were mandatory. In other words, although the *Conseil d'Etat* did not have to rule on this point, the *rapporteur public* concluded that, when an award criterion is mandatory, the courts may rule out a low weighting even if the law does not expressly set a minimum of weighting, but only if it is very low (much less than 10 per cent). So, if a given rule were to set out that an environmental award criterion is obligatory, it is unlikely that the courts would rule out a weighting as being insufficient, unless the weighting would result in rendering the criterion nugatory.

C. Precise SPP Requirements and Contract Drafting

It is common ground that contracting authorities enjoy a wide margin of discretion when drafting the contract as this relates to the definition of their needs. No one can currently challenge the contract subject matter per se. As shown by consistent French case law, only an insufficient definition of the subject matter may be challenged as clarity is required under the Public Procurement Directives. Rules defining specific SPP requirements may result in the fact that courts will become more demanding. For example, in an Italian case, the winning bidder claimed in front of a T.A.R., an administrative court of first instance, that the provisions of Article 34 of the Public Contracts Code were not to be followed rigidly by the

[18] Janssen (n 2).
[19] CE 10 June 2020, *Ministère de la défense*, n° 431194.
[20] Available at www.conseil-etat.fr/arianeweb/#/view-document/?storage=true.
[21] See the 2nd report of the *Chaire de droit des contrats publics* (in French) which regards the links between award rules and bad performance of public contracts, see at chairedcp.univ-lyon3.fr/themes-de-recherches-et-rapports-1.

contracting authority, but rather that the administration could have provided for a duration of the contract different from the one indicated by the Minimum Environmental Requirements (Criteri Ambientali Minimi (CAM)). The Court clarified that the contracting authorities are not only obliged in general terms to fulfil general sustainability objectives, but they must also follow procedures and modalities and minimum criteria under the specific Ministerial Decree having adopted the specific CAM at stake.[22] Furthermore, the Court referred to the margins of discretion of the administration in relation to the CAM, stating that it is absolutely correct and appropriate for a contracting authority to pursue its own needs, but it is not within its discretion to decide whether and how to pursue environmental objectives, given that the law requires it to comply with the CAM. The *Consiglio di Stato* confirmed that the public procurement procedure was unlawful and set it aside.[23]

D. Types of Sustainable Requirements and the Risk of Contradictions Between Them

The question may be posed as to whether a legal claim could be lodged before the courts on the grounds that, despite the presence of an environmental requirement, it is not one of such a nature as to fulfil the goals envisioned, for instance, the fight against climate change. For instance, by 2026, French law will require that award criteria must take into account environmental considerations without defining which type or level of consideration is required. It would be a big improvement if courts were to rule that contracting authorities must combine this obligation with the general obligation to fight climate change following the Paris Agreement of 2015 (COP 21) and require that this criterion must at least refer to the fight against climate change. In some countries, such as France and the Netherlands, courts have already issued injunctions to the governments to act in order to reach the Paris Agreement's goals outside the scope of public procurement (see below section III).

There may also be a risk of contradictions between the science behind sustainable requirements which might complicate the proactive approach. For instance, the use of fair-trade labels – or an equivalent – is legally possible, but it still often means in practice that products are procured from overseas, which is not compatible with a reduction of greenhouse gases.[24] For example, electric cars are virtuous with regard to gas emissions (although this is questionable when one takes into consideration the production stage), but they create other environmental impacts linked to the production and recycling of electric batteries. It is unlikely, however,

[22] Botta (n 2).
[23] Cons. Stato, sec. V, 3 febbraio 2021, n. 972.
[24] F Akoka, 'Contrats publics et environnement' (PhD thesis, Aix-Marseille | 2020) 272.

that this could be challenged, especially since the choice was clearly made by the EU institutions to favour electric vehicles. This complicates the viability of legal claims before the courts, because courts do not have clear-cut answers on what is sustainable and what is not.

E. Risk of Discrimination or Lack of a Link with the Subject Matter of the Contract

In this paragraph, we examine the extent to which a third party could challenge SPP requirements as being too demanding, that is, as creating a risk of discrimination or lacking a link with the subject matter of the contract. This is not specific to SPP requirements, because it may arise every time the need to balance sustainability and competition is present, but the interviews carried out by the Chair of Public Contract Law in Spring 2022 clearly reflect a much higher risk of discrimination in favour of local products and services when SPP considerations are at stake.[25] Under the EU free movement law, discrimination can take two forms: direct or indirect. Requirements may have either the object or the effect of favouring local economic operators. For instance, a proactive approach to de-pollution led a French local authority to demand that food suppliers grow vegetables in local depolluted areas, which is clearly illegal. More generally, GPP is often associated with the development of the local economy.[26]

However, the question is more delicate if, for instance, a contracting authority sets an award criterion on greenhouse gas emissions with a substantial weighting. Would that be considered compatible with the Public Procurement Directives and more generally with the free movement principles enshrined in the Treaty on the Functioning of the European Union (TFEU)? One may think that it might hide localism, but one may also see it as a necessity to take this into account in the fight against climate change. In a 2011 ruling, the French *Conseil d'Etat* admitted that the distance of waste transportation was a lawful sub-criterion, but it is not clear whether this was allowed because it may limit traffic jams or because of the reduction of carbon footprint effects. In this context, the Public Procurement Directives must be clearer because of a potential conflict with fundamental free movement principles and also because of a risk of contradictory assessments by different courts in the Member States.

The indirect risk of discrimination can, furthermore, be illustrated by situations where sustainable requirements leave too much discretion to contracting authorities. This is mainly the case with insufficient transparency of award criteria and the like. The French *Conseil d'Etat* has a clear and regularly applied case law on

[25] See the 4th report of the Chair, available (in French) at chairedcp.univ-lyon3.fr/themes-de-recherches-et-rapports-4.

[26] ibid 100.

the transparency of criteria (and sub-criteria if their weighting may have an impact on the outcome). The Court decided that contracting authorities must design criteria that are sufficiently detailed for the economic operators to draft their bids accordingly and to reduce the margin of appreciation of contracting authorities. For example, the aesthetic criterion for the supply of bus shelters must be precise enough, which is not the case if there are no sub-criteria or details to implement this main criterion.[27] The risk of insufficient transparency is not specific to sustainable criteria but might be increased if the contracting authorities decide to set up vague requirements. It must be noted that, by requiring the application of the principle of transparency, neither the courts nor the *rapporteurs publics* referred to the case law of the CJEU, which was instead referred to by the *rapporteurs publics* when recommending the application of the *Telaustria* or *Teckal* with reference to in house providing.[28]

The assessment of risk of discrimination is, needless to say, necessarily subjective. This is exemplified by the 2011 above-mentioned case, where a *tribunal administratif* (administrative court of first instance in France) had overruled the award procedure, because it was not sufficiently precise regarding the application of the sub-criterion that aimed to diminish the distance between the public works location and the waste area, but the *Conseil d'Etat* ruled otherwise.

Indirect discrimination may also occur in unexpected circumstances. In a very interesting ruling, an Italian T.A.R. ruled that, while it was lawful to require that a percentage of products for catering procurement possessed specific environmental certifications, the contracting authority had failed to conduct an adequate market analysis to check their actual availability of the market. The procedure was therefore deemed to be discriminatory and against open competition.[29] Interestingly, several contracting authorities are at present drafting green criteria and model clauses with the help of local firms' representatives to overcome this problem and to be in line with what is technically and economically feasible, as interviews carried out by the Chair revealed.[30]

Regarding the link between the award criterion and the subject matter of the contract, the risk of the former being found unlawful in the case of mandatory ecological award criterion is nowadays reduced by a more flexible approach by the courts, both at the EU level[31] and at the national level. In a milestone case of 2013, the French *Conseil d'Etat* ruled that

> in the context of a procedure for the award of a contract which, in view of its subject-matter, is likely to be performed, at least in part, by staff engaged in an integration

[27] CE, 28 April 2006, *Ville de Toulouse*, n°280197.

[28] Case C-107/98 *Teckal Srl v Comune di Viano and Azienda Gas-Acqua Consorziale (AGAC) di Reggio Emilia* ECLI:EU:C:1999:562, [1999] ECR I-08121 Case C-324/98 *Telaustria Verlags GmbH and Telefonadress GmbH v Telekom Austria AG* ECLI:EU:C:2000:669, [2000] ECR I-10745.

[29] TAR Lombardia-Milano, sec. IV, 12.02.2019, n. 403.

[30] See 4th report of the Chair (n 25).

[31] Case C-368/10 *Commission v Kingdom of the Netherlands (Max Havelaar)* ECLI:EU:C:2012:284, [2012] ECR I-284.

> process, the contracting authority may legally provide for the assessment of tenders in the light of the criterion of the professional integration of persons in difficulty, provided that this criterion is not discriminatory and enables it to assess these tenders objectively.[32]

Remarkably, the Court checked the feasibility of the requirement when it made reference to a 'contract likely to be performed by staff engaged in an integration process'. In other words, the Court demands that such a criterion is practically possible. This is a step forward from a 2001 case in which the *Conseil d'Etat* ruled that any social award criterion would appear as not having a link with the subject matter of the contract. This 2001 case based its reasoning on a very economical approach to public procurement: public procurement is made to procure what could respond to the primary needs of the contracting authorities but not for promoting horizontal objectives. The condition of a link with the subject matter of the contract has not evolved since then: the *Conseil d'Etat* simply has now a different approach to this condition.[33]

Despite this more flexible approach, the *Conseil d'Etat*, not surprisingly, overturned an award criterion based on the candidates' Corporate Social Responsibility policy, which quite clearly is not subject matter orientated as also explicitly stipulated by Recital 67 to the Public Procurement Directive. After having recalled the legal provisions, it declared

> criteria of a social nature, relating in particular to employment, working conditions or the integration of persons in difficulty into the labour market, may concern all the activities of the tendering undertakings, provided that they contribute to the performance of the services provided for by the contract; these provisions do not, however, have the object or effect of allowing the use of a criterion relating to the general social policy of the undertaking, assessed in the light of its entire activity and applicable without distinction to all the purchaser's contracts, irrespective of the subject matter or conditions of performance specific to the contract in question.[34]

F. Means of Proof for SPP

Any award criterion presupposes that contracting authorities are able to assess the accuracy of the tenders; a criterion which will most likely not be checked jeopardises competition at the award stage if chosen by the contracting authority. This is in essence what the CJEU held in the *EVN* case precisely regarding an environmental criterion.[35]

[32] CE 25 March 2013, *Département de l'Isère*, n° 364950 (Authors' translation).
[33] CE, 25 July 2001, *Commune de Gravelines*, n°229666.
[34] CE, 25 May 2018, *Nantes Métropole*, n°417580 (Authors' translation).
[35] Case C-448/01 *EVN AG and Wienstrom GmbH v Republik Österreich* ECLI:EU:C:2003:651, [2003] ECR I-14527.

A mandatory SPP criterion might render the assessment of the accuracy of tenders more difficult as their assessment is often more subjective than other award criteria, such as more easily quantifiable criteria like price or delivery time. Admittedly, the *EVN* case dealt with renewable electricity and part of the ruling was linked to this peculiar subject matter, but the first condition set by the CJEU for the lawfulness of environmental criteria does apply to any sustainable criterion: it must be 'accompanied by requirements which permit the accuracy of the information contained in the tenders to be effectively verified'.

Since *Max Havelaar*, it is permitted to take into account the green and social impacts at the production stage of any products; however, this may entail difficulties in applying the *EVN* requirement regarding tenders, especially those related to products coming from outside the EU.[36] Is the use of labels or certifications the only paradigm when it comes to technical specifications? Maybe not, as shown by the Italian example of CAM quoted above which sets precise technical specifications in the decrees for the 18 concerned sectors, although it may also lead to challenges. In another Italian case, the appellant claimed that according to the CAM, the components, parts and materials used for the supply of furniture for scientific laboratories should have not contained particular types of additives in a predetermined concentration, or substances identified as 'substances of very high concern' (SVHCs), as provided by Article 59 of REACH Regulation. In order to prove the existence of these characteristics, the tenderer should have submitted a declaration and proof showing compliance. However, the successful tenderer did not produce all of the necessary certifications and declarations. The Court confirmed the first instance decision that the company had to be excluded because it had not complied with the tender requirements.[37] In another relevant Italian case, technical specifications were at stake and required specifically the possession of a 'luminous intensity class' with a value corresponding to at least 'G3-class'. The Court confirmed that this characteristic was not complied with by the products offered by the preferred tenderer and concluded that the conduct of the contracting authority was unlawful.[38] Similarly, the Dutch courts have also placed a high burden of proof on those wanting to challenge the contracting authority assessment as to the sustainability merits of a tender. More specifically, they have avoided such discussions altogether by referring to the broad margin of appreciation for contracting authorities in assessing the means of proof.[39]

III. Civil Society Litigation

Whereas litigation in public procurement has so far been based on economic operators filing claims before the courts, civil society and general interest organisations

[36] *Max Havelaar* (n 31).
[37] Cons. Stato, sec. VI, 4.04.2019, n. 2344.
[38] TAR Toscana, sec. I, 14.05.2018, n. 645.
[39] Heijnsbroek (n 2).

may be interested in challenging public procurement decisions in so far as the environmental – and possibly social – considerations are at stake. In fact, the 'political contestability' of public contracts may lead third parties, especially political opponents and interest groups, such as for instance environmental associations, to challenge these contracts and the award procedures before the courts.[40] It is now well established from a variety of studies that their challenges ensure the accountability of public authorities. In fact, the efficiency of public procurement 'is a substantial component of voters' political choices'.[41] Furthermore, concerned or interested parties and the overall political context influence the way the public agent designs the award and performance of public contracts and management issues may become political issues.[42] Nowadays, the political environment is marked by climate change and by a strong demand for the state to implement efficient environmental policies. It has previously been observed that public contracts have become an instrument for environmental risk management and environmental protection.[43] The contract may, accordingly, be analysed as a substitute for law or law enforcement.[44] Yet, much uncertainty still exists about the relationship between the accountability of contracting authorities and SPP.

There is a growing body of literature that recognises the importance of climate change litigation.[45] NGOs and other concerned/interested parties have gone before the courts to force governments to act against climate change. In fact, 'as of March 2017 climate change cases had been filed in 24 countries (25 if one counts the European Union), with 654 cases filed in the U.S. and over 230 cases filed in all other countries combined'.[46] Courts have condemned states for not respecting the limits for the emission of GHG contained in international conventions, or because national laws are insufficient to fight climate change.[47] They have grounded their

[40] C Cravero, 'Rethinking the Role of Civil Society in Public Procurement' (2019) 14 *European Procurement and Public Private Partnership Law Review* 30.

[41] J Beuve, MW Moszoro and S Saussier, 'Political Contestability and Public Contract Rigidity: An Analysis of Procurement Contracts' (2018) 28 *Journal of Economics & Management Strategy* 316.

[42] MW Moszoro and PT Spiller, 'Political Contestability and Public Contracting' (2018) 21 *Journal of Public Economic Theory* 945.

[43] M Hautereau-Boutonnet, 'Le Contrat Environnemental' [2015] *Recueil Dalloz* 217.

[44] M Hautereau-Boutonnet and E Truilhé-Marengo, 'Regards Thématiques sur le Droit Comparé de l'Environnement' (2015) 40 *Revue juridique de l'environnement* 211.

[45] See, eg, S Maljean-Dubois, 'Climate Change Litigation' in *Max Planck Encyclopedia of Procedural Law* (2019); S Maljean-Dubois, 'A Quand un Contentieux Interétatique sur les Changements Climatiques?' [2021] *Questions of International Law* 17; J Setzer and LC Vanhala 'Climate Change Litigation: A Review of Research on Courts and Litigants in Climate Governance' (2019) 10 *Wiley Interdisciplinary Reviews: Climate Change* 580; J Peel and HM Osofsky, 'A Rights Turn in Climate Change Litigation?' (2018) 7 *Transnational Environmental Law* 37; F Sultana, 'Critical Climate Justice' (2021) 188 *The Geographical Journal* 118; L Wegener, 'Can the Paris Agreement Help Climate Change Litigation and Vice Versa?' (2020) 9 *Transnational Environmental Law* 17.

[46] United Nations Environment Programme & Columbia University, Sabin Center for Climate Change Law, *The Status of Climate Change Litigation: A Global Review* (2017) 10.

[47] M Torre-Schaub, 'Le Contentieux Climatique: du Passé vers l'Avenir' (2022) *7 RFDA* 75.

case law on the Paris Agreement of 2015, and on national laws, in Germany,[48] the Netherlands,[49] the UK,[50] and France.[51]

The standing of representatives of civil society and other concerned parties to challenge public contracts could be a way to enforce the implementation of a mandatory SPP legal framework. In the following paragraphs, we will explore the idea that the political contestability of public contracts could find a new path in the challenge of a public contract by third parties as environmental defenders. Thus, climate change litigation could find a new ground of application in the field of public contracts. We will analyse who can challenge public contracts as interested/concerned parties (A), what can be challenged (B), and what redress can be claimed (C).

A. Typology of Interested/Concerned Parties: Who Can Challenge?

The identification of interested/concerned parties is crucial. We will define them as all of the persons that are neither parties to a public contract nor are having or had an interest in obtaining a particular contract. Therefore, we are not concerned here with economic operators whose interests are protected under Article 1 of the Remedies Directive. In some jurisdictions, such as in France, those interested/concerned parties are also known as 'third parties', meaning that they are not a party to a concluded contract. Public or general interest parties/litigants are also used in this sense.[52] Several applicants may be identified as possible interested/concerned parties who might be able to challenge public contracts for not integrating environmental considerations. To stand before the courts, they have to prove that they have a sufficient stake in the outcome of the case and that their claims are capable of judicial resolution. Moreover, in France, they generally have to prove that they have suffered or will suffer, a loss caused by the public body's allegedly unlawful behaviour. We examine first existing cases already allowing a challenge against public contracts from interested/concerned or third parties in France, and then who could be able to do so in the future.

i. Existing Interested/Concerned/Third Parties

In some countries, such as France, case law and legislation allow third parties to challenge the validity of a contract. This might be a way for third parties to force

[48] A Gaillet and D Grimm, 'La Décision Climat de Karlsruhe' (2022) 31 *AJDA* 166.

[49] *State of the Netherlands v Urgenda Foundation*, Hoge Raad der Nederlanden [Supreme Court of the Netherlands], Dec. 12, 2019, Case No. [2015] HAZA C/09/00456689.

[50] *R (on the application of Friends of the Earth Ltd and others) v Heathrow Airport Ltd* [2020] UKSC 52.

[51] CE, 1 Juillet 2021, *Commune de Grand-Synthe*, n°427301; TA Paris, 14 Octobre 2021, n° 1904967, 1904968, 1904972, 1904976/4-1 (*l'Affaire du siècle*).

[52] HW Micklitz and N Reich (eds), *Public Interest Litigation before European Courts* (Baden-Baden, Nomos, 1996).

contracting authorities to comply with mandatory sustainability requirements and more precisely to consider climate change or social injustice in the award procedure. The United Nations Environment Program (UNEP) identifies 'defenders of the environment' as 'individuals and groups who, in their personal or professional capacity and a peaceful manner, strive to protect and promote human rights relating to the environment, including water, air, land, flora and fauna'.[53] The right of defenders of the environment to access justice is internationally recognised, and we will build on this concept further below. More specifically, the Aarhus Convention of 1998 and the Communication of European Commission Notice on Access to Justice in Environmental Matters of 2017[54] set a common framework of obligations for public authorities and rights for the public, which was widely interpreted by the CJEU in the *Altrip* case.[55] In this regard, environmental associations could be identified as interested/concerned or third parties who can challenge decisions, acts, omissions and contracts from public authorities, including with reference to public procurement. The Aarhus Convention Compliance Committee has already indicated that

> While the Convention relates to environmental matters, there may be legal provisions that do not promote protection of the environment, which can be violated when a decision under article 6 of the Convention is adopted, for instance, provisions concerning conditions for building and construction, economic aspects of investments, trade, finance, public procurement rules, etc. Therefore, review procedures according to article 9, paragraph 2, of the Convention should not be restricted to alleged violations of national law 'serving the environment', 'relating to the environment' or 'promoting the protection of the environment', as there is no legal basis for such limitation in the Convention.[56]

The political contestability of public procurement contracts regarding environmental or social considerations could be inspired by existing remedies against public contracts. For example, in France, the Council of State stated in 2014 that any third party can challenge public contracts.[57] More precisely, third parties may invoke the grounds of illegality directly related to the injured interest they invoke. This decision had some effects, especially on NGOs, who took the opportunity to challenge concession contracts in the field of windmills and water distribution. In several cases, the courts held that individuals as users of the public electricity service do not have a sufficient stake in the outcome of the case whereas environmental associations do. The Administrative Court of Appeal of Nantes ruled that

> the applicant associations, whose aim is either the protection of the maritime environment or the prevention of ecological, technological and sanitary damage, in particular

[53] United Nations Environment Programme, 'Who are environmental defenders?' at www.unep.org/explore-topics/environmental-rights-and-governance/what-we-do/advancing-environmental-rights/who.

[54] Notice on Access to Justice in Environmental Matters C(2017) 2616.

[55] Case C-72/12 *Gemeinde Altrip and Others v Land Rheinland-Pfalz* ECLI:EU:C:2013:712, [2013].

[56] Germany ACCC/C/2008/31; ECE/MP.PP/C.1/2014/8, 4 June 2014, para 78.

[57] CE, 4 Avril 2014, *Département Tarn et Garonne*, n° 358994.

> that linked to the deployment of renewable energies, justify an interest that gives them standing to act against the concession agreement for the use of the public maritime domain.[58]

This conclusion was followed in other similar cases.[59] A different case concerned an agreement outsourcing the public service of production and distribution of drinking water. The Court gave standing to an association whose purpose was to carry out actions for the genuine direct public management of water under the control of the citizens on the whole territory of the local authority.[60] Thus, public contracts in France can be challenged before the courts by an NGO on environmental grounds.

ii. Future Interested/Concerned/Third Parties

We will explore three further options for the enforcement of environmental considerations in public contracts. We will first refer to existing public authorities, then to a defender of the environment, and finally to a possible environmental class or representative action.

In some jurisdictions, specific public authorities may challenge public contracts before the courts, as is the case with the *Préfet* (local state representative) in France. Their role is to review the legality of local authority acts in France and to challenge them before the courts if they are illegal. This authority could bring public contracts to administrative courts for not complying with the GPP legal framework.

One could also imagine the creation of an independent authority as the Defender of Environmental Rights. This authority could oversee the enforcement of environmental law. In fact, in several countries, an Ombudsperson or Defender of Rights already has a power related to environmental considerations. The recent reports of a French member of Parliament enumerate six of these authorities, in Argentina, Belgium, the Czech Republic, Greece, Ontario and Spain.[61] Moreover, the French Citizens' Climate Convention proposed to introduce into French Law an Environmental Defender based on the model of the Defender of Rights.[62] Thus, the Defender of the Environment could be a guardian of green considerations in public procurement if the Parliament so wishes. One can imagine special remedies dedicated to ensuring the enforcement of compulsory green criteria. The same could be set for social considerations.

[58] CAA Nantes, 3 Avril 2018, n° 17NT01851 (Authors' translation).

[59] CAA Nantes, 3 Avril 2018, n° 17NT01735; CAA Nantes, 3 Avril 2018, n°17NT01943; CAA Nantes 17 Juillet 2020, n° 19NT01651.

[60] CAA Marseille, 19 Janvier 2022, n° 19MA05754.

[61] C Muschotti, 'Création d'un défenseur de l'environnement et des générations futures' at cidce.org/wp-content/uploads/2021/07/Rapport-Muschotti-2021.pdf.

[62] Convention citoyenne pour le climat, 'Renforcer le contrôle des politiques environnementales' at propositions.conventioncitoyennepourleclimat.fr/objectif/renforcer-le-controle-des-politiques-environnementales-axe-de-reflexion/.

The French Citizens' Climate Convention has also proposed to broaden the possibility of a class action for environmental damage.[63] Under French law, the possibility for an environmental class action was introduced in 2018.[64] This representative action can concern infringements of legislative provisions relating to the protection of nature and the environment, the improvement of the living environment, the protection of water, air, soil, sites and landscapes, town planning, maritime fisheries, the fight against pollution and nuisances, nuclear safety and radiation protection, commercial practices, and misleading advertising. It can only be brought by registered associations. Accordingly, a small possibility for representative actions exists in environmental matters; NGOs are, however, reluctant to use this procedure even if they could in theory claim damages for environmental harm (see below section III.C).[65]

B. What Can Be Challenged by Interested/Concerned/ Third Parties?

How could defenders of the environment have recourse to law and justice with reference to SPP? On the one hand, one ground of review may be used to challenge every step of the contract award procedure. On the other hand, it is possible to identify two moments of the life cycle of a public contract where third parties can challenge contracts: the award procedure and the execution of the contract.

i. Challenging the Adequacy of Public Contracts in Light of Environmental Objectives

A public contract can be challenged in the light of either the environmental legal framework or the GPP national and international rules. Regarding the environmental legal framework, public contracts could be challenged under the provisions of environmental law for not respecting the national or international objectives of greenhouse gas emissions, or the pollution of water, air and soil etc.

Even if they are not mandatory, international, national and local GPP criteria and requirements offer interesting grounds on which to challenge public contracts before the courts. They set up general objectives that public contracts should reach. Regarding GPP rules, international and national provisions could also be enforced by the courts. The 2012 revision of the WTO Agreement on Government Procurement allowed for the inclusion of environmental considerations in

[63] ibid.
[64] Article L.142-3-1 II du Code de l'environnement.
[65] L Radisson, 'Pourquoi l'action de groupe environnementale ne fonctionne pas' at www.actu-environnement.com/ae/news/action-groupe-environnement-rapport-mission-assemblee-nationale-35684.php4.

technical specifications and tender evaluation criteria.[66] More to the point, international agreements created a common standard, especially regarding the limitation of GHG emissions by the Tokyo agreement of 1997 and the Paris Agreement of 2015, which provide new grounds to challenge public contracts along the lines of what has already happened in several climate justice cases.[67] Furthermore, the national objectives of GPP could be used by third parties to challenge public contracts. For example, in France, there is a national GPP action plan for 2021–25, that sets non-binding objectives. Moreover, there are local action plans for local public buyers (called *SPASER*). The national action plan can be considered as soft law as its drafting is not required by law, whereas a local action plan is compulsory for each local public buyer if the amount of their purchases exceeds €50 million per year (€100 million until 2023). Of the 160 entities obliged to adopt a *SPASER*, however, only 34 have complied with this obligation, whose enforcement is not defined by the law. The question then becomes whether it is possible to challenge the lawfulness of a public contract in the light of either the national scheme or of a *SPASER*. It is conceivable that a court could sanction the failure of a public contract to comply with the objectives and indicators contained in the national plan and more likely so of local plans since they must be adopted.

ii. Challenging the Award Procedure

In addition to what is required by the Remedies Directive, in France, third parties can challenge the award of a public contract (section III.A.ii).[68] They can even argue that a contract should be 'ended' by the contracting authority, either by way of termination (*résiliation*) or by way of annulment (*annulation*) due to illegal content or a serious defect of illegality (*vices d'une particulière gravité*). In any case, the courts can issue an injunction towards a public purchaser to end the contract unless the defect may be amended or unless the general interest requires the contract to be maintained.[69] The already recalled example of the windmill's concession in France shows clearly that this remedy can be used to challenge the award of a concession before the administrative courts although the action was dismissed on its merits. In some Italian cases, indeed the courts found unlawful the lack of application of the required green considerations in the tender and annulled the procedure.[70] The Italian top administrative court has even declared ineffective a contract concluded based on a call for tender breaching the applicable CAM.[71]

[66] Article X.6 of the WTO Agreement on Government Procurement: 'It is understood that a Party, including its contracting entities, may, in accordance with this Article, establish, adopt or apply technical specifications to encourage the conservation of natural resources or protect the environment' at www.wto.org/french/docs_f/legal_f/rev-gpr-94_01_f.pdf.

[67] See (n 49ff).

[68] CE, 4 Avril 2014, *Département de Tarn-et-Garonne*, n° 358994.

[69] CE, 30 Juin 2017, *Syndicat mixte de promotion de l'activité transmanche*, n° 398445.

[70] TAR Lombardia–Milano, sec. I, 24.04.2020, n. 685; Cons. Stato, sec. V, 3.02.2021, n. 972; Cons. Stato, sec. VI, 4.04.2019, n. 2344.

[71] Cons. Stato, sec. III, 14 ottobre 2022, n. 8773; see A Iurascu, 'How Will the Adoption of Mandatory GPP Criteria Change the Game? Lessons from the Italian Experience' (forthcoming).

iii. Challenging the Execution of the Contract

Interested/concerned or third parties may challenge the execution of the contract either because contract clauses were not respected or because the clauses themselves are inconsistent with environmental considerations.

If the environmental clauses of a contract are not respected, civil society or some of its representatives should be afforded some remedy. It could also be a class action or a remedy reserved for NGOs. Courts should, in our opinion, reconsider the French principle of the so-called relative effect of contracts –that is, the effects of a contract are in principle limited exclusively to the parties to the contract – since we would be dealing with public contracts subject to specific sustainable requirements. Still, this would probably require new legislation, as the courts, including administrative courts, are still very much in favour of the 'relative effects' principle.[72]

Moreover, the legality of certain clauses of the contract can be challenged by third parties to the contract (section III.A.i). In French urban planning law, which could serve as a model in this regard, there are three types of relationships between the different urban planning acts: consideration, compatibility and conformity. Thus, the legality of the clauses could be controlled through these different aspects regarding environmental law and the GPP legal framework. For example, we may consider that the clauses of a contract should take into account the national objectives of greenhouse gas emissions and should be compatible with the local objectives of SPP, such as *SPASER* in France, as long as the local objectives are more ambitious than the national objectives. Moreover, the relationship of conformity should be established regarding GPP rules, when the national law sets a minimum of environmental clauses, such as requiring a minimum of recycled furniture, such as in Italy.

To conclude, in France, as is already the case in Italy, mandatory sustainable requirements are likely to be challenged by interested/concerned/third parties other than competitors.

However, there is a risk that the threat of challenges by third parties, especially NGOs, may compromise the willingness to act of contracting authorities, or may overload the courts' agenda, or both. Therefore, the courts are likely to allow the challenge of either public contracts or of their awards by those parties as long as precise sustainable requirements are not fulfilled by the contracting authorities. Allowing challenges against public contracts in so far as they are not sufficient with regard to, for instance, the Paris Agreement of 2015, may require the adoption of specific legislation and this is unlikely to happen due to the above-mentioned risks. Challenges in the general interest should be reserved to a special Ombudsperson. This may also depend on what could be claimed as discussed below.

[72] See F Lichère in *Mélanges Ricci* (forthcoming).

C. What Remedial Action Could Be Taken

Before the contract is signed, it is clear that competitors could claim that some contract clauses are not compatible with mandatory sustainability requirements. However, in France, the argument is usually accepted by the courts as long as the breach affects the claimant's interests. The claimant would, thus, have to prove that its tender had a better chance of being chosen, had the requirement been fulfilled, which renders the challenge more difficult. In France, the state representative (*préfet*) could instead challenge local contracts' award on any grounds. Concerning already signed contracts, an international common legal standard in environmental law is the necessity to restore harm caused to the environment, referred to as environmental harm.[73] Two paths could be followed to make a claim in the environmental remedies against public contracts.

First, the contract could be terminated, for example when the economic operator is condemned for environmental damage. It must be recalled that Article 57(4)(a) of Directive 2014/24/EU sets an exclusion ground

> where the contracting authority can demonstrate by any appropriate means a violation of applicable obligations referred to in Article 18(2)

the latter stating that

> Member States shall take appropriate measures to ensure that in the performance of public contracts economic operators comply with applicable obligations in the fields of environmental, social and labour law established by Union law, national law, collective agreements or by the international environmental, social and labour law provisions listed in Annex X.[74]

However, these provisions have not been implemented in French law so it would need a statute law. On the other hand, the French Code authorises the termination of the contract in case the contractor faces an exclusion ground during the performance of the contract.

In France, the question of whether a public contract could be ended in case it lacks sustainability requirements depends on whether administrative courts would eventually consider the given clauses divisible or not from the rest of the contract. This question is still pending.

Second, concerning damages, the main issue is to ensure that no more environmental harm will be done by means of the execution of the contract either because it directly harms the environment or because it does not comply with environmental legislation. In the French context, two main cases in the field of climate change litigation show what can be claimed by third parties: the *Notre Affaire à*

[73] S Maljean-Dubois, 'L'émergence du développement durable comme paradigme et sa traduction juridique sur la scène internationale' in B Villalba (ed), *Appropriations du développement durable* (Villeneuve d'Ascq, Presses Universitaires du Septentrion, 2009).

[74] Janssen (n 2); Andhov and Muscaritoli (n 15).

Tous case and the *Commune de Grande Synthe* of 2021.[75] In the first case, the liability of the state was engaged before the administrative court of the first instance of Paris.[76] In the second case, the unlawfulness of the refusal to comply with the Paris Agreement of 2015 and the greenhouse gas emission trajectory was claimed by the applicants. The second case led to an expedited decision of the court. An injunction was granted with a financial penalty for delay after 31 March 2022. In line with these cases, litigants could claim damages to restore nature by themselves. Moreover, courts can pronounce an injunction towards public purchasers to force them to take decisions that abide by international and national laws in addition to damages, as recognised recently by the *Conseil d'Etat*.[77]

As a matter of EU law, the availability of damages will depend instead on how the recent judgment in *JP* is read.[78]

IV. Conclusion

One of the more significant findings to emerge from this chapter is that the consistency of public contracts with environmental and social objectives is theoretically possible. It will depend on the activism of NGOs and on the will of the courts to condemn contracting authorities for breaches of international agreements or national law. In fact, applicants could certainly challenge the award procedure and the clauses and the execution of public contracts if the requirements were precise enough.

However, the question is still raised as to whether the courts would adopt such a proactive approach, both in terms of what could be challenged and who could make the challenge. An amendment of the Remedies Directive, which requires standing to the benefit of those having an interest in being awarded the contract only, would be helpful in this regard but is very unlikely to be adopted due to the reluctance of the Member States and the EU principle of procedural autonomy of Member States. A way forward could be to reflect on public enforcement rather than private enforcement. In other words, there is a clear need to ensure that public authorities are in charge of reviewing the award process or the clauses in order to enforce the potential new duties. Competition authorities can be taken as examples in this regard, despite the fact that they are in charge of sanctioning abuse of dominant position and collusive agreements rather than sanctioning a lack of enforcement of positive obligations.

[75] *Commune de Grand-Synthe* (n 51).

[76] *L'Affaire du siècle* (n 51).

[77] CE, 12 Avril 2022, *SCI La Closerie*, n°458176.

[78] Case C-61/21 *JP v Ministre de la Transition écologique and Premier ministre* ECLI:EU:C:2022:1015, [2022].

15

Collective Reflections on the Future of Mandatory Sustainable Public Procurement

ROBERTO CARANTA AND WILLEM JANSSEN

I. Introduction

As the paradigm shift from regulating 'how to buy' towards 'what to buy' is unfolding at the EU and Member State level, the purpose of this book is to gain an understanding of this development and to critically assess it whilst – mostly the EU – seems bound to further stimulate it. This is imperative, because shaping the appropriate balance between mandatory and voluntary requirements will increasingly come to the forefront when assessing the suitability of the legal framework for Sustainable Public Procurement (SPP) in the EU in light of urgent societal challenges like climate change and social injustice.

The richness of the analysis collected in this book makes it difficult to draw conclusions without making some choice about what to include in the final discussion. Building on the structure given to the book itself, we decided to bring together the main findings in the general and sectoral chapters with what experiences and lessons might be drawn from the national chapters in order to, subsequently, assess the reforms flowing from the European Green Deal and other policy initiatives impacting on public procurement. The typology of possible mandatory sustainability requirements in chapter one will be used to organise the discussion. Finally, the analysis of two general themes runs throughout this book. The first being remedies, and the question of how this system of redress is to change in the future. The second being efficiency and effectiveness, which also includes perspectives on alternative modes of regulation and subsidiarity and will close these conclusions.

The importance of the discussion in this book goes beyond the scope of the EU because this is a global phenomenon going well beyond its borders.[1]

[1] G Piga and SL Schooner, 'Transformational Procurement – The Past and Future of Global and Local Public Purchasing – Views from the Expert Community on What Public Money Did and Will Still Need to Buy' (2022) 64 *Government Contractor* 7.

The regulatory toolbox for 'what to buy' comes in many shapes and forms. As indicated in the introduction to this book, mandatory approaches to SPP may be classified as either establishing criteria to be included in the contract documents for a specific procurement or setting percentage targets to be achieved at a more or less aggregate level (individual contracting authority, territorial level or the state in a wide sense).[2] The two approaches merge when the target is set at 100 per cent. This is the case of the Balearic Islands requiring 100 per cent energy of certified renewable energy.[3] Criteria may in turn be differentiated by distinguishing between substantive and procedural requirements, depending on whether they describe what is going to be bought or simply give the contracting authority an indication of how to choose what is bought (eg, by indicating that societal value must be achieved). Structurally akin to substantive criteria is to refer in the contract documents to (general) product requirements. Here, however, SPP very much fades in ordinary public procurement as what is sought is what is lawfully available on the market. Often, as indicated by Andhov and Muscaritoli, we are faced with a 'mixture' of criteria depicting targets and requirements.[4]

The typology of SPP requirements, including minimum mandatory public procurement criteria, (public procurement) targets and product-specific legislation, acts both as a ruler to organise the different approaches to SPP and as a benchmark to evaluate them. The national experiences covered in this book – Italy, the Netherlands and Spain – plus the sectoral studies – transport, textiles, food and construction – in addition to the discussions about primary law, the Public Procurement Directives and other EU secondary legislation, showcase a wide array of different approaches to mandatory SPP.

II. Procedural and Substantive Criteria

As a means to direct the competitive set-up of a procedure, procedural criteria come into two main guises: either as an obligation to consider or to take into account sustainability in general or specific considerations associated with it,[5] or as a duty to give a reason why a more sustainable course is not followed in the buying decision.[6]

A major advantage of this regulatory approach is that it empowers each and every contracting authority with discretion as to how far to engage in SPP, whose exercise is ideally tailored to the specific circumstances – concerning both the

[2] W Janssen, 'Shifting towards Mandatory Sustainability Requirements in EU Public Procurement Law: Context, Relevance and a Typology', ch 1 in this volume, section VI.

[3] X Lazo-Vitoria, 'Spain: Transitioning towards Sustainable Public Procurement Mandatory Requirements', ch 13 in this volume, before the start of section V.

[4] ibid end of section V.

[5] ibid nn 14 and 15.

[6] ibid n 16.

market and its own resources to monitor what is delivered – of each procurement. It is an approach that fits well from the perspective of subsidiarity.[7]

The risk is, of course, that many if not most contracting authorities will treat this as one more fastidious formality. Accordingly, they might resort to rubber stamp reasons explaining away SPP solutions or to include SPP criteria that go no further than what is required by the law. The latter seems to be the case in Spain.[8]

It goes without saying that the width of the discretion actually left to contracting authorities ultimately depends on the litigation patterns in each Member State and on the standard of review adhered to by national courts. If a hard look is given by those courts at the reasons offered by contracting authorities not to go for SPP, most public buyers will rather not take the risk. If instead rubber stamping by courts is the prevailing judicial style, green mouthing will be prevalent.[9]

Unsurprisingly, some proposed EU measures seem to move away from procedural requirements towards hard requirements. One example is provided by the Old Energy Efficiency Directive. Article 6(1) (*Purchasing by public bodies*) provided that

> central governments purchase only products, services and buildings with high energy-efficiency performance, insofar as that is consistent with cost-effectiveness, economical feasibility, wider sustainability, technical suitability, as well as sufficient competition.

One way to strengthen SPP in the Proposed recast has been to do away with conditionality.[10] In the detailed explanation of the specific provisions of the proposal the Commission argues that

> Article 7 strengthens the public procurement provisions by extending the obligation to take into account the energy efficiency requirements by all public administration levels, and by removing conditionalities with regard to cost-effectiveness, technical and economic feasibility.[11]

A variation of this approach is the indication to Spanish contracting authorities to insert in each public contract 'at least' one environmental or social (or innovative) condition.[12] Interestingly, this move between regulatory approaches has also

[7] And this is even if the CJEU tends not to assess the subsidiarity of individual provisions in larger legislative measures as those discussed in T van den Brink, 'Subsidiarity Lost Along the Way? EU Public Procurement Legislation on the Road to Sustainability', ch 3 in this volume n 25.

[8] Lazo-Vitoria (n 3) n 23.

[9] The standard of review is notoriously very diverging in the Member States, see PP Craig, 'Judicial Review of Questions of Law: A Comparative Perspective' in SR Ackerman and P Lindseth (eds), *Comparative Administrative Law*, 2nd edn (Cheltenham, Edward Elgar, 2019). Also, on the hesitant stance of the courts to review open norms, see, P Heijnsbroek, 'The Netherlands: Obligations to Justify the Lowest Price and to Create as Much Societal Value as Possible', ch 12 in this volume.

[10] D Gruyaert and V Pissierssens, 'Transforming the Construction Sector through Minimum Requirements', ch 10 in this volume after n 33.

[11] Proposal for an Energy Efficiency Directive (recast) COM(2021) 558, 20; in the impact assessment preceding its Proposal for a recast, the Commission has also referred to simplification as one reason to do away with conditionality: 'Removing conditionalities of cost-effectiveness, technical or economic feasibility as regards energy efficiency requirements in public procurement will simplify the implementation of the energy efficiency requirements, as they will apply equally to all public authorities.'

[12] These should be contract performance conditions, see Lazo-Vitoria (n 3) n 19.

materialised in a different manner, namely from procedurally requiring the use of technical specifications and/or award criteria towards targets under the Clean Vehicles Directive. More attention should be paid to the underpinning of such regulatory changes, which at present does not seem to attract much thought.[13]

Substantive criteria are the more muscular approach to regulating SPP by mandating the level of sustainable public procurement. These criteria could in fact benefit internal budgetary discussions that question if sustainable public procurement should be put more towards the forefront. Mandatory requirements of this sort direct the policy course without the need for such discussions, because the 'what to buy' decision is to some extent taken away from the contracting authorities and transferred to the EU lawmakers. As is well known, under Article 5(3) Treaty on European Union (TEU), this competence shift is only allowed when

> the objectives of the proposed action cannot be sufficiently achieved by the Member States, either at central level or at the regional and local level, but can rather, by reason of the scale or effects of the proposed action, be better achieved at Union level

As the Circular Economy Action Plan avows, the shift towards mandatory criteria is born out of the realisation that instruments such as the EU GPP criteria 'have reduced impact due to the limitations of voluntary approaches'.[14] Pouikli has highlighted the existing

> misbalance between the discretion assigned to contracting authorities within the existing voluntary GPP regime and the role of the public procurement as a mechanism to increase compliance of MS with environmental objectives.[15]

Two very different approaches are given to mandatory-substantive SPP criteria. One is the use of very open-worded clauses. An example is provided by Article L 3.1 of the French Public Contracts Code as added by the 2021 Climate Law. It provides that public procurement is to contribute to the attainment of sustainable development in its three components.[16]

The most substantial limit in using very open-worded clauses is that (some) contracting authorities will content themselves with introducing in turn very vague – and unenforceable – stipulations in the contract documents or with including reference to requirements which are already mandatory under the applicable legislation.[17] This is also the result of a broad open norm that was included

[13] A Semple, 'Charge of the Light Brigade? The Clean Vehicles Directive and the Batteries Regulation', ch 7 in this volume.

[14] A New Circular Economy Action Plan, COM(2020) 98 para 2.1.

[15] K Pouikli, 'Towards Mandatory Green Public Procurement (GPP) Requirements under the EU Green Deal: Reconsidering the Role of Public Procurement as an Environmental Policy Tool' (2021) 21 *ERA Forum* 699, 701.

[16] F Lichère and O Sulpice, 'Mandatory Requirements in Public Procurement Law: The Role of Remedies, Courts and Public Interest Litigation', ch 14 in this volume, section II.A.

[17] XLazo-Vitoria (n 3) n 23.

in the Netherlands, which requires contracting authorities to procure based on a vague notion of 'as much societal value as possible'.[18] On the other hand, decisions by sustainability-minded contracting authorities might be challenged as having too thin a basis in the legislation.[19] A variation of the approach based on procedural requirements combines more or less vague clauses with a mandate to comply or explain.[20] Here again, there is some risk of contracting authorities resorting to standard formulas to explain away SPP when not fearing some form of supervision, including litigation.[21]

The other approach to substantive SPP criteria consists in laying down detailed prescriptions for the contracting authorities to include in their procurement documents. This approach is followed in Italy. The Minimum Environmental Requirements (CAMs) include technical specifications and contract performance conditions that must be adopted by contracting authorities for both below and above the EU thresholds contracts.[22]

The most striking instance among the recent Commission's proposals is Article 19 of the Net Zero Industry Act. The proposed provision binds contracting authorities and entities to include sustainability and supply security in their award criteria, such as 'environmental sustainability going beyond the minimum requirements in applicable legislation'.[23]

The Proposal for a European Critical Raw Materials Act provides for mandatory SPP award criteria via national programme implementation. Under its Article 25, the Member States will have to adopt and implement national programmes containing inter alia measures designed to 'increase the use of secondary critical raw materials in manufacturing, including, where appropriate, by taking recycled content into account in award criteria related to public procurement'.[24]

Interestingly, a few of the presently proposed EU measures give the Commission the power to enact mandatory SPP criteria through delegated legislation. This is the case for instance with the Construction Products Regulation[25] and the Batteries Regulation.[26] This is interesting as it provides more regulatory space for the Commission without having to go through the full EU legislative process. Problematically, it might be deemed an illegitimate delegation, should it ultimately

[18] Heijnsbroek (n 9).

[19] Lazo-Vitoria (n 3) n 23 and after reference to n 41; Lichère and Sulpice (n 16) after reference to n 11.

[20] F Schotanus and R Nicholas, 'Coercive, Memetic and Normative Influences on the Uptake of Sustainable Public Procurement: An Institutional Perspective', ch 5 in this volume, nn 28 and 43.

[21] ibid nn 28 and 30.

[22] G Botta, 'Italy: Leading the Way towards Mandatory Sustainable Public Procurement through Minimum Environmental Criteria', ch 11 in this volume, section III.C.

[23] Proposal for a Net Zero Industry Act COM(2023) 161.

[24] Proposal for a Regulation on critical raw materials COM(2023) 160.

[25] Art 84 of Proposal for a Revision of the Construction Products Regulation COM(2022) 144; See Gruyaert and Pissierssens (n 10) after reference to n 47; see also R Caranta, 'Towards Mandatory SPP for Buildings/Works' (2022) 4 *Eur. Journal of Public Proc. Markets* 9.

[26] Art 70 of Proposal for a Batteries Regulation (COM)2020 798; see Semple (n 13) n 35.

prove to be an essential instead of a non-essential part of the regulatory framework based on the Schengen Border Case.[27]

Finally, to avoid criteria becoming outdated, binding substantive criteria need to be updated on a rolling base, which might be a costly exercise.[28] This is what is already happening on a rolling basis with the EU GPP criteria. Somewhat surprisingly, the European Commission proposals flowing from the European Green Deal seem oblivious to the work already done in this area, which has been taken up in a number of Member States, such as Italy.[29]

III. Horizontal and Sectoral Criteria

The regulatory choice between horizontal cross-cutting criteria versus sectoral criteria also proves relevant in the move to regulating 'what to buy'. It comes to the forefront as a choice between tailor-made rules and generic rules. For instance, a recurrent example of horizontal procedural SPP criterion concerns limitations to the use of the lowest price/cost. The lowest price/cost award criteria depress not just quality but might lead tenderers to squeeze their workforce. This led the European Parliament to ask for the Most Economically Advantageous Tender (MEAT) to become the only award criterion, but the lowest price/cost is still there for instance in Article 67 of the Classic Directive.[30] However, a number of Member States are taking advantage of the option left to them by the last phrase in Article 67(2) to limit recourse to the lowest price/cost or require justification to have recourse to them.[31] However, the problem remains that very low weight is given to quality. To avoid this issue, Spain provides that quality shall account for at least 51 per cent of the award of contracts for 'services to the person'.[32] In this respect, the Netherlands currently forces contracting authorities to motivate the choice to award contracts based on the lowest life cycle costs, which is surprising to say the least considering the advantage for the environment of the use of such award criteria.[33]

Somewhere between horizontal and sectoral are often requirements flowing from legislation enacted to fight climate change. Those requirements tend to focus on contracts relating to specific goods or services, but often, as is the case with Spain, the list of relevant contracts is very long.[34] Similar considerations apply to

[27] See more on this, WA Janssen, 'On Discretion & Sustainability in EU Public Procurement Law: From Room for Diversity to Unity?' in T van den Brink and V Passalaqua (eds), *Diversity and Unity in the European Union* (Cheltenham, Edward Elgar, forthcoming, 2023).

[28] Schotanus and Nicholas (n 20) phrase after reference to n 22.

[29] Bott (n 22) n 25.

[30] See A Semple, 'Article 67 Contract Award Criteria' in R Caranta and A Sanchez-Graells (eds), *Commentary on Directive 2014/24/EU* (Cheltenham, Edward Elgar Publishing, 2021) 709.

[31] See, eg, Lazo-Vitoria (n 3) n 16.

[32] Lazo-Vitoria (n 3) n 17.

[33] Heijnsbroek (n 9).

[34] Lazo-Vitori a (n 3) paragraph after n 28.

provisions related to procurements passed in the implementation of EU grants from the Recovery and Resilience Facility.[35]

At present, most mandatory SPP measures that are in effect or tabled before the EU legislature are, ultimately, sectoral. While procedural criteria may in theory be included in horizontal public procurement provisions, such as those in the Public Procurement Directives, substantive criteria, targets and product requirements can only be specific, tailored to the specific characteristic of a given product or sector. For instance, mandatory SPP targets are laid down in the Energy Performance of the Buildings Directive and the Clean Vehicles Directive. Furthermore, mandatory SPP (substantive) criteria are foreseen in the Proposal for a Revision of the Construction Products Regulation[36] and Proposal for a Batteries Regulation.[37]

IV. (Public Procurement) Targets

As a second broad category of mandatory sustainability requirements, setting targets is the less intrusive approach to SPP, because it leaves it to the Member States to decide how to achieve the targets themselves. Therefore, it complies with the gravity effect of the subsidiarity principle and leaves decisions to the governance level closer to the people.[38]

Targets may be plotted along a line between two poles.[39] On the one hand, we have targets referring directly to improvements to a general sustainability goal (eg, reduction of global warming or of unemployment in minority populations). This is the case, for instance, with the Climate Act, setting a target of at least a 55 per cent reduction of net emissions of greenhouse gases as compared to 1990.[40] SPP rules may be instrumental in reaching – but are not normally designed with reference to – these broad targets. SPP is, however, often mentioned in national planning documents adopted on the basis of EU targets. The targets set in the EU Climate Act are spread over the Member States according to the Efforts Sharing Regulation, while the Governance Regulation requires the Member States to adopt national energy and climate plans (NECPs). All the Member States referred to SPP in their plans, and some went on to require percentages of sustainable goods to be procured.[41] On the other hand, we have targets referred to the acquisition of specific and well-defined 'sustainable goods'. The latter is the case with the new Clean Vehicles Directive. It sets binding targets for each Member State in terms of the number of low and zero-emissions vehicles procured as a percentage of overall

[35] ibid section V.
[36] Gruyaert and Pissierssens (n 10) end of section II.D.
[37] Semple (n 13) section IV.
[38] van den Brink (n 7) first page of the chapter.
[39] See also M Andhov and F Muscaritoli, 'Climate Change and Public Procurement: Are We Shifting the Legal Discourse?', ch 2 in this volume section VI.
[40] ibid section IV.B.
[41] For detailed analyses see Andhov and Muscaritoli (n 37).

vehicle procurement.[42] The same applies to the purchase of buses by a public transport company according to the Belgian NECP.[43] Somewhere in between the two poles are those targets requiring some action necessarily implying the conclusion of public contracts. This is the case with energy upgrade targets in the Energy Efficiency Directive which will be translated into procurements for works and maintenance services.[44]

As noted before, targets may also be a fallback position from more ambitious or at least more stringent mandatory SPP criteria. This is the story of the revised Clean Vehicles Directive. The old Clean Vehicles Directive gave contracting authorities the choice between (not very demanding) technical specifications and rather complex – or at least novel for most contracting authorities – award criteria based on life cycle costing.[45]

Mandatory SPP by targets entails an accrued need for monitoring and possibly enforcement at the central (EU) level. Monitoring is necessarily premised upon reporting requirements for the Member States. Such requirements were already laid down in Article 24 of the Energy Efficiency Directive.[46] One of the weak points of the old Clean Vehicles Directive was the lack of reporting obligations.[47] The revised Clean Vehicles Directive mitigates the problem by providing for reporting periods, even if arguably rather long.[48] Still, how to enforce targets is not so clear.[49] It might also be more suitable to include reporting obligations in terms of demanding that the Member States include how they will achieve the report and how they will distribute the obligations amongst their contracting authorities.[50]

In the case of targets, technical indications as to the desired 'sustainable' requirements are still needed at the national level if not at the EU level, but their level of detail might fall short of full-fledged SPP criteria.[51] Schebesta and Palan Casado rightly remark that 'The competing dimensions of sustainability make it very complex for individual contracting authorities to draft specifications that will actually meet policy objectives relating to sustainability'.[52] As Gruyaert and Pissierssens also point out (Article 5 of the Proposal for an Energy Performance of the Buildings Directive)

> The obligation for MS to lay down minimum requirements on the energy performance of new buildings and of large existing buildings that are subject to major renovation,

[42] Semple (n 13) n 28.
[43] See Andhov and Muscaritoli (n 37) section IV.B.
[44] See Gruyaert and Pissierssens (n 10) n 30; Andhov and Muscaritoli (n 37) n 64.
[45] Semple (n 13) section II.
[46] Gruyaert and Pissierssens (n 10) n 30.
[47] Semple (n 13) section II.
[48] ibid n 33.
[49] ibid end of section III.
[50] M Andhov, R Caranta, WA Janssen and O Martin-Ortega, 'Shaping Sustainable Public Procurement Laws in the European Union', EP Greens Report, November 2022 (forthcoming, 2023).
[51] This is the case again with the revised Clean Vehicles Directive, see Semple (n 13) n 29.
[52] H Schebesta and MJ Plana Casado, 'Food: Mandatory EU Public Procurement Criteria for Food after the Farm to Fork Strategy', ch 8 in this volume, beginning of section IV.

will affect the definition of the subject matter and technical specifications of the works contract.[53]

If this is the case, we end up with substantive GPP criteria anyway, but possibly at the national – or subnational – level rather than at the EU level. This is in line with those advocating lesser EU influence on the discretion of contracting authorities to procure as they see fit subsidiarity, it is also potentially more suitable for sustainability as more ambitious Member States may go beyond EU-depicted sustainability levels. It is, however, less positive for the internal market that is at risk of fragmentation and possibly also for sustainability as some Member States might instead choose weak criteria and in the end fall short of reaching the target.

Arguably, unlike requirements, targets may easily be set down at the national level in soft law or guidance documents, which has been the case already in Member States like the Netherlands.[54] While legally speaking their enforceability through litigation may be doubtful, the bureaucratic culture in many countries might still nudge those working in contracting authorities into striving to achieve the targets set in soft law instruments.[55]

The case of Spain is interesting in this light because many approaches are followed at the same time. Targets are set by soft law,[56] while many substantive and procedural requirements are set by horizontal rules.[57]

V. Product-Specific Requirements

Under Article 26 Treaty on the Functioning of the European Union (TFEU), establishing and ensuring the functioning of a 'market without internal frontiers in which the free movement of goods, persons, services and capital is ensured' is one of the main (shared) competencies of the EU. The principle of mutual recognition has proven insufficient to this end. As a result, Article 114 TFEU gives EU institutions the power to

> adopt the measures for the approximation of the provisions laid down by law, regulation or administrative action in the Member States which have as their object the establishment and functioning of the internal market.

The Ecodesign Directive is the most relevant example of product requirements covering a wider area of energy consumption and energy-related products. In the framework of the SPI, the Commission Proposal for a Regulation on Ecodesign for

[53] Gruyaert and Pissierssens (n 10) few lines before reference to n 38.
[54] Heijnsbroek (n 9).
[55] Piga and Schooner (n 1); Lazo-Vitoria (n 3) n 12.
[56] Lazo-Vitoria(n 3) n 12.
[57] ibid n 12ff.

Sustainable Products, widening both the coverage and the ambitions of the present rules (and scaling up its EU binding force).[58]

Sectoral instances of harmonisation are provided by the textiles and clothing sector. Textiles Regulation on fibre names and related labelling and marking of the fibre composition of textiles and Regulation on Personal Protective Equipment are two examples.[59]

These measures regulate the producer rather than the procurer, thereby emphasising the need to also balance the regulatory burden between actors in the EU. Laying down (universally applicable) sustainable product requirements, as envisaged under the SPI, might make all procurement sustainable, and is therefore seen as a suitable solution for some.[60] Still, as is the case with sustainability criteria, product requirements need to be developed product by product as well, in a time-consuming process.[61]

Arguably, SPP and mandatory SPP might still be relevant even after product requirements have been laid down. Indeed, as Backes and Bouve convincingly argue, SPP and the SPI can go hand in hand and are complementary tools.[62] We can of course – and rather we must – raise the bar and clamour for less polluting and generally more sustainable vehicles as well. Still, because of the competition among automakers and the ensuing innovation, there will for sure be less polluting and somehow more sustainable vehicles on the market. However high the bar, contracting authorities – as well as consumers – will always be in a position to aim higher, and be nudged and even directed to do so and contribute more in the fight against climate change and in achieving other societal goals. As Semple has clearly indicated,

> On the one hand, progressive tightening of industry-wide emissions limits on vehicles may be considered a more direct and effective way of promoting clean transport than measures targeting public procurement. On the other hand, the widespread impact of emissions limits means that they are inevitably the target of industry lobbying and, as illustrated by the Dieselgate scandal, may also be subject to industry evasion. Using public contracts as a complementary measure – by mandating public authorities to choose vehicles with environmental performance better than minimum regulatory standards – has the potential to act as a carrot, increasing demand and returns to research and development (R&D) for more sustainable vehicles, rather than the stick of emissions regulations.[63]

[58] C Backes and M Boeve, 'Regulating the Producer instead of the Procurer – The EU Sustainable Products Initiative and Extended Producer Responsibility as Ways to Foster the Transition to a Circular Economy', ch 6 in this volume, section II.

[59] M Koszewska and JS Ligte, 'Textiles and Clothing: Mandatory Social Requirements as the Way Forward?', ch 9 in this volume, section III.A.

[60] Including Gruyaert and Pissierssens (n 10); but see Schotanus and Nicholas (n 20) reference to n 22.

[61] Backes and Boeve (n 56) after reference to n 16 and section II.C.

[62] ibid section I.

[63] Semple (n 13) n 6.

As illustrated by Koszewska and Svensky Ligte, harmonisation may also be very one-sided and, therefore, not in line with sustainable development as a trifold approach including environmental and social progress. So far, in the textile sector, mandatory standards focus on the protection of the environment, human health and consumer rights more generally. Social aspects such as workers' well-being and rights are instead not considered in harmonisation measures.[64] The more recent proposal on prohibiting products made with forced labour on the Union market might make a first start in filling this regulatory crevice.[65] Regulating the producers does not make it impossible to regulate the procurer, however. For instance, Articles 4(3)(h) and 58 of the Proposal for a Regulation on Ecodesign for Sustainable Products gives the Commission the power to draw requirements applicable to public contracts, including mandatory ones.[66]

From a different perspective, laying down product requirements does not by itself prevent Member States and contracting authorities to pursue higher or additional goals and therefore actually engaging in SPP. Unless, that is to say, full harmonisation is chosen.[67]

The risks of full harmonisation in this area – as the one envisaged in the CPR – are enormous and this is even more so if – to accommodate less innovative Member States – the bar is kept low.[68] More sustainable-minded Member States or even contracting authorities risk losing drive and momentum.[69] Or worse, they may find their procurement decision challenged by less performant and/or innovative tenderers. Alarmingly enough, the chapter by Van den Brink shows that not even subsidiarity is an argument that may be opposed to total harmonisation.[70]

Which, as a matter of proportionality, leads to a preference for legislative measures characterised as minimal harmonisation.[71] We strongly argue in favour of this within this context. The chapters in this book lead to the same conclusion that was penned by economists and public purchasing scientists. More specifically, these approaches converge in recommending a degree of discretion or flexibility to the benefit of contract authorities and public buyers (and even more so to the Member States) at least in so far as their professional level is high.[72] Consequently,

[64] Koszewska and Ligte (n 57) section III.B.
[65] Proposal for a Regulation on prohibiting products made with forced labour on the Union market' COM(2022).
[66] Backes and Boeve (n 56) last phrase of section II.B.
[67] See N de Sadeleer, 'Environmental Measures as an Obstacle to Free Movement of Goods in the Internal Market' in E Maitre-Ekern, C Dalhammar and H Bugge (eds), *Preventing Environmental Damage from Products: An Analysis of the Policy and Regulatory Framework in Europe* (Cambridge, Cambridge University Press, 2018).
[68] Caranta (n 23) 20.
[69] Schotanus and Nicholas (n 20) reference to n 22.
[70] van den Brink (n 7) paragraph after reference to n 21.
[71] ibid n 24.
[72] E Carreras and D Vannoni, 'Mandatory Requirements in Sustainable Public Procurement: The Economic Perspective', ch 4 in this volume, n 62.

in this conceptual frame, Schotanus and Nicolas advocate for procedural requirements such as 'comply or explain'.[73] Still, from the point of view of mitigating litigation risks, more stringent mandatory SPP requirements might in the end be preferable.[74]

VI. Remedies

As a regulatory closing piece, remedies must come to the forefront after the introduction of mandatory sustainability criteria to ensure enforcement. Remedies for breaches of procurement rules have been the object of an early codification already in 1989.[75] Enforceable rights given to economic operators – the *Mobilisierung des Einzelnen* – were a necessary tool to open up national public contracts markets to EU-wide competition.[76] The rather basic remedial rules enacted in 1989 soon had their scope of application widened to utilities procurement in 1992. In 2007, the rules were supplemented by additional remedies which were regulated in their finer details.[77]

Under Article 1(3) of Directive 89/665/EEC, the first Remedies Directive,

> the Member States shall ensure that the review procedures are available, under detailed rules which the Member States may establish, at least to any person having or having had an interest in obtaining a particular public supply or public works contract and who has been or risks being harmed by an alleged infringement.

(Some) economic operators might well have an interest in challenging award decisions taken in breach of applicable SPP rules. As it was indicated, 'green and social suppliers have an actual incentive' to challenge tender documents and procurement decisions not complying with mandatory SPP rules.[78] The incentive is stronger in those Member States where not inserting required SPP criteria in the contract documents might lead to contract termination[79] or ineffectiveness.[80]

[73] Schotanus and Nicholas (n 20) reference to n 43.

[74] Lichère and Sulpice (n16) n 25.

[75] See, also for further references A Sánchez-Graells, 'If ain't broke, don't fix it'? EU requirements of administrative oversight and judicial protection for public contracts' in L Folliot-Lalliot and S Torricelli (eds), *Contrôles et contentieux des contrats publics. Oversight and Challenges of public contracts* (Bruylant, Bruxelles, 2018) 495ff.

[76] See the very compelling analysis in Wollenschläger 'Deutschland' in U Neergaard, C Jackson and GS Ølykke (eds), *Public Procurement Law: Limitations, Opportunities and Paradoxes. The XXVI FIDE Congress in Copenhagen, 2014 Congress Publications* Vol 3 (DJØF, Copenhagen 2014) 390ff.

[77] See also for further references R Caranta, 'The Interplay Between EU Legislation and Effectiveness, Effective Judicial Protection and the Right to an Effective Remedy in EU Public Procurement Law' (2019) 12 *REALaw* 63.

[78] Schotanus and Nicholas (n 20) n 28.

[79] Lazo-Vitoria (n 3) n 20.

[80] Cons. Stato, sec. III, 14.10.2022, n. 8773; see A Iurascu, 'How Will the Adoption of Mandatory GPP Criteria Change the Game? Lessons from the Italian Experience' EPPPL 1/2023, 1.

Importantly, it is not just about award procedures. Not delivering on SPP clauses during contract performance might also amount to an (implicit) illegal contract award under Article 72 of the Classic Procurement Directive. This is, however, something seldom litigated before the courts, because economic operators lack both the information and even more so incentives to mount challenges against contract changes which might or might not lead to retendering, also depending on whether the changes have already been implemented.[81]

However, as shown by Lichère and Sulpice, other actors, such as NGOs, might have an even greater incentive to litigate and this concerns both individual award procedures and illegal contract modifications.[82] NGOs might more easily have an interest also in challenging procurement practices and trends – going beyond individual award procedure – as contracting authorities collectively come short of national or other targets. Public contracts might become an area for climate and wider sustainability litigation.[83]

NGOs are clearly not the only ones in charge of enforcing mandatory requirements. More traditionally speaking, manufacturers of more sustainable products might have an interest in bringing to courts states or contracting authorities missing their targets.[84]

Finally, as Lichère and Sulpice have indicated, giving standing to an independent ombudsperson-like authority could increase vigilance on the uptake of mandatory SPP rules by contracting authorities and entities.[85] Enlisting public procurement in the fight against climate change and in the pursuit of other relevant societal goals means that litigation cannot be confined to economic operators protecting their merely economic interests as it is currently provided under Article 1(3) of the Remedies Directive.

In this novel framework, one advantage of mandatory SPP – and especially of mandatory substantive criteria and requirements – will lie in the limited risk that sustainably oriented choices are challenged by competitors alleging the lack of the link to the subject matter required under EU law.[86] As the experience in France, the Netherlands, and Spain shows, the use of vague SPP mandates instead translates itself into litigation and potentially in very conservative case laws.[87]

VII. Effectiveness and Efficiency

As Carrera and Vannoni have shown, there is very little hard economic evidence about the actual effectiveness and efficiency (or lack thereof) of SPP in general

[81] See, eg, Case C-263/19 *T-Systems Magyarország Zrt. and BKK Budapesti Közlekedési Központ v Közbeszerzési Hatóság Közbeszerzési Döntőbizottság* ECLI:EU:C:2020:373, [2020].
[82] Lichère and Sulpice (n 16) section II.D.
[83] Andhov and Muscaritoli (n 37) section VI.
[84] Semple (n 13) end of section III.
[85] Lichère and Sulpice (n 16) section III.A.ii.
[86] ibid section II.D; see the benign data on litigation from Italy in Botta (n 22) section V.
[87] Lazo-Vitoria (n 3) after reference to n 41; Lichère and Sulpice (n 16) after reference to n 11.

and of mandatory SPP specifically.[88] The few studies we have on GPP seem to disprove general theoretical economic assumptions strongly tilted against regulatory action.[89] Carreras and Vannoni provide a very articulated analysis of the different degrees of effectiveness and efficiency expected from GPP and SRPP and, within the latter, from *hardcore* social objectives (eg, respect for human and labour rights) and the goals of promoting inclusion and supplier diversity.[90] Schotanus and Nicolas are more positive in pointing towards the potential benefits of SPP.[91]

We share Gimeno Feliu's take on procurement as an investment rather than as an expense, the latter being more typical of a bureaucratic, economic vision of bidding processes.[92] Accordingly, we need to focus on the real costs – including societal and environmental costs – and not so much on the price tag of what is bought through public procurement.[93]

Assuming, along with mainstream policy indications, that SPP measures indeed deliver societal benefits, then mandatory SPP has the capacity to increase the number of public contracts incorporating environmental and/or social considerations.[94]

As illustrated above, criteria (both procedural and substantive), targets and product-specific requirements, individually taken all show some shortcomings. Targets and procedural requirements are fast to enact, but their effectiveness may be easily dented. Procedural and substantive criteria are quite constraining on contracting authorities, they should act as a baseline, but enacting them is a time-consuming resource-intensive effort. Arguably, different types of measures should be combined, and constantly weighed up with advantages and disadvantages.[95] Targets and especially procedural criteria should act as default rules, applicable waiting for the development of requirements and substantive criteria.[96] Accordingly, they could be included in the Public Procurement Directives.

Adoption of product or sector-specific criteria might be sped up by working on already existing EU GPP criteria, instead of having to wait for the EU legislature to swing the pendulum. While the EU GPP criteria are only focusing on the environmental aspects and lack attention to social ones, as Schebesta and Plana Casado

[88] Carreras and Vannoni (n 69) after reference to n 17.

[89] ibid between reference to nn 18 and 22. But SRPP is a different matter, see reference to n 51ff.

[90] Carreras and Vannoni (n 70) after reference to n 30 and at reference to n 60.

[91] Schotanus and Nicholas (n 20) section I; Carreras and Vannoni (n 69) after reference to n 22 which indicates 'management scholars and business strategists are more positive about the effects of environmental regulation in shaping the environmental strategies and performance of firms'.

[92] JM Gimeno Feliu, 'La visión estratégica en la contratación pública en la LCSP: hacia una contratación socialmente responsable y de calidad' (2020) 415 *Revista Economía Industrial* 89.

[93] SL Schooner and M Speidel, 'Warming Up to Sustainable Procurement' (2020) 60 *Contract Management* 32, 37ff; see also R Caranta 'Public Procurement for the SDGs – Rethinking the Basics' in L Mélon (ed), *Sustainability in Public Procurement, Corporate Law and Higher Education* (Routledge, forthcoming, 2023).

[94] For data from Spain, see Lazo-Vitoria (n 3) n 25.

[95] Schotanus and Nicholas (n 20).

[96] Targets are also recommended for non-hardcore SRPP, see Carreras and Vannoni (n 70) reference to last phrase in conclusion.

rightly underline, they could serve as a starting point when they are well developed enough.[97] A major issue affecting the efficacy of SPP provisions is the fact that substantive criteria often require more detailed rules to be operationalised. Enacting those rules is a time and effort-intensive job, which is often delayed as it is shown by the case of the measures that should have been enacted in the wake of the Spanish law on climate change and energy transition.[98] Still, the list of minimum (partially mandatory) environmental criteria – CAMs is constantly updated in Italy and CAMs are routinely updated in Italy.[99] It would seem that institutional choices impact the efficiency of the process of laying down mandatory SPP criteria. Relying on the work already done with the EU GPP criteria would accelerate the process, and could be the template for legislation based on the delegated acts that are likely to be given to the Commission in the future.

Our contributors have more or less strongly emphasised that by itself changing the legal provisions will not be enough to guarantee a strong uptake of SPP. As shown in the previous section, judicial or quasi-judicial remedies have a role to play, but targets are harder to enforce through litigation by economic operators and the Remedies Directives need reform, which would be an argument in favour of stronger national enforcement authorities.

Mandatory requirements are just one component of supporting institutional forces. Best practices and professional norms must be involved too.[100] Unsurprisingly, many contributors have stressed the importance of guidance and training to really enhance the uptake of SPP.[101] This today includes 'basic carbon literacy'.[102] More generally, updating professional norms and knowledge seems necessary.[103]

As Gruyaert and Pissierssens have stressed, effective mandatory SPP also requires close monitoring of the outcomes.[104] This is of course true of public procurement in general. However, some of the benefits from SPP accrue not just to the contracting authority, but to the environment and/or to the wider society, which might prove difficult to measure in economic terms. Again, this is also true of some procurement, such as those benefiting members of the general public, but in many cases, it is the contracting authorities benefiting from the goods and services purchased. In the latter case, incentives to check the quality of what is delivered are stronger. Still, since all and every public procurement, including SPP, is in the end expected to benefit society at large, contractors must be made accountable. The baseline is that the required benefits from procurement must

[97] Which is an issue concerning food, see Schebesta and Plana Casado (n 50) section III.A.
[98] Lazo-Vitoria paragraph after n 28.
[99] Botta (n 22) section IV.
[100] Schotanus and Nicholas (n 20) section I after reference to n 14; see also D Klingler and S Schooner, 'Promoting Sustainable Public Procurement through Economic Policy Tools: From Moral Suasion to Nudging' (2022) 4 *Eur. Journal of Public Proc. Markets* 69.
[101] Lazo-Vitoria (n 3) n 39; Botta (n 22) n 48.
[102] Andhov and Muscaritoli (n 37) reference to the last phrase of section VII.
[103] Schotanus and Nicholas (n 20) section IV.
[104] Gruyaert and Pissierssens (n 10) section III.

be measurable.[105] Contracting authorities need to draft contract clauses allowing them to check that benefits are indeed delivered. Schotanus and Nicolas take a step further, highlighting that monitoring must lead to the identification of best practices to be spread for adoption by other contracting authorities.[106]

Another aspect related to the effectiveness of mandatory SPP concerns the impacts on litigation patterns. Apparently, in some jurisdictions, a strict understanding by courts of the link to the subject matter of strategic considerations.[107] Arguably that may be an issue when lawmakers choose wide-worded and high-sounding mandates. Italy instead shows that opting for articulated criteria has a negligible impact on litigation.[108]

As Carreras and Vannoni indicate, 'understanding the effectiveness and cost-effectiveness of GPP is for a large part an empirical task. Unfortunately, the empirical literature on the effects of specific GPP policies is rather scant'.[109] We wish for more of such studies.[110]

VIII. Final Thought

In light of climate change and social injustice as pressing societal challenges, the debate on the effective regulatory design of public procurement must remain at the forefront. The study contained in this book provides the first coherent analysis of the ongoing development of the paradigm shift from 'how to buy' towards 'what to buy'. What is clear is that it is necessary to act to face these challenges through all possible tools, SPP included. The situation where, *dum Romae consulitur, Saguntum expugnatur*, must be avoided. Simply talking about issues is not and never was a wise strategy. The discussions in this book have debated a new way to approach regulating public procurement in order to make it future proof.[111] Many of the discussed pitfalls, hurdles, opportunities and benefits of regulating SPP in this way, relate to 'how' it will be regulated in the end, either through minimum sustainability requirements, targets, or product-specific legislation. In any event, as the European Green Deal train continues to ride out its term, more mandatory sustainability requirements are likely to be needed sooner than later.[112]

[105] See also Carreras and Vannoni (n 70) reference to phrase after reference to n 29.
[106] Schotanus and Nicholas (n 20) reference to nn 26 and section IV.B.
[107] Lazo-Vitoria (n 3) n 42.
[108] Botta (n 22) reference to the start of section V.
[109] Carreras and Vannoni (n 70) reference n 37.
[110] ibid reference to phrase after reference to n 43.
[111] Caranta (n 91); see WA Janssen, 'Verplicht Maatschappelijk Verantwoord Aanbesteden: een eerste Verkenning van een Paradigmaverandering' (2020) 1 *Tijdschrift Aanbestedingsrecht & Staatssteunrecht* 19, 24.
[112] See also SL Schooner, 'No Time to Waste: Embracing Sustainable Public Procurement to Mitigate the Accelerating Climate Crisis' (2021) 61 *Contract Management* 24.

Most prominently, it has come to the forefront that the existence of a solely procedural regulation of public procurement will soon be a thing of the past in the EU, because more substantive regulation is to complement the current pallet. It means that the search for an optimal mix of voluntary and mandatory sustainability requirements has commenced ensuring the effectiveness of EU public procurement law, and its relationship with sustainability, in the future.

INDEX

Milton Keynes UK
Ingram Content Group UK Ltd.
UKHW020217081123
432156UK00005B/71

9 781509 963959